# Educational Neuro

# Educational Neuroscience

Edited by

Denis Mareschal
Brian Butterworth
Andy Tolmie

**WILEY** Blackwell

This edition first published 2013
© 2014 John Wiley & Sons, Ltd

*Registered Office*
John Wiley & Sons, Ltd, The Atrium, Southern Gate, Chichester, West Sussex, PO19 8SQ, UK

*Editorial Offices*
350 Main Street, Malden, MA 02148–5020, USA
9600 Garsington Road, Oxford, OX4 2DQ, UK
The Atrium, Southern Gate, Chichester, West Sussex, PO19 8SQ, UK

For details of our global editorial offices, for customer services, and for information about how to apply for permission to reuse the copyright material in this book please see our website at www.wiley.com/wiley-blackwell.

The right of Denis Mareschal, Brian Butterworth, and Andy Tolmie to be identified as the authors of this work has been asserted in accordance with the UK Copyright, Designs and Patents Act 1988.

*Library of Congress Cataloging-in-Publication Data*
Educational neuroscience / edited by Denis Mareschal, Brian Butterworth, Andy Tolmie.
     pages   cm
   Includes bibliographical references and index.
     ISBN 978-1-119-97319-5 (cloth) – ISBN 978-1-118-72589-4 (pbk.)   1. Educational psychology–Handbooks, manuals, etc.   2. Learning–Physiological aspects–Handbooks, manuals, etc.   3. Cognitive neuroscience–Handbooks, manuals, etc.   4. Neurosciences–Handbooks, manuals, etc.   I. Mareschal, Denis, editor of compilation.   II. Butterworth, Brian, editor of compilation.   III. Tolmie, Andrew, editor of compilation.
     LB1051.E348 2013
     370.15–dc23
                                        2013025391
A catalogue record for this book is available from the British Library.
Cover image: the concept of learning process of children © VLADGRIN/Shutterstock
Cover design by Cyan Design

Set in 11/13.5pt Minion by SPi Publisher Services, Pondicherry, India
CEN Logo Designer : Storm Thorgerson at Stormstudios
Printed and bound in Malaysia by Vivar Printing Sdn Bhd

2  2016

# Dedication

*To all the learners and teachers who contributed to the work described in this book*

# Contents

List of Contributors      ix

Preface      xi

Foreword: Imaging the Future      xii
*Michael I. Posner*

1. Introduction      1
*Brian Butterworth and Andy Tolmie*

2. Neuroimaging Methods      13
*Frederic Dick, Sarah Lloyd-Fox, Anna Blasi, Clare Elwell, and Debbie Mills*

3. Computational Modeling of Learning and Teaching      46
*Michael S. C. Thomas and Diana Laurillard*

4. Genetics for Education      77
*Yulia Kovas, Sergei Malykh, and Stephen A. Petrill*

5. Research Methods in Educational Psychology      110
*Andy Tolmie*

6. Language Development      134
*Victoria Knowland and Chris Donlan*

7. Literacy Development      172
*Liory Fern-Pollak and Jackie Masterson*

8. Mathematical Development      201
*Brian Butterworth and Sashank Varma*

9.  The Development and Application of Scientific Reasoning                    237
    *Jonathan Fugelsang and Denis Mareschal*

10. Social Development                                                          268
    *Sarah-Jayne Blakemore, Kathrin Cohen Kadosh,*
    *Catherine L. Sebastian, Tobias Grossmann, and Mark H. Johnson*

11. Emotional Development                                                       297
    *Alice Jones*

12. Attention and Executive Control                                            325
    *Michelle de Haan*

    Afterword                                                                   349
    *John T. Bruer*

Index                                                                          364

# List of Contributors

**Sarah-Jayne Blakemore**, *Institute of Cognitive Neuroscience, University College London*

**Anna Blasi**, *Centre for Brain and Cognitive Development, Birkbeck University of London*

**John T. Bruer**, *James S. McDonnell Foundation*

**Brian Butterworth**, *Institute of Cognitive Neuroscience, University College London*

**Kathrin Cohen Kadosh**, *Department of Experimental Psychology, University of Oxford*

**Michelle de Haan**, *University College London Institute of Child Health*

**Frederic Dick**, *Birkbeck/UCL Centre for NeuroImaging, Birkbeck University of London*

**Chris Donlan**, *Division of Psychology and Language Sciences, University College London*

**Clare Elwell**, *Department of Medical Physics and Bioengineering, University College London*

**Liory Fern-Pollak**, *Centre for Cognition and NeuroImaging, Brunel University*

**Jonathan Fugelsang**, *Department of Psychology, University of Waterloo*

**Tobias Grossmann**, *Max Planck Institute for Human Cognitive & Brain Sciences*

**Mark H. Johnson**, *Centre for Brain and Cognitive Development, Birkbeck University of London*

**Alice Jones**, *Department of Psychology, Goldsmiths College, University of London*

**Victoria Knowland**, *Language and Communication Sciences, City University, London*

**Yulia Kovas**, *Department of Psychology, Goldsmiths College, University of London*

**Diana Laurillard**, *London Knowledge Lab, Institute of Education, University of London*

**Sarah Lloyd-Fox**, *Centre for Brain and Cognitive Development, Birkbeck University of London*

**Sergei Malykh**, *Laboratory for Cognitive Investigations and Behavioral Genetics, Tomsk State University; Laboratory of Developmental Behavioral Genetics, Psychological Institute of Russian Academy of Education*

**Denis Mareschal**, *Centre for Brain and Cognitive Development, Birkbeck University of London*

**Jackie Masterson**, *Department of Psychology and Human Development, Institute of Education, University of London*

**Debbie Mills**, *School of Psychology, Bangor University*

**Stephen A. Petrill**, *Department of Human Development and Family Science, Ohio State University*

**Michael I. Posner**, *Department of Psychology, University of Oregon*

**Catherine L. Sebastian**, *Department of Psychology, Royal Holloway, University of London*

**Michael S. C. Thomas**, *Developmental Neurocognition Lab, Birkbeck University of London*

**Andy Tolmie**, *Department of Psychology and Human Development, Institute of Education, University of London*

**Sashank Varma**, *Department of Educational Psychology, University of Minnesota*

# Preface

*Educational Neuroscience* is intended as a reference tool for use by active researchers and practitioners alike. It reflects the activities of the Centre for Educational Neuroscience (CEN), a joint venture between Birkbeck University of London, University College London, and the Institute of Education, all based in Central London. We are very grateful to these institutions for their continuing support of the CEN, whose mission is not just to further our understanding of how neural and biological processes can help understand learning in the classroom, but also to ensure that there is a real dialogue between educational practitioners and basic science researchers. We are also grateful to the following individuals for their help in reading and fine-tuning the chapters within this volume: Caspar Addyman, Gizelle Anzures, Jasmine Cockcroft, Teodora Gliga, Victoria Knowland, Nick Lange, Manuela Mielke, Greg Pascoe, Daisy Powell, Angelica Ronald, Michael Thomas, and Rachel Wu.

# Foreword: Imaging the Future

## Michael I. Posner

It is the goal of this book to summarize the methods employed and the evidence so far collected to support educational neuroscience. Each chapter deals with infancy, childhood, and adult education. A foreword, however, is free to attempt to imagine an educational system that may never really exist, but could be reasonably implied by what is already known. Below I have tried to help the reader separate fantasy from reality by using real references to mark what has actually taken place and separate it from what I think might someday happen.

One could imagine young parents taking their 10-month-old daughter to the pediatric specialist for an educational checkup. Records of electrical activity at the scalp are taken to see how well native phonemes are solidifying their representation in the brain (Guttorm et al., 2005; Molfese, 2000). At the same time Mandarin phonemes are studied to see if the parents' goal of preparing their daughter for a Chinese emersion school is likely to be worthwhile (Kuhl, 1994; Kuhl, Tsao, & Liu, 2003). A new robot tutor is available to help the family reach their goal. Entry to school might depend upon having developed a strong enough phonemic organization to support learning to read. To obtain more information on this the reader should examine the chapters by Victoria Knowland and Chris Donlan, as well as Liory Fern-Pollak and Jackie Masterson, on language and literacy. These chapters may help you decide how likely these events are.

A research laboratory at the NATO center for brain and education has released a new report comparing English children with Chinese children in the brain mechanisms involved in simple number comparison with Arabic digits. It has previously been found that English-speaking and Chinese-speaking adults, equally familiar with Arabic digits, use entirely different brain pathways to make simple numerical comparisons (Tang et al., 2006). The new functional magnetic resonance imaging (fMRI) study, not yet conducted, could show that following extensive exposure to special lessons adapted from Chinese classrooms, English-speaking children use the Chinese pathways. Could such studies lead to changes designed to raise success and to close the achievement gap between Asian and Western children? To find out whether this could work, even in theory, read Butterworth and Varma on mathematical development.

There has been widespread panic about increases in the prevalence of autism and attention deficit hyperactivity disorder (ADHD) in the United States of America. There is also worry among the parents of typically developing children that in the digital age their child will not be able to resist distraction and focus on their school subjects. Research has discovered specific attention networks that underlie our ability to focus attention on sensory information as is needed in reading and arithmetic (Posner & Rothbart, 2007). One of these attention networks, involved in orienting to sensory stimuli, is disrupted in children with autism (Townsend, Keehn, & Westerfield, 2011) but not in children with ADHD (Johnson et al., 2008). ADHD children have shown deficits in other attention networks involved in alerting and voluntary control of responses (Johnson et al., 2008). Moreover, the connectivity of the network involved in voluntary control of response is also important in control of emotion and of the social world. Chapters by Blakemore and colleagues and Jones show how important such controls are to the development of children.

Research to be published shortly by the London Center for Educational Neuroscience has shown that the different attention networks can be suppressed or enhanced with drugs that influence the chemicals that modulate them. However, drugs might not be the only or even the best alternative. A number of recent studies of children with ADHD and those developing typically have improved aspects of their attention by training exercises that might use computers or live classroom instruction (Diamond, Barnett, Thomas, & Munro, 2007; Klingberg, 2011; Rueda, Rothbart, McCandliss, Saccamanno, & Posner, 2005). It is not yet known whether such training really makes a long term improvement in disorders such as ADHD, or whether strengthening of attention networks can prevent disorders and improve performance in schools. We can imagine a future where it is possible to tailor these exercises to enhance the performance of all children and perhaps to close achievement differences based on social class. Background for these ideas can be obtained by reading the chapter by Michelle de Haan.

An important development in cognitive science is that concepts based on clear rules are often less important in human thinking than fuzzy sets in which semantic categories are represented by typical instances (Rosch, 1975). The consequences of such categories have been elaborated and applied to a wide range of human thought through the study of metaphorical thinking (Lakoff & Johnson, 2003). Imaging has begun to explore the neural basis of how the brain supports Roschian concepts and metaphorical thinking. Expertise in a large number of domains produces activation of a posterior brain area related to the visual system, which can automatically deal with relevant written words. Many humans are experts in face perception (Kanwisher, 2000) and most are in reading (McCandliss, Cohen, & Dehaene, 2003). These activate parts of the fusiform gyrus, which plays a crucial role in both fluent face recognition and reading. As new skills are learned they can also develop such areas and allow the person to automatically interpret new input in light of old knowledge (Posner 2013, in press; Righi, Tarr, & Kingon, in press; Tanaka & Curran, 2001). The study of the brain mechanisms of experts may help us determine if a given teaching method is establishing genuine expertise. The chapter by Jonathan Fugelsang and Denis Mareschal provides the background by discussing the importance of training in conceptual thinking and reasoning in science.

To foster the development of an educational system related to neuroscience it will be important for the next generation of educational researchers to understand the methods and ways of thinking in neuroscience. Neuroscience results do not dictate curricular development; rather, they require creative application by designers to synthesize the results into appropriate curricula. To do this means understanding how neuroscience ideas (Fred Dick and colleagues, Chapter 2) are brought together in the formation of computational models (Michael Thomas and Diana Laurillard, Chapter 3), and in addition how those neural networks that are common to all people relate to network efficiency, which differs among individuals and within individuals from time to time. Genetic variations in interaction with the environment are one of the influences on such individual differences (Chapter 4, Yulia Kovas and colleagues). As a link to curricular development, education researchers need to know how to study and evaluate preliminary designs of educational interventions to see which can be integrated into the overall curriculum (Chapter 5, Andy Tolmie).

Although not all of these educational applications of neuroscience may come to pass, I hope this book will play a role in conveying the exciting present and future possibilities of educational neuroscience.

## References

Diamond, A., Barnett, S., Thomas, J., & Munro, S. (2007). Preschool improves cognitive control. *Science, 30*, 1387–1388.

Guttorm, T. K., Leppanen, P. H. T., Poikkeus, A. M., Eklund, K. M., Lyytinen, P., & Lyytinen, H. (2005). Brain event-related potentials (ERPs) measured at birth predict later language development in children with and without familial risk for dyslexia. *Cortex, 41*(3), 291–303.

Johnson, K. A., Robertson, I. H., Barry, E., Mulligan, A., Daibhis, A., Daly, M., Watchorn, A., Gill, M., & Bellgrove, M. A. (2008). Impaired conflict resolution and alerting in children with ADHD: Evidence from the ANT. *Journal of Child Psychology and Psychiatry, 49,* 1339–1347.

Kanwisher, N. (2000). Domain specificity in face perception. *Nature Neuroscience, 3,* 759–763.

Klingberg, T. (2011). Training working memory and attention. In M. I. Posner (Ed.), *Cognitive neuroscience of attention* (2nd ed., pp. 475–486). New York: Guilford.

Kuhl, P. K. (1994). Learning and representation in speech and language. *Current Opinion in Neurobiology, 4,* 812–822.

Kuhl, P. K., Tsao, F. M., & Liu, H. M. (2003). Foreign-language experience in infancy: Effects of short-term exposure and social interaction on phonetic learning. *Proceedings of the National Academy of Sciences of the United States of America, 100*(15), 9096–9101.

Lakoff, G., & Johnson, M. (2003). *Metaphors we live by.* Chicago, IL: University of Chicago Press.

McCandliss, B. D., Cohen, L., & Dehaene, S. (2003). The visual word form area: Expertise for reading in the fusiform gyrus. *Trends in Cognitive Sciences, 7*(7): 293–299.

Molfese, D. L. (2000). Predicting dyslexia at eight years of age using neonatal brain responses. *Brain and Language, 72,* 238–245.

Posner, M. I. (2013). The expert brain. In J. J. Staszewski (Ed.), *Expertise and skill scquisition: The impact of William G. Chase.* New York: Psychology.

Posner, M. I., & Rothbart, M. K. (2007). *Educating the human brain.* Washington, DC: APA Books.

Righi, G., Tarr, M. J., & Kingon, A. (in press). Category-selective recruitment of the fusiform gyrus with chess expertise. In J. J. Staszewski (Ed.), *Expertise and skill acquisition: The impact of William G. Chase.* New York: Psychology.

Rosch, E. (1975). Cognitive representation of semantic categories. *Journal of Experimental Psychology: General, 104,* 192–233.

Rueda, M. R., Rothbart, M. K., McCandliss, B. D., Saccamanno, L., & Posner, M. I. (2005). Training, maturation and genetic influences on the development of executive attention. *Proceedings of the National Academy of Sciences of the United States of America, 102,* 14931–14936.

Tanaka, J. W., & Curran, T. (2001). A neural basis for expert object recognition. *Psychological Science, 12,* 43–47.

Tang, Y. Y., Zhang, W. T., Chen, K. W., Feng, S. H., Ji, Y., Shen, J. X., Reiman, E. M., & Liu, Y. Y. (2006). Arithmetic processing in the brain shaped by cultures. *Proceedings of the National Academy of Sciences, 103*(26), 10775–10780.

Townsend, J., Keehn, B., & Westerfield, M. (2011). Abstraction of mind in autism. In M. I. Posner (Ed.), *Cognitive neuroscience of attention* (2nd ed., pp. 357–373). New York: Guilford.

# Chapter 1

# Introduction

## Brian Butterworth and Andy Tolmie

### The Nature of the Discipline

Education is about enhancing learning, and neuroscience is about understanding the mental processes involved in learning. This common ground suggests a future in which educational practice can be transformed by science, just as medical practice was transformed by science about a century ago.

Report by the Royal Society, UK, 2011

The mission statement of the Centre for Educational Neuroscience in London, the affiliation of all but two of the lead authors in this book, states how this transformation can be brought about:

**What**: Our vision is to bring together three previously distinct disciplines [education, psychology and neuroscience] – to focus on a specific common problem: how to promote better learning. This will mean building a new scientific community and a new discipline, educational neuroscience.

**Why**: We now understand better how learning organizes and reorganizes the brain, but there is very little research so far that has had an impact on educational delivery. What is lacking is a body of researchers who are expert in education, psychology, and neuroscience, and to create these researchers is a primary aim of the project.

*Educational Neuroscience*, First Edition. Edited by Denis Mareschal, Brian Butterworth and Andy Tolmie.
© 2014 John Wiley & Sons, Ltd. Published 2014 by John Wiley & Sons, Ltd.

**How**: We believe we can do this by building on existing research collaborations and creating new initial training, post-graduate research, and continuing professional development opportunities for becoming expert in educational neuroscience.

**Impact**: Bringing education, psychology, and neuroscience together can help in designing better learning environments through the lifespan, and this will lead to more fulfilled and more effective learners.

## Three Disciplines: Education, Psychology, Neuroscience

The goal of educational neuroscience is to work out how all learners can be helped to achieve their learning potentials and to make learning more effective for all learners. This has meant in practice that education seeks answers to two main questions.

What are the sources of individual differences in learning?
What are the optimal contexts for the learner?

In an attempt to answer these questions, educational neuroscience has evolved through three key phases of enquiry, which we discus in turn below. See Figure 1.1.

### Phase 1. Education and psychology

Prior to the emergence of educational neuroscience as a separate discipline, in what we call Phase 1, educational research had a long history of collaboration with

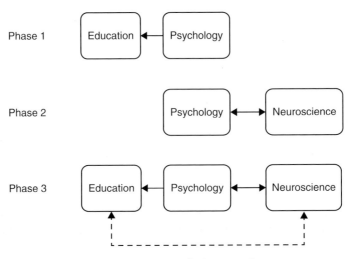

**Figure 1.1**   Three phases in the emergence of educational neuroscience.

psychology in trying to achieve these goals. This is especially true in curriculum relevant areas such as learning to read and learning mathematics. Psychology first pointed to two main sources of individual differences in learning. First, there were differences in intrinsic cognitive capacity, for example as measured by IQ tests or tests of working memory, and more recently differences in cognitive styles. Another approach has revealed evidence for domain-specific cognitive differences in language acquisition (see Chapter 6), learning to read (see Chapter 7) and learning arithmetic (see Chapter 8). Second, psychological as well as sociological studies revealed experiential sources of individual variation, for example differences in home environment using socioeconomic status or parental education as proxy measures (e.g., Melhuish et al., 2008). Finally, with regard to optimal learning contexts, psychology has provided methodologies for investigating and comparing teaching methods, but it has also made proposals, mostly for mathematics and reading, and to some extent for science.

In mathematics, there was the classic debate between Thorndike and Brownell. In *The Psychology of Arithmetic*, Thorndike (1922) took ideas from associationist theories of psychology, and emphasized drilling simple number bonds. In the 1930s, Brownell, in several important papers, applied psychological ideas about meaningful practice to how math should be taught. In the 1950s and 1960s, Piaget's "constructivist" theories about the nature of cognitive development were very influential. Constructivism emphasizes the child's construction of new schemas (accommodation) when new stimuli cannot be understood using existing schemas (see Chapter 8).

In the case of learning to read, perhaps the most striking impact of psychology is in differentiating dyslexic learners from other learners. Here careful psychological assessment revealed that some children found it hard to learn to read despite good vision, high general intelligence, appropriate teaching, and supportive home environment. Critically, it was found that dyslexic learners suffered from a deficit in analyzing the phonological structure of their language and indeed that phonological training could help (Bradley & Bryant, 1978).

Nevertheless, the debate continues as to whether there is a single underlying phenotype (Elliott, 2005) or whether there are a variety of separable causes of delays and differences in learning to read. Much ink has been spilled in the so-called "reading wars" about which method of teaching reading is most effective. Evidence, until recently, has been entirely based on psychological studies of reading performance. On one side, there are those who have proposed the *whole-word* or whole-language method, in which letter–sound associations are not drilled, but rather children are encouraged to recognize whole words, sound them out, and interpret them. On the other side, there is *phonics*, based precisely on drilling letter–sound correspondences (Ehri, Nunes, Stahl, & Willows, 2001) Unfortunately, many proponents of the two approaches appear to have a political agenda in which left-leaning child-centered proponents prefer the former, and conservative exam-focused proponents prefer the latter. Of course, in an orthography such as English, with many irregular and exceptional pronunciations, the learner needs to have a grasp of both letter–sound correspondences and whole-word pronunciations and meanings. Learners certainly need to know that *pint* is not pronounced to rhyme with *print*. It may be that it will be helpful for the teacher to encourage the learner to recognize whole letter strings, rather than simply insist on sounding out the letters. Nevertheless, children can and do learn to read irregular and exception words by "self-teaching": that is, by using context to figure out what must be meant and thereby get a plausible pronunciation of *pint*, which will then be stored in the mental lexicon of meaningful letter strings (Share, 1995).

## Phase 2. Psychology and neuroscience

This phase is characterized by the collaboration between neuroscience and the cognitive, affective, and developmental branches of psychology, to create cognitive neuroscience. In the course of this collaboration, questions arising from education were raised, notably in the neural basis of reading and its disorders, and in mathematics and its disorders, but also in more general issues of attention, executive function, and memory.

The neural underpinnings of cognition and learning in particular have also been the subject of studies of neurological patients. This is perhaps most striking in the case of learning and memory, where selective deficits in patients revealed much about the structure of memory, distinguishing short from long-term memory, declarative from procedural memory, encoding from retrieval, and so on. Even the first steps in revealing the neural bases of curriculum-relevant cognitive processes owe much to the study of patients. The identification of selective reading and spelling problems and evidence for their neural basis dates back to Dejerine in 1892, and modern multiroute models of normal reading were due initially to studies of patients (see Shallice, 1988, for the classic account). Similarly, the basic anatomy and functional organization of mathematical cognition was identified from studies of selective deficits in patients (Caramazza & McCloskey, 1987; Dehaene & Cohen, 1995; Warrington, 1982).

However, the critical impetus for the most relevant aspect of neuroscience for education, *cognitive neuroscience*, came with availability of *in vivo* imaging of neural processes as they happened (see Chapter 2 for a discussion of these methodologies). Neuroimaging has revealed important aspects of domain-general cognitive processes, such as performance on IQ tests, even the developmental trajectory of verbal and non-verbal IQ (Ramsden et al., 2011) and the neural basis of verbal working memory (Paulesu, Frith, & Frackowiak, 1993) and spatial working memory (Petrides, 2000; van Asselen et al., 2006). Other domain-general capacities that contribute to individual differences, such as attention and goal-directed behavior, social and emotional development are now better understood from neuroimaging studies (see Chapter 2). The capacity to understand other minds has also become clearer (see Frith, 2007, and Chapter 10).

Advances have also been made in curriculum-relevant cognitive capacities. For example, the reading network in the brain as revealed by neuroimaging clearly links visual recognition in the inferior temporal region with speech in the inferior frontal gyrus and with word meanings in the middle temporal lobe. This has enabled a better understanding of individual differences in the ability to learn to read in dyslexia. This has been shown to be related to abnormalities in this network: decreased activation in the left inferior temporal region (Paulesu et al., 2001) and abnormal structure in the left middle temporal lobe (Silani et al., 2005). These findings may help to resolve the skepticism that still surrounds the classification of learners as dyslexics.

Note that, without neuroimaging, it might be thought that learning different orthographies, such as alphabetic English or Italian as compared with character-based Chinese or Japanese, might depend on very different neural circuits. However, we now know from neuroimaging that all orthographies depend on similar neural networks (Dehaene, 2009) and indeed that dyslexia is due to similar neural abnormalities (Paulesu et al., 2001).

It has now become feasible to carry out large-scale studies of the development of the brain, and to understand better the genetic and environmental factors that affect it.

## Phase 3. Emergence of educational neuroscience

Phase 3 is where we are now: we are seeking to use neuroscience to inform educational practice as a way to improve learning. In 1997, John Bruer famously argued that this was "a bridge too far."

> Currently, we do not know enough about brain development and neural function to link that understanding directly, in any meaningful, defensible way to instruction and educational practice. … There is a well-established bridge, now nearly 50 years old, between education and cognitive psychology. There is a second bridge, only around 10 years old, between cognitive psychology and neuroscience. This newer bridge is allowing us to see how mental functions map onto brain structures. When neuroscience does begin to provide useful insights for educators about instruction and educational practice, those insights will be the

result of extensive traffic over this second bridge. Cognitive psychology provides the only firm ground we have to anchor these bridges. It is the only way to go if we eventually want to move between education and the brain.

Bruer based this position on critiques of three aspects of very basic neuroscience usually derived from studies of non-human species: the time course of *synaptogenesis* and *synaptic pruning*, *critical periods* for learning, and the role of *enriched early environments*. He quite sensibly notes that the evidence from these aspects is not sufficient to inform formal education. However, Since Bruer's (1997) paper, there has been rapid expansion of the "pontoon" between the two bridges – cognitive neuroscience. This discipline deploys the resources of brain imaging to develop and refine our understanding of cognitive processes, including those that underpin educational attainment, such as working memory and learning processes, and also curriculum-relevant cognitions involved in language, reading, motivation, and mathematics. This in itself would still be the two-bridge solution that Bruer alluded to.

In 2005, *Nature* published a skeptical editorial questioning the contribution that even cognitive neuroscience could make to education. It warned

> Researchers are planning to use magnetic resonance imaging to "look under the hood" at the development of skills such as numeracy and reading. It's fascinating stuff, but how the results will inform educational practice remains, for now, largely a matter of speculation. Making meaningful connections between brain activity and behaviour is difficult, even under controlled lab settings. Brain imaging is seductive, and has an unfortunate tendency to spawn breathless, overreaching media coverage. Care will be needed to ensure that these projects don't encourage ill-informed "experts" to design yet more pseudoscientific educational tools…. There's also a strong case for putting the educational tools derived from research in neuroscience to more rigorous empirical tests. For instance, researchers who have evidence that dyslexics have problems with auditory processing have developed a program called Fast ForWord to help them learn to read. But the scientists' company is now marketing the software as a learning aid for children with no specific reading deficits, before they have gathered evidence that it helps anyone other than dyslexics. For now, providing this sort of evidence is where the emphasis should remain (Editorial, 2005, p. 1138).

Nevertheless, these new methodologies have enabled us to explore both individual differences in children and education in new ways, suggesting a direct bridge from neuroscience to education. For example, dyslexic readers can be identified through abnormal neural structures and patterns of activation in the reading network (see Chapter 7), even in very young children before they have begun learning to read using neural responses to speech sounds (Lyytinen et al.,

2001). Dyscalculic learners can be identified by abnormal neural structures and patterns of activation (see Chapter 8), and these can turn out to be more discriminating than purely behavioral measures (Dumontheil & Klingberg, 2011). Even individual differences in language development (see Chapter 6), reasoning, and social and emotional development (see Chapters 10 and 11 respectively) can also be revealed by neuroimaging. Moreover, links between genetics and neuroimaging, as well as between genetics and cognitive capacity, are strengthening very rapidly (see Chapter 4).

In fact, new methodologies have enabled scientists to plot the developmental trajectories with much more precision than previously. It will become possible in the near future to identify not just neural differences at a particular ontogenetic time point, which may resolve and be simply a delay in development, but also track differences in the developmental trajectories of educationally relevant cognitive functions. It is possible to use mathematical models of trajectory differences to classify learners, and these "learner models" can inform the design of individualized learning contexts in teaching and in learning technologies (see Chapter 3).

Of course, three disciplines are involved, each with their own methodologies, that cannot easily be unified. Therefore, the critical move is what Laurillard has termed "methodological interoperability" (Laurillard, 2007). That is, although the methods of the three disciplines are different, it is possible, and indeed necessary, for each discipline to test the findings of the others. For example, when the cognitive neuroscience theory leads to new pedagogic design, the theory will be tested by more effective learning. More generally, methodological interoperability can be mediated through explicit computational models of a learning process (see, for example, Chapter 3).

## Issues and Problems in Developing Educational Neuroscience

The earlier sections of this chapter have spelled out something of the objectives of educational neuroscience. From a *scientific* perspective, the rationale is clear cut, even if the collaboration between – and ultimately integration of – disciplines that it requires presents a range of theoretical and methodological challenges. The diversity of empirically driven theorizing that there has been about learning over the past 150 years can be seen as an indication of the highly complex nature of learning-related phenomena, which for a long while seemed as if they could only be captured in fragmentary fashion. More recently, however, educational psychologists and cognitive neuroscientists have recognized that it is possible to build more integrated models of learning, which do better justice to this complexity by bringing together social and cognitive or cognitive and neural processes within single accounts (for examples of the former, see Philips & Tolmie, 2007, or for the latter, Klingberg, 2010; McNab et al., 2009). If we want to achieve any full account of learning, the logical conclusion is that this will depend on bringing *all* of these strands together in a nonreductionist framework that retains description at the environmental, cognitive, and neural levels, and seeks to understand how these interact with and impact on each other to produce observed outcomes in both formal and informal educational settings. It is this framework that educational neuroscience aims to deliver.

The picture becomes more complex, however, when we turn to *educational* perspectives on the purpose of this enterprise. Education is itself a hugely complex activity with social, economic, political, and individual goals – and a corresponding variety of views on how successful outcomes should be defined. There are in fact some interesting (and, as we shall see, potentially useful) parallels between education and public health (cf. the opening quote in this chapter): defining precisely *why* we promote either is difficult, beyond perhaps a central concern with enabling populations to realize their potential either intellectually or physically, and removing avoidable impediments to this outcome. Nevertheless, despite this fuzziness as to end purpose, it seems reasonable to argue that a full scientific understanding of learning processes and the constraints upon them, and the optimal coordination of this understanding with teaching practices, are shared concerns for educators *and* researchers. The implication is that *translational* research in this sense and the implementation of its lessons are ultimately the fundamental objectives of educational neuroscience. The further implication is that at present the key building blocks necessary to achieve this are held by diverse communities, and not just scientific ones, but also those involving educators, administrators, and policy makers, since they too will have crucial parts to play if genuine translation is to happen.

A serious analysis of what putting these building blocks together is likely to require is critical if we are to understand how to progress, but such an analysis suggests that the scientific challenges may actually be less than the organizational ones. The development of public health as a discipline and a practice provides some indication of what may be involved, as well as some clues as to the structures that we may need to evolve in order to achieve our translational objectives. The origins of modern public health are frequently traced to the work of John Snow during the 1854 cholera outbreak in London. Polluted water and poor waste disposal had long been recognized as being involved in the occurrence of certain forms of disease, but up to this point thinking on the mechanism involved was dominated by miasma theory – essentially the notion that the origin of these diseases lay in airborne emanations from rotting organic matter. The response to outbreaks of disease was therefore driven by concerns with the circulation of air, the location of cemeteries, and so on. Snow's application of germ theory (which had by then gradually garnered a range of supportive evidence) suggested instead that specific microorganisms were responsible for the spread of cholera. This led in turn to his identification of a polluted public water well as the source of the outbreak. This notable success resulted in a rapid extension of germ theory to a range of infectious diseases, a marked growth in public sanitation works, and over the ensuing decades a broadening of activity to include the development of programs relating to public education (e.g., on infant health), vaccination, road safety, occupational safety, and drug control, to cite but a few instances. Public health is now an established part of daily life in developed countries, and an explicit objective of developing ones due to the growth of governmental and international agencies promoting good practice (e.g., the Surgeon-General's office, and the World Health Organisation).

If the translational goals of educational neuroscience parallel those of public health science, then the implication would seem to be that we should (a) begin by targeting a key area of educational need where good theory is able to make an obvious difference, (b) build outward from this initial example via core teams of individuals representing the different contributing strands of activity (i.e., the equivalent to epidemiologists, biostatisticians, local and national government officials, and health service professionals), whose activity is focused on mutually identified areas of need or risk and methods of counteracting these, (c) promote public knowledge of effective practices (without necessarily worrying *too* much about grasp of why these are effective), and (d) let governments take control ultimately, whilst continuing to feed them good, relevant evidence. The key step in this sequence is almost certainly the second one, which depends on building a consensus across key players in multidisciplinary teams within different professional backgrounds, based on (within bounds) shared knowledge of the relevant science – whilst as far as possible avoiding bias towards any one approach which may undermine that consensus.

This is a complex and difficult balancing act. To start with the science itself, the public health model suggests that researchers have a critical role to play in providing reliable and systematic evidence that can steer effective action. However, educational neuroscience research to date is piecemeal and unevenly developed, with much work on dyslexia that is beginning to inform both remedial and mainstream teaching of literacy (see, e.g., Hulme & Snowling, 2009), but few other areas approaching this level of activity, and some (e.g., conceptual growth in science, gifted and talented children) having been addressed by only a handful of researchers. Arguably, of course, public health science was in a similar position in the 1850s, but it did at least have a unifying framework in germ theory that had amassed supporting evidence in a range of areas of work, and which was capable of driving further work. It is hard to point to any framework within educational neuroscience that has similar coherence; to the extent that there is a consensus across researchers, this is based primarily on a shared belief that a full understanding of learning processes demands consideration of the neural level, but not what form the resulting models or framework should take. A consensus of this kind will be hard to achieve without a more coordinated program of research, covering typical *and* atypical learning in a range of key curriculum areas including language and literacy, number and mathematics, conceptual development and causal understanding in science, and socioemotional development. Only by garnering evidence that encompasses a breadth of phenomena using the different disciplinary approaches at our disposal – including intervention work that shows it is possible to bring about specific outcomes – is a bigger picture likely to emerge. One purpose of this book is to encourage the development of a research program of this kind, by illustrating something of what its different elements will look like.

Equally important is the need to progress as a community in a number of different senses. One aspect of this will be researchers from different disciplinary backgrounds working as equal partners, as discussed earlier. The research community needs to become coherent and self-sustaining, however, and this entails not just dialogue and collaboration between existing researchers but the creation of a transdisciplinary environment for the training of students and researchers, who will become the first fully fledged educational neuroscientists by dint of having been schooled to think about the field holistically from the outset.

As noted already, though, to be effective we need to recognize that researchers can only be one part of a wider community of engagement and exchange that helps set the research agenda, and maintains a focus on the implications for practice, including delivery. This wider community will need to encompass teachers, trainee teachers, teacher training agencies, professional educational and school psychologists, speech and language therapists, pediatric neurologists, and members of other professions involved in implementing evidence-based support for learning and remediation of learning difficulties. Moreover, if we take the public health model seriously, then the function of this wider community extends far beyond an advisory or consultative role: it needs to be an active partnership of researchers and professionals working *together* to identify issues, improve understanding through rigorous research, and develop solutions. In other words, practitioners will need to be involved at the heart of the research – and researchers will need to engage with issues of delivery. The implied roles are largely unfamiliar to all concerned, so even setting up a small number of functioning teams will require members to make an unusual commitment, which may need to be based in the first instance on belief in the potential of the work rather than substantial concrete evidence of benefit.

Finally, there will also need to be engagement with policy makers and policy shapers, in order to help ensure that educational neuroscience has socially perceived value, and that team members are therefore in some sense sanctioned to contribute to the development and deployment of novel forms of provision. Given an environment within which politicians and policy specialists are subjected to constant streams of lobbying by organizations with competing vested interests, success on this front will depend on standing out in some way – hence the importance of good science and a convincing application based upon it. If this was true for public health science, it is even more so now.

# References

Bradley, L., & Bryant, P. (1978). Difficulties in auditory organisation as a possible cause of reading backwardness. *Nature, 271*, 746–747.

Bruer, J. T. (1997). Education and the brain: A bridge too far. *Educational Researcher, 26*(8), 4–16.

Caramazza, A., & McCloskey, M. (1987). Dissociations of calculation processes. In G. Deloche & X. Seron (Eds.), *Mathematical disabilities: A cognitive neuropsychological perspective*. Hillsdale, NJ: LEA.

Dehaene, S. (2009). *Reading in the brain: The science and evolution of a human invention*. New York: Penguin.

Dehaene, S., & Cohen, L. (1995). Towards an anatomical and functional model of number processing. *Mathematical Cognition, 1*, 83–120.

Dumontheil, I., & Klingberg, T. (2011). Brain activity during a visuospatial working memory task predicts arithmetical performance 2 years later. *Cerebral Cortex, 22*(5), 1078–1085. DOI: 10.1093/cercor/bhr175

Editorial. (2005). Bringing neuroscience to the classroom. *Nature, 435*, 1138.

Ehri, L. C., Nunes, S. R., Stahl, S. A., & Willows, D. M. (2001). Systematic phonics instruction helps students learn to read: Evidence from the National Reading Panel's meta-analysis. *Review of Educational Research, 71*(3), 393–447.

Elliott, J. (2005). The dyslexia debate continues. *The Psychologist, 18*(12), 728–730.

Frith, C. D. (2007). *Making up the mind: How the brain creates our mental world*. Oxford: Blackwell.

Hulme, C., & Snowling, M.J. (2009). *Developmental disorders of language learning and cognition*. Chichester: Wiley-Blackwell.

Klingberg, T. (2010). Training and plasticity of working memory. *Trends in Cognitive Sciences, 14*(7), 317–324.

Laurillard, D. (2007). *Making the link between neuroscience and teaching methods*. Paper presented at the Numbra Summer School *Numeracy and brain development: progress and prospects*.

Lyytinen, H., Ahonen, T., Eklund, K., Guttorm, T. K., Laakso, M.-L., Leinonen, S., Leppanen, P. H. T., Lyytinen, P., Poikkeus, A.-M., Puolakanaho, A., Richardson, U., &

Viholainen, H. (2001). Developmental pathways of children with and without familial risk for dyslexia during the first years of life. *Developmental Neuropsychology*, *20*(2), 535–554.

McNab, F., Varrone, A., Farde, L., Jucaite, A., Bystritsky, P., Forssberg, H., & Klingberg, T. (2009). Changes in cortical dopamine D1 receptor binding associated with cognitive training. *Science*, *323*(5915), 800–802.

Melhuish, E. C., Sylva, K., Sammons, P., Siraj-Blatchford, I., Taggart, B., Phan, M. B., & Malin, A. (2008). Preschool influences on mathematics achievement. *Science*, *321*, 1161–1162.

Paulesu, E., Démonet, J.-F., Fazio, F., McCrory, E., Chanoine, V., Brunswick, N., Cappa, S. F., Cossu, G., Habib, M., Frith, C. D., & Frith, U. (2001). Dyslexia: Cultural diversity and biological unity. *Science*, *291*(5511), 2165.

Paulesu, E., Frith, C. D., & Frackowiak, R. S. J. (1993). The neural correlates of the verbal component of working memory. *Nature*, *362*, 342–345.

Petrides, M. (2000). The role of the mid-dorsolateral prefrontal cortex in working memory. *Experimental Brain Research*, *133*, 44–55.

Philips, S., & Tolmie, A. (2007). Children's performance on and understanding of the Balance Scale problem: The effects of parental support. *Infant and Child Development*, *16*, 95–117.

Ramsden, S., Richardson, F. M., Josse, G., Thomas, M. S. C., Ellis, C., Shakeshaft, C., Seghier, M. L., & Price, C. J. (2011). Verbal and non-verbal intelligence changes in the teenage brain [10.1038/nature10514]. *Nature*, *479*(7371), 113–116.

Shallice, T. (1988). *From neuropsychology to mental structure*. Cambridge: Cambridge University Press.

Share, D. L. (1995). Phonological recoding and self-teaching: sine qua non of reading acquisition. *Cognition*, *55*(2), 151–218.

Silani, G., Frith, U., Demonet, J. F., Fazio, F., Perani, D., Price, C., Frith, C. D., & Paulesu, E. (2005). Brain abnormalities underlying altered activation in dyslexia: A voxel based morphometry study. *Brain*, *128*(10), 2453–2461.

Thorndike, E. L. (1922). *The psychology of arithmetic*. New York: Macmillan.

van Asselen, M., Kessels, R. P. C., Neggers, S. F. W., Kappelle, L. J., Frijns, C. J. M., & Postma, A. (2006). Brain areas involved in spatial working memory. *Neuropsychologia*, *44*(7), 1185–1194.

Warrington, E. (1982). The fractionation of arithmetical skills: A single case study. *Quarterly Journal of Experimental Psychology*, *34A*, 31–51.

# Chapter 2

# Neuroimaging Methods

## Frederic Dick, Sarah Lloyd-Fox, Anna Blasi, Clare Elwell, and Debbie Mills

The last decade has seen remarkable growth in the use of neuroimaging tools to explore the development of brain structure and function in typically and atypically developing child populations, from infancy through adolescence. Because neuroimaging methods necessarily play a major role in educational neuroscience, it is important to understand what a given methodology can – and cannot – tell us about how children's brains change. In this chapter, we review the three major neuroimaging techniques currently used with children, namely electroencephalography (EEG) and associated event-related potentials (ERPs), near-infrared spectroscopy (NIRS), and magnetic resonance imaging (MRI). We lay out in turn each method's theoretical bases and practical issues, and highlight some key developmental findings associated with each technique.

## Electroencephalography and Event-Related Potentials

Since the mid-1960s, electroencephalography (EEG) and the EEG-derived event-related potential (ERP) have been one of the most widely used methods for studying brain activity linked to sensory, attentional, and cognitive processes across the lifespan. In the last two decades, developmental EEG/ERP studies have contributed a plethora of information on how the organization of the brain changes as children get older and learn new skills. EEG/ERPs are relatively inexpensive to

*Educational Neuroscience*, First Edition. Edited by Denis Mareschal, Brian Butterworth and Andy Tolmie.

record and do not require an overt response from the participant. It is currently the most practical neuroimaging method for studying developmental changes in brain activity in individuals such as infants and young children who are not easily tested using other brain imaging techniques. With the recent availability of easy-to-use packaged ERP systems, many developmental and educational scientists are setting up electrophysiology laboratories. The great promise of this new wave of research lies in the nature of the developmental questions being asked. However, the technique also has its limitations. This section addresses some of the promising approaches and common problems EEG/ERP researchers encounter when collecting, analysing, and interpreting electrophysiological data in developmental populations.

## Principles of EEG recording and averaging ERPs

Different parts of the brain communicate by sending minute electrochemical signals between brain cells called neurons. When large groups of neurons fire at the same time, they generate electrical activity. By placing small metal sensors (electrodes) at different locations over the scalp, scientists can record and analyse the electrical activity of the brain. Electroencephalography records changes in brain activity over time by measuring the difference in voltage between two electrode sites sampled at regular time intervals. Neural activity oscillates at various frequencies linked to different states of alertness, leading to the popular name for EEG of "brain waves." EEG is typically characterized as a function of frequency, measured in cycles per second or hertz (Hz), over time in milliseconds. Most adult brain activity is within 1–100 Hz. Slower brain wave frequencies (between 1 and 13 Hz) are associated with sleep or relaxation. Frequencies of 13–100 Hz are associated with alertness and a variety of mental functions from attention to problem solving.

In contrast to EEG, which measures ongoing brain activity, ERPs are *averages* of epochs of EEG at each electrode site, time-locked in response to specific stimuli, such as pictures or sounds. By averaging across several epochs, the activity unrelated to the stimuli averages out. The resulting ERP reflects brain activity that is time-locked to a specific event. ERPs are characterized by a series of positive- and negative-going waveforms. Typically, and as seen in Figure 2.2, ERPs are illustrated as changes in voltage (measured in microvolts along the *y*-axis) over time (in milliseconds along the *x*-axis). Fluctuations in voltage that are linked to specific sensory or cognitive events are called ERP components. The amplitude, latency, and distribution of these components provide information about the nature, timing, and organization of the neural systems mediating cognitive processes resulting from specific kinds of stimulus.

Recording EEG and averaging ERPs involves a series of steps that are common across different electrophysiological hardware and software packages. This includes placement of the electrodes, amplifying and filtering the EEG, determining the sampling rate for digitization, selecting a reference, time-locking the EEG to particular categories of stimuli, detecting artefacts, rejecting or correcting for artefacts, and averaging and plotting the ERPs. When and how to conduct each of these activities can be constrained by the choice of hardware and software, but also depends to a large extent on the ERP philosophy in the laboratory.

The procedures used for filtering, referencing, and treatment of artefacts are particularly important and can affect interpretation of the findings. However, best practice for these procedures can be a source of disagreement across laboratories. An in-depth discussion of each point is beyond this chapter, but a few of these issues will be addressed. For more information on recording, signal averaging, and interpreting ERPs there are several excellent sources available (de Haan, 2007; Handy, 2005; Luck, 2005; Luck & Kappenman, 2012).

*Placement of electrodes*   The 10–20 international system for standardizing electrode placements was established in the late 1950s (Jasper, 1958). It was based on relative measurements between electrode sites and landmarks on the head, i.e., the nasion (bridge of the nose) and the inion (bump on the back of the head). Current high-density systems, some with up to 250 electrode sites, have led to modifications of this system using spherical coordinates to define specific sites. However, the 10–20 (or later 10–10 or 10–5) placement system is still a widely used method for communicating electrode locations in publications. Electrode application time varies markedly depending on the number of electrodes and the type of system. The ideal number of electrodes to use depends on the research questions being asked. Studies using source localization programs will require a large number of electrodes. In contrast, studies examining modulation of an ERP component with a wide distribution may elect to record from fewer electrodes.

Most current systems use an elastic cap (see Figure 2.1) or net designed to fit securely on the head. Electrode locations are fixed in the cap or net, and size is determined by head circumference. An additional electrode for measuring eye movement may be part of the cap or applied separately. Gel or saline solution is used to facilitate a connection between each of the electrodes and the scalp. For developmental populations, the amount of time spent placing electrodes on the participant can have a major impact on the data recorded. Entertaining younger participants can be quite helpful. Completing electrode placement in 10 or 15 minutes greatly enhances the quality of the EEG.

*EEG recording*   As noted above, EEG is measured as the difference in voltage between two electrodes. To obtain these recordings, most systems select one of

**Figure 2.1**    Infant wearing ERP cap while being engaged with play theatre.

the electrode sites as a reference channel, i.e., an electrode channel that is subtracted from the other active electrode sites during data acquisition. Because the signals generated by brain activity are minute, they must be amplified approximately 10 000–50 000-fold to be measured. These voltage differentials are measured at each electrode site at regular intervals. The rate at which most modern systems can sample EEG tends to range from 500 to 2000 Hz or higher. That is, a data point is recorded at each site every 0.5–2 ms.

To eliminate electrical noise not related to brain activity, high- and low-pass filters are also frequently applied during recording. Somewhat counterintuitively, filters are described according to the frequencies they *allow to pass* for recording. Therefore, high-pass filters are used to eliminate contamination of the signal from low-frequency artefact such as movement and skin potentials. In contrast, low-pass filters are used to eliminate high-frequency noise caused by external sources such as electrical equipment. So-called "bandpass" filters set both high- and low-pass filter settings. It is important to note that filtering during data acquisition *permanently* eliminates certain frequencies from the recordings. Filtering can distort the EEG and resulting ERPs. Therefore, it is a good idea to record with as wide a bandpass setting as possible. Some ERP systems can record reference and filter-free data, so these filtering procedures are conducted in software during the analysis and not the data acquisition process. Additional filters and rereferencing can also be applied offline during signal averaging. This is beyond the scope of the chapter, but the reader can learn more about these procedures in the sources cited above.

*Event-related potential signal averaging* In contrast to EEG, ERPs reflect changes in brain activity across a specific time period (epoch) of activity elicited by a specific set of stimuli such as pictures of familiar versus unfamiliar faces. ERPs are created by averaging together epochs of EEG that are time-locked to the onset of a particular category of stimuli (e.g., familiar faces). The averaging process entails segmenting the EEG data into epochs or "chunks" of time that are linked to the presentation of particular types of stimulus and experimental conditions, identifying and rejecting or correcting artefacts linked to movement or other sources of noise, and averaging activity across time at each electrode site.

The epoch length includes a prestimulus interval for a baseline, and a specific amount of time following the stimulus. For example, developmental studies of language development may use a 200 millisecond (ms) prestimulus baseline with a 1000–1500 ms post-stimulus epoch. Determining the epoch length of the ERP depends on the cognitive processes being measured, as well the age of the participant. Components linked to sensory processes occur earlier in the epoch than higher cognitive processes. Infants and children have slower brain responses than adults, and may require longer epochs. The number of trials per condition is another important consideration. The larger the number of EEG trials included in an ERP average, the higher the signal-to-noise ratio. In general, ERP components that are large in amplitude and widely distributed require fewer trials per condition than smaller and earlier sensory potentials.

One limitation of this technique for use with infants and children is that it is sensitive to movements. Consideration must be given to how to treat different types of artefact such as movement, blinks, and horizontal eye movements. The rationale behind signal averaging is that, by averaging large numbers of EEG epochs together, only the signals time-locked to the sensory or cognitive event remain in the average. Therefore, if there are a sufficient number of trials per condition, much of the artefact within the range of amplitudes of brain activity will average out of the data. However, ERPs can be markedly distorted by large artefacts and particularly by artefacts that are time-locked to the stimuli – e.g., if the participant blinks each time s/he hears a sound.

Blinks are readily detected with an ocular electrode, as they are opposite in polarity over and under the eye. For developmental populations, a colourful sticker placed over the electrode can help infants and children tolerate the extra electrode below the eye. Each software package has its own approaches and algorithms for detecting different types of artefact. There are two common approaches for artefact removal, although which method to use can be controversial. Traditionally, trials contaminated with artefact are eliminated from the averages through artefact rejection. Because infants and children have large EEG signals, rejecting trials based on the same thresholds (e.g., ±100 μV) can be problematic in that they can reject trials containing large voltage frontal brain activity. Additionally, variability across participants, or across trials in the same participants, can increase the likelihood of including trials that contain artefact but fall below the threshold set for all participants. Therefore, setting individual thresholds is more time consuming but a better practice.

Other researchers prefer to model artefact – e.g., using independent component analyses – and thereby correct the average by subtracting the modeled signal. Because of variability in the morphology of artefact across trials, there are difficulties with modeling artefact in infants and young children. Even the best artefact rejection or correction procedures cannot replace the need for clean, artefact-free recordings. To obtain the best recordings and maximize signal-to-noise ratio, it is critical to keep the time for electrode placement to a minimum, and to keep experiments short and interesting for the participants. Providing the child participant with periodic breaks, colourful moving attention grabbers between blocks of trials, and reinforcements for sitting still are all effective tools for improving the quality of the EEG and resulting ERP.

## Making sense of ERP components

Establishing the functional significance of ERP findings can be mystifying to the newcomer and expert alike. This section will describe how ERP researchers display, measure, and interpret brain waves. ERPs are illustrated as a series of positive and negative deflections in voltage across time. As noted above, amplitude in microvolts is plotted along the *y*-axis, and time in milliseconds is plotted along the *x*-axis (see Figure 2.2). Note that when reading ERP papers, negative-going voltage can be plotted either above or below the *x*-axis. (In Figure 2.2, negative going voltage is plotted upwards.)

Fluctuations in voltage that have been linked with sensory and psychological processes across multiple experiments are called ERP components. ERP components are commonly named from their polarity (P for positive or N for negative) and their peak latency (e.g., at what time a component hits its highest or lowest peak). For example, one negative component elicited by semantic processing typically peaks around 400 ms and is labeled N400. Components are also often named for the order in which they occur in the waveform (e.g., the average voltage fluctuation for an electrode over the entire ERP epoch). For example, the first positive component in a waveform is often labeled P1.

Measurements of ERP components typically reflect the latency (the time in milliseconds at which the maximum positive or negative activity occurred), peak or mean amplitude (the maximal or mean positive or negative going activity in microvolts within a given time window), and distribution of the

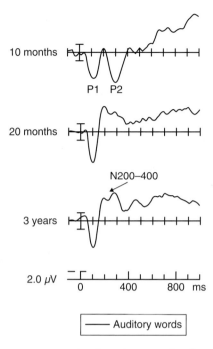

**Figure 2.2**   ERP components to words, changing over development.

activity across the scalp (the location of electrode sites at which the activity is observed). It is important to note that the relation between measurements of ERP components and changes in the underlying neural activity is not completely understood. A simplified explanation is that the latency, amplitude, and distribution of ERP components can provide information about the timing, amount, and to some extent physiological source of the underlying neural activity.

*Latency*   ERP latencies provide information about the timing of different cognitive processes. Longer latencies are thought to reflect slower processing. As a rule of thumb, sensory processes are associated with peaks within the first 200 ms after stimulus onset, whereas higher cognitive processes are associated with longer latencies. Comparing the latencies of ERPs associated with different experimental conditions can provide information about the time course of different cognitive events. For example, ERPs have been used to provide information about the time course of semantic and phonological encoding in adults (Desroches, Newman, & Joanisse, 2009; Rodriguez-Fornells, Schmitt, Kutas, & Munte, 2002), children (Coch, Grossi, Skendzel, & Neville, 2005), and even infants (Conboy & Mills, 2006; Friedrich & Friederici, 2010, 2011; Mani, Mills, & Plunkett, 2012; Mills et al., 2004).

*Amplitude*    ERP amplitudes can provide information about the relative amount of neural activity elicited by different experimental conditions, or by different groups. In general, larger amplitudes are thought to reflect more neural activity, specifically in the number of neurons firing in response to a particular stimulus event. For example, focused attention can modulate the amplitude of certain ERP components, with larger amplitudes observed in attended than nonattended conditions. Recently, in three- to eight-year-old children the amplitude of attention-related ERP components (within 100 ms of stimulus onset) was linked to the child's ability to suppress irrelevant information (Stevens, Lauinger, & Neville, 2009).

*Distribution*    ERPs are also characterized by their distribution across the scalp. Distribution refers to the area (e.g., left or right; anterior or posterior) in which a given ERP component or ERP effect (difference in ERPs between conditions) is observed or is the largest. For example, in the study by Stevens et al. (2009) cited above, the difference in ERP amplitudes between the attended and nonattended conditions was observed over anterior regions of the left hemisphere. This ERP effect would be described as having a left anterior distribution. To some extent, the distribution of ERP components reflects the physiological source. Cognitive events that elicit ERPs differing in latency and distribution are often interpreted as reflecting nonidentical brain systems.

   *It is very important not to conflate patterns of ERP distribution across the scalp with the location of generators in the brain*. A left anterior distribution, as noted above, means that the ERP amplitude differences elicited by the attended versus nonattended condition were observed at electrode sites located over the left frontal region. It does *not* mean that the source of this activity was generated in left frontal brain regions. In fact, the distribution of ERP components can be quite different from the underlying source. For example the N400, a negative-going wave that peaks around 400 ms and is associated with semantic integration, typically displays a right posterior distribution. However, fMRI and magnetoencephalography (MEG) studies have localized the source of the N400 to left temporal regions (Lau, Phillips, & Poeppel, 2008; Van Petten & Luka, 2006).

## ERPs and development

The popularity of electrophysiological methods to address developmental questions has dramatically increased over the last 30 years. Figure 2.3 shows changes in the numbers of peer-reviewed papers identified in a search of PsycINFO using the terms "event-related potentials, ERP, EEG, or electrophysiology" limited to developmental populations between birth and 17 years of age. In the 1970s and

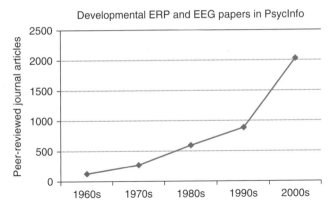

**Figure 2.3** Growth in number of developmental ERP articles.

1980s there were only a few hundred developmental EEG/ERP papers published across two decades. In contrast, there have been over 1000 ERP/EEG papers with developmental populations in 2010 and 2011 alone (not shown on graph). Early studies of ERPs tended to focus on the ERP components themselves, and whether or not ERP components observed in adults could also be elicited in infants and children. More recently, there have been a large number of developmental psychologists using the ERP technique to answer more detailed questions about brain and cognitive development. The ERP technique has been widely used to study different aspects of developmental change across several domains. A few examples include charting the maturation of different cortical areas (see, e.g., Ceponiene, Rinne, & Näätänen, 2002; Kurtzberg, Stone, & Vaughan, 1986; Segalowitz & Davies, 2004), assessing the integrity and development of auditory and visual sensory systems (Atkinson, 2001; Coch, Skendzel, Grossi, & Neville, 2005; Dubois et al., 2008; Kushnerenko et al., 2002; Kurtzberg et al., 1984; Wunderlich, Cone-Wesson, & Shepherd, 2006), development of attention (Reynolds, Courage, & Richards, 2010; Richards, Reynolds, & Courage, 2010), speech perception and language (Conboy & Mills, 2006; Friedrich & Friederici, 2010, 2011; Kuhl & Rivera-Gaxiola, 2008; Mills et al., 2004), social and cognitive development (Carver & Bauer, 2001; Itier & Taylor, 2004), the direct effects of learning (Key, Molfese, & Ratajczak, 2006; Mills, Plunkett, Prat, & Schafer, 2005), predictors of later development (Kuhl, Conboy, Padden, Nelson, & Pruitt, 2005; Molfese, Molfese, & Pratt, 2007), assessment of different interventions (Neville, Stevens, & Pakulak, 2011; Stevens et al., 2011; Vanderwert, Marshall, Nelson, Zeanah, & Fox, 2010), identification of children at risk (Nelson & McCleery, 2008), and many others. It is beyond the scope of this chapter to provide a comprehensive review of current studies of ERPs with children and infants. However, there are a number of excellent content- or methodologically oriented review articles (de Haan, Johnson, & Halit, 2003; Karmiloff-Smith, 2010; Kuhl & Rivera-Gaxiola, 2008; Nelson & McCleery, 2008; Thierry, 2005), book chapters (Coch & Guillick, 2012; Mannel, 2008; Mills & Conboy, 2009; Nelson & Monk, 2001), and books (de Haan, 2007; de Haan & Gunnar, 2009; Johnson, 2005; Nelson & Luciana, 2008) available.

It is important to keep in mind that there are marked changes in the timing and morphology of ERPs across infancy, childhood, adolescence, and even throughout adulthood. Caution must be taken when interpreting the functional significance of an ERP effect at different points in development. The polarity (negative/positive-going), timing, amplitude, and distribution of ERPs elicited by a specific experimental manipulation can change as a function of age. For example, in adults a negative-going component at 170 ms observed over occipitotemporal regions (N170) is larger in response to faces than to many other objects (Bentin et al., 1996; see also Mercure et al., 2008). In infants, two components thought to be precursors of the N170 – the N290 and P400 – show similar responsiveness to faces, but peak much later and show marked differences in their distribution compared with the N170 (Halit, de Haan, & Johnson, 2003).

It is not known if the infant and adult components are functionally equivalent. Moreover, it is not clear if some components evident in infancy have correlates in children and adults. For example a late negative-going wave called the Nc is modulated by familiarity and attention in infants and children (Courchesne, Ganz, & Norcia, 1981), but a direct correlate is not observed in adults. Other ERP components such as the N1 to auditory (Wunderlich et al., 2006) or visual (Mitchell & Neville, 2004) stimuli are slow to develop, and are only reliably elicited in middle or late childhood. In contrast, other ERP components, such as the N400, appear quite early in the first year of life and seem to reflect a similar functional significance to that in adults (Friedrich & Friederici, 2011). An excellent resource for discussion of the functional significance of ERP components in developmental populations is provided by Coch & Guillick (2012).

## Strengths and limitations of the ERP technique with developmental populations

The ERP technique has a number of advantages over behavioural approaches for use in studying developmental questions. First, ERPs do not require an overt response. Behavioural studies typically require the child to make an overt action such as point to a picture, imitate a set of actions, manipulate objects, show a looking preference, etc. A child's willingness to perform a task on a given day may be influenced by a number of factors unrelated to competence on the task, such as motivation, temperament, and social inhibition. ERPs measure brain activity linked to specific cognitive processes without requiring the child to do anything except see or hear the stimuli. Second, ERPs are particularly well suited to studying comprehension independent of production. Children often understand more than they can produce. However, assessing comprehension alone can be difficult in young children. For example, children cannot be asked to perform a grammaticality judgement, but ERPs to grammatically incorrect sentences can tell us if the brain notices a violation. Third, ERPs provide an online measure of cognitive processing. Behavioural measures suitable for children typically measure the end result of cognitive processing. ERPs reflect changes in brain activity over time during the course of processing. Thus ERPs can be used to chart the time course of neural activation to sensory, attentional, and higher cognitive processes elicited as children are engaged in a particular task. Fourth, ERPs can be used to compare changes in brain activity across the lifespan using the same dependent measure. Behavioural paradigms used to test cognition in infants and children, such as habituation, high-amplitude sucking, preference looking, and deferred imitation, may be useful only for a limited period of development. Different paradigms elicit different behaviours. This makes studying age-related changes in the same dependent measure impossible. In contrast, ERPs can be recorded at all ages from newborns, infants, children, adolescents, and throughout adulthood. Although there are some caveats in comparing infant with adult ERP components, this technique can be useful in examining changes in brain activity related to maturational and experiential factors across the lifespan. Fifth, the temporal resolution of ERPs is one of its greatest strengths. Current ERP systems can measure brain activity with a resolution of a fraction of a millisecond. Comparing the latencies of ERP components elicited by different experimental conditions or participant groups provides precise information about the timing of different cognitive events. Moreover, in contrast to fMRI and NIRS, which measure the hemodynamic response – an indirect and temporally lagged correlate of neural activity – EEG provides a direct and instantaneous measure of neural activity. This removes an additional level of inference in interpreting the response to experimental manipulations. Finally, EEFG and ERPs can reveal information about the brain that cannot be measured by behaviour or other cognitive neuroscience techniques. For example, even when two groups show the same level of accuracy and reaction times in behavioural responses, ERPs may show qualitative differences in the way the information is processed. Mills et al. (2000) showed that the brain systems mediating recognition of upright versus inverted faces was markedly different between participants with Williams syndrome and controls, even though both groups showed a similar inversion effect in behaviour alone.

ERPs also have some limitations. In contrast to their excellent temporal resolution, the spatial resolution of ERPs is quite limited. Because of volume conduction, neural activity from one site can travel though brain tissue and be recorded at different regions across the scalp. That is, electrical activity recorded at a given electrode is a measure of signals produced throughout the brain at that one location. In addition, the skull acts as a barrier, resulting in further spreading of the signal. There are computer programs available designed to localize the source of ERP components for high-density ERP systems, but this practice can be controversial (see Luck, 2005). Another limitation of EEG/ERPs is that the precise relation between the physiological source of the brain activity and the resulting surface potentials is not completely understood. Therefore, the functional significance of differences in ERP amplitude, latency, and distribution is not simple or transparent, and can be subject to misinterpretations.

In the section above, descriptions of these measurements are simplified for purposes of clarity. However, it is again important to emphasize that there is *not* a one-to-one correspondence between activity generated in different locations in the brain and the ERPs observed at the scalp. The latencies and amplitudes of the underlying activity can sum in a variety of different ways. Additionally, variability in latency and amplitudes across trials can interact to produce misleading results. For example, variability in peak latency across trials can result in smaller peak amplitudes. For a more complete discussion of strengths and limitations of ERPs the reader is directed to several books on ERP methods cited earlier. Nevertheless, the strengths of the technique, and the practical benefits outlined above, have helped to make ERPs the most widely used methods for linking brain and cognitive development in developmental and atypical populations.

## Near-Infrared Spectroscopy (NIRS)

Over a decade has passed since near-infrared spectroscopy (NIRS) was first applied to functional brain imaging in infants (Meek et al., 1998). In order to map hemodynamic responses (e.g., changes in local blood flow and volume) associated with neural activity, NIRS relies upon the relative transparency of biological tissue to near-infrared light as well as the differential absorption of oxy- and deoxyhemoglobin. NIRS systems are relatively portable, inexpensive, and particularly suited for use with infants, as they are noninvasive, operate silently, and do not require the participant to be completely motionless.

In 1993 the first reports were published of the use of NIRS to detect the hemodynamic response to cortical activation. Since then, the technology has been used to investigate cortical function in a range of age groups including adults (Ferrari & Quaresima, 2012) and children (Nagamitsu, Yamashita, Tanaka, &

Matsuishi, 2012). It is relatively recently that researchers have realized the potential of NIRS as an assay of infants' neuronal activity and brain organization (Lloyd-Fox, Blasi, & Elwell, 2010). There is a range of commercially produced as well as "in-house" manufactured NIRS systems available. The choice of which system to use is often driven by the cost and availability of infant- or child-appropriate probes and headgear (for more detailed reviews of available systems and their application in infancy research, see Lloyd-Fox et al., 2010; Wolff, Ferrari, & Quaresima, 2007). This section will provide an overview of the NIRS methodology and its relative advantages and disadvantages, and will provide some examples of what it has helped us to understand about infants' neural organization for perceptual and cognitive tasks.

## General principles and applications of NIRS

When neurons fire, their metabolic demands change, provoking a complex set of changes in oxygen and glucose consumption, local cerebral blood flow, and blood volume (Buxton, 2009). To a first approximation, a typical hemodynamic response to cortical neuronal activation in adults drives an increase in local blood flow that is disproportionate to the local oxygen demand, thus leading to an increase in oxy-hemoglobin ($HbO_2$) and a (smaller) decrease in deoxyhemoglobin (HHb) as it is displaced from the veins, and hence an increase in total hemoglobin (HbT) (Villringer and Chance, 1997; for a complete treatment, see Buxton, 2009). (Hemoglobin is the protein in red blood cells that transports oxygen and contains iron.) This change in local hemoglobin concentrations is the basis of NIRS. Biological tissue is relatively transparent to light in the near-infrared part of the spectrum, allowing several centimeters of tissue to be illuminated. This fortuitous "optical window" coincides with the favourable differential absorption spectra of oxy- and deoxyhemoglobin, thus allowing near-infrared absorption spectroscopy methods to provide a noninvasive measure of tissue oxygenation and hemodynamics.

With this optical technique, the light migrates from sources to detectors located on the head by traveling through the skin, skull, and underlying brain tissue (Elwell, 1995; Jöbsis, 1977; see Figure 2.4). The attenuation (or loss) of this 650–1000 nm wavelength light will be due to both absorption and scattering effects within these tissues. Further, blood oxy- and deoxy-hemoglobin chromophores (the aspect of the compound that is responsible for the characteristic colour) have different absorption properties of near-infrared light, so blood oxygenation can be measured. If scattering is assumed to be constant during the recording time, the measured changes in the attenuation of the near-infrared light can therefore be used to calculate the changes in blood oxyhemoglobin

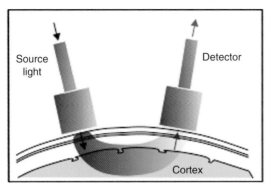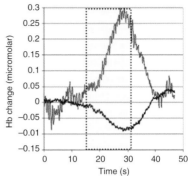

**Figure 2.4** The left panel shows a schematic representation of a source and detector illustrating the absorption and most likely path of scattered light that eventually reaches the detector. Note that this is not an accurate model of light transport but for illustrative purposes only. The right panel shows a typical hemodynamic response to cortical neuronal activation with an increase in HbO$_2$ (red) and a decrease in HHb (blue) leading to an overall increase in blood flow.

(HbO2), deoxyhemoglobin (HHb) and total hemoglobin (HbT = HbO$_2$ + HHb) in the illuminated tissue. With knowledge of the optical pathlength in tissue (see Delpy & Cope, 1997), the changes in the concentrations of HbO$_2$, HHb, and HbT can be quantified, and used as surrogate markers of brain blood flow and neuronal activation.

In a basic NIRS experiment, the onset of a stimulus (for instance a flashing checkerboard) triggers neuronal activation, which thereby induces an increase in the concentration of HbO$_2$ and a lesser decrease in HHb concentration. The particular amplitude and timing of this activation-induced vascular response is known as the *hemodynamic response function* (HRF). The shape of the signal may vary according to the evoking stimuli (i.e., differences in amplitude are observed between brief and prolonged stimulus presentation) as well as the underlying neural activity. (Figure 2.4 shows the typical changes in HbO$_2$ and HHb during functional activation of the adult brain.)

A major advantage of functional NIRS (also known as fNIRS) compared with EEG is that it is less susceptible to data corruption by movement artefacts, and offers a somewhat more spatially resolved image of activation, thereby allowing the localization of brain responses to cortical regions. In addition, when compared with functional magnetic resonance imaging or fMRI (see below), fNIRS has much superior temporal resolution, is silent (allowing for less masked presentation of auditory stimuli), and can measure both oxy- and deoxyhemoglobin concentrations, providing a more complete measure of the hemodynamic response relative to fMRI. Though fMRI and fNIRS measure the same hemodynamic response, generally fMRI techniques have a limited acquisition rate (with typical whole-brain fMRI acquiring an image every 2 s), whereas fNIRS systems can acquire data at greater than 100 Hz, thus providing superior temporal resolution (Huppert, Hoge, Diamond, Franceschini, & Boas, 2006). However, the temporal resolution of fNIRS is lower than that of EEG (see above), and the depth resolution is dependent on the age of the infant and the optical properties of the tissue (see Fukui, Ajichi, & Okada, 2003). Further, the technique offers lower spatial resolution compared with MRI, and detailed images of anatomical structure are beyond the capabilities of the technique (see Minagawa-Kawai, Mori, Hebden, & Dupoux, 2008, for further discussion of these limitations). However, it is possible to co-register fNIRS and structural MRI images for better understanding of structure–function relationships.

## Studies of development using NIRS

The use of NIRS to study infant functional brain activation is a rapidly increasing research area with increasing diversity of design, cortical regions of interest, and cognitive process under investigation. Whereas in early fNIRS studies the main aim was typically to detect the neural response to basic stimuli in primary cortical areas, such as response to acoustic tones in the auditory cortex (Sakatani, Chen, Lichty, Zuo, & Wang, 1999) or stroboscopic flashing light in the visual cortex (Hoshi et al., 2000; Zaramella et al., 2001), more recently researchers have focused on more complex stimuli activating multiple cortical regions (Lloyd-Fox et al., 2010). An increasing number of researchers have focused on the study of awake infants to address topics such as object processing (Watanabe et al., 2008; Wilcox et al., 2005, 2008), social communication (Grossman et al., 2008; Minagawa-Kawai et al., 2009), human action processing (Lloyd-Fox et al., 2009; Lloyd-Fox, Blasi, Everdell, Elwell, & Johnson, 2011a), voice processing (Blasi et al., 2011; Lloyd-Fox, Blasi, Mercure, Elwell, & Johnson, 2011b), action observation (Shimada and Hiraki, 2006), and face processing (Blasi et al., 2007; Carlsson, Lagercrantz, Olson, Printz, & Bartocci, 2008; Otsuka et al., 2007). In these studies, fNIRS has been used to characterize hemodynamic responses in broad cortical regions such as the superior temporal region (eye gaze/human action processing), orbitofrontal cortex (maternal face/emotion recognition), sensorimotor areas (action observation), prefrontal cortex (object permanence), and occipitotemporal cortex (dynamic objects).

As an example of recent fNIRS work in one domain of development (action perception), Lloyd-Fox et al. (2009) found that five-month-old infants activate the posterior superior temporal cortex in response to dynamic human movements such as "peek-a-boo" but not in response to dynamic non-human mechanical movements such as toys rotating, thus suggesting a bias for human-action-specific responses. In a related fNIRS study, Lloyd-Fox et al. (2011a) found that five-month-old infants' cortical responses to seeing isolated human movements of either the eyes, hand, or mouth were already quite spatially segregated across frontal and temporal cortex detectors (see Figure 5 of Lloyd-Fox et al., 2011a).

There has been recent technical progress in NIRS implementation, with development of multiple source–detector separation arrays to aid depth discrimination of the hemodynamic response, additional detector channels, and advances in headgear design leading to improved optical signals. Current directions for the development of fNIRS techniques include (a) the refinement of probe and headgear to reduce movement (particularly important when studying visual paradigms where the infant is awake), (b) new experimental designs to address effects of boredom, anticipation, and the synchronization of systemic/ biorhythmic responses, (c) better characterization and interpretation of infants' hemodynamic response, and (d) and co-registration between the hemodynamic response measured at the surface of the head and the underlying cortical anatomy (for a review of these issues see Aslin & Mehler, 2005; Meek, 2002).

## Magnetic Resonance Imaging (MRI)

### Background and safety

The phenomenon of nuclear magnetic resonance has been used as a basic research tool in the physical sciences for more than 50 years. However, it was only in the 1970s that innovations by Paul Lauterbur and Sir Peter Mansfield allowed for magnetic resonance to be used to create two-dimensional images of physical structures. Numerous theoretical and technical advances since their initial discoveries have made magnetic resonance imaging (MRI) the dominant medical imaging tool today. MRI has several major advantages over other imaging technologies such as computerized tomography (CT) and positron emission tomography (PET), including safety, flexibility, and speed of data acquisition.

First, MRI is a truly noninvasive imaging technique, something that is especially important for paediatric imaging. As we will explain below, MRI uses strong magnetic fields and nonionizing radiofrequency (RF) energy to generate a signal from the body. In contrast, the use of ionizing radiation is central to both CT (X-rays) and PET (injected radionuclides). When ionizing radiation passes through the body, it is energetic enough to strip electrons off atoms and molecules such as water. This can create free radicals in the form of ionized water, which can in turn remove electrons or hydrogen atoms from other molecules in the body. In sufficient doses, this process can cause damage or death to cell machinery. By contrast, nonionizing radiation – such as that used for transmitting mobile phone signals, radio broadcasts, or microwave transmissions, as well as for MRI – transmits much less energy, and only excites electrons to a higher-energy state, rather than removing them from their orbits. When the electrons fall back to their less-energetic state, they give off their excess energy in the form of heat. However, it takes a lot of radiofrequency or microwave energy to create significant heating, and MRI scanners are carefully calibrated to avoid depositing too much energy in a given amount of tissue.

The magnetic fields used in MRI are also safe – several decades of experiments have shown no deleterious effects of long-term exposure to high-strength magnetic fields in developing or adult organisms (for an extensive list of studies, see http://mrisafety.com/research_summary.asp). In recognition of this evidence, the US Food and Drug Administration has declared MRI safe for children and infants aged more than one month for magnetic field strengths up to 8 T (see below), and for neonates ages less than one month for magnetic field strength up to 4 T.

MR is also a flexible and fast imaging method. Less than one hour of scan time will provide a vast amount of data on various aspects of brain structure and function. Indeed, it can take as little as 4–5 min to acquire a single high-resolution scan showing the structure of the whole brain. Similarly, basic functional MRI protocols can be used to localize primary visual, auditory, motor, and sensory regions with 4–8 min of scanning. While using MRI with children does present some special challenges (as we outline below), these qualities make it very attractive as a research tool for understanding links between brain and behaviour and how these might change over developmental time.

## Basic components of MRI

While modern MRI scanners are extremely complex pieces of equipment (see Figure 2.5 for an example of a typical MRI scanner used for research), they can be broken down into four basic components. The first of these is the main magnet itself. It is made of several thin, large-diameter spools of coiled wire in a sealed cylinder, which is cooled by liquid helium so that the wire loses all electrical resistance and becomes 'superconducting'. To generate a magnetic field, a very strong electrical current is injected into the coil; remarkably, this current will continue to flow around the coil without any additional energy input, assuming that the liquid helium keeps the coil sufficiently cool to retain its superconductivity. The electrical current moving around the coil generates a very strong magnetic field, measured in units of tesla. Standard MRI scanners have magnetic field strengths

*Frederic Dick et al.*

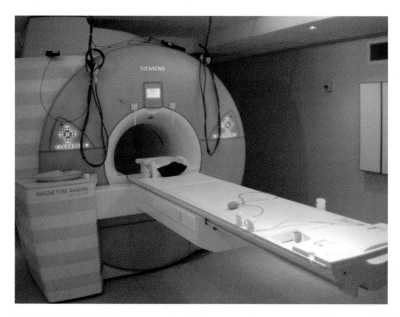

**Figure 2.5** A 1.5 T MRI scanner, fitted for research purposes. (Courtesy Birkbeck/ UCL Centre for NeuroImaging.)

of 1.5, 3.0, 4.0, and now even 7.0 T (as a comparison, the magnetic field right next to the pole of a small bar magnet is about 0.01 T). Because the magnetic field is so strong, ferromagnetic metallic objects (keys, coins, tools) that are brought into the scanner room can be sucked in to the bore of the magnet at very high speeds, endangering whomever is near or in the magnet, as well as potentially damaging the scanner itself. This is one of the major safety concerns when using MRI; thus, when in the vicinity of an MRI scanner, it is important to remember that the magnet is always on, even when the scanner is not in operation.

In addition to the main magnet, MRI scanners also have three magnetic gradient coils that pulse on and off at different times depending on the type of scan; the coils are arranged so that they generate gradients in the strength of the magnetic field in the left–right direction, the front–back direction, and the head–toe direction. The magnetic field generated by these coils is not as strong as that of the main magnet, but unlike that of the main magnet the magnetic field varies in strength from one end of the coil to another, for reasons explained below. In the presence of the main magnetic field, the fast-switching electrical currents in these gradient coils generate a magnetic field that results in force on the coils, causing them to vibrate at the switching rate. This vibration in the gradient coils causes the loud "clanging" or "beeping" noises characteristic of MRI scanning. Fortunately, recent advances in scanner technology have helped reduce this noise significantly.

The third major scanner component is the radiofrequency (RF) transmit coil, which sends out brief pulses of RF energy, in much the same way that mobile phones transmit signals back and forth. The fourth component is the RF receiver coil. The position of this coil, or set of coils, will depend on the particular part of the body being imaged. For brain imaging, the coils tend to be arranged in a kind of "birdcage" configuration that surrounds the head of the participant. The coils pick up faint RF signals from the body, which are then amplified and processed by computers connected to the scanner.

## Basic physics of MRI

How do the four components of the MRI scanner work together to create such a wide variety of functional and structural images of the brain and body? The answer to this question lies in some fundamental properties of atoms and their interactions with each other. Medical MRI exploits the fact that the nucleus of the most abundant element in the body – hydrogen, with only one proton – acts like a small magnet with a north and a south pole. The magnetic dipoles of the billions and billions of hydrogen protons in a small tissue volume are usually oriented randomly, meaning that they do not have an overall net magnetization. However, when the tissue is placed in a very strong magnetic field such as the one in an MRI scanner, a tiny proportion of the hydrogen protons in the tissue will align with the field, thereby forming a very weak but detectable magnetization that is aligned with the magnet's bore (the "longitudinal" magnetization).

Each hydrogen proton also has an intrinsic property called "spin", somewhat like a top or dreidel spinning on a hard surface. Just like a top in the earth's gravitational field, the spinning protons will tend to be oriented within the main magnetic field. If a top is spinning rapidly on a table, and then is tilted away from the main axis of the earth's gravitational field (e.g., straight up and down), it will start to swivel slowly around that axis. Constantly "spinning" hydrogen protons do the same thing in a magnetic field. Interestingly, the speed with which the protons precess is completely predictable given the strength of the main magnetic field; this precession rate is termed the "Larmor frequency".

Even though the hydrogen protons aligned with the magnetic field are rotating or precessing at the same rate or frequency around the magnetic axis, they are not all in sync. Instead, they are out of phase with each other, and not all pointing in the same direction at the same time. However, if we beam in an electromagnetic pulse (an RF pulse) that oscillates at the same frequency as that at which the protons are precessing, then they will all start to point in the same direction as they swivel around.

If the RF pulse is the correct length, it will tip all of the spinning protons completely over so that they are swivelling around in sync in the plane perpendicular to the main magnetic orientation. (Imagine a table full of spinning tops that have been tipped over on their sides and are miraculously swivelling just above the table's surface, all in unison.) Recall that when the hydrogen protons are aligned, they generate their own small magnetic field. When the precessing protons are tipped over on their sides, their net magnetization is rotating perpendicular to the main magnetic field. As long as they are tipped over and are not aligned with the main magnetic field, this little rotating magnetization will induce electrical current in a surrounding coil of wire. This is the signal that MRI scanners detect.

Eventually, the protons will start to tip back up (or relax) and align with the main magnetic field, and will also get out of phase with each other. (This is a little harder to visualize with real tops; it is as if the proton "tops" have no friction and never slow down, but are constantly colliding with each other, with the end result that their coordinated swivelling returns to an uncoordinated swivelling.) This means that the electrical current that they induce will also decrease and eventually disappear. The speed with which the spinning protons dephase and relax – and therefore the speed with which the electrical signal decays – depends upon the chemical composition of the surrounding tissue. This difference in the rate of decay of the protons' signal is what makes it possible for MRI to detect different tissue types, in that the signal from the precessing protons in white matter, gray matter, and cerebrospinal fluid will decay at different rates.

The preceding paragraphs essentially lay out the most basic MR experiment. An object – in our case, a person – is put into a large magnetic field, the person's protons become slightly more aligned with the magnetic field, and an RF pulse is applied at the Larmor frequency, making the spinning protons tip over and precess in unison. This in turn generates a small electrical current in the wire coil around the person; the speed with which this current decays tells us something about the chemical composition of the tissue surrounding the hydrogen protons.

## How are MR images generated?

While the MR experiment described above is very useful for finding out the chemical properties of a given sample, it does not tell us anything about the spatial layout of different substances within this sample. As we noted above, it was Mansfield's and Lauterbur's innovations in the 1970s that made it possible to use magnetic resonance techniques to create two-dimensional pictures of objects such as the human body. The key insight to creating MR "pictures" was taking advantage of the relationship between magnetic field strength and precession (Larmor) frequency. Recall that MRI scanners not only have a very strong static magnetic field, but also have three magnetic gradient coils arranged along perpendicular axes (*X*, *Y*, and *Z*) along the main bore of the magnet. Introduction of current into one of these coils creates a magnetic gradient that is slightly weaker at one end, and slightly stronger at the other end. This means that the Larmor frequency will change from one end of the magnetic gradient to the other.

This systematic change in hydrogen protons' precession frequency can be used to encode spatial information in the MRI signal in what is generally a three-stage process. The first is the 'slice-select' stage, where one magnetic gradient is switched on, thus creating a 'gradient' of Larmor frequencies along the *Z*-axis parallel with the bore of the magnet. A precisely calibrated RF pulse is then delivered that will only tip over protons with a narrow range of Larmor frequencies – and thus excite protons in a thin slice of tissue. After these protons within one slice are tipped and are precessing in unison, a second, perpendicular magnetic gradient is turned on momentarily, thereby changing the phase of the precessing protons systematically along the *Y*-axis. Finally, the last perpendicular gradient is turned on along the *X*-axis, again systematically changing the Larmor frequency along the *X*-axis while the MR signal is collected.

By repeating this process many times, with many different variants of magnetic gradient, the spatial composition of the entire sample can be recorded. Perhaps the most remarkable thing about the process is the *decoding* of this signal. The brain image is reconstructed by applying a Fourier transform to the entire set of measurements. A Fourier transform reconstructs an image (such as a brain slice) by adding together a large number of stripe patterns of different spacings and different orientations (Fourier components), each with a particular weighting. Each data point from the head coil corresponds to a single Fourier component and represents the extent to which the brain slice resembles a stripe pattern of a certain orientation and spacing. Remarkably, despite the fact that each such measurement originates from the whole head, a detailed picture can nevertheless be reassembled. The gradients are essentially used to create all the different stripe patterns.

### Varieties of MR images

MRI is an especially powerful imaging technique, partly because it can reveal so many different tissue properties. There are three general families of MR images that are commonly used in neuroscientific and clinical research: structural,

*Frederic Dick et al.*

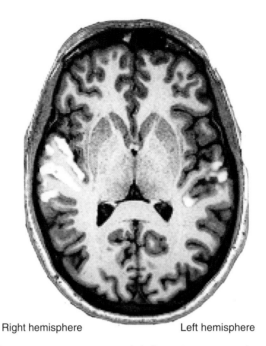

Right hemisphere                    Left hemisphere

**Figure 2.6** f MRI activation in a young adult listening to complex auditory stimuli. Note that the brain is shown in "radiological convention", where the left side of the image shows the right side of the brain. The grayscale image is a high-resolution (1 × 1 × 1 mm³) $T_1$-weighted scan, where (in general) white-colored pixels show white (myelinated) tissue, gray-colored pixels show gray matter (cortex or subcortical nuclei), and dark pixels show cerebrospinal fluid or bone. The heatscale overlay shows a gently smoothed statistical map of f MRI activation along the right and left superior temporal gyri.

functional, and diffusion-tensor imaging (see Figure 2.6). Structural images can be thought of as a "snapshot" of the brain at one point in time. Structural scans for research purposes are usually quite high resolution (often down to 1 × 1 × 1 mm³ or less), and can be used to measure the volume, shape, and position of tissues of interest. These scans can also be used to reconstruct the cortical surface, which can then be measured in terms of its thickness and relative curvature at different locations in the brain. Just as in film photography, the relative brightness of a given tissue in a structural MR image is determined by how that tissue absorbs and gives off energy during the time the image is acquired. Furthermore, the choice of structural scan type will determine whether a given tissue shows up as bright or dark. For instance, in so-called $T_1$-weighted scans, cortical gray matter (primarily composed of neuronal cell bodies, glial cells, capillaries, and dendrites) will look gray, whereas white matter (predominantly myelinated axons) will tend to look white, and cerebrospinal fluid (CSF) will be very dark. On the other hand, $T_2$-weighted images will tend to show white matter as dark, gray matter as gray, and CSF as bright.

Unlike the high-resolution, single-snapshot view of the brain provided by structural scans, fMRI scans reflect transient changes in the brain occurring over a period of seconds and minutes, ones that are thought to reflect changes in neuronal activity. Thus, fMRI can be used to assess and compare the pattern of functional activation of brain regions in given cognitive tasks. By far the most frequently used fMRI method is that based on "blood oxygenation level dependent" (BOLD) image contrast. This technique, developed in the early 1990s, cleverly uses the change in the ratio of oxygenated to deoxygenated hemoglobin in the blood as an indirect measure of changes in the location of neuronal firing – exactly the same physiological phenomenon that is used in fNIRS, as discussed above. The logic of BOLD imaging is as follows: about 2–3 s after a population of neurons increases its firing rate, there is a transient (from 12 to 20 s) change in the amount of oxygenated hemoglobin delivered to this region of tissue by the brain's circulatory system. This oxygenated hemoglobin replaces some of the deoxygenated hemoglobin that was previously in that region. This slight change in the ratio of oxygenated to deoxygenated hemoglobin can be picked up by a standard clinical MR scanner. Because deoxygenated hemoglobin is paramagnetic, it "spoils" the coherence of the MR signal to some degree. Oxygenated hemoglobin, on the other hand, is less paramagnetic, so when it replaces the deoxygenated blood the overall coherence of the signal in that region increases. These small, transient increases and decreases in signal due to the influx of blood after neuronal activation are what allow us to visualize – albeit indirectly – changes in neural activation over time.

The third type of MR imaging commonly used for brain research is diffusion-weighted, or diffusion tensor imaging (DTI). This MRI technique uses another physical phenomenon – the directions that water diffuses in brain tissue – in order to reveal the location and orientation of white-matter tracts such as the corpus callosum and the superior longitudinal fasciculus, both very important for allowing different brain regions to "talk" to each other. DTI techniques take advantage of two basic facts: (1) water molecules move randomly (e.g., Brownian motion), and (2) water diffuses differently around white and gray matter. Water will meander slowly through gray matter, in many different directions, but will move more quickly along white-matter pathways, and will not diffuse through them very easily, since they are ensheathed in water-repelling myelin. We can use MRI to track the diffusion of water molecules over time, in many different directions, and thereby reconstruct the likely location and orientation of white-matter tracts.

## The challenges of studying children using MRI

While MRI is a powerful and versatile tool, it comes with its own set of challenges and limitations when applied to developmental cognitive neuroscience (like all other research methodologies). Many of these are practical difficulties. For instance, MRI is quite resource intensive, both in terms of the cost per hour for scanning itself, and in the time and experience required to process and analyse MRI data. Furthermore, some children either cannot be scanned – e.g., those with metal in their bodies, including orthodontic devices – or find the scanner environment aversive, because of either claustrophobia (the magnet bore can be quite narrow), the loud scanner noise, or the clinical atmosphere of many MRI suites. MRI also requires participants to remain still for 5–10 min intervals. Not only is this difficult for some children, but also differences in the extent of head movement between age groups (leading to profound effects on image quality) can introduce major confounds in the experimental design and analysis (Power, Barnes, Snyder, Schlaggar, & Petersen, 2012). In functional imaging, participants must also attend for long periods of time – age differences in levels of attention or task compliance are sometimes hard to detect in the scanner, but can have considerable impact on patterns of brain activation (Kotsoni, Byrd, & Casey, 2006; Power et al., 2012). These and other issues are addressed in several recent reviews of the developmental neuroimaging literature, such as that by Karmiloff-Smith (2010).

## Studies of development using MRI

The study of structural and functional brain development using MR techniques in infants and young children presents methodological as well as the practical challenges described above (Berl, Vaidya, & Gaillard, 2006). Many of the techniques used in the analysis of neuroimaging data were developed for adult brains, and had to be modified and adapted for use with children. In the remaining section we outline a few recent advances MRI and fMRI have made in the study of brain development and function in young children.

*Structural brain development* In the early years of life the progressive development of cognitive function is accompanied by ongoing structural change in the brain. In the first published studies of brain development, MRI was used to describe the qualitative changes of gray and white matter in the neonatal brain, and up to the first two years of life. These studies delineate the changes in cerebral tissue composition that take place in the first months, as myelination processes set in (Barkovich & Kjos, 1988; McArdle et al., 1987). More recently,

MRI techniques have been used in quantitative cross-sectional and longitudinal studies of brain development in children as young as three months of age into young adulthood. These changes are typically quantified in terms of brain size, cortical thickness, and gray and white matter volume (Lenroot & Giedd, 2006). A study by Sowell and colleagues (Sowell, Thompson, Leornard, Welcome, Kan, & Toga, 2004) found that in normally developing children between the ages of 5 and 11 years brain volume expands at a rate of up to 1 mm per year. This expansion of brain volume, which is found predominantly in the prefrontal region, is accompanied by underlying changes in gray and white matter composition. Namely, as brain size expands (in right-frontal and parietal and occipital regions bilaterally) gray matter thins (at least as it is observed in MR images) and white matter increases due to myelin proliferation, a process that improves the speed and efficiency of processing between cortical regions. In fact, the cortical "thinning" of the frontal and parietal lobes observed with MR was found to correlate with better performance on measures of verbal skill. Increases in cortical thickness also occur, but are more selective, and appear to be localized mainly within the left anterior and posterior perisylvian regions.

As children mature, the proportion of gray and white matter in the brain changes. Approaching puberty, the rate of gray and white matter maturation accelerates. Whilst white-matter volume typically shows a linear increase throughout childhood, changes in gray-matter volume are nonlinear, in that they decrease in post-adolescence (Giedd et al., 1999; Gogtay et al., 2004; Sowell et al., 1999). Interestingly, gray-matter volume appears to peak in the frontal and parietal regions of the brain approximately one year earlier in females than males, which corresponds with the earlier onset of puberty in females, suggesting an influence of gonadal hormones upon brain development (Giedd et al., 1999). In tracking the sequence of gray-matter development in different brain regions in young individuals aged 4–21 years, Gogtay et al. (2004) found that the process of gray-matter maturation appears to follow a similar sequence to how the brain regions evolved, with phylogenetically older regions maturing first. Moreover, the sequence of structural development was also similar to that of functional development, whereby primary sensorimotor cortices and the frontal and occipital poles mature first, followed by the remainder of the cortex in a posterior to anterior direction, with the superior temporal cortex being the last area to mature. In infants, Deoni et al. (2011) used a quantitative MRI technique to examine the development of subcortical myelination, showing regional differences in the regionalization and rate of myelination from 3 to 11 months of age.

Functional MRI has also been an exciting tool for exploring brain development, with the breadth and number of studies too great to detail here (for reviews of several cognitive domains of interest, see Karmiloff-Smith, 2010; Luna, Padmanabhan, & O'Hearn, 2010; Schlaggar & McCandliss, 2008). Many of the

other chapters in this volume will describe fMRI work with children. One especially interesting recent set of studies investigated functional regionalization in
newborn infants (~2 days old) when listening to speech and music stimuli
(Perani et al., 2010, 2011). Amongst other results, the authors found that newborn infants showed a substantially right-lateralized response in primary and
secondary auditory regions for naturally produced speech and music, whereas
altered speech and music showed a bilateral or even slightly left-lateralized profile of activation.

## Other Neuroimaging Techniques

One other noninvasive neuroimaging technique increasingly used in developmental studies is MEG. MEG detects magnetization changes related to electrical
currents generated by neurons (the electrical signals detected by EEG), and like
EEG has very fine temporal resolution with potentially finer spatial resolution. For
a review and an exciting example of new developmental research using MEG, see
Hari and Salmelin (2012) and Travis et al. (2011). An established *invasive* neuroimaging technique that is used in adults and clinical developmental settings is PET
(mentioned above). Because this technique deposits small quantities of ionizing
radiation, it is generally not used for studies of typical development, but has been
very important for understanding patterns of brain activity in atypical development
such as after perinatal focal brain injury (Müller et al., 1998, 1999).

## Conclusions

Noninvasive neuroimaging techniques have proved an invaluable addition to
our understanding of brain development and functional reorganization. While
it is important to note what they *cannot* currently tell us (e.g., what a child is
thinking about, or the kinds of skill she or he is or will be proficient in), there is
no question that these imaging methodologies will considerable contributions
to uncovering the mechanisms underlying neural and cognitive development.

## References

Aslin, R., & Mehler, J. (2005). Near-infrared spectroscopy for functional studies of brain
    activity in human infants: Promise, prospects, and challenges. *Journal of Biomedical
    Optics, 10*, 011009-1–3.
Atkinson, J. (2001). Assessing visual function and prognosis in the developing visual
    brain. *Investigative Ophthalmology and Visual Science, 42*, S312.

Barkovich, A., & Kjos, B. (1988). Normal postnatal development of the corpus callosum as demonstrated by MR imaging. *American Journal of Neuroradiology, 9*, 487–491.

Bentin, S., Allison, T., Puce, A., Perez, E., & McCarthy, G. (1996). Electrophysiological studies of face perception in humans. *Journal of Cognitive Neuroscience, 8*, 551–565.

Berl, M., Vaidya, C., & Gaillard, W. (2006). Functional imaging of developmental and adaptive changes in neurocognition. *NeuroImage, 30*, 679–691.

Blasi, A., Fox, S., Everdell, N., Volein, A., Tucker, L., Csibra, G., Gibson, A., Hebden, J., Johnson, M. H., & Elwell, C. (2007) Investigation of depth dependent changes in cerebral haemodynamics during face perception in infants. *Physics in Medicine and Biology, 52*, 6849–6864.

Blasi, A., Mercure, E., Lloyd-Fox, S., Thomson, A., Brammer, M., Sauter, D., Deeley, Q., Barker, G. J., Renvall, V., Deoni, S., Gasston, D., Williams, S. C. R., Johnson, M. H., Simmons, A., & Murphy, D. (2011) Early specialization for voice and emotion processing in the infant brain. *Current Biology, 21*, 1220–1224.

Buxton, R. (2009). *Introduction to functional magnetic resonance imaging: Principles and techniques* (2nd ed.). Cambridge: Cambridge University Press.

Carlsson, J., Lagercrantz, H., Olson, L., Printz, G., & Bartocci, M. (2008). Activation of the right fronto-temporal cortex during maternal facial recognition in young infants. *Acta Paediatrica, 97*, 1221–1225.

Carver, L. J., & Bauer, P. J. (2001). The dawning of a past: The emergence of long-term explicit memory in infancy. *Journal of Experimental Psychology: General, 130*, 726–745.

Ceponiene, R., Rinne, T., & Näätänen, R. (2002). Maturation of cortical sound processing as indexed by event-related potentials. *Clinical Neurophysiology, 113*(6), 870–882.

Coch, D., Grossi, G., Skendzel, W., & Neville, H. (2005a). ERP nonword rhyming effects in children and adults. *Journal of Cognitive Neuroscience, 17*, 168–182.

Coch, D., & Guillick, M. M. (2012). Event-related potentials and development. In S. J. Luck & E. S. Kappenman (Eds.), *The Oxford handbook of event-related potential components* (pp. 475–511). New York: Oxford University Press.

Coch, D., Skendzel, W., Grossi, G., & Neville, H. (2005b). Motion and color processing in school-age children and adults: An ERP study. *Developmental Science, 8*(4), 372–386.

Conboy, B. T., & Mills, D. L. (2006). Two languages, one developing brain: Event-related potentials to words in bilingual toddlers. *Developmental Science, 9*, F1–F12.

Courchesne, E., Ganz, L., & Norcia, A. M. (1981). Event-related brain potentials to human faces in infants. *Child Development, 52*, 804–811.

de Haan, M. (2007). *Infant EEG and event-related potentials.* New York: Psychology.

de Haan, M., & Gunnar, M. R. (Eds.). (2009). *Handbook of developmental social neuroscience.* New York: Guilford.

de Haan, M., Johnson, M. H., & Halit, H. (2003). Development of face-sensitive event-related potentials during infancy: A review. *International Journal of Psychophysiology, 51*, 45–58.

Delpy, D. T., & Cope, M. (1997). Quantification in tissue near-infrared spectroscopy. *Philosophical Transactions of the Royal Society of London, B Biological Sciences, 352*, 649–659.

Deoni, S. C. L., Mercure, E., Blasi, A., Gasston, D., Thomson, A., Johnson, M., Williams, S. C. R., & Murphy, D. G. M. (2011). Mapping infant brain myelination with magnetic resonance imaging. *Journal of Neuroscience, 31*(2), 784–791.

Desroches, A. S., Newman, R. L., & Joanisse, M. F. (2009). Investigating the time course of spoken word recognition: Electrophysiological evidence for the influences of phonological similarity. *Journal of Cognitive Neuroscience, 21*(20), 1893–1906.

Dubois, J., Dehaene-Lambertz, G., Soarès, C., Cointepas, Y., Le Bihan, D., & Hertz-Pannier, L. (2008). Microstructural correlates of infant functional development: Example of the visual pathways. *The Journal of Neuroscience, 28*(8), 1943–1948.

Elwell, C. E. (1995). *A practical users guide to near infrared spectroscopy.* London: Hamamatsu Photonics, UK.

Ferrari, M., & Quaresima, V. (2012). A brief review on the history of human functional near-infrared spectroscopy (fNIRS) development and fields of application. *NeuroImage.* DOI: 10.1016/j.neuroimage.2012.03.049

Friedrich, M., & Friederici, A. D. (2010). Maturing brain mechanisms and developing behavioral language skill. *Brain and Language, 114,* 66–71.

Friedrich, M., & Friederici, A. D. (2011). Word learning in 6-month-olds: Fast encoding–weak retention. *Journal of Cognitive Neuroscience, 23,* 3228–3240.

Fukui, Y., Ajichi, Y., & Okada, E. (2003). Monte Carlo prediction of near-infrared light propagation in realistic adult and neonatal head models. *Applied Optics, 42,* 2881–2887.

Giedd, J. N., Blumenthal, J., Jeffries, N. O., Castellanos, F. X., Liu, H., Zijdenbros, A., Paus, T., Evans, A. C., & Rapoport, J. L. (1999). Brain development during childhood and adolescence: A longitudinal MRI study. *Nature Neuroscience, 2,* 861–863.

Gogtay, N., Giedd, J. N., Lusk, L., Hayashi, K. M., Greenstein, D., Vaituzis, A. C., Nugent, T.F., III, Herman, D. H. Clasen, L. S., Toga, A. W. Rapoport, J. L., & Thompson, P. M. (2004). Dynamic mapping of human cortical development during childhood through early adulthood. *Proceedings of the National Academy of Sciences, 101*(21), 8174–8179.

Grossmann, T., Johnson, M. H., Lloyd-Fox, S., Blasi, A., Deligianni, F., Elwell, C., & Csibra, G. (2008). Early cortical specialization for face-to-face communication in human infants. *Proceedings of the Royal Society, B, 275,* 2803–2811.

Halit, H., de Haan, M., & Johnson, M. H. (2003). Cortical specialisation for face processing: Face-sensitive event-related potential components in 3 and 12 month-old infants. *NeuroImage, 1*(9), 1180–1193.

Handy, T. C. (Ed.). (2005). *Event-related potentials: A methods handbook.* Cambridge, MA: MIT Press.

Hari, R., & Salmelin, R. (2012). Magnetoencephalography: From SQUIDs to neuroscience. NeuroImage 20th anniversary special edition. *NeuroImage, 61*(2), 386–396.

Hoshi, Y., Kohri, S., Matsumoto, Y., Kazutoshi, C., Matsuda, T., Okajima, S., & Fujimoto, S. (2000). Haemodynamic responses to photic stimulation in neonates. *Pediatric Neurology, 23,* 323–327.

Huppert, T. J., Hoge, R. D., Diamond, S. G., Franceschini, M. A., & Boas, D. A. (2006). A temporal comparison of BOLD, ASL and NIRS haemodynamic responses to motor stimuli in adult humans. *NeuroImage, 29,* 368–382.

Itier, R. J., & Taylor, M. J. (2004). Face recognition memory and configural processing: A developmental ERP study using upright, inverted and contrast-reversed faces. *Journal of Cognitive Neuroscience, 16*(3), 1–15.

Key, A. P., Molfese, D. L., & Ratajczak, E. D. (2006). ERP indicators of learning in adults. *Developmental Neuropsychology, 29*(2), 379–395.

Kuhl, P. K., Conboy, B. T., Padden, D., Nelson, T., & Pruitt, J. (2005). Early speech perception and later language development: Implications for the 'critical period'. *Language Learning and Development, 1*(3/4), 237–264.

Jasper, H. (1958). The ten–twenty electrode system of the International Federation. *Electroencephalography and Clinical Neurophysiology, 10*, 371–375.

Jöbsis, F. F. (1977). Noninvasive, infrared monitoring of cerebral and myocardial oxygen sufficiency and circulatory parameters. *Science, 198*, 1264–1267.

Johnson, M. H. (2005). *Developmental cognitive neuroscience.* Malden, MA: Blackwell.

Karmiloff-Smith, A. (2010). Neuroimaging of the developing brain: Taking "developing" seriously. *Human Brain Mapping, 31*, 934–941.

Kotsoni, E., Byrd, D., & Casey, B. J. (2006). Special considerations for functional magnetic resonance imaging of pediatric populations. *Journal of Magnetic Resonance Imaging, 23*(6), 877–886.

Kuhl, P., & Rivera-Gaxiola, M. (2008). Neural substrates of language acquisition. *Annual Review of Neuroscience, 31*, 511–534.

Kurtzberg, D., Stone, C. L., & Vaughan, H. G., Jr. (1986). Cortical responses to speech sounds in the infant. In R. Q. Cracco & I. Bodis-Wollner (Eds.), *Evoked potentials* (pp. 513–520). New York: Liss.

Kurtzberg, D., Vaughan, H. G., Courchesne, E., Friedman, D., Harter, R., and Putnam, L. E. (1984). Developmental aspects of event-related potentials. *Annals of the New York Academy of Sciences, 425*, 300–318.

Kushnerenko, E., Ceponiene, R., Balan, P., Fellman, V., Huotilainen, M., and Näätänen, R. (2002). Maturation of the auditory event-related potentials during the 1st year of life. *Neuroreport, 13*, 47–51.

Lau, E. F., Phillips C., & Poeppel, D. (2008). A cortical network for semantics: [de]constructing the N400. *Nature Reviews Neuroscience, 9*, 920–933.

Lenroot, R. K., & Giedd, J. N. (2006). Brain development in children and adolescents: Insights from anatomical magnetic resonance imaging. *Neuroscience and Biobehavioral Reviews, 30*(6), 718–729.

Lloyd-Fox, S., Blasi, A., & Elwell, C. E. (2010). Illuminating the developing brain: The past, present and future of functional near infrared spectroscopy. *Neuroscience and Biobehavioural Reviews, 34*(3), 269–284.

Lloyd-Fox, S., Blasi, A., Everdell, N., Elwell, C. E., & Johnson, M. H. (2011a). Selective cortical mapping of biological motion processing in young infants. *Journal of Cognitive Neuroscience, 23*(9), 2521–2532.

Lloyd-Fox, S., Blasi, A., Mercure, E., Elwell, C. E., & Johnson, M. H. (2011b). The emergence of cerebral specialisation for the human voice over the first months of life. *Social Neuroscience, 7*, 317–330.

Lloyd-Fox, S., Blasi, A., Volein, A., Everdell, N., Elwell, C., & Johnson, M. H. (2009). Social perception in infancy: A near infrared spectroscopy study. *Child Development, 80*, 986–999.

Luck, S. J. (2005). *An introduction to the event-related potential technique.* Cambridge, MA: MIT Press.

Luck, S. J., & Kappenman, E. S. (Eds.). (2012). *Oxford handbook of event-related potential components.* New York: Oxford University Press.

Luna, B., Padmanabhan, A., & O'Hearn, K. (2010). What has fMRI told us about the development of cognitive control through adolescence? *Brain and Cognition, 72*(1), 101–113.

Mani, N., Mills, D. L., & Plunkett, K. (2012). Vowels in early words: An event-related potential study. *Developmental Science, 15*, 2–11.

Mannel, C. (2008). The method of event-related potentials in the study of cognitive processes. In A. Friederici & G. Thierry (Eds.), *Trends in language acquisition research: Early language development* (pp. 1–22). Amsterdam: Benjamins.

McArdle, C. B., Richardson, C. J., Nicholas, D. A., Mirfakhraee, M., Hayden, C. K., & Amparo, E. G. (1987). Developmental features of the neonatal brain: MR imaging. Part I. Gray–white matter differentiation and myelination. *Radiology, 162*, 223–229.

Meek, J. (2002). Basic principles of optical imaging and application to the study of infant development. *Developmental Science, 5*, 371–380.

Meek, J. H., Firbank, M., Elwell, C. E., Atkinson, J., Braddick, O., & Wyatt, J. S. 1998. Regional haemodynamic responses to visual stimulation in awake infants. *Pediatric Research, 43*, 840–843.

Mercure, E., Dick, F., Halit, H., Kaufman, J., & Johnson, M. H. (2008). Differential lateralization for words and faces: Category or psychophysics? *Journal of Cognitive Neuroscience, s*(*11*), 2070–2087.

Mills, D. L., Alvarez, T. D., St. George, M., Appelbaum, L. G., Neville, H., & Bellugi, U. (2000). Electrophysiological studies of face recognition in Williams syndrome. *Journal of Cognitive Neuroscience, 12*, 47–64.

Mills, D., & Conboy, B. (2009). Early communicative development and the social brain. In M. de Haan & M. Gunnar (Eds.), *Handbook of developmental social neuroscience* (pp. 175–207). New York: Guilford.

Mills, D. L., Plunkett, K., Prat, C., & Schafer, G. (2005). Watching the infant brain learn words: Effects of language and experience. *Cognitive Development, 20*, 19–31.

Mills, D. L., Prat, C., Zangl, R., Stager, C. L., Neville, H. J., & Werker, J. F. (2004). Language experience and the organization of brain activity to phonetically similar words: ERP evidence from 14- and 20-month-olds. *Journal of Cognitive Neuroscience, 16*, 1452–1464.

Minagawa-Kawai, Y., Matsuoka, S., Dan, I., Naoi, N., Nakamura, K., & Kojima, S. (2009). Prefrontal activation associated with social attachment: Facial-emotion recognition in mothers and infants. *Cerebral Cortex, 19*, 284–292.

Minagawa-Kawai, Y., Mori, K., Hebden, J. C., & Dupoux, E. (2008). Optical imaging of infants' neurocognitive development: recent advances and perspectives. *Developmental Neurobiology, 68*, 712–728.

Mitchell, T. V., & Neville, H. J. (2004). Asynchronies in the development of electrophysiological responses to motion and color. *Journal of Cognitive Neuroscience, 16*(8), 1363–1374.

Molfese, D. L., Molfese, V. J., & Pratt, N. L. (2007). The use of event-related evoked potentials to predict developmental outcomes. In M. de Haan (Ed.), *Infant EEG and event-related potentials*. Hove, UK: Psychology (pp. 199–225).

Müller, R. A., Rothermel, R. D., Behen, M. E., Muzik, O., Chakraborty, P. K., & Chugani, H. T. (1999). Language organization in patients with early and late left-hemisphere lesion: A PET study. *Neuropsychologia, 37*(5), 545–557.

Müller, R. A., Rothermel, R. D., Behen, M. E., Muzik, O., Mangner, T. J., & Chugani, H. T. (1998). Differential patterns of language and motor reorganization following early left hemisphere lesion: A PET study. *Archives of Neurology, 55*(8), 1113–1119.

Nagamitsu, S., Yamashita, Y., Tanaka, H., & Matsuishi, T. (2012). Functional near-infrared spectroscopy studies in children. *BioPsychoSocial Medicine, 6*, 7. DOI: 10.1186/1751 0759-6-7

Nelson, C., & Luciana, M. (Eds.). (2008). *Handbook of developmental cognitive neuroscience*. Cambridge, MA: MIT Press.

Nelson, C. A., & McCleery, J. P. (2008). Use of event-related potentials in the study of typical and atypical development. *Journal of the American Academy of Child and Adolescent Psychiatry, 47*, 1252–1261.

Nelson, C. A., & Monk, C.S. (2001). The use of event-related potentials in the study of cognitive development. In C. Nelson & M. Luciana (Eds.), *Handbook of developmental cognitive neuroscience* (pp. 125–136).Cambridge, MA: MIT Press.

Neville, H., Stevens, C., & Pakulak, E. (2011). Interacting experiential and genetic effects on human neurocognitive development. In Battro A. M., Dehaene, S., & Singer, W. J. (Eds.), *Human neuroplasticity and education* (pp. 167–181). Vatican City: Pontifical Academy of Sciences.

Otsuka, Y., Nakato, E., Kanazawa, S., Yamaguchi, M. Y., Watanabe, S., & Kakigi, R. (2007). Neural activation to upright and inverted faces in infants measured by near infrared spectroscopy. *NeuroImage, 34*, 399–406.

Perani, D., Saccuman, M. C., Scifo, P., Awander, A., Spada, D., Baldoli, C., Poloniato, A., Lohmann, G., & Friederici, A. D. (2011). Neural language networks at birth. *Proceedings of the National Academy of Sciences of the United States of America, 108*, 16056–16061.

Perani, D., Saccuman, M. C., Scifo, P., Spada, D., Andreolli, G., Rovelli, R., Baldoli, C., & Koelsch, S. (2010). Functional specializations for music processing in the human newborn brain. *Proceedings of the National Academy of Sciences of the United States of America, 107*(10), 4758–4763.

Power, J. D., Barnes, K. A., Snyder, A. Z., Schlaggar, B. L., & Petersen S. E. (2012). Spurious but systematic correlations in functional connectivity MRI networks arise from subject motion. *NeuroImage, 59*, 2142–2154.

Reynolds, G. D., Courage, M. L., & Richards, J. E. (2010). Infant attention and visual preferences: Converging evidence from behavior, event-related potentials, and cortical source localization. *Developmental Psychology, 46*, 886–904.

Richards, J. E., Reynolds, G. D., & Courage, M. I. (2010). The neural bases of infant attention. *Current Directions in Psychological Science, 19*, 41–16.

Rodriguez-Fornells, A., Schmitt, B. M., Kutas, M., & Munte, T. M., (2002). Electrophysiological estimates of the time course of semantic and phonological encoding during listening and naming. *Neuropsychologia, 40*, 778–787.

Sakatani, K., Chen, S., Lichty, W., Zuo, H., & Wang, Y. (1999). Cerebral blood oxygenation changes induced by auditory stimulation in newborn infants measured by near infrared spectroscopy. *Early Human Development, 55*, 229–236.

Schlaggar, B. L., & McCandliss, B. D. (2007). Development of neural systems for reading. *Annual Review of Neuroscience, 30*(1), 475–503.

Segalowitz, S. J., & Davies, P. L. (2004). Charting the maturation of the frontal lobe: An electrophysiological strategy. *Brain and Cognition, 55*, 116–133.

Shimada, S., & Hiraki, K. (2006). Infant's brain responses to live and televised action. *NeuroImage, 32*, 930–939.

Sowell, E. R., Thompson, P. M., Holmes, C. J., Batth, R., Jernigan, T. L., & Toga, A. W. (1999). Localizing age-related changes in brain structure between childhood and adolescence using statistical parametric mapping. *NeuroImage, 9*, 587–597.

Sowell, E. R., Thompson, P. M., Leonard, C. M., Welcome, S. E., Kan, E., & Toga, A. W. (2004). Longitudinal mapping of cortical thickness and brain growth in children. *The Journal of Neuroscience, 24*(38), 8223–8231.

Stevens, C., Harn, H., Chard, D., Currin, J., Parisi, D., & Neville, H. (2011). Examining the role of attention and instruction in at-risk kindergarteners: Electrophysiological measures of selective auditory attention before and after an early literacy intervention. *Journal of Learning Disabilities.* DOI: 10.1177/0022219411417877

Stevens, C., Lauinger, B., & Neville, H. (2009). Differences in the neural mechanisms of selective attention in children from different socioeconomic backgrounds: An event-related brain potential study. *Developmental Science, 12*(4), 634–646.

Thierry, G. (2005). The use of event-related potentials in the study of early cognitive development. *Infant and Child Development, 14*, 85–94.

Travis, K. E., Leonard, M. K., Brown, T. T., Hagler, D. J., Curran, M., Dale, A. M., Elman, J. L., & Halgren, E. (2011). Spatiotemporal neural dynamics of word understanding in 12- to 18-month-old-infants. *Cerebral Cortex, 21*(8), 1832–1839.

Van Petten, C., & Luka, B. J. (2006). Neural localization of semantic context effects in electromagnetic and hemodynamic studies. *Brain and Language, 97*, 279–293.

Vanderwert, R. E., Marshall, P. J., Nelson, C. A., Zeanah, C. H., & Fox, N. A. (2010). Timing of intervention affects brain electrical activity in children exposed to severe psychosocial neglect. *PLoS ONE, 5*(7), 1–5.

Villringer, A., & Chance, B. (1997). Noninvasive optical spectroscopy and imaging of human brain function. *Trends in Neuroscience, 20*, 435–442.

Watanabe, H., Homae, F., Nakano, T., & Taga, G. (2008). Functional activation in diverse regions of the developing brain of human infants. *NeuroImage, 43*, 346–357.

Wilcox, T., Bortfeld, H., Woods, R., Wriuck, E., & Boas, D. A. (2005). Using near-infrared spectroscopy to assess neural activation during object processing in infants. *Journal of Biomedical Optics, 10*, 1010–1019.

Wilcox, T., Bortfeld, H., Woods, R., Wruck, E., & Boas, D. A. (2008). Haemodynamic response to featural changes in the occipital and inferior temporal cortex in infants: A preliminary methodological exploration. *Developmental Science, 11*, 361–370.

Wolf, M., Ferrari, M., & Quaresima, V. (2007). Progress of near-infrared spectroscopy and topography for brain and muscle clinical applications. *Journal of Biomedical Optics, 12*, 062104-1–14.

Wunderlich, J. L., Cone-Wesson, B. K., & Shepherd, R. (2006). Maturation of the cortical auditory evoked potential in infants and young children. *Hearing Research, 212*, 185–202.

Zaramella, P., Freato, F., Amigoni, A., Salvadori, S., Marangoni, P., Suppjei, A., Schiavo, B., & Chiandetti, L. (2001). Brain auditory activation measured by near-infrared spectroscopy (NIRS) in neonates. *Pediatric Research, 49*, 213–220.

## Further Reading

Buxton, R. (2009). *Introduction to functional magnetic resonance imaging: principles and techniques* (2nd ed.). Cambridge: Cambridge University Press.

Luck, S. J. (2005). *An introduction to the event-related potential technique.* Cambridge, MA: MIT Press.

Meek, J. (2002). Basic principles of optical imaging and application to the study of infant development. *Developmental Science, 5*, 371–380.

Weishaupt, D., Kchli, V. D., & Marincek, B. (2008). *How does MRI work? An introduction to the physics and function of magnetic resonance imaging.* Berlin: Springer.

# Chapter 3

# Computational Modeling of Learning and Teaching

## Michael S. C. Thomas and Diana Laurillard

## Introduction

In this chapter, we consider how computer models are being used to advance our understanding of learning within education. By the notion of 'model', we mean a simplified representation and implementation of a phenomenon that captures the key theoretical principles of its operation. In the case of computer models, the implementation of the model is in the form of a computer program.

In educational neuroscience, computers are employed as model systems in two different but related ways. First, computers are used to understand the *cognitive mechanisms* that underlie the learning process. Second, computers are used as *teaching tools* that model the interaction of the teacher with the learner; these tools can take the form of *intelligent tutoring systems* or *adaptive microworlds*. Cognitive models and computer-based teaching tools are related in that both require an understanding of the learner and the way in which particular sets of experiences and kinds of feedback can advance the learner's knowledge. Indeed, some computer programs have been employed both as cognitive models and as the basis of intelligent tutoring systems (see the later example of ACT-R). The two uses differ in that for cognitive models the target of the model is the learning process taking place within the child or adult, while for the teaching tools the target of the model is the behavior of the human teacher and his or her interactions with the learner.

*Educational Neuroscience*, First Edition. Edited by Denis Mareschal, Brian Butterworth and Andy Tolmie.
© 2014 John Wiley & Sons, Ltd. Published 2014 by John Wiley & Sons, Ltd.

Both approaches are concerned with *individual differences*. Cognitive modeling seeks to understand the causal mechanisms – be they of genetic or environmental origin – that lead to differences in learning outcomes. For the teaching tools, intelligent tutoring systems seek to tailor the knowledge and tasks that the individual learner must revisit to acquire a specific domain, given the successes and failures he or she has exhibited on previous tasks (an *instructivist* pedagogic model). Adaptive microworlds contain a model of how a user can interact with a domain to construct an object or event; the program then adapts the difficulty of the task goal to the individual learner's performance on the last task (a *constructionist* pedagogic model).

In terms of the dialogue between education and neuroscience, cognitive modeling demonstrates one active interface between the disciplines. *Artificial neural networks* are used to build models of learning based on the computational principles observed in actual neural circuits. To the extent that these cognitive models are successful, they will uncover the nature of knowledge representations in the learner, as well as the sequence of knowledge development. In the future, they may thus inform computer-based teaching programs.

Our review of computational methods is structured as follows. In the first half of the chapter, we discuss the use of computers as cognitive models. We discuss why building explicit, implemented models is an effective way to advance our understanding of the nature of learning, and we summarize the general principles and aims of building such models. We discuss two of the main approaches to building models of the cognitive system, the *symbolic* and *subsymbolic* approaches. The subsymbolic approach makes widespread use of artificial neural network models. We consider the way in which such models have been inspired by neuroscience research into the principles of computation in the brain and how artificial neural networks have certain properties that make them well suited to modeling cognitive mechanisms of learning. By way of illustration, we describe research in which a large population of artificial neural networks is used to simulate individual differences in rates of language development, and which addresses the specific educational issue of why language delay, when diagnosed early in children, sometimes disappears of its own accord, but other times persists and requires intervention. We finish the first half of the chapter with a look to the future, in how computational models of learning may advance beyond current limitations to enrich our understanding of the plethora of phenomena that represent the educational experience.

In the second part of the chapter we discuss the use of computers as teaching tools. We summarize the key properties of educational models of teaching and learning. We then describe the components of two different digital learning environments, intelligent tutoring systems and adaptive microworlds. In each case, we make reference to the pedagogical theories that they embody.

We illustrate the second of these approaches with an example of an adaptive microworld designed to address weaknesses in the understanding of number sense found in children with dyscalculia, a specific deficit in the learning of mathematical skills.

Finally, although the approaches of cognitive modeling and computer-based teaching tools are conceptually related, it will become apparent that they sometimes use terms and ideas in different ways, and approach their account of the process of learning from different directions. We use the example of *feedback* to highlight where the approaches line up and where they do not. We finish with a summary of the main points of the chapter.

## Computational Models of Cognition

### The use of models to understand mechanisms of learning

At the heart of education lies the concept of learning – facilitating change in knowledge and abilities over time. Computational systems can provide models to understand the cognitive processes underlying learning. Such models are formal systems that track the changes in information processing that take place as a behavior or skill is acquired. Models are generally implemented as psychologically constrained computer simulations, which learn tasks such as reasoning, concept formation, and language and literacy skills.

To date, models have mainly been applied to the study of cognitive development, focusing in particular on how transitions are achieved from one level of competence to the next via experience and/or maturation. Models have been used to probe questions such as how much 'preprogrammed' or innate knowledge exists in the infant mind, and how the sophistication of reasoning can increase in children with age and experience. Education differs from cognitive development with respect to the assumed learning environment. Whereas development reflects what the learner discovers through interaction with his or her natural physical and social environments, formal education concerns the acquisition of knowledge and skills accumulated by a culture across many generations. The extended, structured learning environments provided by education are powerful enough to sculpt new brain systems, such as those involved in reading and mathematics. Education is built on the foundation of cognitive development, and, with respect to the innate component of cognitive development, education both takes advantage of inherited mechanisms of brain plasticity and is also constrained by the types of knowledge representation that the mind can support.

Computer models have proved invaluable tools to help developmental psychology shift from a descriptive science into a mature explanatory science

(Mareschal & Thomas, 2007). A descriptive science deals in summaries of observations of what happens – in the case of development, the abilities that children exhibit at different ages. An explanatory science deals in mechanism – revealing the underlying causal processes that give rise to the observed behavior. The construction of computer models has aided the shift to an explanatory science of development because, when researchers have to translate their underlying theories into explicit computer models, they must specify precisely what is meant by the various terms in the causal theory. Terms such as *representations, symbols, variables,* and *learning* must have an exact definition to allow implementation. The degree of precision required to construct a working computer model avoids the possibility of arguments arising from the misunderstanding of imprecise verbal theories. For example, the idea of "attention" conveniently summarizes a cluster of human behaviors. Yet it is another thing to build a processing system that has the ability to select certain sorts of information for enhanced processing. How does the system select what information to attend to, and how is the processing of attended (and unattended) information altered? There is no longer room for vagueness when building a working model of the process.

## General principles and aims of computational models of learning

A cognitive computational model of the learning process usually comprises the following four elements. First, there is a *computational system,* of which there are different varieties. A computational system is a mechanism that acquires, stores, and manipulates information, which it can use to drive behavior. Second, there are *representations of information.* Some of these representations are specified by the modeller and correspond to the information supplied to the system by its simulated environment, along with the output responses that are required to generate the requisite behavior (e.g., behaviors such as naming a word, giving the number that is the answer to a mathematic problem, or inferring the intended meaning of an analogy). Other representations of information may be developed by the computational system itself during the learning process – this is the information the system needs in order to generate the appropriate behavior, given the input with which it is supplied. Third, the model has a *learning algorithm.* This is a process by which the system alters its internal structures to improve its performance on the target problem, given feedback on its current performance (see the later section on Feedback for more detail on types of feedback in computer learning systems). Fourth, there is a *training set,* corresponding to the problem domain that the model must learn. Training sets can be supplied externally by the modeler. Alternatively, the modeler can construct an artificial microworld in which the model generates its own training set by its behavior and subsequent experiences in the artificial microworld. The microworld may contain other individuals (or *agents*) with which the model can interact. In addition, modellers sometimes test the learning system on a *generalization set*, corresponding to novel problems within the target domain. Success on a generalization set ensures that the model has learnt the general principles of the problem domain, rather than just memorizing the individual items in the training set.

There is a wide range of possible computational systems that can serve as models for learning in the cognitive system (see, e.g., Mitchell, 1997, and Sun, 2008, for introductions to different types of machine learning system). These include concept learning, decision tree learning, artificial neural networks, Bayesian (probabilistic) learning, instance-based learning, genetic algorithms, and reinforcement learning. One broad distinction that has characterized computational models of development in particular is that between *symbolic* and *subsymbolic* models. Researchers using *symbolic* models maintain that cognition is best characterized as a rule-governed physical symbol system, such as a conventional computer program. In this view, cognitive development consists in the construction and modification of mental rules. By contrast, researchers using *subsymbolic* models view cognition in terms of a highly interactive dynamic system, such as an artificial neural network. An artificial neural network contains simple processing units, each with an activation level analogous to the firing rate of a neuron. The processing units are wired together in networks with weighted connections. The strength of the connection between any two units determines how much the activity of one unit can affect the subsequent activity of the other. Networks can learn tasks as transformations between different activation states. They do so by gradually changing the strength of the connection weights to produce the appropriate activation states, based on information from the environment. In this type of system, the causal entities are not rules but continuous activation states distributed across the network, states that sometimes cycle over time. Such networks do not operate as physical symbol systems, or at best approximate them in certain narrow circumstances. That is, the networks sometimes show *rule-following* behavior, without being *rule driven*. In a subsymbolic framework, both learning and development consist in the continuous tuning of the underlying parameters of the cognitive system (for a network, these parameters are the connection weights), in order to bring the responses of the system closer to the desired behaviors.

In symbolic models, encoded knowledge can be clear and transparent. In some cases, it corresponds to a rule-based description of the observed behavior (e.g., the rules for addition and subtraction in a system that performs arithmetic). Rules can be very powerful in producing a range of complex behaviors (e.g., the rules of grammar can be used to generate an infinite variety of sentences). In subsymbolic models, it can be less obvious what knowledge is encoded, since dynamic patterns of activation across a network of simple processing units may not be directly relatable to behavior. Given the task presented at input, the activation patterns must simply serve to provide the correct answer at output. Most symbolic models have emphasized the transparency of knowledge representations involved in cognitive development at the expense of implementing mechanisms for the acquisition of new knowledge and abilities. That is to say, it has proved difficult to understand how systems that run according to rules learn new sets of rules, particularly rules that are more sophisticated than those previously operating in the system. In contrast, most subsymbolic models have emphasized the specification of a learning mechanism for incrementally improving behavior on a problem domain, at the expense of the transparency of the knowledge representations that the system acquires. In short, symbolic models have more transparent workings but do not readily capture the process of learning, while subsymbolic models are good at learning but their internal functioning is more opaque.

For researchers in psychology who investigate the nature of the mind and the nature of development, the different learnabilities of, respectively, rules and activation patterns has led to a conundrum. To the extent we think that the human mind needs complicated and densely structured mental representations to deliver a cognitive skill, it is hard to fathom how these representations are learned. There are three ways out of this conundrum (Mareschal & Thomas, 2006). *Either* complex behavior is generated by representations that are in large part innate (i.e., not learned at all; Chomsky's theory of universal grammar would provide one example of such an approach in the field of language development – this is the idea that humans easily acquire complex language because we are born with a blueprint for grammar), *or* we do not yet understand the full repertoire of learning mechanisms available to the human mind (that is, somehow complex mental representations are learnable in a way we have not yet understood), *or* we are currently overestimating the complexity of the representations that the human mind needs to generate its complex behaviors.

How does a researcher tell if he or she has constructed a good model of a certain cognitive process? Certainly the model should reproduce the behaviors observed in people. A model of learning should be able to learn the skills that people can learn, be unable to learn the skills that people cannot learn, and should exhibit the same trajectory of learning, including the same kinds of errors that people make when they are going through the process of learning.

However, the evaluation of a model can be more nuanced. A model must be constrained by empirical psychological evidence. No "unrealistic" components or processes should be included to make the model work. For instance, a model of learning to read should encode written words (orthography) in the way we believe children do, and encode spoken words (phonology) in the way we believe children do. This does not necessarily mean it should have a visual system to recognize the written words and a mouth to pronounce the spoken words. It does mean that the information it receives about written words should be similar to what we know the visual system extracts from the page, and the information it outputs should respect the structure of spoken sounds, in terms of articulatory features. Next, the model should be exposed to the same kinds of learning experience that children are, such as the juxtaposition of written and spoken letters and words. Moreover, the model should contain a learning mechanism that we think could plausibly operate in the mind. However, a model will necessarily contain simplifications (such as the lack of eyes to read words and a mouth to speak them). It is, after all, a model intended to capture the key principles of the process under study, rather than duplicating the system in every regard.

A cognitive model should be evaluated according to several criteria. (i) Does the model simulate human behavior in the target domain? (ii) Does it help *explain* why the human behavior occurs? (This requires that the modeller understands why the model works!) (iii) Is the model successful in simulating the target behavior due to its key design principles – the theory that the model embodies – or due to its design simplifications (fixes that the researcher has used to get the model to work)? If the answer is the former, the model can be viewed as a demonstration of the viability of the theory it embodies. (iv) Does the model explain a range of behaviors rather than just one (i.e., is it parsimonious)? Finally, (v) can the model generate any new behaviors observable under different conditions (e.g., in novel situations, or perhaps when the model is damaged in certain ways); that is, does the model generate novel predictions that can be corroborated by subsequent psychological experiments with people?

Examples of symbolic and subsymbolic cognitive models:<br>ACT-R and artificial neural networks

One widely used symbolic model of cognitive processing is called ACT-R (Anderson, 2007; Anderson & Lebiere, 1998). ACT-R stands for Adaptive Control of Thought – Rational. The system is intended as an overarching cognitive architecture, capturing how the whole mind works. The key components of ACT-R are inspired by processing distinctions observed in the brain, and in particular the distinction between declarative memory (explicit facts and knowledge) and procedural memory (implicit knowledge and skills). The system has different specialized components that reflect this distinction.

At the heart of ACT-R lie procedural IF–THEN rules. If a certain set of conditions hold, then a certain behavior is produced. The system has working memories or buffers of current knowledge, reflecting both new inputs and its previous processing states. The system's library of rules competes to find the rule that most closely matches the current state of the buffers. The winning rule then produces the subsequent behavior. When the rule is executed, it may then alter the knowledge in the buffers, which triggers the next winning rule, and so forth. In ACT-R, cognition proceeds as a succession of rule operations. ACT-R is symbolic in the sense that it contains discrete variables and syntactic rule-based operations, although the performance of the system may also depend on what is referred to as 'subsymbolic quantities', such as the strength of productions, and the base level of activation for a chunk of knowledge (Anderson & Schunn, 2000). ACT-R has been used to model a variety of cognitive processes including memory, attention, executive control, language, and problem solving.

Two further points are of note. First, as we saw in the previous section, cognitive models that rely on rule-based representations struggle to find a ready means to learn new rules. In keeping with this, ACT-R has found relatively little application to modeling cognitive processes involved in learning and development. Second, as we shall see in the second half of the chapter, ACT-R has nevertheless been successfully used as the engine on which intelligent tutoring systems are based.

One widely used subsymbolic model of cognitive processing is the artificial neural network (Rumelhart & McClelland, 1986; Spencer, Thomas, & McClelland, 2009; Thomas & McClelland, 2008). As we have seen, artificial neural networks are abstractions that capture some of the key properties of computation carried out in neural circuits. The brain comprises a large number of neurons that electrically signal to each other via highly connected networks. Artificial neural networks contain simple processing units, each with an activation value, and a network of connections through which the activity of each processing unit can influence the activity of other processing units. A key property of neural systems is that they are adaptive. The strengths of the connections between units can be altered incrementally to bring the network's output closer to the desired behavior given its inputs. Many of the artificial neural network learning algorithms are based on *Hebbian learning* (Hebb, 1949), the principle that "units that fire together should wire together". In other words, if two units are firing at the same time, they are probably both involved in performing the same computation; therefore, the connection between them should be strengthened so that they encourage each other to fire when the units receive equivalent inputs the next time around.

As they learn, artificial neural networks are able to develop their own internal representations of knowledge over their banks of processing units. Artificial neural networks are subsymbolic in the sense that information is encoded as continuous patterns of activation. As we saw in the previous section, these representations of knowledge are not necessarily transparent in what information they contain. When used as cognitive models, artificial neural networks therefore emphasize the learning of new abilities at the expense of the transparency of the exact knowledge that is being acquired. Artificial neural networks have been used to model a wide range of developmental phenomena, including perceptual learning and object-oriented behaviors in infants, language and literacy acquisition in children, and the development of reasoning in children (Elman et al., 1996; Mareschal & Thomas, 2007). In addition, these models have begun to provide a platform to understand development and individual differences within the same explanatory framework: that is, why children of the same age should differ in their abilities, and the respective role of genetic variation and environmental variation in generating these differences (see, e.g., Thomas, Baughman, Karaminis, & Addyman, 2012a; Thomas, Forrester, & Ronald, in press; Thomas, Knowland, & Karmiloff-Smith, 2011). In the next section, we outline an example of an artificial neural network model of language development that illustrates these points, as well as more general principles of the construction and evaluation of cognitive models.

## An example of cognitive modeling in educational neuroscience: individual differences in language development

One central concern of cognitive modeling within educational neuroscience is the issue of *individual differences.* What are the genetic and/or environmental causes of differences in learning outcomes? An understanding of these causes may help us optimize learning outcomes for children with different abilities or from different backgrounds. So why do children learn at different rates? While it is long established that individual differences can have both environmental and genetic causes, there is a lack of detailed cognitive modeling that stipulates how these influences unfold in generating behavior. For example, there has been a recent renewal of interest in how *socioeconomic status* (SES) affects children's development and their educational outcomes (Hackman & Farah, 2009). However, SES is associated with many differences in children's physical and social environments, and it is unclear which causal pathways are responsible for the observed variation in developmental outcomes. One possibility considered within the field of language development is that SES is associated with differences in the quality and quantity of the *information* (in this case, language input) to which the child is exposed (see Chapter 6, this volume, for a wider review of relevant issues in language development). In lower-SES families, there is simply less language directed towards the child (Hart & Risley, 1995). Targeting the role of language input more precisely, Huttenlocher, Vasilyeva, Cymerman, and Levine (2002) found that the proportion of complex sentences produced by teachers

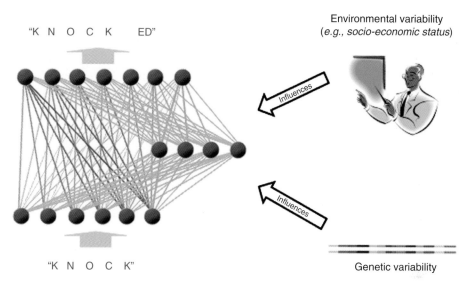

**Figure 3.1**    An example of a cognitive model of one aspect of language acquisition, based on an artificial neural network. The model learns to form the past tense of English verbs. The model simulates a population of learners who show individual differences in their learning due to variations in learning abilities and environments.

predicted 18% of the variance in the improvement in children's performance on a syntax comprehension task over a year of preschool. Differences in language input appear to be an important (if not sole) contributor to differences in rates of language development across the SES range of developed countries.

Thomas et al., (in press) built a cognitive model of the acquisition of one aspect of English grammar, the English past tense. The model was designed to capture the range of developmental trajectories of a large population of simulated children, and incorporated individual differences from both intrinsic sources (i.e., the power of the learning mechanism each child had) and extrinsic sources (the quality of the environment to which the child was exposed, by hypothesis influenced by SES). Population-level modeling is a relatively recent innovation, which has become possible through increases in computational power that allow thousands of models to be run rather than just a few (Thomas et al., 2012a). The Thomas, Forrester, and Ronald model is illustrated in Figure 3.1. It comprised an artificial neural network, with a phonological representation of the English verb stem at input, along with information about the verb's meaning, and a phonological representation of the past tense at the output. The network was exposed to verb stem–past tense pairs for both regular and irregular English verbs (e.g., knock–knocked; think–thought), and underwent an extended developmental trajectory as it acquired this aspect of grammar. The model aimed to capture empirical data from Bishop (2005), which reported the effects of SES on the acquisition of English past tense for a sample of 300 six-year-old children. For these children, regular past tenses were produced more accurately than irregular past tenses. SES explained around 1% of the variation in children's regular-verb performance but around 5% of the variation in irregular-verb performance.

The model succeeded in capturing the predictive power of SES that was observed in the empirical data, and in particular the greater predictive power of SES on irregular than regular verbs. The model suggested that the empirical data were best captured by relatively wide variation in learning abilities of children and relatively narrow variation in (and good quality of) environmental information. The model served as a demonstration of the viability of the theory that variations in language input are one causal pathway through which SES may operate. In addition, the model generated a novel prediction not previously considered by any researcher: it predicted that SES should reliably predict *gifted* performance in children (e.g., whether a child would fall in the top 10% of the population) but not *delayed* performance (e.g., whether the child would fall in the bottom 10%). This surprising prediction was subsequently borne out by the Bishop (2005) data set.

In a follow-up paper, Thomas and Knowland (submitted) used the model to focus on an important current issue in the field of developmental language disorders. It is optimal to diagnose language delay in children early on (say, at three or four years of age) in order to optimize chances for effective intervention. However, of the children diagnosed with delay at this young age, over half subsequently have their delay resolve of its own accord without the need for intervention. Early intervention is therefore optimal but risks treating children in whom (potentially costly) intervention is unnecessary. Thomas and Knowland used the population-modeling technique to focus on the issue of the outcome of early-diagnosed delay. Figure 3.2 shows how simulated children were diagnosed with delay (here defined as falling more than one standard deviation below the population mean) at five different developmental time points. Figure 3.3 summarizes the number of simulated children with delay at each time point – and confirms that in the model, too, the number of cases of delay fell by over half from the first to the fifth time point. Thomas and Knowland then examined the cases of persisting early delay and resolving early delay in more detail, tracing individual trajectories. Several of these trajectories are displayed in Figure 3.4. There were in fact four patterns of development: typical development, persisting delay, resolving delay with low–average final outcome, and resolving delay with good final outcome.

At this point, the investigation focused on what properties differed between these four groups, in terms of both the environmental conditions and the learning properties of the artificial neural networks. Artificial neural networks have a

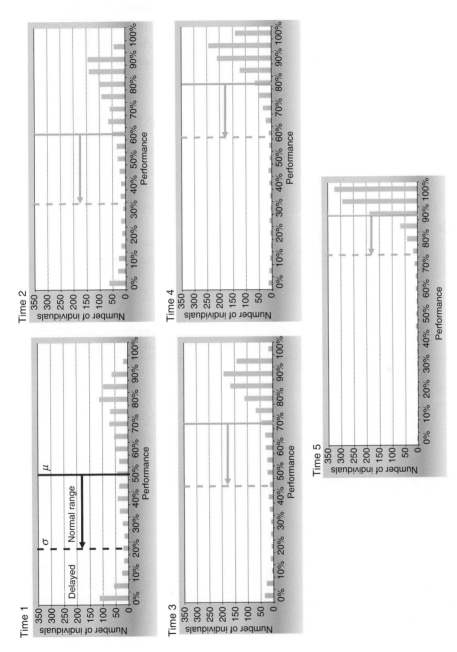

**Figure 3.2** Frequency distributions of the number of simulated children performing at each level of accuracy, at five points in development. Individuals exhibiting delay are diagnosed at each time point as falling more than one standard deviation ($\sigma$) below the mean ($\mu$). The proportion of delayed individuals reduces over time, suggesting that some cases of delay must resolve.

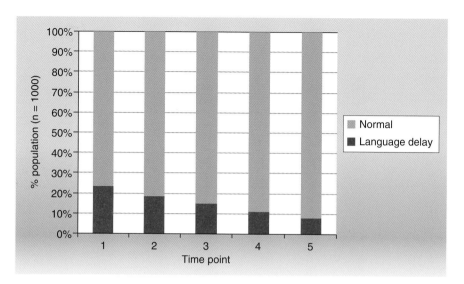

**Figure 3.3**    The proportion of the simulated population showing developmental delay at each time point.

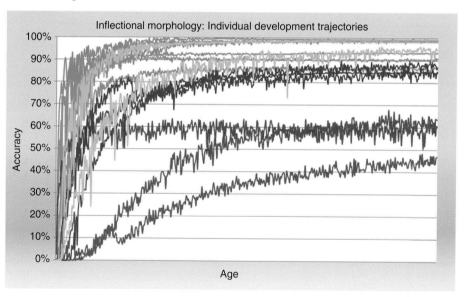

**Figure 3.4**    Example developmental trajectories showing four different patterns: typical development (green); persisting developmental delay (red); resolving delay with low–average final outcome (dark blue); and resolving delay with good final outcome (turquoise).

range of properties that can alter how much information they can learn and how quickly they can learn it. We can refer broadly to these properties as the *capacity* and *plasticity* of the system. Capacity is affected by, for example, how many units and connections there are inside the network. Plasticity is affected by how quickly

**Table 3.1**    Computational causes of the four types of developmental trajectory.

| | | Computational Plasticity | Computational Capacity | Environment |
|---|---|---|---|---|
| | Normal | Okay | Okay | Okay |
| | Persistent deficit | Okay / low | Poor | Okay |
| | Resolving low-normal | Low | Okay | Poor |
| | Resolving normal | Low | Okay | Good |

connection weights can alter their strength when the network is required to change its behavior. Combined with the quality of the learning environment, the properties of capacity and plasticity allowed Thomas and Knowland to distinguish between the four groups.

The results are shown in Table 3.1. When development was delayed, this could arise from limitations in capacity or plasticity. Persisting delay was associated with limitations in capacity, while environmental conditions seemed unimportant. Resolving delay was associated with limitations in plasticity, i.e., it took these learners longer to adapt and they learned at a slower rate. Crucially, for this second group, the quality of the environment then predicted the final level of performance after the delay had resolved. A rich environment (high SES) was associated with good final outcome, while poorer environments (lower SES) were associated with low–average final outcome. Once more this was a prediction that had not arisen from any previous theory, and once more the prediction was confirmed in the data set of Bishop (2005), for a large sample of British children who were diagnosed as at risk of language delay aged four, and whose past-tense abilities were then tested at age six. The next step of this research program is to isolate behavioral or neural markers that can distinguish low capacity from low plasticity in the early diagnosis of language delay, and so narrow the focus of language interventions.

This example of a cognitive model illustrates several of the design principles we introduced earlier. The model was aimed towards capturing the acquisition of a specific task domain. It comprised a computational system – an artificial neural network; representations of information – phonological encodings of English verb stems and past tenses, along with information about their meaning; a learning algorithm – in this case backpropagation, a supervised learning algorithm (see later, in "Feedback"), which is itself a variant of Hebbian learning (Thomas & McClelland, 2008); and a training set – pairs of English verb stems and their associated past tenses. The model was evaluated according to how well it simulated real empirical data – children's ability to learn regular and irregular English past tenses, and the influence of SES on individual differences in this ability. It was evaluated by the extent to which it achieved this success via its design principles rather than simplifications – in this case, the theory being implemented was the idea that SES corresponded to differences in the richness of the language information in the environment to which the child was exposed, against a background of individual differences in learning ability. The model was further evaluated against its ability to explain a range of phenomena – in this case, both normal language development, gifted language development, and delayed language development. Moreover, the model was evaluated against its ability to produce novel empirical predictions, which were then borne out by real empirical data – in this case, the model predicted differential effects of SES on gifted versus delayed language development, and on different types of delayed development, both of which were subsequently confirmed.

## The broader perspective: neuroconstructivism and education

In the previous section, we described a cognitive model aimed at capturing the influence of variations in the environment on children's language development. This model used an artificial neural network as its basic computational system. Such networks embody principles derived from neuroscience, and in this way cognitive-level modeling provides a link between neuroscience and the overt aspects of children's behavior that are the central concern of education. Nevertheless, this is only one model, targeting a fairly circumscribed aspect of language acquisition. It is also important to consider the broader perspective that this theoretical approach implies, and its potential impact on educational theories.

The idea that neuroscience principles should influence cognitive-level theories of learning amounts to the proposal that the way a cognitive system (the "mind") is implemented in the brain makes certain ways of thinking and learning easier and others harder. Under this view, one cannot, therefore, derive a theory of cognition without reference to how the brain delivers cognition. *Neuroconstructivism* is one theoretical approach that has recently attempted to flesh out this idea (Elman et al., 1996; Mareschal et al., 2007). In particular, neuroconstructivism builds on the Piagetian view that development corresponds to the progressive elaboration in the complexity of mental representations via experience-dependent processes, enabling new competences to develop based on earlier, simpler ones (*constructivism*). *Neuro*-constructivism also incorporates recent theories of functional brain development, proposing that the increase in representational complexity is realized in the brain by a progressive elaboration of functional cortical structures (see Sirois et al., 2008; Thomas et al., 2008; Westermann et al., 2007; Westermann, Thomas, & Karmiloff-Smith, 2010).

One might well ask, then, which principles of brain function should influence the formation of cognitive theory? Here are five such principles. (1) The brain uses *partial representations of knowledge*: whole concepts are rarely used, only the dimensions of knowledge required to drive particular behaviors relevant to the current context of action. Whole concepts may, indeed, be rarely acquired. (2) *Contextualisation*: mechanisms always act in context – genes operate in the context of other genes, neurons operate within the context of a neural network, brain regions operate within the context of a set of brain regions, the brain operates within the context of the body, and the individual operates within the context of a culture and society. (3) *Timing*: the timing of developmental events can be crucial, so that the same event happening at different times can have different consequences. (4) *Emergent specialization* (and brain localization): systems become more specialized with development, tuning their function to particular domains depending on experience. For example, within vision, dedicated systems for face recognition and written word recognition are experience-dependent specializations of an initially more general object recognition system. (5) Developmental events in the brain must be construed within the wider framework of *evolutionary developmental biology*: an adaptive framework informs the functions established during brain development. What has evolution designed the system to do, and what are the neural constraints fashioned into the structure of the brain that allow the individual to achieve that goal when the child is raised in a normal environment? How can these constraints respond to novel environments, such as the evolutionary novel (cultural environment) of literacy and numeracy?

These ideas are recent enough that their implications for educational theory have not yet been fully explored. In respect of *timing*, for example, research has begun to focus on what sensitive periods in brain development may mean for the timing of the delivery of educational curricula (e.g., Thomas, 2012; Thomas & Knowland, 2009). In some cases, this work has once more relied on the use of computational modeling to connect neuroscience principles to high-level behavior (Thomas & Johnson, 2006). However, it is likely that there are more deep-seated implications for education to be derived from the neuroconstructivist thesis. For example, the notion of *partial representations* of knowledge suggests that different dimensions of a concept are activated according to context. This means that knowledge may be intrinsically bound by context, including during its acquisition.[1] In turn, this implies that the acquisition of a full, abstract concept requires exposure to all contexts of its usage. To give a concrete example, a child may learn that 5 is a number that falls between 4 and 6; that 5 is the result of summing 1 and 4; that 5 is the result of dividing 10 by 2. But each of these reflects the use of the number 5 in a given context. The ultimate goal of learning is to acquire the decontextualized concept: to learn that 5 is just 5. Constrained by modes of brain function, the child will always begin by acquiring concepts in a perceptual and contextually bound fashion. This predicts that multiple contexts of presentation must be deployed to liberate concepts from the shackles of context and the sensorimotor conditions of their acquisition, in order to construct the abstract idea. The abstract idea is then applicable across a range of situations including ones that the child is yet to encounter.

### The future of cognitive modeling in education

Although cognitive modeling is a powerful method to advance our theories of learning and development, there are a number of reasons why this approach is currently somewhat limited with respect to education. This is because many of the central phenomena in education are among the most psychologically complex – involving the social context of the classroom, the dynamics of the interaction between learner and teacher, and the combination of knowledge and motivation. Current models are limited for several reasons: because they are insufficiently complex – though, as we saw earlier, models must retain some degree of simplicity to serve their explanatory goals – and because models currently target individual cognitive systems or components within that system, which makes it hard to capture the dynamics of learner–teacher interaction, or the community phenomenon of a classroom. Finally, there also remain unresolved debates within the study of cognition: what do representations of high-level conceptual knowledge look like? How does meta-cognition work? How do emotions, rewards, and motivation mediate learning?

Nevertheless, one can sketch out a picture of how the cognitive modeling approach could contribute to education in the future. Its ultimate aim will be to optimize the timing, regimes, and contexts of learning by understanding

---

[1]   See Thomas, Purser, & Mareschal (2012b) for a computational modeling treatment of this idea, and in particular the proposal that the importance of language in problem-solving is that it allows the individual to bring to bear information that is not suggested by the individual's immediate context.

mechanistic principles of how the brain acquires, consolidates, and abstracts knowledge. It will contribute an understanding of how representations of knowledge form in the learner, how learners interact to develop a shared understanding in a classroom context, the role of attention and motivation in this process, how other factors may affect the learning properties of the brain (such as the role of sleep in consolidating memories, or of aerobic fitness in modulating brain plasticity), and the factors that may alter changes in brain plasticity with age, in order to optimize learning across the lifespan. Cognitive modeling will also contribute an understanding of cognitive mechanisms in the teacher: how the teacher represents the current state of the learner, how the teacher uses this knowledge to present information relevant to the task domain to the advance learner's knowledge, how the teacher generates feedback that is meaningful to the learner given the current state of knowledge, and how the teacher's emotional and motivational states modulate these processes. Finally, cognitive modeling will contribute an understanding of how each of these processes can vary across individuals, from the least to most gifted.

Cognitive modeling is a computational approach in neuroscience to understanding the process of learning and development. We now consider computational approaches in education that use our, albeit partial, understanding of the process of learning to develop a computational model of teaching. Here, there are two distinct approaches: intelligent tutoring systems and adaptive microworlds.

## Computers as Teaching Systems

### Educational models of teaching and learning

From the educational point of view, any teaching–learning environment includes a set of properties that must be present to make it possible for students to learn. The terminology is different, but the properties found in the educational literature all have their counterparts in the neuroscience account of learning developed above. These are referenced in parentheses in the following educational account, where a teaching–learning environment must specify a *learning outcome* (requisite/target behavior), a *method of assessment* of achievement of the learning outcome (*generalization set*, i.e., the test that learning has occurred), and a *set of task activities* (*training set*) the learner is to work through in order to achieve the outcome, where each activity consists of *learner actions* (*output responses*) to achieve a *goal* (*target problem*), and *meaningful feedback* (*feedback*) on the actions in relation to the goal. The teaching–learning environment may also give learners access to *peer learners* (*agents*). These properties are common both to conventional human/physical learning environments and to digital teaching–learning environments that attempt to emulate the human teacher. The digital version is a computer program in which the role of the teacher, the task activities, the goal, and the feedback all take place through the learner interacting with a either an "intelligent teaching system" or an "adaptive microworld".

The remaining correspondence is between the *computational system* that models learning in a cognitive system, and the *teacher's model of learning*, which is meant to correspond to the way their learners learn. In a digital teaching–learning environment in education, the model of learning draws on one or more theories of learning, such as constructivism, social constructivism, constructionism, and conceptual, experiential, collaborative learning (Laurillard, 2012), none of which have clear equivalents in the computational system models of learning above: concept learning, decision tree learning, artificial neural networks, Bayesian (probabilistic) learning, instance-based learning, genetic algorithms, and reinforcement learning. This is probably because the computational system models are relevant for learning the elements of knowledge or skills (such as the link between the verb stem and the past tense), whereas the educational theories operate at a different level of description of the curriculum (such as "the different forms of verb conjugation", "the laws of motion", or "the causes of the first world war"). However, the educational models of learning are much less well specified in terms of clearly agreed parameters and mechanisms, and lack synergy (Bransford et al., 2006).

One advantage of trying to construct a digital teaching–learning environment is that, just as with the cognitive modeling discussed above, the process demands specificity about exactly what the model of learning consists in. By combining the expectations on teacher and learner of all the current educational models of learning, it is possible to derive an explicit model, the "conversational framework," for describing the teaching–learning process in education (Frederickson, Reed, & Clifford, 2005; Laurillard, 2002). This model defines the process as a continual iteration between teacher and learner, between learner and peer, and between each participant's concepts and actions. Figure 3.5 illustrates the relationships between teacher, learner, and peer, and with the practice environment, real or virtual.

The iterations between the teacher's conceptual knowledge (TC) and the learner's conceptual knowledge (LC) are mediated by forms of representation such as language, symbols, diagrams, animations, and so on, through reading, listening, watching, debating, discussing, and so on, at the conceptual level. At the practice level, the teacher generates a modeling environment that emulates the world (TME), such as exercises, labs, fieldwork, and so on, in which the learner can use his or her practice repertoire (LP), in the form of goal-oriented actions, feedback, and revised actions, at the action level. Peer learning is represented in terms of discussions with peers about their concepts (PC) and exchanges of their practice outputs (PP). The within-participant iterations represent the generation of

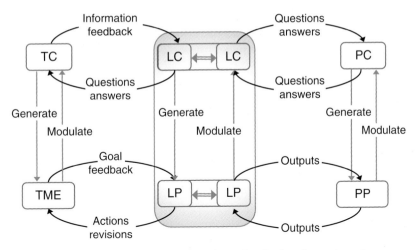

**Figure 3.5** The conversational framework for individual and peer learning.

actions in the light of their current concepts and the modulation of their concepts in the light of feedback on actions. This includes the teacher generating a practice environment in the light of learners' discussions and questions, and modulating his or her own discourse in the light of learners' actions. The framework attempts to capture the dynamics of teacher–learner–peer interactions both within and beyond the classroom. The theories of learning currently used in education can each be mapped onto all or part of the framework.

In terms of the two types of model discussed above, the iterative nature of this model and the adaptive nature of the processes of generating actions and modulating concepts make it closest to the learning mechanism for incrementally improving behavior that is based on *subsymbolic* models. In the conversational framework, the knowledge representations that constitute the learner's concepts and actions are similarly opaque – they can only be detected in terms of what the learner produces as conceptual representations in their interactions with the teacher and peers, or the actions performed at the practice level.

In the next sections we look at the two main approaches to computational modeling in education: intelligent tutoring systems and adaptive microworlds.

### Computational modeling of teaching and learning: intelligent tutoring systems

Intelligent tutoring systems (ITSs) use a symbolic model, and derive from theories of human information processing. A computational model of cognitive processing, such as ACT-R, enables an intelligent tutoring system to make inferences about what and how students are learning, as it monitors their outputs on a set of activities provided by the system (Sawyer, 2006).

The intelligent tutoring system has three components that are critical for aligning the student and teacher.

The *learning model* is the network of declarative chunks and production rules that generate responses to the problem set, i.e., the equivalent of the *computational system* in neuroscience, and the *teacher's model of learning* in education.

The *diagnosis* of the student's current needs is carried out by the system monitoring the student's behavior (*learner actions* or *output responses*) and comparing it with the behavior predicted by the model, in order to deduce which declarative knowledge chunks and production rules are being used. For example, if a student is making mistakes, it deduces the erroneous knowledge the student is using that would generate such mistakes.

The *teacher feedback* deals with the discrepancies diagnosed between the actual and predicted behavior, and is provided by the system in the form of help, scaffolding, and "dynamic instruction to repair the holes in their knowledge" (Anderson & Schunn, 2000, p. 19).

This account does not make any explicit reference to the other components of the cognitive model, although they are present in an intelligent tutoring system: the *task activities* or *training set* take(s) the form of the actions the student has to take to achieve the *goals* set by the system. So there is a good correspondence between the cognitive model and the computational modeling offered by the intelligent tutoring system.

Research on the intelligent tutoring system approach has some features in common with cognitive modeling, therefore, but was overtaken in the 1990s by the explosion of alternative forms of computer-based learning activities such as web resources, multimedia, user-generated content methods, and online communications technologies (Laurillard, 2010), and it has not progressed to having any major mainstream impact.

## Computational modeling: adaptive microworlds

By contrast, an adaptive microworld has no explicit model of learning, being closer to the subsymbolic model of learning, and is built on Papert's ideal of "learning without being taught" (diSessa, 2001; Papert, 1980). A microworld is an interactive computational model of an aspect of the world, with its own constraints and assumptions, in which learners can experience the relevant concepts by using the program "to engage tasks of value to them, and in doing so … come to understand powerful underlying principles" (diSessa, 2001). It is adaptive (i) when it responds to the learner by showing the result of their actions in that world, and (ii) when it is designed to adjust the difficulty of the task in the light of the learner's current performance.

The microworld approach has fared better, and the fundamental idea of "constructionism" as a model of how learning can succeed is still current. Pioneered by Seymour Papert at MIT, and influenced by Piagetian psychology, "constructionism" embodies the theory that we learn complex concepts and ideas best by constructing representations that use them (Papert, 1980; Papert & Harel, 1991). The idea was applied to curriculum topics in science, but had most impact in school maths in the form of "Logo" for learning geometry, in many different countries (Hoyles & Noss, 2003). The fundamental concept of learning through construction is applicable across a wide range of discipline areas, at all levels of learning. The concept has now been implemented as "NetLogo", a modeling tool that enables learners to set up and investigate models of the behavior of systems such as population growth, electrical circuits, and climate change, wherever a computational model is possible (Gilbert & Troitzsch, 2005).

## The computational modeling of pedagogy

To provide a teaching–learning environment, a computer program must include all the properties defined above, which a simple modeling environment such as Logo or NetLogo does not. A simple modeling environment is adaptive to students' actions, but not to their level of performance. It is important also to embed the role of the teacher who monitors and sets up the task activities. Thus an *adaptive microworld* combines the task model with rules for monitoring student performance and adapts the difficulty of the next task according to the learner's needs. Figure 3.6 shows how the two contrasting computational environments for teaching and learning can be mapped onto the framework.

In Figure 3.6(a) the ITS uses the model of the teacher's modeling environment (TME) to generate the task goal (1, 2); the learner uses his or her concept knowledge to generate an action to achieve the goal (3, 4); the ITS monitors the learner's action and modulates the extrinsic feedback or guidance (5, 6), allowing the learner to adapt his or her concept knowledge to generate a revised action (7, 8).

In Figure 3.6(b) the teacher's modeling environment is a microworld (TME) that sets the task goal (1); the learner uses his or her concept knowledge to generate an action to achieve the goal (2, 3); the microworld models and shows the result of the action (4); the learner uses the feedback to modulate his or her concept knowledge (5) and generate a revised action (6, 7); an adaptive microworld monitors the learner's actions and modulates the selection of the teacher's concept (8) to generate a more, or less, challenging task goal (9, 10).

(a)

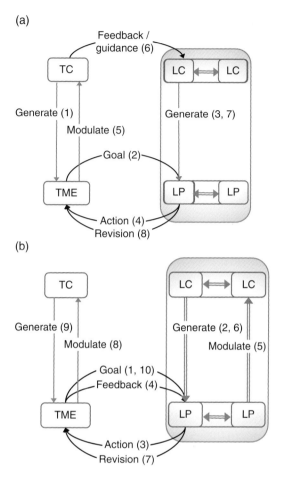

(b)

**Figure 3.6**    (a) An intelligent tutoring system, and (b) an adaptive microworld mapped to the conversational framework.

The point of adapting to the learner's performance is to make the learning situation challenging, to keep the learners in the "zone of proximal development" (Vygotsky, 1978), where inevitably they will make errors. We know that the response to errors is critical in the neural basis of learning. The brain mechanisms try to reduce the difference between the organism's response and the correct or optimal outcome through *prediction error learning* (Dayan & Abbott, 2001). Similarly, the "constructionist" pedagogy relies on the learner being able to interpret the nature of the error (i.e., that the feedback is meaningful to him or her), and then construct the correct response, thereby recruiting the "prediction error learning" mechanisms to dealing with the task set. For this to be possible, the task set must be within the current repertoire, so it is important for the program to monitor the *learner actions* or *output responses,* provide *meaningful feedback* so he or she can change the action or response until it matches the *goal*, and if still having difficulty, adapt the *goal* or *target problem* by changing the *task activity* or *training set*.

## An example of an adaptive microworld

As we have seen, neuroscience can help us understand the process of learning by providing cognitive models such as *prediction error learning*, or learning algorithms based on machine learning systems, which can inform the approach a human teacher or a tutoring program might take and are compatible with educational models such as constructionism. It can also help with identifying the type of knowledge that must be targeted. An example of this is the identification of "dyscalculia" as a particular type of neural deficit, sometimes referred to as a "lack of number sense" (see Chapter 8). Children and adults who are dyscalculic need to spend time making sense of how numbers work, and teachers of special needs (SEN) classes have developed materials and techniques to help tackle this specific deficit (Butterworth & Yeo, 2004). Working with, for example, rods of different lengths to represent numbers (such as Cuisenaire rods), learners work on tasks such as constructing the relations between sets (e.g., finding any two rods that make up the length 10, or finding which two identical rods make 10). The same approach has now been implemented as a digital environment by modeling the teacher in the form of an adaptive microworld, which embodies the assumption that the learner is using the cognitive mechanism of *prediction error learning*. One such example is a program for learning the number bonds of ten. Its properties are as follows:

*learning outcome* – able to compute, e.g., $3 + ? = 10$;
*method of assessment* – tasks such as $3 + ? = 10$, etc.
*set of task activities* – find the correct number bond for 10 for a given number (rods fall within a 10 unit wide column; the sequence of tasks progresses from rods with colour + length, to length only, colour + length + digit, length + digit, digit only; rods fall more slowly if performance is poor);
*learner actions* – select a rod to fit the column from the pile of 10 rods;
*goal* – select the rod that fits;
*meaningful feedback* – rods overlap or show a gap or wriggle into place.

This program provides no peer interaction, and is designed for the individual learner working without a teacher (see www.number-sense.co.uk for other examples). The teacher's model of learning embodied in the program is the idea of "constructionism", that by trying to construct a pairing that fits, and by seeing the result of this action, and then attempting to improve it, the learner will begin to make sense of the relationship between the cardinalities of the numbers 0 to 10 in

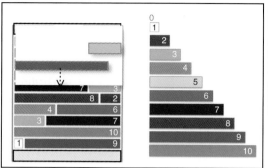

As a rod falls, the learner must select the appropriate rod to make a length of 10. The feedback shows an overlap, gap, or fit, and if incorrect, the same rod falls again, so the learner can improve their response in the light of the feedback.
Task difficulty varies according to whether the objects display length, colour, digit, in different combinations, or, at the highest level, only digits.

**Figure 3.7**    Learning the number bonds of 10.

terms of their representation as lengths, and eventually in terms of their representation as digits (see Figure 3.7 for a representation of the interface[2]). Like the human teacher, the program adapts the next task item to the pace and accuracy of the response, and the next task set to the learner's ability, proposing that the learner repeat the same task if he or she was very slow or very inaccurate (although the learner can override this). Tests with learners in SEN classes (the *method of assessment*, or *generalization set*) in primary and secondary school (ages 8–13) show that, for example, (i) their performance improves over the short term (two weeks), and (ii) the number of tasks completed is significantly more than in an SEN class of three learners: 4–11 trials per minute were completed by individual learners, while only 1.4 trials per minute were completed on average during ten-minute observations of the classes (Butterworth, Varma, & Laurillard, 2011).

Like the cognitive modeling example above, and the intelligent tutoring system in this section, therefore, this approach also addresses the essential properties for a teaching–learning system. The principal differences between the computational modeling in neuroscience and in education are that in the former the learning process is being modelled by the system, the output of which is to be the same as that of the human learner, whereas in the latter there is only an assumed model of how the human learner is learning, and it is the human teacher whose behavior is modelled by the systems. To examine this in more detail we consider in the next section how the concept of "feedback" is used in the two types of system.

## Contrasting perspectives on "feedback"

Computational modeling in neuroscience and education sometimes uses similar terminology, but the concepts behind this terminology do not always directly line up. The notion of feedback offers an instructive example. Feedback is crucial

[2]   Now available in the App Store as 'Number Bonds by Thinkout'.

in education, to improve performance on a given task and thereby build an understanding of the topic. Based on the student's current performance on a set of activities, the teacher offers a form of feedback, of which there are two types – "extrinsic", where the teacher interprets what the student needs to be told in order to improve their performance, and "intrinsic", where the environment provides information about the result of their action in relation to their intended goal. In both cases, feedback must be meaningful to the learners if they are to make use of it. The distinction is important because classroom research strongly suggests that intrinsic motivation and reward are more effective than extrinsic (Deci, Koestner, & Ryan, 2001).

Intelligent tutoring systems endeavour to capture and automate the role of the teacher in providing the appropriate *extrinsic* feedback, given the actions of the learner in the task environment of the system. For example, in a system tutoring multiplication, the student attempts a set of problems. Based on the characteristics of the errors displayed, the tutoring system will infer the student's current (erroneous) understanding of the multiplication procedure and provide direct *extrinsic* feedback to repair the gaps in knowledge and rules, and then set further problems to enable the student to improve his or her performance.

Adaptive microworlds create a practice environment that provides *intrinsic* feedback on the learner's actions on a task, based on its model of the world, although by modeling a specific aspect of the real world it focuses the learner's attention on the concepts and skills relevant to the learning outcome. It then selects further tasks, according to the learner's level, to enable him or her to improve in performance.

Cognitive modeling considers how feedback operates inside learning mechanisms. Models are generally addressed to mechanisms for acquiring particular behaviors (such as learning to read, or as we saw above learning aspects of English grammar or aspects of number). Acquisition occurs through exposure to the problem domain. For artificial neural networks, feedback is usually construed as falling into three different classes. In *self-organizing learning* mechanisms, the goal is for the system to develop categories that capture the key dimension of the problem domain, without necessarily generating overt behavior. Self-organizing systems require no external feedback, but instead attempt to optimize some property of their internal knowledge representations as they are exposed to more and more examples of the problem domain. One such property would be how concise or parsimonious the representations are.

In *supervised learning*, very detailed feedback is given to the learning mechanism to improve its performance. For a given input (i.e., example from the problem domain), the mechanism must learn to output a given response (i.e., the right answer, or a step toward the right answer to be fed into another mechanism in the wider cognitive system). Learning occurs in the following way. For the given input, the mechanism outputs its current "best guess" of the appropriate response. This is compared with the actual desired response. The disparity between the two is used as an *error signal* to adjust the connection strengths of the network in such a way that the next time the network encounters this problem its output will be closer to the desired answer. Through repeated exposure to examples, along with detailed feedback, the network gradually acquires the required knowledge. From the point of view of the learning mechanism, the source of the desired response is simply viewed as external to the mechanism – it might originate either from another part of the cognitive system, or as informational feedback from the environment, or from a teacher. As a type of learning algorithm, therefore, supervised learning would be neutral as to whether the feedback was intrinsic or extrinsic.

The third type is called *reinforcement learning*, and falls in between self-organized learning (no feedback) and supervised learning (detailed feedback). In reinforcement learning, the mechanism offers its best guess as to the required response, but the feedback it receives is much more vague. It is similar to a game of locating a hidden object, where one is told "warmer, warmer, cooler, cooler" to encourage looking in one place but discourage looking in other places. This type of learning mechanism is less powerful for learning detailed knowledge. However, researchers have used this type of mechanism to build models of the development of decision making and behavioral control, based on whether the child finds the outcome of each decision to be good or bad; and models of how decision-making abilities can differ in disorders such as attention deficit hyperactivity disorder (see, e.g., Williams & Dayan, 2005). Because this type of learning operates by attempting to minimize the disparity between the expected reward of an action (e.g., whether you will be told "warmer" or "cooler" in the find-a-hidden-object game) and the actual reward, it is sometimes called *prediction error learning*.

The example of feedback shows that all forms of computational modeling discussed here require very detailed specification of the information provided to the learner to improve performance on a task. In the case of intelligent tutoring, providing feedback requires a model of the learner that enables the system to match the output to the presumed input, and thereby direct the feedback to the behavior that produced the erroneous output. In the case of adaptive microworlds the model of the task interaction must provide appropriate informational feedback on the action that enables the learner to interpret how to improve the action. In the case of cognitive models, feedback considers ways in which information is directed to specific mechanisms to alter their knowledge and thereby incrementally improve subsequent behavior.

## Conclusion

This chapter has reviewed recent work on the use of computational models in educational neuroscience, in the related methods of cognitive modeling and digital teaching tools. We highlighted the strength of the modeling method, in making explicit theories of learning and teaching. We demonstrated that there are several points of similarity between the approaches of cognitive modeling and digital teaching tools, even though they have different goals and different theoretical origins. Cognitive modeling aims to understand the learning process in the brain; within the teaching tools, intelligent tutoring systems aim to model the learner's knowledge as a version of the domain knowledge in order to generate appropriate remedial tutoring; adaptive microworlds aim to use our understanding of the learning process in the brain to model an environment in which the learner can use this process to learn formal concepts and skills. The theoretical origins of the contrasting approaches draw primarily on neuroscience, information processing, and constructionism, respectively.

We have shown that the two approaches identify a common set of properties that a learning environment must have. This is encouraging for the future of the interdisciplinary field of educational neuroscience. Despite their very different goals and theoretical origins, the computational models have identified something like the essence of what it takes to learn, and formalized it as the set of conditions that make learning possible. From this analysis we can begin to envisage the transfer of a learning model, or task activity, or feedback type from one discipline to the other; or the transfer of a finding from one to being tested in the other. Mutually contesting the terminology and precise definitions could also help to advance the disciplines of education and neuroscience separately while beginning to bind them together. In short, we are moving towards the potential of integrating educational, neuroscience, and psychological approaches in our developing understanding of learning.

We conclude that the two types of modeling provide the basis for the constructive interdisciplinary dialogue that can now take place between neuroscience-informed cognitive models and education-informed teaching systems.

## Acknowledgements

This work was supported by ESRC grant RES-062-23-2721. We would like to thank Kaska Porayska-Pomsta and Ed Hubbard for helpful discussions during the writing of this chapter, as well as the helpful comments of three anonymous reviewers.

## References

Anderson, J. R. (2007). *How can the human mind occur in the physical universe?* New York: Oxford University Press.

Anderson, J. R., & Lebiere, C. (1998). *The atomic components of thought.* Mahwah, NJ: Erlbaum.

Anderson, J. R., & Schunn, C. D. (2000). Implications of the ACT-R learning theory: No magic bullets. In R. Glaser (Ed.), *Advances in instructional psychology: Educational design and cognitive science* (Vol. 5) (pp. 1–34). Mahwah, NJ: Erlbaum.

Bishop, D. V. M. (2005). DeFries–Fulker analysis of twin data with skewed distributions: Cautions and recommendations from a study of children's use of verb inflections. *Behavior Genetics, 35*(4), 479–490.

Bransford, J., Vye, N., Stevens, R., Kuhl, P., Schwartz, D., Bell, P., Meltzoff, A., Barron, B., Pea, R., Reeves, B., Roschelle, J., & Sabelli, N. (2006). Learning theories and education: Toward a decade of synergy. In P. Alexander & P. Winne (Eds.), *Handbook of educational psychology* (2nd ed.) (pp. 209–244). Mahwah, NJ: Erlbaum.

Butterworth, B., Varma, S., & Laurillard, D. (2011). Dyscalculia: from brain to education. *Science, 332,* 1049–1053.

Butterworth, B., & Yeo, D. (2004). *Dyscalculia guidance: Helping pupils with specific learning difficulties in maths.* London: nferNelson.

Dayan, P., & Abbott, L. F. (2001). *Theoretical neuroscience: Computational and mathematical modeling of neural systems.* Cambridge, MA: MIT Press.

Deci, E. L., Koestner, R., & Ryan, R. M. (2001). Extrinsic rewards and intrinsic motivation in education: Reconsidered once again. *Review of Educational Research, 71*(1), 1–27. DOI: 10.3102/00346543071001001

diSessa, A. A. (2001). *Changing minds: Computers, learning and literacy.* Cambridge, MA: MIT Press.

Elman, J. L., Bates, E. A., Johnson, M. H., Karmiloff-Smith, A., Parisi, D., & Plunkett, K. (1996). *Rethinking innateness: A connectionist perspective on development.* Cambridge, MA: MIT Press.

Frederickson, N., Reed, P., & Clifford, V. (2005). Evaluating web-supported learning versus lecture-based teaching: Quantitative and qualitative perspectives. *Higher Education Research and Development, 50,* 645–664.

Gilbert, N., & Troitzsch, K. G. (2005). *Simulation for the social scientist.* Maidenhead, UK: McGraw-Hill.

Hackman, D. A., & Farah, M. J. (2009). Socioeconomic status and the developing brain. *Trends in Cognitive Sciences, 13*(2), 65–73.

Hart, B., & Risley, T. R. (1995). *Meaningful differences in the everyday experience of young American children.* Baltimore, MD: Brookes.

Hebb, D. O. (1949). *The organization of behavior.* New York: John Wiley & Sons, Inc.

Hoyles, C., & Noss, R. (2003). What can digital technologies take from and bring to research in mathematics education? In A. J. Bishop, M. A. Clements, C. Keitel, J. Kilpatrick, & F. K. S. Leung (Eds.), *Second international handbook of research in mathematics education* (pp. 323–349). Dordrecht: Kluwer.

Huttenlocher, J., Vasilyeva, J., Cymerman, E., & Levine, S. (2002). Language input and child syntax. *Cognitive Psychology, 45*, 337–374.

Laurillard, D. (2002). *Rethinking university teaching: A conversational framework for the effective use of learning technologies* (2nd ed.). London: RoutledgeFalmer.

Laurillard, D. (2010). Effective use of technology in teaching and learning in HE. In Peterson, P., Baker, E., & McGaw, B. (Eds.), *International encyclopedia of education* (Vol. 4, pp. 419–426). Oxford: Elsevier.

Laurillard, D. (2012). *Teaching as a design science: Building pedagogical patterns for learning and technology.* New York: Routledge.

Mareschal, D., Johnson, M., Sirios, S., Spratling, M., Thomas, M. S. C., & Westermann, G. (2007). *Neuroconstructivism: How the brain constructs cognition.* Oxford: Oxford University Press.

Mareschal, D., & Thomas, M. S. C. (2006). How computational models help explain the origins of reasoning. *Computational Intelligence Magazine, IEEE, 1*(3), 32–40.

Mareschal, D., & Thomas M. S. C. (2007) Computational modeling in developmental psychology. *IEEE Transactions on Evolutionary Computation (Special Issue on Autonomous Mental Development), 11*(2), 137–150.

Mitchell, T. M. (1997). *Machine learning.* New York: McGraw-Hill.

Papert, S. (1980). *Mindstorms: Children, computers, and powerful ideas.* Brighton, UK: Harvester.

Papert, S., & Harel, I. (1991). Situating constructionism. In I. Harel & S. Papert (Eds.), *Constructionism: Research reports and essays, 1985–1990.* Norwood, NJ: Ablex.

Rumelhart, D. E., & McClelland, J. L. (1986). *Parallel distributed processing. Volume 1.* Cambridge, MA: MIT Press.

Sawyer, K. (Ed.). (2006). *Cambridge handbook of the learning sciences.* Cambridge: Cambridge University Press.

Sirois, S., Spratling, M., Thomas, M. S. C., Westermann, G., Mareschal, D., & Johnson, M. H. (2008). Précis of neuroconstructivism: How the brain constructs cognition. *Behavioral and Brain Sciences, 31*, 321–356.

Spencer, J., Thomas, M. S. C., & McClelland, J. L. (2009). *Toward a new unified theory of development: Connectionism and dynamical systems theory re-considered.* Oxford: Oxford University Press.

Sun, R. (2008). *Cambridge handbook of computational cognitive modelling.* Cambridge: Cambridge University Press.

Thomas, M. S. C. (2012). Brain plasticity and education. *British Journal of Educational Psychology – Monograph Series II: Educational Neuroscience, 8*, 142–156.

Thomas, M. S. C., Baughman, F. D., Karaminis, T., & Addyman, C. (2012a). Modelling development disorders. In C. Marshall (Ed.), *Current issues in developmental disorders* (pp. 93–124). Hove, UK: Psychology.

Thomas, M. S. C., & Johnson, M. H. (2006). The computational modelling of sensitive periods. *Developmental Psychobiology, 48*(4), 337–344.

Thomas, M. S. C., & Knowland, V. (2009). Sensitive periods in brain development: Implications for education policy. *European Psychiatric Review, 2*(1), 17–20.

Thomas, M. S. C., & Knowland, V. C. P. (in press). Modelling mechanisms of persisting and resolving delay in language development. Manuscript submitted for publication.

Thomas, M. S. C., Knowland, V. C. P., & Karmiloff-Smith, A. (2011). Mechanisms of developmental regression in autism and the broader phenotype: A neural network modeling approach. *Psychological Review, 118*(4), 637–654.

Thomas, M. S. C., & McClelland, J. L. (2008). Connectionist models of cognition. In R. Sun (Ed.), *Cambridge handbook of computational cognitive modelling* (pp. 23–58). Cambridge: Cambridge University Press.

Thomas, M. S. C., Purser, H. R. M., & Mareschal, D. (2012b). Is the mystery of thought demystified by context-dependent categorisation? Towards a new relation between language and thought. *Mind and Language, 27*(5), 595–618.

Thomas, M. S. C., Forrester, N. A., & Ronald, A. (2013). Modelling socio-economic status effects on language development. *Developmental Psychology*.

Thomas, M. S. C., Westermann, G., Mareschal, D., Johnson, M. H., Sirois, S., & Spratling, M. (2008). Studying development in the 21st century. *Behavioral and Brain Sciences, 31*, 345–356.

Vygotsky, L. S. (1978). *Mind in society: The development of higher psychological processes.* Cambridge, MA: Harvard University Press.

Westermann, G., Mareschal, D., Johnson, M. H., Sirois, S., Spratling, M. W., & Thomas, M. S. C. (2007). Neuroconstructivism. *Developmental Science, 10*(1), 75–83.

Westermann, G., Thomas, M. S. C., & Karmiloff-Smith, A. (2010). Neuroconstructivism. In U. Goswami (Ed.), *Blackwell handbook of child development* (2nd ed.) (pp. 723–748). Oxford: Blackwell.

Williams, J. O. H., & Dayan, P. (2005). Dopamine, learning and impulsivity: A biological account of ADHD. *Journal of Child Adolescent Psychopharmacology, 15*(2), 160–179.

## Further Reading

Laurillard, D. (2012). *Teaching as a design science: Building pedagogical patterns for learning and technology.* New York: Routledge.

Mareschal, D., Johnson, M., Sirios, S., Spratling, M., Thomas, M. S. C., & Westermann, G. (2007). *Neuroconstructivism: How the brain constructs cognition.* Oxford: Oxford University Press.

Sawyer, K. (Ed.). (2006). *Cambridge handbook of the learning sciences.* Cambridge: Cambridge University Press.

Thomas, M. S. C., Baughman, F. D., Karaminis, T., & Addyman, C. (2012). Modelling development disorders. In C. Marshall (Ed.), *Current issues in developmental disorders* (pp. 93–124). Hove, UK: Psychology

# Chapter 4

# Genetics for Education

## Yulia Kovas, Sergei Malykh, and Stephen A. Petrill

Education is the clearest example of an environmental influence on a person's development. Curricula, teacher training, teaching methods, class settings, educationally relevant cultural norms and values – are all examples of environmental factors that have a profound effect on what, when, and how we learn. However, *behavioral genetic research* shows that these and other educational environments interact with people's unique genetic profiles, leading to huge individual differences in motivation, learning, ability, and achievement (e.g., Kovas, Haworth, Dale, & Plomin, 2007). In this chapter, we outline the methodological tools used in *behavioral genetics* to study educationally relevant phenomena, such as variation in reading, mathematics, language, and other cognitive, motivational, and behavioral traits. Such traits are called *phenotypes* in behavioral genetic research, to refer to observable, quantifiable expression of underlying gene–environment processes. We have included a basic technical detail box (Box 4.1) and glossary (Box 4.2) in this chapter introducing a number of important behavioural genetic terms and concepts.

Although this is a volume on educational neuroscience, we will not discuss the links between brain and behavior directly. There are two reasons. First, there are several recent publications on this topic, which cover the current state of affairs in this very young field (e.g., Kovas & Plomin, 2006; Plomin, Kovas, & Haworth, 2007). Second, from the point of view of behavioral genetic research, the brain and brain-related parameters (such as brain volume, connectivity, and function) are simply a collection of phenotypes. Therefore, the same methods

*Educational Neuroscience*, First Edition. Edited by Denis Mareschal, Brian Butterworth and Andy Tolmie.

**Box 4.1   *What does* everyone *need to know about genetics?***

This box could include some basic information about the molecule of DNA, about amino acids, chromosomes, the double helix, the laws of genetic transmission described by Mendel, gene expression, or *epigenetic regulation*. However, such information is easily and freely available in numerous online resources, including excellent animations (e.g., The Gene Almanac, http://www.dnalc.org/home.html; background on the Human Genome Project, http://www.genome.gov/Education/; the Genetics Learning Science Centre, http://learn.genetics.utah.edu/index.html). Moreover, many excellent textbooks provide introduction to each of the many facets of genetic research (e.g., Plomin et al., 2012). Accompanying this chapter, we have also included a glossary of some concepts and technical terms.

Just as the basic messages from neuroscience can be understood without detailed understanding of brain organization or functioning, or the complex methods used in studying the brain, the basic messages from the latest genetic research can also be understood by nonexperts. Here we highlight three important messages:

1.  Each individual has a *unique genetic profile*, contributing to the unique phenotypic profile. This includes the unique sequence of the DNA code, the unique pattern of genetic expression, and a unique product of the gene–environment interplay. Millions of DNA differences (variants, polymorphisms) exist in the human genome, and each one of them may contribute to the observed differences among us. Each DNA variant is likely to contribute only a little to the variation in each trait. This makes the quest of linking genes and behavior difficult, but new methods and technologies make this task possible.

2.  Just like environmental effects, *genetic effects are not deterministic*. Genes contribute to outcomes through complex patterns of gene–environment interplay. The same genes may have completely different effects depending on the environments in which they express themselves. A gene may be silent or active, depending on multiple factors. Genetic effects can be moderated by environments, and therefore are not in themselves an explanation for any complex behavior. The same trait (e.g., cognitive ability) can be highly heritable in one culture, and highly environmental in another – depending on the environments (e.g., access to education). Genetic information about complex traits is

probabilistic. Just as knowing something about a person's home environment may provide only probabilistic information about their educational potential, so knowing about their DNA sequence can provide only probabilistic information. With advances in *behavoural genomic* research, such probabilistic information should become more and more precise and useful.

3. *Genetic effects are not static*, but unravel and change across development. It is commonly believed that genetic effects are "pre-programed", "stable", and "permanent". Instead, they are probabilistic, changeable, and malleable. Some genes become active only at certain stages of development, and sometimes only in the presence of a particular stressor. In addition, the same behavioral trait may be under a weaker or stronger genetic influence at different stages of development. For example, in today's Western societies, individual differences in general intelligence are largely due to environmental factors during early childhood, but under a strong genetic control in adulthood (Haworth et al., 2010). Knowing the unique DNA sequence of an individual will never be enough to understand how genes affect behavior. We will need to learn about a complex path from each gene to each behavior at each important point in development.

## Box 4.2 *Glossary*

**Behavioral genetics** The study of behavior through the use of *quantitative genetic* and *molecular genetic* methodology.

**Behavioral genomics** The study of how genes in the genome function, including the processes of gene–environment interplay.

**Bivariate heritability** The genetic contribution to the phenotypic correlation between traits.

**Cholesky decomposition (procedure, analysis, model)** A statistical method used in *quantitative genetics*, which allows us to assess the overlap and specificity of genetic and environmental influences on two or more phenotypically correlated traits.

**DNA** (deoxyribonucleic acid) The double-stranded molecule that encodes genetic information. The two strands are held together by hydrogen bonds between two of the four bases, with adenine bonded to thymine, and cytosine bonded to guanine.

**DNA sequence**   The order of base pairs on a single chain of the DNA double helix. The human set of DNA sequences (the *genome*) consists of about three billion base pairs, counting just one chromosome from each pair of chromosomes. The three billion base pairs contain about 25 000 protein-coding genes, which range in size from about 1000 bases to two million bases.

**DNA variation**   Although the human DNA sequence is largely the same for all people, it nevertheless includes millions of DNA polymorphisms – locations where different people may have different variants. The most common type of DNA variation is *single-nucleotide polymorphism (SNP)*, which involves a mutation in a single nucleotide. Other types of variation include CNVs (copy number variants), which involve duplication of long stretches of DNA as well as other types of deletion, substitution, and insertion.

**DZ twins**   Dizygotic (literally, "two zygotes"), fraternal twins share on average 50% of their segregating (variable) DNA.

**Epigenetics**   DNA modifications that affect gene expression without changing DNA sequence.

**Epigenetic regulation**   includes processes by which genes may be expressed or silenced under the influence of environments.

**Genetic correlation**   The extent to which genetic effects on one trait are correlated with genetic effects on another trait.

**Gene–environment correlation (GE correlation)**   Genetic influence on exposure to environment experiences that are correlated with genetic propensities.

**Gene–environment interaction**   Genetic sensitivity or susceptibility to environments.

**Genome**   All the DNA sequences of an organism. The human genome contains about three billion DNA base pairs.

**Group genetic correlation**   The extent to which the same genetic effects operate on one learning disability (e.g., reading disability) and another ability (e.g., mathematical ability) (see Knopik, Alarcón, & DeFries, 1997, for details).

**Group heritability**   In a multivariate extremes analysis this indicates the extent to which genetic effects mediate the phenotypic covariance between one (e.g., reading) disability and another (e.g., mathematical) ability.

**GWAS (genome-wide association study)**   A molecular genetic method that assesses DNA variation throughout the genome in an attempt to link multiple DNA variants with the variation in a particular trait.

**Heritability**   The proportion of the phenotypic differences in a particular trait among individuals in a particular population that can be attributed to genetic differences. It is important to note that heritability is a population-based statistic: the same trait may be more or less heritable at a different time in development, in a different population, or under the influence of different environments.

**Methylation**   DNA methylation is an epigenetic process by which gene expression is inactivated by adding a methyl group.

**Microarray (gene chip)**   A surface the size of a postage stamp with hundreds of thousands of DNA sequences that serve as probes to detect single-nucleotide polymorphisms (SNPs) in molecular association studies or gene expression in expression studies.

**Molecular genetics**   The search for associations between specific genes and specific outcomes.

**MZ twins**   Monozygotic (literally, "one zygote"), identical twins have identical DNA sequences.

**MZ differences design**   As MZ twins have an identical DNA sequence, any behavioral differences between them are attributed to environmental factors (or epigenetic effects, by which different environments lead to differences in the expression of the same genes). Studying MZ twins who differ on a particular trait (e.g., who are discordant for a learning disability) in relation to differences in their experiences is an effective tool in the search for the true causal environmental factors. The method can also be used in assessing the effectiveness of educational methods and interventions, as MZ twins are perfect controls for each other.

**Nonshared environment**   Environmental influences that do not contribute to resemblance between family members.

**Phenotype**   An observed characteristic of an individual that results from the combined effects of (multiple) genotypes and (multiple) environments.

**Phenotypic variance**   An observed (measured) variation (individual differences) in any trait (e.g., brain mechanism, cognitive ability, academic achievement level)

**Pleiotropy**   Multiple effects of a gene. The same gene has multiple functions and affects different organs via the same or different mechanisms.

**Pleiotropic associations**   Observed correlations between different traits (phenotypes) that are due to effects of the same gene(s).

**Quantitative genetics**   Quantitative genetic methods (such as twin and adoption studies) estimate genetic and environmental contribution to the observed (phenotypic) variation (individual differences) in a trait in a particular population at a particular time, as well as the genetic and environmental contributions to the covariance among different traits.

**Quantitative trait locus (QTL)**　Genes of various effect sizes in multiple gene systems that contribute to quantitative (continuous) variation in a phenotype, as opposed to a single gene causing an outcome.

**Shared environment**　Environmental factors responsible for resemblance between family members, *not* the objectively shared factors. Some "objectively shared" environments (e.g., the same SES for two children growing up in the same home) may act by contributing to their dissimilarity through interactions with other influences.

**Single-nucleotide polymorphism (SNP)**　　see **DNA variation**

**Structural equation modeling (model fitting)**　In quantitative genetics, a method to test the goodness of fit between a model of genetic and environmental relatedness and the observed data is used. Different models can be compared, and the best-fitting model is used to estimate genetic and environmental parameters.

**Triplet code of DNA**　The DNA is written in an alphabet consisting of four letters (A, T, C, G), with three-letter words (codons). These three-letter words code for amino acids, the organic molecules that build polypeptides, which are the building blocks of enzymes and other proteins. For example, "CGA" codes for alanine, whereas "CCA" codes for glycine.

**Whole-genome sequencing**　The procedure by which an individual's entire genomic sequence is genotyped, so that all the common and rare variants of all kinds are known.

apply to the genetically sensitive investigations of the brain traits as for behavioral traits, which are the focus of this chapter.

Some of the points that we will make in this chapter may seem obvious. However, in our experience, it is still useful to cover basic issues, as there are many persistent myths and misunderstandings surrounding genetics and its relation to behavior. In fact, we talked to many nonbehavior geneticist colleagues about the themes covered in this chapter and identified several major misunderstandings about genetics even among professional psychology researchers. Broadly speaking, these misunderstandings may be summarized as viewing genetic influences as static and deterministic. For example, a typical "lay" interpretation of the observed high *heritability* for academic achievement is a fundamentally erroneous assumption that one's achievement levels are determined by one's genetic makeup, with little scope for educational intervention. In reality, heritability only reflects the influence made by genetic factors in specific environments. Moderate to high heritability of most educationally relevant traits in the United Kingdom may reflect the uniformity of the UK curriculum and teaching standards (Kovas et al., 2007). Indeed, there is some evidence from international comparison, suggesting that, with a higher degree of variation in school types and quality, genes explain less variation in academic ability and achievement (e.g., Petrill, Deater-Deckard, Thompson, Schatschneider, & DeThorne, 2007).

Providing everyone with equal educational opportunities is arguably the greatest challenge of a modern society. As a consequence of universal availability of education, a large proportion of individual differences in educational outcomes is explained by genetic variation. Recognizing that different people require different approaches and different amounts of time to reach certain educational milestones, today's educational policies continuously attempt to individualize educational approaches. However, despite these attempts, which include for example extra support to underperforming children in schools, the enormous amount of variation remains in all aspects of motivation, ability, and achievement. This is true of all cultures. For example, in China, where children consistently outperform children from other countries in mathematics, an enormous amount of variation in mathematical ability and achievement nevertheless exists (see, e.g., PISA, 2009; Rodic et al., in press). Clearly, it is very important to understand factors driving this wide variation, and behavioral genetic research already has shown that these factors involve complex interactive processes between *variation in DNA* and variation in environment.

Genetic effects are dynamic. Genes contribute to both stability and change in ability and achievement, with genetic effects on ability increasing with age (see, e.g., Haworth, Kovas, Petrill, & Plomin, 2007; Haworth et al., 2010; Kovas et al., 2007). The realization that genetic effects are not static – that the same genes may be expressed differently in different environments and at different stages of development – is of fundamental relevance to education.

Genetic research *does not* undermine the importance of education, but rather it can help improve educational practice. Societies that have achieved universal access to education face a new, even more difficult challenge: that of creating educational systems that allow all individuals to fully utilize their unique genetic profiles – the unique structure and function of their DNA sequence – in order to make the most of education. In the future, education may indeed be able to reduce the variation in achievement by successful prevention of many of the learning problems, and to shift the whole achievement distribution in the positive direction. We believe that this can only be achieved through understanding the mechanisms by which genes respond to environments, and through individualizing education in ways that we are not currently able to fully conceptualize.

However, the process of integrating genetics into educational research and practice has begun. In the following sections we review the methods and findings that, in our opinion, have already made important contributions to this process.

## Genetics for Education: What is in the Toolkit?

Many specialized tools of high precision and quality are available to today's *behavioral genetics* researchers. *Quantitative genetics* uses twin, adoption, and other family studies to quantify the relative contributions of genes and environments to the variance in different traits and to the relationships between traits. Today, quantitative genetic research involves large representative samples and utilizes the latest analytic and statistical methodology – providing deeper and deeper insights into the mechanisms underlying child development. The rapidly advancing *molecular genetics* aims to identify the actual genes that are involved in variation in traits. Quantitative and molecular genetics, the two branches of *behavioral genetics*, lead to further *behavioral genomic* investigations, which aim to clarify the complex paths from each gene to behavior, including the complex interplay with environmental influences.

In this chapter we provide examples of quantitative and molecular genetic methodology, as well as of genetically sensitive cross-cultural designs – applied to educationally relevant questions. We begin with the overview of the twin method – the most commonly used method of quantitative genetics. We then provide several specific applications of the twin methodology to the educationally relevant questions: estimating the relative contributions of genetic and environmental factors to individual differences; evaluating genetic and environmental sources of gender differences; evaluating the teacher/classroom effect; examining the etiology of learning disabilities; studying the sources of the relationships among different traits and of the change and continuity in the same traits; and using genetically sensitive approaches to understanding environmental influences. We then go on to a brief overview of the current breakthroughs in educationally relevant molecular genetic research, and to an outline of the genetically sensitive cross-cultural studies. We conclude with our predictions about the uses of genetic research for the benefit of education of the future.

## Quantitative Genetics for Education

The field of *quantitative genetics* has moved on from the methodological "stone age", when small numbers of *monozygotic* (genetically identical) and *dyzygotic* (sharing on average 50% of variable DNA) twins were compared to estimate the relative contribution of genes and environments to certain traits. Advanced statistical methods have been developed to utilize the large, multivariate, longitudinal twin and other family datasets in order to address important questions for education, such as the following. Are the same environments important for mathematical and verbal learning? Do the same genes contribute to mathematical learning at the beginning of formal education (e.g., early arithmetic) and at later stages (e.g., algebra, geometry, advanced mathematics)? What are the etiological links between motivation and achievement?

Twins have been described as the ideal natural experiment. The use of both *identical (monozygotic, MZ)* and *nonidentical (dizygotic, DZ)* twin pairs in the classical twin design allows the relative contributions of genetic and environmental factors to the educationally relevant traits to be determined. The twin design, especially applied to large representative samples, can also be used to achieve the following. (1) Produce estimates of genetic influence (heritability) and distinguish two types of environmental influence (shared and nonshared). (2) Provide a perfectly controlled sibling study for molecular genetic investigations. (3) Investigate environmental influences whilst controlling for genetics (e.g., determining the extent to which environmental correlates of motivation and achievement are truly causal). (4) Investigate *epigenetic* differences whilst controlling for genetics (for example, by identifying epigenetic differences within pairs of MZ twins, who show different (discordant) educational achievement levels). Epigenetic differences here refer to the differences in how genes are expressed, presumably under the influences of environments, rather than the differences in the structure of DNA. (5) Unravel the interaction between genes and environments (for example, the extent to which the effectiveness of a particular educational method depends on genetics). (6) Understand genetic and environmental contributions to heterogeneity and comorbidity (for example, whether subtypes of a learning disability are etiologically different). (7) Track genetic and environmental influences as they unfold during the life course (for example, by identifying how early genetic influences emerge; how the relative contribution of genes and environments change throughout life; and the role of *epigenetics* with increasing age). In the following six sections we provide examples of twin research designs and findings addressing these important educational questions.

Although different types of experimental design, with varying degrees of family relatedness, are used in quantitative genetic research (e.g., sibling studies, adoption studies, virtual twins – unrelated people who show a high degree of observed similarity), the twin method remains the most commonly used, as it allows for large representative samples and consequently affords a high precision in statistical parameter estimates. Like any other methodology, the twin method also has its limitations (see Boomsma, Busjahn, & Peltonen, 2002; Martin, Boomsma, & Machin, 1997; Plomin, DeFries, McClearn, &

McGuffin, 2008, for a full discussion of these issues). Despite the limitations, the twin method provides solid and reliable results, which have been validated not only through multiple replications in different samples, but also through convergence with results from other methods, such as adoption studies and molecular genetics (Bates, 2008; Visscher et al., 2006; Wray, Goddard, & Visscher, 2008). For this reason, we will focus primarily on the twin method and its current uses.

### Estimating the relative contributions of genes and environments to variation in educationally relevant traits

The twin method addresses the origins of individual differences by estimating the proportion of variance that can be attributed to *genetic, shared environment*, and *nonshared environment factors* (Plomin et al., 2008). In the case of complex traits that are likely to be influenced by multiple factors, the *genetic component of variance* (*heritability*) refers to the influence of alleles (gene variants) at all gene loci (positions in the *DNA sequence*) that affect the trait. The similarity between twins for any particular trait can be due, wholly or in part, to these shared genetic effects. Twin similarity may also be due, wholly or in part, to *shared environment*. This refers to environmental influences that vary in the population but are experienced similarly by members of pairs of twins. For example, pairs of twins experience similar conditions during gestation, have the same socio-economic status, live in the same family, and usually go to the same school. These factors could reasonably be expected to increase similarity between co-twins. *Nonshared environment* refers to any aspect of environmental influence that is experienced differently by the two twins and contributes to phenotypic differences between them, including measurement error. Such influences involve aspects of experience that are specific to an individual, such as traumas and diseases, idiosyncratic experiences, different peers, differential treatment by the parents and teachers, and, importantly, different perceptions of experiences, even if the events appear to be ostensibly the same for the two children.

Genetic influence can be estimated by comparing intraclass correlations for *identical* (*MZ*) *twins* and *fraternal* (*DZ*) *twins*. The *phenotypic variance of a trait* can be attributed to genetic variance to the extent that the MZ twin correlation exceeds the DZ twin correlation. Specifically, heritability (the proportion of phenotypic variance attributed to genetic variance), can be estimated as twice the difference between the MZ and DZ twin correlations. The relatedness for shared (common) environmental influences is assumed to be 1.0 for both MZ and DZ twin pairs who grow up in the same family, because they experience equally similar prenatal and postnatal environments. Shared environmental influences are evidenced to the extent that the DZ twins' correlation is significantly more than half of the MZ correlation. Nonshared environment is estimated by subtracting MZ correlation from the total variance $(100 - r_{MZ})$ and indexes everything that can contribute to dissimilarity between the genetically identical twins growing up together.

*Structural equation model fitting* is a comprehensive way of estimating variance components of a given trait or of the covariance between traits based on the principles of the twin method. The fundamental quantitative genetic model is the so-called ACE model. It apportions the phenotypic variance into genetic (A), shared environmental (C), and nonshared environmental (E) components, assuming no effects of nonadditive genetics or nonrandom mating. The ACE parameters and their confidence intervals can be estimated by fitting the models to variance/covariance matrices using the model-fitting program Mx (Neale, Boker, Xie, & Maes, 2006).

In recent years this methodology has been applied to investigating many educationally relevant traits, from achievement in different areas of learning (e.g., Hart, Petrill, & Kamp Dush, 2010; Keenan, Betjemann, Wadsworth, DeFries, & Olson, 2006; Kovas et al., 2007), to motivation and self-perceived ability (e.g., Luo, Kovas, Haworth, & Plomin, 2011), to cognitive abilities and disabilities (e.g., Plomin & Kovas, 2005). These studies have definitively demonstrated that genes contribute to every investigated trait.

## Etiology of sex differences

Extensions of the basic twin methodology, such as sex-limitation models, have been applied to questions about etiology of any observed sex differences in ability, motivation, and achievement. There are three possibilities with respect to the causes of individual differences in boys and girls, regardless of mean differences between the sexes (Neale et al., 2006). The first possibility is that different genetic and environmental factors are responsible for individual differences in a trait (for example, reading ability) for boys and girls – these are called *qualitative differences*. Such sex-specific effects may be associated with sex chromosomes (e.g., genes on the X or Y chromosomes). Alternatively, they can also involve genes on the autosomal chromosomes that affect boys and girls differently, for example because the genes interact with sex hormones. The second possibility, not mutually exclusive with the first, is that the same etiological influences contribute to individual differences in boys and girls, but that they do so to a different extent – these are known as *quantitative differences*. The third possibility is that there are no differences in the etiology of individual differences for boys and girls; the same genes and environments operate to the same extent in both sexes, even if there are mean differences between boys and girls. That is, for example, mean reading scores are lower for boys than girls, but the factors that make one boy different from another can be the same as those that make one girl different from another girl. It should be noted that quantitative genetics with its focus on individual differences has little to say about the origins of mean differences between boys and girls.

These three possibilities (qualitative differences, quantitative differences, and no differences) can be assessed using sex-limitation structural equation modeling (Neale et al., 2006). Each possibility is associated with a set of parameters in the sex-limitation models. Qualitative differences are evidenced in the genetic relatedness ($r_g$) between DZ opposite-sex twins. In DZ same-sex pairs, the assumption is that on average the twins share 50% of their varying DNA, and the coefficient of genetic relatedness is therefore 0.5. If there are qualitative differences in etiology between boys and girls (different genetic and environmental factors), the genetic relatedness in DZ opposite-sex twins will be less than 0.5. If there are quantitative differences (the same factors, but exerting different magnitudes of effect) rather than qualitative differences, the genetic relatedness for DZ opposite-sex pairs will still be 0.5, but the parameter estimates for the A, C, and E components will be significantly different for male–male pairs and female–female pairs. If there are no qualitative or quantitative differences between boys and girls, the genetic relatedness of DZ opposite-sex (DZos) pairs will be 0.5 and the A, C, and E estimates for male–male and female–female pairs will be the same. However, the phenotypic variance might nonetheless differ for the two sexes because mean differences are often associated with variance differences (i.e., higher means have higher variances).

Applying this methodology, most research to date found no quantitative or qualitative differences in the etiology of individual differences in educationally relevant traits for boys and girls, despite the presence of small average differences (e.g., Kovas et al., 2007). For example, in the Twins Early Development Study, involving approximately 10 000 pairs of twins followed from birth, no etiological gender differences were found for different aspects of school achievement or motivation in early school years – at ages 7, 9, 10, and 12 – for the entire ability range (see, e.g., Haworth et al., 2009; Kovas et al., 2007). Similarly, no etiological sex differences were found later in development, for example for normal or low mathematical performance in 17/18-year-old Dutch twins (Markowitz, Willemsen, Trumbetta, van Beijsterveldt, & Boomsma, 2005), or for mathematical achievement and numerically relevant cognitive traits in 16-year-old UK twins (Tosto et al., in press).

## The contribution of the teacher and the classroom to individual variation

Recently, a similar methodology to that of the sex-limitation model has been applied to address another question of great relevance to education. Several studies tested whether studying in the same classroom or with the same teacher increases similarity in ability among children in that class (Byrne et al., 2010; Kovas et al., 2007). These studies compared similarity in scores on many different traits separately for two groups of twins: those attending the same class and those in different classes. The pattern of correlations in these studies revealed a striking finding: being in the same class and studying with the same teacher did not seem to significantly increase the similarity between the twins in any of the examined traits, including reading, mathematics, science, general cognitive ability, self-perceived ability, and liking of the school subjects. The increased similarity was absent when the twins were currently sharing a class and a teacher, as well as when examining possible effects of previously attending the same class (e.g., the same first mathematics teacher).

Beyond examining the pattern of twin correlations for the two groups, studies (e.g., Kovas et al., 2007) reported model-fitting analyses, applying the so-called "teacher heterogeneity model", to test whether any small differences in estimates for the two groups (in a very few cases when they were observed) were statistically significant. The model, used for these analyses, was similar to that of the sex-limitation model used to test for quantitative sex differences. The full model allowed A, C, and E parameters to vary between the groups. The null model equated the A, C, and E parameters for the two groups (same versus different teacher/classroom). A systematic report of such model-fitting analyses in the Twins Early Development Study concluded that studying in the same classroom in the United Kingdom does not increase similarity between children in any of the examined academically relevant traits at ages 7–16.

These finding require serious consideration. The initial (erroneous) conclusion from these findings might be that teachers are unimportant. However, there is a different interpretation. This lack of a shared classroom environment effect reflects the achievements of modern education: as a society we have developed good teaching methods and programs and provide all children access to quality teaching. This allows most children to reach a certain level, beyond which the differences are explained largely by genetic differences and unique experiences. In a less egalitarian society, the influence of educational shared environment on motivation and achievement would likely be much greater. A less optimistic conclusion can also be drawn. As the UK children's overall academic achievement level is not at the top of many international comparisons (e.g., PISA, 2009), it is possible that the lack of the teacher effect reflects the absence of effective individualized educational methods that lead to strong effects on each child's development.

## Conceptualizing learning disability

The twin methodology has also been applied to the important question of whether learning disability should be conceptualized as categorically different or etiologically linked to the normal individual variation. Large community twin samples make it possible to study disability in the context of ability by selecting children at the low end of the normal distribution (see, e.g., Oliver & Plomin, 2007). Different theoretical perspectives can be used to select probands (individuals performing below or above expected norms) for these studies. For example, mathematical disability can be conceptualized as stemming from specific problems, such as low estimation performance in the presence of the normal IQ. Alternatively, probands could be all children who fall behind what is expected by the educational standard at a particular age. Proband-wise concordances (the ratio of the number of probands in concordant pairs to the total number of probands) represent the risk that a co-twin of a proband is affected, and can be calculated separately for each measure and each of the five sex-by-zygosity groups. Greater MZ than DZ concordances suggest the importance of genetic influences (Plomin et al., 2008).

Another statistical method that allows us to address these etiological questions is called DF extremes analysis (DeFries & Fulker, 1985). This analysis assesses genetic links between disability and ability by bringing together dichotomous diagnoses of disability with quantitative traits of ability. Rather than assessing twin similarity on a quantitative trait of ability or in terms of concordance for a diagnostic cut-off, DF extremes analysis assesses twin similarity as the extent to which the mean standardized quantitative trait score of co-twins of selected extreme or diagnosed probands is below the population mean and approaches the mean standardized score of those probands (see Plomin & Kovas, 2005, for a detailed explanation of DF extremes analysis and for discussion of alternative methods). This measure of twin similarity is called a group twin correlation (or transformed co-twin mean) in DF extremes analysis because it focuses on the mean quantitative trait score of co-twins rather than individual differences.

Genetic influence is implied if group twin correlations are greater for MZ than for DZ twins, that is, if the mean standardized score of the co-twins is lower for MZ pairs than for DZ pairs. Doubling the difference between MZ and DZ group twin correlations estimates the genetic contribution to the average phenotypic difference between the probands and the population. The ratio between this genetic estimate and the phenotypic difference between the probands and the population is called group heritability. It should be noted that group heritability does not refer to individual differences among the probands – the question is *not* why one proband is slightly more disabled than another but rather why the probands as a group have lower scores than the rest of the population.

Finding group heritability implies first that disability and ability are both heritable, and second that there are genetic links between the disability and normal variation in the ability. That is, group heritability itself, not the comparison between group heritability and the other estimates of heritability, indicates genetic links between disability and ability. If a measure of extremes (or a diagnosis) were not linked genetically to a quantitative trait, group heritability would be zero. For example, this situation could occur if a severe form of learning disability is due to a single-gene disorder that contributes little to normal variation in learning ability. However, most researchers now believe that common disorders such as learning disabilities are caused by common genetic variants – the common disease/ common variant hypothesis (e.g., Plomin, Haworth, & Davis, 2009) – rather than by a concatenation of rare single-gene disorders. To the extent that the same genes contribute to learning disability and normal variation in learning ability, group heritability will be observed, although the magnitude of group heritability depends on the individual heritability for normal variation and the heritability of disability gleaned from concordances for disability.

Research using this method suggests that learning disabilities (for example, very low mathematical performance) lie on the same etiological continuum as ability. In other words, the *same* genetic and environmental influences are involved in placing someone at the very low end of the continuum as are involved in placing one person just slightly below another in terms of achievement at the high end. It is the number and combination of such factors that determine each particular position (see, e.g., Plomin & Kovas, 2005; Plomin et al., 2009).

### Etiology of the links across abilities and ages

Multivariate extension of the quantitative genetic method is one of the most under-recognized advantages of the quantitative genetic design. Multivariate genetic designs extend the principles of the twin method to address theoretically meaningful questions about the relationships between measures of educational interest. In contrast to univariate quantitative genetic analysis, which decomposes the variance of a single trait into genetic and environmental sources of variance, multivariate genetic analysis decomposes the covariance between traits into genetic and environmental sources of covariance (Martin & Eaves, 1977). In other words, multivariate genetic analysis assesses genetic and environmental factors responsible for the phenotypic correlation between two traits. For example, if the same genes affect different traits (a biological phenomenon called *pleiotropy*), a *genetic correlation* will be observed between the traits.

For twin studies, multivariate genetic analysis is based on cross-trait twin correlations for two or more traits. That is, rather than comparing one twin's score on variable $X$ with the co-twin's score on the same variable $X$, one twin's $X$ is correlated with the co-twin's $Y$. The phenotypic covariance between two traits is attributed wholly or in part to their genetic overlap to the extent that the MZ cross-trait twin correlation exceeds the DZ cross-trait twin correlation. Shared environmental influences are indicated to the extent that DZ twins' correlation is more than half of the MZ correlation. As with the univariate analyses, *structural equation modeling*, based on the same principles, is used as a more comprehensive way of estimating the proportion of covariance. A typical model (called *Cholesky decomposition*) is commonly used in multivariate twin methodology to test for common and independent genetic and environmental effects on variance in two different traits. The Cholesky procedure is similar to hierarchical regression analysis in nongenetic studies, where the independent contribution of a predictor variable is assessed after accounting for its shared variance with other predictor variables. In the bivariate case, the first factor assesses genetic, shared, and nonshared environmental influences on trait 1, some of which may also influence trait 2. The second factor estimates genetic, shared, and nonshared environmental influences unique to trait 2. The same logic applies to more than two factors.

Another important statistic that can be derived from Cholesky analyses is *bivariate heritability*. This statistic indexes the extent to which the phenotypic correlation between $X$ and $Y$ is mediated genetically. That is, *univariate heritability* is the extent to which the variance of a trait can be explained by genetic variance; *bivariate heritability* is the extent to which the covariance between two traits (or the same trait at two ages) can be explained by genetic covariance. *Bivariate heritability* is the genetic correlation (see below) weighted by the product of the square roots of the heritabilities of $X$ and $Y$ and divided by the phenotypic correlation between the two traits (Plomin & DeFries, 1979). The rest of the phenotypic correlation is explained by bivariate shared environment and bivariate nonshared environment.

In addition, the paths from the model can be transformed to obtain the estimates of genetic, shared, and nonshared environmental correlations between each pair of factors. *Genetic correlations* index the extent to which genetic influences on one measure correlate with genetic influences on a second measure. In other words, genetic correlations indicate the extent to which individual differences in the two measures reflect the same genetic influences. This correlated factors model is merely an algebraic transformation of the Cholesky model. The take-home point here is that there are two important statistics: *bivariate herita-bility*, which is the genetic contribution to the phenotypic correlation between traits, and *genetic correlation*, which is the extent to which genetic effects on one trait are correlated with genetic effects on another trait.

It is also possible to extend DF extremes analysis (described above) to address multivariate issues – analyzing two traits on the same measurement occasion, or the same trait on two measurement occasions (Plomin & Kovas, 2005). For example, group heritability can indicate the extent to which genetic factors account for the mean difference between probands selected on reading and the population on mathematics. In other words, in this case, *group heritability* in a multivariate extremes analysis indicates the extent to which genetic effects mediate the phenotypic covariance between reading disability and mathe-matics ability. Such covariance would be observed if co-twins of children with low reading scores (reading probands) had co-twins whose mathematics scores were on average lower than the population mean.

The *group genetic correlation* indicates the extent to which the same genetic effects operate on reading disability and mathematics ability. Analysis in both directions is required to estimate a DF extremes genetic correlation – that is, probands need to be also selected from the lowest 15% of mathematics performance and analyzed with their co-twin quantitative trait scores on reading.

Many important educational questions have been recently addressed using multivariate twin methodology. For example, the Simple View of Reading (Gough & Tunmer, 1986) holds that reading comprehension results from the intersection of text-decoding- and language-based skills. The reading literature suggests that, although there is considerable shared variance between decoding- and language-based skills, these factors also contribute unique variation to reading comprehen-sion (e.g., Catts, Hogan, & Adlof, 2005; Cutting & Scarborough, 2006; Kendeou, van den Broek, White, & Lynch, 2009). Multivariate genetic designs have been used to examine the etiology of the overlapping, yet independent, contribution of decoding- and language-based skills to reading comprehension. There are sev-eral possibilities. First, genetic influences among decoding- and language-based skills may overlap, but shared or nonshared environmental factors may be independent. In this case, individual differences in reading comprehension are influenced by a common underlying set of genetic factors influencing multiple skills, whereas the environmental skills related to reading comprehension arise through separate environmental pathways. Conversely, decoding- and language-based skills may influence reading comprehension through separate genetic pathways, whereas the shared or nonshared environment may influence overlap between decoding- and language-based skills.

Results suggest that genetic influences on decoding- and language-based skills, although overlapping, also show independent genetic variance as they relate to reading comprehension. In contrast, shared environmental influences are almost completely overlapping (Harlaar et al., 2010; Keenan et al., 2006). Put another way, the distinction between decoding- and language-based skills is due to independent genetic factors, not independent sources of variance related to the home environment or instruction.

This general approach has been employed to address other fundamental questions in education, such as the relationship between reading and maths skills (Hart et al., 2010a; Hart, Petrill, Thompson, & Plomin, 2009; Kovas et al., 2007); the association between reading, maths, and attentional skills (Hart et al., 2010b); and relationship between reading and measures of the environment (Harlaar, Deater-Deckard, Thompson, & Petrill, 2011).

For learning disabilities, multivariate genetic twin research generally suggests substantial genetic co-morbidity, in that genetic correlations are high (about 0.70) between reading, mathematics, and language disabilities (Plomin & Kovas, 2005).

Cross-sectional, prospective, and retrospective longitudinal analyses can be performed using the multivariate twin methodology to assess etiological age-to-age change and continuity. For example, it is commonly assumed that changes in academic attitudes or in performance across age are due to environmental changes (e.g., a new teacher) or stressors (e.g., illness). However, the relative contributions of genes and environment change across time, and therefore any improvements or decreases in performance may occur for either genetic or environmental reasons (Haworth et al., 2010).

Behavioral genetics students are often asked to solve the following paradox: the heritability of a trait (e.g., general intelligence) is 30% … but it is also 70%! How can this be? Usually, students are perplexed by this question, but after some consideration, they can at least partially solve the puzzle, for example by mentioning development. The same trait can be highly environmental at one age and highly heritable at another. This has been shown to be the case for general cognitive ability ($g$), for which heritability increases with age (Haworth et al., 2010; Malykh, Iskoldsky, & Gindina, 2005). Once there is an intellectual breakthrough with solving this paradox, students usually suggest other potential sources of these differences in the relative contribution of genes and environments to the same trait, such as cultural or generational effects.

Behavioral genetic studies suggest that genetic factors explain a significant proportion of the longitudinal stability in reading skills (e.g., Byrne et al., 2005, 2009; Harlaar, Dale, & Plomin, 2007; Petrill et al., 2007; Wadsworth, Corley, Hewitt, Plomin, & DeFries, 2002) as well as math skills (Haworth et al., 2007; Kovas et al., 2007).

Taken together, multivariate genetic designs suggest that the environment is important to the relationships between different measures of educational interest, both concurrently and longitudinally. These studies also suggest that genetic influences help explain the relationships among reading, math, language, attention, and other skills, as well as how these skills develop. Thus, to fully understand how children's educational outcomes unfold, it is also necessary to understand the genetic and neurological underpinnings of how these skills develop and relate to one another.

Finally, the multivariate methods can be extended to study the etiology of cross-trait cross-time associations. For example, one recent study examined the genetic and environmental origins of individual differences in mathematical self-evaluation over time and its association with later mathematics achievement in a UK sample of 2138 twin pairs at ages 9 and 12 (Luo et al., 2011). Self-evaluation indexed how much children liked mathematical activities, and how good they thought they were at those activities. In contrast to the commonly held view (see, e.g., Krapp, 2005; Wigfield & Eccles, 2000), individual differences in mathematical self-evaluation are driven by genetic and nonshared environmental factors rather than by shared environment, not only in middle childhood but also in early adolescence. Self-evaluation of mathematical abilities and interest is moderately heritable at both 9 and 12 years (40% and 43% respectively), suggesting that genetic influence on mathematical self-evaluation is largely stable in magnitude from middle childhood to early adolescence.

The large influences of nonshared environment found in this study suggest that siblings – in this case, twins – do not develop similar mathematical self-evaluation beyond their genetic similarity, despite environmental factors shared by them, such as parents' beliefs, attitudes, and behaviors. The nonshared experiences or perceptions contributing to motivational traits remain poorly understood and require further investigation. Other potential candidate factors include peer pressure, childhood illnesses, differential expectations, and treatment by parents and teachers. Interestingly, these results are also supported by the *same* versus *different* teacher analysis on these data. Twins in this large sample were no more similar in terms of their self-perceived ability or liking of different academic subjects when they studied in the same versus different classes.

The main findings of this study come from the *cross-lagged analyses* of the links between self-evaluation and achievement (where both traits are measured at both ages in the same children). The study found reciprocal influences over time, in that earlier self-evaluation contributed to later achievement and earlier achievement also contributed to later self-evaluation. In other words, there was a small but significant correlation between self-evaluation at age 9 and mathematical achievement at age 12, after controlling for contemporaneous self-evaluation and achievement and for IQ. Similarly, there was a significant correlation between mathematical achievement at 9 and self-evaluation at 12. The most novel finding was that both cross-lagged relationships were genetically mediated. What does it mean that the cross-lagged contribution from mathematical self-evaluation at 9 years to mathematics achievement at 12 years is almost entirely attributed to genetic effects (98%)? This genetic mediation means that, if we were able to identify the genes responsible for the heritability of self-evaluation at age 9, some of these genes would not be associated with mathematics achievement at age 9 but they would be associated with mathematics achievement at age 12. Although there is considerable genetic stability for mathematics achievement from age 9 to age 12, some new genetic effects on mathematics achievement emerge at age 12, and the cross-lagged genetic effects from self-evaluation at age 9 contribute to this new genetic variance. Clearly, we are far from understanding the mechanisms of such *pleiotropic associations* (the same genes affecting different traits), but the results of such studies help to clarify the nature of cross-age cross-trait associations. In the study by Luo et al. (2011) no environmentally determined causal link was found between earlier self-evaluation and later mathematics achievement, at least in the United Kingdom.

## Understanding of the role of the environment

Research on the environment is in many ways more difficult than research on genetics. Genetics is entering a golden post-genomic era in which the structure and function of the entire *genome* will be known (see the section on *molecular genetics*). In contrast, there is no "environome" project. Indeed, there are no laws of environmental transmission and there is nothing comparable to the *triplet code of DNA*. Another important factor in the slow progress towards understanding the role of the environment has been the dominant tendency of the social sciences to view environmental influences in opposition to genetics. However, three of the most important recent discoveries about environmental mechanisms, described below, have come from twin research (Plomin et al., 2008).

*Family environment does not make children similar to each other.* Contrary to most environmental theories, and as demonstrated with several earlier examples in this chapter, environmental influences are largely of the nonshared type (Plomin & Daniels, 1987). That is, effective environments make children growing up in the same family no more similar than children growing up in different families. In other words, environmental influences do not operate on a family-by-family basis but rather on an individual-by-individual basis. Although a priority for environmental research is to identify these nonshared environmental factors, little is known as yet about them (Plomin, Asbury, &

Dunn, 2001; Turkheimer & Waldron, 2000). However, the very realization of the importance of nonshared environments has implications for further research in education (e.g., Plomin, Kovas, & Haworth, 2007).

*Environments are partly heritable.* The second major finding about environments comes from dozens of twin studies demonstrating that when measures of psychological environments (such as parenting, stress, social support) are treated as dependent measures they show substantial genetic influence, a phenomenon that has been called the *nature of nurture* (Plomin & Bergeman, 1991). How can measures of the environment show genetic influence given that environments have no DNA? The answer is that psychological environments can be considered as extended phenotypes of individuals, reflecting genetic differences among individuals as they select, modify, and construct their environments (Plomin, 1994).

To date, hardly any research has been conducted treating educational environments as traits to be decomposed in terms of genetic and environmental etiology. One study (Walker & Plomin, 2006) analysed the data collected using a modified version of children's perceptions on the School Life Questionnaire (Ainley & Bourke, 1992) for 1162 pairs of nine-year-old twins, part of the Twins Early Development Study (Oliver & Plomin, 2007), and found significant genetic influence (average heritability of 30%) for six scales, with the Adventure scale (the extent to which the classroom is fun, exciting, interesting) and the General Satisfaction scale showing the strongest genetic influence (heritabilities of 44% and 45%, respectively) (Walker & Plomin, 2006). Heritabilities were similar regardless of whether members of twin pairs were in the same classroom or in different classrooms.

In education, even though children are assigned to teachers and classrooms, their self-perceived strengths and weaknesses, their interests and values, and the peers they select may, in part for genetic reasons, make them active participants in accepting and creating learning experiences. In order to investigate *gene–environment correlation* in education, learning environments need to be studied in genetically sensitive designs. Most measures of educational environments are passive in relation to the child, such as teacher quality and class size, and are thus unlikely to reflect genetic influences evoked or created by children (although such measures could involve passive gene–environment correlation to the extent that children attend schools that differ in teacher quality and class size on the basis of genetically influenced characteristics of their parents). However, in order to fully consider the interplay between school environments and children's genetic strengths and weaknesses, it is necessary to develop measures that capture children's active role in selecting, modifying, and creating their educational environments, both within and beyond schools.

*The links between environments and outcomes are partly genetic.* The third, related to the second, major finding regarding the role of the environment concerns the often implied causal links between environment and outcomes. If environmental measures and developmental outcome measures show genetic influence, it is possible that associations between environmental measures and measures of educational outcomes are at least in part mediated genetically. Multivariate genetic designs (described in the previous section) are able to decompose the covariance between environmental measures and developmental outcome measures in order to investigate the extent to which their association is mediated genetically (e.g., Pike, McGuire, Hetherington, Reiss, & Plomin, 1996). The typical finding from such research is that genetic factors mediate about half of the association between measures of family environment and children's behavioral outcomes (Plomin, 1994). A prerequisite for such analyses is that there is phenotypic covariance between the environmental measure and the outcome measure, which often is not the case. For example, in one of the largest educationally relevant twin samples in the world, TEDS, such analyses were not possible using the School Life Questionnaire because the phenotypic correlations between this measure and children's academic achievement were too small (0.05 on average for the six scales) to warrant multivariate genetic analyses (Walker & Plomin, 2006).

The explanation for these results – showing genetic mediation of correlations between environmental measures and outcome measures – lies in a process of *genotype–environment (GE) correlation*, in which children's genetic propensities are correlated with their experiences (see, e.g., Plomin et al., 2008). That is, children evoke parental responses in part for genetic reasons (sometimes called evocative GE correlation); and children actively create environments that foster their genetic propensities (sometimes called active GE correlation). This research has contributed to a change in thinking about the relationship between children's experiences and their behavioral development. A passive model in which the environment directly causes differences in children's development has given way to an active model in which children create their own experiences, for example by selecting and modifying their environments and by constructing perceptions of their experience and re-constructing their experiences in memory (Plomin, 1994).

One highly effective method to study environmental influences is the so-called *MZ differences design*, which allows users to identify nonshared environmental factors while controlling for genetic influences. The only influences that make monozygotic (MZ) twins different from one another are their unique environmental experiences, such as different friends, teachers, and life events. One recent study used the basic logic of this design to assess the degree of monozygotic twins' dissimilarity in their perceptions of the classroom environment (such as pupil–teacher relationship and general satisfaction), and in their behavior problems (such as conduct problems and peer problems) reported by their teachers (Oliver, Pike, & Plomin, 2008). The study found that the MZ twin correlations were much less than 100% (22–52%) for both classroom experiences and behavior, indicating a considerable nonshared environmental influence on classroom experiences and behavior problems. The same study showed that between 1 and 5% of the differences in behavior could be explained by the differences in classroom experience between the MZ twins (or, alternatively, the behavioral differences could explain a portion of the classroom experience). Whatever the direction of this association, the initial differences have to be due to environmental rather than genetic factors.

*Using genetically sensitive approaches to evaluate educational methods*  The MZ differences design, and other methods using MZ twins, can also be applied to the assessment of educational methods and interventions. This application of the twin method is not new. As early as the 1930s, Russian psychologist Luria and his colleagues conducted studies using the method of "control twin" to assess the effectiveness of particular educational methods, such as literacy training, in pre-school children. In one such study, Luria and Mirenova (1936) taught block building and other constructing tasks using different methods with co-twins from several MZ pairs. Controlling for genetic differences, the authors were able to establish a more effective teaching method. Another study (Mirenova, 1934) assessed physical performance (e.g., high jump, throwing a ball at a target) in pairs of four-year-old MZ twins. Having established a twin with worse performance in each pair, a particular training regime was introduced for that twin. The effectiveness of the regime on different aspects of psychomotor development could be then assessed, controlling for any genetic effects. Although this method requires careful ethical and practical considerations, we believe that it can be very useful for education purposes.

*Applying MZ differences design to extending the search for nonshared environment beyond school or family experiences*  A whole new field of genetic research – epigenetics – is dedicated to the study of *DNA methylation* across the *genome*. DNA methylation is a mechanism through which genes are expressed or silenced under the influence of environments (Mill & Petronis, 2007; Petronis, 2004). Although this mechanism is as yet poorly understood, the study of methylation is particularly promising: unlike the structure of the DNA, methylation is dynamic, and is responsive to environmental intervention. Recent research found that MZ twins differ in their degree of methylation, suggesting that epigenetic processes are influenced by nonshared environments (e.g., Mill & Petronis,

2007; Petronis, 2006). Understanding epigenetic mechanisms may lead to personalized interventions involving nutritional, chemical, physical, and psychosocial programs (see, e.g., Dolinoy, Weidman, & Jirtle, 2007; Feil, 2006).

To summarize, far from becoming irrelevant with advances in molecular biology, the twin design is increasingly valuable and provides a more refined genetic investigation of educationally relevant traits. Twin studies can also point the way for molecular genetic studies in terms of selecting well-defined phenotypes or groups of phenotypes, selecting probands for case–control association studies, and in terms of raising awareness of changes in genetic influence across development (McCarthy et al., 2008).

## Molecular Genetics for Education

Today's behavioral geneticists have at their disposal a whole range of molecular genetic tools. These include new and continuously improving technologies (e.g., *microarrays* that allow to genotype hundreds of thousands of DNA markers simultaneously), statistical methodologies (e.g., *whole-genome sequencing* analyses), and increasing understanding of the biological processes (e.g., *epigenetic regulation*, by which environments regulate genetic effects). *Molecular genetics* is possibly the fastest developing area in the history of human science – the area is still in its infancy, but has already provided many important insights into the origins and mechanisms of individual differences. We have no doubt that this area holds great promise for education of the future. Consequently, in this section we briefly outline important concepts and methods employed in molecular genetics and provide several examples of the contribution that has already been made by this field.

### The QTL perspective

Recent molecular genetic research has provided much evidence in support of the hypothesis that genetic factors contribute to individual differences in all complex traits, such as learning abilities, disabilities, motivation, and achievement (e.g., Davies et al., 2011; Docherty, Kovas, & Plomin, 2011; Plomin et al., 2009). Moreover, this genetic research provides firm support for the polygenic conceptualization of the heritability of complex traits: many DNA markers contribute to variation in any complex trait and the effect of any such marker on the outcome is very small. These genetic markers (areas of the genome that contribute to normal variation) are often referred to as *quantitative trait loci* (QTLs); QTL theory is the molecular genetic reflection of quantitative genetic theory that underlies the twin method (Plomin et al., 2008; Plomin, Owen, & McGuffin, 1994). The implications of the QTL theory are profound. If many DNA markers of very small effect contribute to any complex trait, this means that each person's educational profile may be a product of unique combinations of many genetic markers, environments, and interactions between them.

For *molecular genetics*, twin study evidence for genetic links between qualitative diagnoses and quantitative distributions supports the value of switching from case–control designs to a quantitative traits and a QTL perspective (Plomin, DeFries, Knopik, & Neiderhiser, 2012). In addition to its implications for *genome-wide association studies*, the QTL perspective has profound implications for diagnosis, treatment, and prevention of learning disabilities and low motivation. However, the QTL analyses require very large samples that are representative of the populations from which they are drawn, and in which qualitative diagnoses can be studied in the context of quantitative trait distributions.

## Genome-wide association studies (GWAS)

The human genome is largely invariant: all people largely share the same *sequence of DNA*. If the human genome were a book, it would be the same fascinating novel for all people, with the same number of pages and the same words on each page. However, the number of mistakes that can occur when a book is copied manually again and again is enormous. When a copy of a copy that contains errors (mutations) is made, then this copy will also contain errors. The next copy will contain old errors and new (de novo) errors. These errors are the source of our unique individualities and the building blocks for evolution. Our individual genomes contain millions of such errors (variants or polymorphisms). Some of them are common, as they come from the same old source; while others are very rare as they have only occurred for just one copy (person). Some are dramatic – such as when a whole page is missing or inserted – this usually leads to dramatic consequences (e.g., Down syndrome). Still others are almost unnoticeable, such as when only one letter (single nucleotide) is substituted – *single-nucleotide polymorphisms (SNPs)*. Some SNPs may have no functional significance, such as when a spelling mistake does not change the meaning of a word or sentence, or they may have important consequences, just as one letter may change the meaning of a word, a sentence, or the entire text.

Today, we are in an unprecedented position: by carefully sequencing the genomes of thousands of people, millions of common variants in our genomes have been documented. Of the functional variants (those that have any effect on any phenotype), each is hypothesized to have only a very small effect on any trait. What needs to be done now is to relate each of these variants to the variation in people's behavior. This is not an easy task. We currently still only have a very limited understanding of the biological mechanisms underlying individual variation in ability, motivation, and achievement. This might mean that we will need to examine each of the millions of variants to determine their role in individual differences in educationally relevant traits.

Until recently, this task was not considered possible. However, with rapidly advancing technology, molecular genetic research is moving towards the ability to identify all DNA markers, even of extremely small effects, including rare genetic variants. The latest *microarray* technology allows for simultaneous assessment of millions of DNA markers from an individual. Within a few hours, one's genome can be examined for millions of variants. Then, genomes of hundreds or thousands of people are compared to establish any points of differences in the genomes associated with observed differences in any particular trait (see, e.g., Plomin et al., 2012; McCarthy et al., 2008). These so-called *genome-wide association studies* have begun to identify DNA polymorphisms (variants) associated with educationally relevant traits, such as reading (e.g., Meaburn, Harlaar, Craig, Schalkwyk, & Plomin, 2007), mathematics (Docherty et al., 2009), and general cognitive ability (e.g., Butcher, Davis, Craig, & Plomin, 2008; Davies et al., 2011). The Davies et al. (2011) study not only provides information on the genetic variants involved in individual differences in human intelligence, but also provides firm support for the conclusions drawn from the twin method: a large portion of individual differences in cognitive abilities can be explained by the combined effects of multiple genes, each of small individual effect.

It is likely that the information on our complete genomic profiles will be available long before we can truly utilize this knowledge. The process of tracing a path from each genetic variant to behavior may take a long time. Indeed, at the same time as the search for DNA markers associated with educationally relevant traits, research into the exact mechanisms by which each gene affects a trait is also taking place. This work is complex and involves multiple levels: from gene expression profiles, to specific protein functions, to physiology, and often to the structure and function of the brain (Plomin et al., 2009). Foreseeing the specific applications of molecular genetic research to education is difficult at this stage, but it is even more difficult to imagine that this wealth of knowledge about our uniqueness will not contribute to ways of maximizing our unique potential.

## Cross-Cultural Behavioral Genetic Research

In this very brief section we describe another important method that we believe offers great promise for education. Examining the extent to which the same genes are expressed in different cultures will provide new insights into the mechanisms of *gene–environment interaction*. Cross-cultural comparisons have already yielded some important findings. Many recent data suggest that the patterns of genetic and environmental influences on many traits are similar across cultures. For example, the increase of heritability of general intelligence has been documented in many different countries (see, e.g., Haworth et al., 2010; Malykh et al., 2005).

Nevertheless, some etiological differences have also been documented. For example, several studies have found that some aspects of reading and mathematical ability are influenced by shared environment more than by genes in US school children (e.g., Petrill et al., 2012) rather than in UK children. The variation in school types and quality is much greater in the United States than in the United Kingdom, which might explain the observed differences in the relative contributions of genes and environments to educational phenotypes in these two countries. However, it is important to note that the actual levels of academic performance of the population are not necessarily related to the relative contributions of genes and environments to the individual differences. For example, children in the United Kingdom and in the United States perform below average on the latest international comparisons of mathematical achievement (PISA, 2009).

Cross-cultural differences could be driven both by average differences in the frequency of particular genetic variants across populations and by average differences in the relevant environments. We think that it is unlikely that many of the observed differences between populations in educational achievement will be explained by genetic differences among populations. One recent study, which compared early numerical development of children from several countries (China, Kyrgyzia, Russia, and the United Kingdom), found significant differences in performance across the countries (Rodic et al., in press). As the study included two different populations in Kyrgyzia – Kyrgyz and Dungan – the authors were able to test several important hypotheses regarding these observed differences. Kyrgyzstan is the second poorest country in Central Asia, and Kyrgyz and Dungan people, who live in Kyrgyzia, share the same socio-economic background. Kyrgyz and Dungan children both follow the Russian educational system and study in Russian, but both also speak their own languages in their homes. Dungan people have migrated from China, are closely genetically related to Chinese, speak a variant of Chinese, but do not use Chinese characters, using the Cyrillic alphabet instead. The study found that Kyrgyz and Dungan children showed very similar performance in early arithmetic skills, lagging behind UK, Russian, and Chinese children. The Chinese children showed the best performance. In other words, Dungan children did not show any advantage in arithmetic over Kyrgyz children. These results suggest that, although genetic differences explain a large proportion of the individual differences in mathematical ability, the observed cross-cultural differences are likely to be explained by nongenetic factors, such as cultural norms or the structure of the written language. However, the authors call for further empirical investigations into potential differences, including careful documenting of the relevant environments, molecular and epigenetic research, and intervention work embedded in the twin design.

The same processes that are involved in cross-cultural differences may also be involved in individual variation within cultures, and in the group differences within countries. For example, even within a culture, heritability of the same trait can differ across generations or groups of society, reflecting economic and political changes, the societal organization, and cultural norms. As environments change, so do the genetic effects. This is in particular relevant for educational settings. Today's children are significantly different from children several generations ago. For example, through access to the latest gadgets, today's child has access to more knowledge in the palm of the hand than the greatest educationalists of the past. This change in access to information may lead to cognitive and motivational changes, and to changes in the role of the teacher. Genetic contribution to academic success may dramatically change in these new circumstances. Studying these processes using genetically sensitive cross-cultural approaches may help in the complex task of adapting education of the future to new demands.

## Conclusion

We believe that these examples of behavioral genetic methods and findings illustrate the far-reaching impact that this field can have on education, in terms of prevention of learning disabilities and improving general levels of educational success through highly personalized educational approaches. In order to address important educational challenges with high precision, we need large representative samples of twins, latest molecular genetic methodology, and cross-cultural behavioral genomic comparisons. We believe that embedding the research described in this volume into cross-cultural genetically sensitive designs will lead to rapid advances in our understanding of the mechanisms underlying individual variation in learning. In turn, this new understanding should contribute to implementation of successful individualized educational programs in the future.

## Acknowledgements

The authors gratefully acknowledge support from the UK Medical Research Council (program grant G0500079), the US National Institutes of Health (grants HD44454, HD46167, and HD059215), and the Government of the Russian Federation (grant 11.G34.31.0043).

# References

Ainley, J., & Bourke, S. (1992). Students' views of primary school. *Research Papers in Education, 7,* 107–128.

Bates, T. C. (2008). Current genetic discoveries and education: Strengths, opportunities, and limitations. *Mind, Brain, and Education, 2*(2), 74–79.

Boomsma, D., Busjahn, A., & Peltonen, L. (2002). Classical twin studies and beyond. *Nature Reviews Genetics, 3* Nov(11), 872–882.

Butcher, L. M., Davis, O. S. P., Craig, I. W., & Plomin, R. (2008). Genome-wide quantitative trait locus association scan of general cognitive ability using pooled DNA and 500 K single nucleotide polymorphism microarrays. *Genes, Brain and Behavior, 7,* 435–446.

Byrne, B., Coventry, W. L., Olson, R. K., Samuelsson, S., Corley, R., Willcutt, E. G., Wadsworth, S., & DeFries, J. C. (2009). Genetic and environmental influences on aspects of literacy and language in early childhood: Continuity and change from preschool to grade 2. *Journal of Neurolinguistics, 22,* 219–236.

Byrne, B., Coventry, W. L., Olson, R. K., Wadsworth, S., Samuelsson, S., Petrill, S. A., Willcutt, E. G., & Corley, R. (2010). "Teacher effects" in early literacy development: Evidence from a study of twins. *Journal of Educational Psychology, 102*(1), 32–42.

Byrne, B., Wadsworth, S., Corley, R., Samuelsson, S., Quain, P., DeFries, J. C., Willcutt, E., & Olson, R. K. (2005). Longitudinal twin study of early literacy development: Preschool and kindergarten phases. *Scientific Studies of Reading, 9*(3), 219–236.

Catts, H., Hogan, T., & Adloff, S. (2005). In H. Catts & A. Kamhi (Eds.), *The connections between language and reading disabilities* (pp. 25–40). Mahwah, NJ: Erlbaum.

Cutting, L. E., & Scarborough, H. S. (2006). Prediction of reading comprehension: Relative contributions of word recognition, language proficiency, and othr cognitive skills can depend on how comprehension is measured. *Scientific Studies of Reading, 10*(3), 277–299.

Davies, G., Tenesa, A., Payton, A., Yang, J., Harris, S. E., Liewald, D., Ke, X., Le Hellard, S., Christoforou, A., Luciano, M., McGhee, K., Lopez, L., Gow, A. J., Corley, J., Redmond, P., Fox, H. C., Haggart, P., Whalley, L. J., McNeill, G., Goddard, M. E., Espeseth, T., Lundervold, A. J., Reinvang, I., Pickles, A., Steen, V. M., Ollier, W., Porteous, D. J., Horan, M., Starr, J. M., Pendleton, N., Visscher, P. M., & Deary, I. J. (2011). Genome-wide association studies establish that human intelligence is highly heritable and plygenic. *Molecular Psychiatry, 16,* 996–1005.

DeFries, J. C., & Fulker, D. W. (1985). Multiple regression analysis of twin data. *Behavioral Genetics, 15,* 467–473.

Docherty, S. J., Davis, O. S. P., Kovas, Y., Meaburn, E. L., Dale, P. S., Petrill, S. A., Schalkwyk, L. C., & Plomin, R. (2009). A genome-wide association study identifies multiple loci associated with mathematics ability and disability. *Genes, Brain and Behavior, 9,* 234–247.

Docherty, S. J., Kovas, Y., & Plomin, R. (2011). Gene–environment interaction in the etiology of mathematical ability using SNP sets. *Behavioral Genetics, 41,* 141–154.

Dolinoy, D. C., Weidman, J. R., & Jirtle, R. L. (2007). Epigenetic gene regulation: Linking early developmental environment to adult disease. *Reproductive Toxicology, 23*, 297–307. DOI: 10.1016/j.reprotox.2006.08.012

Feil, R. (2006). Environmental and nutritional effects on the epigenetic regulation of genes. *Mutation Research: Fundamental and Molecular Mechanisms of Mutagenesis, 600*, 46–57. DOI: 10.1016/j.mrfmmm.2006.05.029

Gough, P. B., & Tunmer, W. E. (1986). Decoding, reading and reading disability. *Remedial and Special Education, 7*, 6–10.

Harlaar, N., Cutting, L., Deater-Deckard, K., Dethorne, L. S., Justice, L. M., Schatschneider, C., Thompson, L. A., & Petrill, S. A. (2010). Predicting individual differences in reading comprehension: A twin study. *Annals of Dyslexia, 60*(2), 265–288.

Harlaar, N., Dale, P. S., & Plomin, R. (2007). From learning to read to reading to learn: Substantial and stable genetic influence. *Child Development, 78*(1), 116–131.

Harlaar, N., Deater-Deckard, K., Thompson, L. A., & Petrill, S. A. (2011). Associations between reading achievement and independent reading in early elementary school: A genetically-informative cross-lagged study. *Child Development, 82*(6), 2123–2137.

Hart, S. A., Petrill, S. A., & Kamp Dush, C. M. (2010a). Genetic influences on language, reading, and mathematic skills in a national sample: An analysis in the National Longitudinal Survey of Youth. *Language, Speech, and Hearing Services in Schools, 41*, 118–128.

Hart, S. A., Petrill, S. A., Thompson, L. A., & Plomin, R. (2009). The ABC's of math: A genetic analysis of mathematics and its links with reading ability and general cognitive ability. *Journal of Educational Psychology, 101*(2), 388–402.

Hart S. A., Petrill S. A., Willcutt E., Thompson L. A., Schatschneider C., Deater-Deckard K., & Cutting L. E. (2010b). Exploring how symptoms of attention-deficit/hyperactivity disorder are related to reading and mathematics performance: General genes, general environments. *Psychological Science, 21*(11), 1708–1715.

Haworth, C. M. A, Kovas, Y., Harlaar, N., Hayiou-Thomas, M. E., Petrill, S. A., Dale, P. S., & Plomin, R. (2009). Generalist genes and learning disabilities: A multivariate genetic analysis of low performance in reading, mathematics, language and general cognitive ability in a sample of 8000 12-year-old twins. *Journal of Child Psychology and Psychiatry, 50*(10), 1318–1325.

Haworth, C. M. A., Kovas, Y., Petrill, S. A., & Plomin, R. (2007). Developmental origins of low mathematics performance and normal variation in twins from 7 to 9 years. *Twin Research and Human Genetics, 10*(1), 106–117.

Haworth, C. M. A., Wright, M. J., Luciano, M., Martin, N. G., de Geus, E. J. C., van Beijsterveldt, C. E. M., Bartels, M., Posthuma, D., Boomsma, D. I., Davis, O. S. P., Kovas, Y., Corley, R. P., DeFries, J. C., Hewitt, J. K., Olson, R. K., Rhea, S.-A., Wadsworth, S. J., Iacono, W. G., McGue, M., Thompson, L. A., Hart, S. A., Petrill, S. A., Lubinski, D., & Plomin, R. (2010). The heritability of general cognitive ability increases linearly from childhood to young adulthood. *Molecular Psychiatry, 15*, 1112–1120.

Keenan, J. M., Betjemann, R. S., Wadsworth, S. J., DeFries, J. C., & Olson, R. K. (2006). Genetic and environmental influences on reading and listening comprehension. *Journal of Research in Reading, 29*, 79–91.

Kendeou, P., van den Broek, P., White, M. J., & Lynch, J. (2009). Predicting reading comprehension in early elementary school: The independent contributions of oral language and decoding skills. *Journal of Educational Psychology, 101*, 765–778.

Knopik, V. S., Alarcon, M., & DeFries, J. C. (1997). Comorbidity of mathematics and reading deficits: Evidence for a genetic etiology. *Behavior Genetics, 27*, 447–453.

Kovas, Y., Haworth, C. M. A., Dale, P. S., & Plomin, R. (2007). The genetic and environmental origins of learning abilities and disabilities in the early school years. *Monographs of the Society for Research in Child Development, 72*, 1–144.

Kovas, Y., & Plomin, R. (2006). Generalist genes: Implications for cognitive sciences. *Trends in Cognitive Science, 10*, 198–203.

Krapp, A. (2005). Basic needs and the development of interest and intrinsic motivational orientations. *Learning and Instruction, 15*(5), 381–395. DOI: 10.1016/j.learninstruc.2005.07.007

Luo, Y., Kovas, Y., Haworth, C., & Plomin, R. (2011). Cross-lagged analyses of mathematical achievement and mathematical self-evaluation in children at 9 and 12 years of age. *Learning and Individual Differences, 21*(6), 710–718.

Luria, A. R., & Mirenova, A. N. (1936). Экспериментальное развитие конструктивной деятельности. Дифференциальное обучение однояйцевых близнецов [Experimental development of constructive activity. Differential education of monozygotic twins]. *Труды Медико-биологического института [Works of the Medico-Biological Institute], 4*, 487–505.

Malykh, S. B., Iskoldsky, N. V., & Gindina, E. D. (2005). Genetic analysis of IQ in young adulthood: A Russian twin study. *Personality and Individual Differences, 38*(6), 1475–1485.

Markowitz, E. M., Willemsen, G., Trumbetta, S. L., van Beijsterveldt, T. C. E. M., & Boomsma, D. I. (2005). The etiology of mathematical and reading (dis)ability covariation in a sample of Dutch twins. *Twin Research and Human Genetics, 8*, 585–593.

Martin, N., Boomsma, D. I., & Machin, G. (1997). A twin-pronged attack on complex traits. *Nature Genetics, 17*, 387–392.

Martin, N. G., & Eaves, L. J. (1977). The genetical analysis of covariance structure. *Heredity, 38*, 79–95.

McCarthy, M. I., Abecasis, G. R., Cardon, L. R., Goldstein, D. B., Little, J., Ioannidis, J. P. A., & Hirschhorn, J. N. (2008). Genome-wide association studies for complex traits: Consensus, uncertainty and challenges. *Nature Reviews Genetics, 9*, 356–369.

Meaburn, E. L., Harlaar, N., Craig, I. W., Schalkwyk, L. C., & Plomin, R. (2007). Quantitative trait locus association scan of early reading disability and ability using pooled DNA and 100 K SNP microarrays in a sample of 5760 children. *Molecular Psychiatry, 13*, 729–740.

Mill, J., & Petronis, A. (2007). Molecular studies of major depressive disorder: The epigenetic perspective. *Molecular Psychiatry, 12*, 799–814. DOI: 10.1038/sj.mp.4001992

Mirenova, A. N. (1934). Миренова А.Н. Психомоторное обучение дошкольника и общее развитие. Некоторые эксперименты на близнецах [Psychomotor education of pre-schoolers and general development. Several experiments with twins].

*Труды медико-биологического института* [Works of the Medico-Biological Institute], *3*, 86–103.

Neale, M. C., Boker, S. M., Xie, G., & Maes, H. H. (2006). *MX: Statistical modeling* (7th ed.) (Available from Department of Psychiatry, VCU, Box 900126, Richmond, VA 23298, USA)

Oliver, B., Pike, A., & Plomin, R. (2008). Nonshared environmental influences on teacher-reported behaviour problems: Monozygotic twin differences in perceptions of the classroom. *Journal of Child Psychology and Psychiatry, 49*, 646–653.

Oliver, B., & Plomin, R. (2007). Twins Early Development Study (TEDS): A multivariate, longitudinal genetic investigation of language, cognition and behaviour problems from childhood through adolescence. *Twin Research and Human Genetics, 10*, 96–105.

Petrill, S. A., Deater-Deckard, K., Thompson, L., Schatschneider, C., & DeThorne, L. (2007). Longitudinal genetic analysis of early reading: The Western Reserve Reading Project. *Reading and Writing, 20*(1/2), 127–246.

Petrill, S. A., Logan, J. A. R., Hart, S. A., Vincent, P., Thompson, L., Kovas, Y., & Plomin, R. (2012). Math fluency is etiologically distinct from untimed math performance, decoding fluency, and untimed reading performance: Evidence from a twin study. *Journal of Learning Disabilities, 45*(4), 371–381.

Petronis, A. (2004). The origin of schizophrenia: Genetic thesis, epigenetic antithesis, and resolving synthesis. *Biological Psychiatry, 55*, 965–970.

Petronis, A. (2006). Epigenetics and twins: Three variations on the theme. *Trends in Genetics , 22*, 347–350. DOI: 10.1016/j.tig.2006.04.010

Pike, A., McGuire, S., Hetherington, E. M., Reiss, D., & Plomin, R. (1996). Family environment and adolescent depressive symptoms and antisocial behavior: A multivariate genetic analysis. *Developmental Psychology, 132*(4), 574–589.

PISA. (2009). *PISA 2009 key findings*. Retrieved June 10, 2013, from http://www.oecd.org/pisa/pisaproducts/pisa2009keyfindings.htm

Plomin, R. (1994). *Genetics and experience: The interplay between nature and nurture.* Thousand Oaks, CA: Sage.

Plomin, R., Asbury, K., & Dunn, J. (2001). Why are children in the same family so different? Nonshared environment a decade later. *Canadian Journal of Psychiatry, 46*(3), 225–233.

Plomin, R., & Bergeman, C. S. (1991). The nature of nurture: Genetic influences on "environmental" measures. *Behavioral and Brain Sciences, 14*, 373–427.

Plomin, R., & Daniels, D. (1987). Why are children in the same family so different from each other? *Behavioral and Brain Sciences, 10*, 1–16.

Plomin, R., & DeFries, J. C. (1979). Multivariate behavioral genetic analysis of twin data on scholastic abilities. *Behavioral Genetics, 9*, 505–517.

Plomin, R., DeFries, J. C., Knopik, V. S., & Neiderhiser, J. M. (2012). *Behavioral genetics* (6th ed.). New York: Worth.

Plomin, R., DeFries, J. C., McClearn, G. E., & McGuffin, P. (2008). *Behavioral genetics* (5th ed.). New York: Worth.

Plomin, R., Haworth, C. M. A., & Davis, O. S. P. (2009). Common disorders are quantitative traits. *Nature Reviews Genetics, 10*, 872–878.

Plomin, R., & Kovas, Y. (2005). Generalist genes and learning disabilities. *Psychological Bulletin, 131*, 592–617.

Plomin, R., Kovas, Y., & Haworth, C. M. A. (2007). Generalist genes: Genetic links between brain, mind, and education. *Mind, Brain, and Education, 1*(1), 11–19.

Plomin, R., Owen, M. J., & McGuffin, P. (1994). The genetic basis of complex human behaviors. *Science, 264*(5166), 1733–1739.

Rodic, M., Zhou, X., Tikhomirova, T., Wei, W., Malykh, S., Ismatulina, V., Sabirova, E., Davidova, Y., Tosto, M., Lemelin, J.-P., & Kovas, Y. (in press). Cross-cultural perspective on cognitive underpinning of individual differences in early mathematics. *Developmental Science.*

Tosto, M. G., Petrill, S. A., Halberda, J., Trzaskowski, M., Tikhomirova, T. N., Bogdanova, O. Y., Ly, R., Wilmer, J. B., Naiman, D. Q., Germine, L., Plomin, R., & Kovas Y. (in press). Why do we differ in number sense? Evidence from a genetically sensitive investigation. *Intelligence.*

Turkheimer, E., & Waldron, M. (2000). Nonshared environment: A theoretical, methodological, and quantitative review. *Psychological Bulletin, 126*, 78–108.

Visscher, P. M., Medland, S. E., Ferreira, M. A., Morley, K. I., Zhu, G., Cornes, B. K., Montgomery, G. W., & Martin, N. G. (2006). Assumption-free estimation of heritability from genome-wide identity-by-descent sharing between full siblings. *PLoS Genetics, 2*, e41.

Wadsworth, S. J., Corley, R. P., Hewitt, J. K., Plomin, R., & DeFries, J. C. (2002). Reading performance at 7, 12 and 16 years of age in the Colorado Adoption Project: Parent–offspring analyses. *Journal of Child Psychology and Psychiatry, 43*, 769–774.

Walker, S. O., & Plomin, R. (2006). Nature, nurture, and perceptions of the classroom environment as they relate to teacher assessed academic achievement: A twin study of 9-year-olds. *Educational Psychology, 26*, 541–561.

Wigfield, A., & Eccles, J. S. (2000). Expectancy-value theory of achievement motivation. *Contemporary Educational Psychology, 25*(1), 68–81. DOI: 10.1006/ceps.1999.1015

Wray, N. R., Goddard, M. E., & Visscher, P. M. (2008). Prediction of individual genetic risk of complex disease. *Current Opinion in Genetics and Development, 18*, 257–263.

## Further Reading

Plomin R., DeFries, J. C., Knopik, V. S., & Neiderhiser, J. M. (2013). Behavioral Genetics (6th Ed.). London UK: Worth.

Scerif, G., & Karmiloff-Smith, A. (2005). The dawn of cognitive genetics? Crucial developmental caveats. *Trends in Cognitive Sciences, 9*, 126–135.

Taylor, J., Roehrif, A. D., Hensler, B. S., Connor, C. M., & Schatschneider, C. (2010). *Teacher quality moderates the genetic effects on early reading. Science, 328*, 512–514.

# Chapter 5

# Research Methods in Educational Psychology

## Andy Tolmie

### Different Types of Approach to Educational Research

Taken generically, mainstream educational research spans an extremely wide range of concerns, including school organization and effectiveness, pedagogy and classroom processes, educational technology and other forms of support for learning, special and inclusive education, and a variety of cross-cutting curricular specializations, such as science, mathematics, and literacy education. Given the importance attached to education and over a century's history of active investigation of factors affecting educational outcomes, this diversity is unsurprising, though challenging for any attempt to summarize the research methods that have been employed.

However, there is a more fundamental distinction between what may be termed "pure" educational research and psychological research in education. The former tends to be characterized by a concern with specific educational systems and structures, and the outcomes these produce. The latter is typically much less concerned with specific systems and contexts, being driven instead by a focus on the processes by which learning occurs, the factors that shape these processes, and how an understanding of both might be deployed within educational settings. Much research of this kind does not even take place within formal educational contexts, for instance making use of out-of-class or laboratory settings (e.g., Huss, Verney, Fosker, Mead, & Goswami, 2011; Philips & Tolmie, 2007), or concentrating on informal learning that takes place outside of school (e.g., Pino-Pasternak, Whitebread, & Tolmie, 2010).

*Educational Neuroscience*, First Edition. Edited by Denis Mareschal, Brian Butterworth and Andy Tolmie.
© 2014 John Wiley & Sons, Ltd. Published 2014 by John Wiley & Sons, Ltd.

There is an inherently greater affinity between the methods and theoretical concerns of the neuroscience of learning and educational psychology: both are directed at understanding the basic processes of learning and the factors facilitating or constraining these. If educational neuroscience seeks to find points of convergence between the different research traditions, these are more likely to be found here than between neuroscience and pure educational research, at least at this point in time. This chapter will consequently focus predominantly on the methodologies employed within educational psychology. The next section deals with the issue of measurement, and the strategies that have evolved over time for capturing learning processes. The following section moves on to consider how these measurement techniques are deployed within different types of study design, including school-based interventions. Throughout the chapter a central goal will be to highlight the specific constraints that limit potential approaches to research in educational psychology as compared to the work in experimental cognitive neuroscience that features in other chapters.

## Deciding What to Measure

Research in educational psychology is primarily concerned with measuring two types of variable, learning outcomes and factors that predict or constrain these outcomes, in order to draw inferences about the processes connecting them. Because of an interest in *specific* learning phenomena, the emphasis is also typically on fine-grained measures of conceptual understanding or skill rather than general achievement in terms of curricular objectives, and on the impact of proximal factors such as learners' academic self-concepts, teacher dialogue, and parental support during learning activities rather than structural predictors of outcome such as socioeconomic status (SES). This creates pressure to devise novel measures for each piece of research, albeit working to precedent and agreed principles, rather than relying on established instruments. The implications of this are considered below with respect to the two main types of instrument, behavioral and report measures. The section concludes with a consideration of demographic and environmental measures, and the ways in which these have been utilized in educational psychology.

### Behavioral measures

Behavioral measures fall into two broad categories, *performance* (what individuals are actually observed to do under typical circumstances) and *competence* (what individuals show themselves to be capable of doing under controlled conditions).

Each has its problems. Measures of performance ostensibly have greater authenticity, but the level of learning achieved in a given area may remain hidden unless circumstances call for it to manifest. Measures of competence appear to avoid this problem, but may simply reflect performance under test conditions and nowhere else (see, e.g., Nunes, Schliemann, & Carraher, 1993, on conceptions of situated learning that elucidate this problem). The present chapter is not the context for enlarging further on these issues, but I will touch on practical approaches that help navigate the difficulties they present.

*Measures of observed performance*   Observational measures take a variety of forms, but the standard approach that defines the basic framework is known as *systematic observation* (see, e.g., Croll, 1986). This rests on the core principle that observations of behavior should be made using predefined categories of theoretical importance, in order to avoid the subjectivity that may color spontaneous judgments. Aspects of behavior that are of focal interest are operationalized into precise variables in advance of the research, and these are adhered to throughout. Observations are also typically made at fixed intervals and for fixed durations, to ensure a common baseline for comparison of individuals.

When systematic observation is used in classroom settings, a number of learners (probably only a subset of those present) are identified at the outset as targets for observation, and then watched in turn by an observer for one or more predetermined periods of time (usually some minutes at least), as far as possible under comparable circumstances. During this period, the occurrence of behaviors in the agreed categories will be recorded, using either *event-sampling* or *time-sampling* techniques. In event sampling, the categories of behavior are limited in number and type (e.g., instances of children responding to teacher questions in a specific way), and the incidence of these at any point during the observational period will simply be recorded. Time-sampling techniques aim for a more complete record of activity, dividing the observational period up into fixed time intervals (e.g., 15 s), with the researcher noting which behaviors within a broad set of possible categories are exhibited in each interval. For example, in research on the effects of collaborative group work in primary school science by Christie, Tolmie, Thurston, Howe, and Topping (2009), the observational categories were particular types of dialogue indicative of productive engagement with the collaborative tasks, such as proposition of ideas, use of explanations, disagreements, and so on. It is common practice within this kind of approach to have observation windows alternating with recording windows, to ensure there is time to note observations down correctly.

The underlying rationale of systematic observation is that, since it is impossible to record *all* of a learner's behavior, we need to focus instead on representative and perhaps contrasting subsamples. In the work of Christie et al. (2009), for instance, the dialogue of target children in group-work lessons was compared with that in whole-class lessons on related topics in order to establish how far dialogue type was a function of the setting. Similarly, by using three time points, spread over four months, they were able to demonstrate increases in the incidence of productive dialogue in group-work lessons which were absent from whole-class lessons, indicating that context-specific learning had occurred.

Systematic observation is not without problems. There are resource overheads associated with conducting observations in real time, and ensuring that researchers are suitably trained to carry out what is a taxing activity with the necessary care. There are also issues regarding the validity of the measures obtained, given the potential impact on behavior of having an observer present. Some researchers make video recordings of the target activity and code these afterwards, rather than having observers present (e.g., Blatchford, Baines, Rubie-Davies, Bassett, & Chowne, 2006). However, children often regard the presence of a camera as more novel than that of a researcher taking notes, so the former may actually be more intrusive, as well as presenting technical challenges around sight lines and recording quality. Video is only the better option where the coding scheme is complex and hard to employ in real time; in out-of-class settings where there are fewer issues regarding recording quality and the presence of a fixed camera typically becomes rapidly forgotten (see, e.g., Howe, Rodgers, & Tolmie, 1990); or with adult learners, who are less liable to distraction.

Systematic observation also requires a *reliability check* to be made in order to demonstrate that the observations are not researcher dependent, creating another overhead. Given the demands of specifying exactly which behaviors should be treated as an instance of "use of explanation" or "proposition of idea", the need for such checks is a real one. Precise definitions are usually too abstract to be of much practical value, so most researchers fall back on lists of examples. This makes variation in interpretation across individuals inevitable, especially where the focus is on nonverbal behavior, which is often more fleeting. These reliability checks are usually conducted by two researchers. Both record the same behavior of a subset of targets (10% is adequate), and compare their coding to ensure that the agreement rate is sufficiently high (70% or more), and above chance levels. Since much data collection in educational psychology requires researchers to make judgements about responses or behaviors, checks of this kind are commonplace. It is also common practice to use coding schemes derived from those that have already been demonstrated to be effective – the coding used by Christie et al. (2009), for instance, drew on nearly 20 years' prior research on dialogue in group work settings.

Systematic observation has the advantage of yielding quantitative frequency counts of target categories of behavior, which are amenable to statistical analysis. However, there are potential problems of loss of information and false equivalence: for instance, is it legitimate to treat two different explanations of why a toy car rolls faster down a steep slope than a shallow one (e.g., "it's not affected so much by the surface" versus "it's more affected by gravity") as being of identical importance within a group work exercise? In fact, in this case, the empirical answer to the question may be yes, since the frequency of explanations is associated with learning regardless of content (Howe et al., 2007). Nevertheless, some researchers eschew the use of systematic observation in favor of detailed case-study observations, in which the activity of individual learners is followed over an extended period of time, with points of apparent importance being noted in qualitative terms either as they arise or during later inspection of video records (see, e.g., Meard, Bertone, & Flavier, 2008). Such approaches present their own challenges in terms of establishing that an impartial analysis has been conducted, usually met by presenting the verbatim details of statements and/or events from which conclusions have been drawn as *warrants* for these. They do have the capacity to yield insights that may be hard won using quantitative methods, though. A common strategy within educational psychology is to use case-study approaches during the earlier stages of a program of work, devising more "grounded" quantitative behavioral measures on the basis of these.

*Measures of competence: test and psychometric measures*    Educational psychology's concern with measuring learning creates some particular problems when it comes to constructing measures of competence. Take primary-school children's understanding of object flotation in physics as an example. Children of this age rarely possess any explicit and generalizable account of what leads some objects to float in water while others sink. Their response to any single question on the topic (for instance, presenting them with a piece of wood and asking them to predict whether or not it is likely float and justify their answer, as in Howe et al., 1990) is therefore unlikely to be especially informative. Learning in this area and others generally proceeds incrementally – though not necessarily smoothly – and while this is happening learners exhibit differing understanding depending on the context of testing, and the specific question asked (see, e.g., Karmiloff-Smith, 1992; Siegler, 1996). Moreover, it is seldom possible to hypothesize with confidence which specific questions or contexts will reveal learning gains, even following a targeted intervention.

As a result, test-based measures of learning in educational psychology lean on basic psychometric principles: (a) use of a range of items covering different contexts in which understanding might be applied, (b) use of schemes for scoring responses that go beyond simple pass/fail, to enhance sensitivity, and (c) checking of response profiles across items to ensure each adds additional discriminating power. Provided responses to sets of such items show a reasonable degree of correlation, confirming they are all measuring the same thing, they can be used to generate a composite index of understanding (see Tolmie, Muijs, & McAteer, 2011, for more detail). Once a suitable index has been constructed, it can be used to assess the extent of learning over time or in response to a specific intervention with considerable reliability and sensitivity. For example, Howe et al. (2007) used measures of understanding of forces and evaporation designed in this way that generated statistically reliable differences between intervention and control samples on margins of around 5% of the scale range – differences that were still detectable 18 months later.

This approach inevitably provokes questions about how many items should be employed, and what their scope should be. There are no definitive answers to these questions, since they depend on the area of measurement and the objective of making it. In the Howe et al. (2007) research, for example, the objective was to test the impact of a broad-based intervention in primary science group work on conceptual understanding of forces and evaporation, and grasp of the procedures required to systematically investigate each. The pre- and postintervention measures therefore comprised items relating to both conceptual and procedural understanding in the two areas. The forces and evaporation measures were of different lengths (29 and 16 items respectively), since there is a greater range of phenomena relating to forces than to evaporation. Where there is a more clearly defined taxonomy of mental operations to be acquired, as in mathematics (see, e.g., Dowker & Sigley, 2010), this may provide an alternative basis for determining the focus and number of items required, though there may then be issues regarding item difficulty (e.g., single- versus multiple-digit addition).

There are also pragmatic concerns regarding administration to be considered. Class-based administration in questionnaire format offers obvious efficiencies, but may have limitations in terms of participants' engagement and potential collusion over responses. Employing written responses may also entail use of multiple-choice items in order to obviate the demands involved in composing free-text answers, thereby reducing detail. One-to-one administration by a trained researcher is likely to produce more reliable data, and may make it possible to use fewer items because of the richer nature of verbal responses. It also facilitates measurement of nonverbal responses (see, e.g., Pine, Lufkin, & Messer, 2004, on the use of gesture as a measure of implicit understanding of balance). It carries a much greater overhead in terms of time, though, and this is often the overriding concern. Whichever method is used, there are also issues about how long respondents' attention is likely to be sustained. Ideally, then, any measure should be the focus of detailed pilot work prior to being actually deployed, in order to check its usability, unless it is based on well-established precedents.

Although the psychometric approach to measurement of competence has become dominant, purely descriptive nonquantitative methods have substantial precedent in Piaget's "critical method". In this approach, children were presented with a specific problem or observation and then subjected to individualized questioning regarding their thoughts about the target phenomenon (see, e.g., Piaget, 1929, on children's understanding of dynamic tension in the context of twisted string). Piaget employed this method almost exclusively throughout his life's work, triangulating detail from different individual interviews to produce extremely detailed – and still hugely influential – accounts of the development of children's knowledge in a wide range of areas. This method suffers from two connected limitations, however: the constraints on comparison resulting from the use of different questions with different children; and the fact that any coordinated picture is only apparent at the level of the sample, not the individual learner. Since variation at the individual level, both between learners and within them over time, provides a crucial means of tracking the influence of the factors shaping learning, it is hard to escape the need for comparable data at this level.

A potentially more useful extension to the psychometric approach, which does address individual variation, is *dynamic assessment*. This has its basis in Vygotsky's (1978) notion of the zone of proximal development – defined as the difference between what learners can do unaided, and what they can do when assisted by a more expert other – and his observation that individual children could appear to be at the same level of competence with respect to the former, and yet perform differently when assisted. Vygotsky concluded that assessment that ignored the developmental capacity of the child – the ability to learn and to change – missed a fundamental dimension of capability, "for 'it is only in movement that a body shows what it is'" (Vygotsky, 1978, p. 65). Dynamic assessment is founded on this principle, and characterized by a phased approach to measurement, in which behavior is recorded during preteaching, teaching and often post-teaching stages, all within single sessions (see, e.g., Tzuriel & Shamir, 2010). This approach does not preclude the use of quantitative indices or systematic item design, but utilizes these as a point of departure to capture data on learning itself. It is also more resource intensive as a result.

While the use of bespoke measures of competence is prevalent, educational psychology does make use of standardized tests, and in many instances bespoke measures gradually evolve into a more standardized form (e.g., the Working Memory Test Battery for Children of Pickering & Gathercole, 2001). However, standardized measures do present two particular difficulties. First, developing them is a labor-intensive activity. They require much greater attention to be paid to item design and item selection, since the final measure has to be robust enough to stand up to repeated use over an extended period of time under a variety of circumstances. Variability in the performance of individual items must therefore be reduced to a minimum. These requirements typically entail a number of cycles of design, testing and weeding out of items until a robust and coherent set has been derived. Once this point has been reached, it is still necessary to collect data from a large and representative standardization sample, in order to obtain norms for performance against which future participants can be judged.

The second problem is that this process inevitably results in a general measure that is poorly tailored to the specific requirements of any individual piece of research. It is therefore extremely unusual for standardized measures to be used as outcome measures, or as the sole predictors of learning. They are almost exclusively employed instead as a source of (a) baseline measures to establish the comparability of different groupings within and across samples, (b) covariates, which allow variance attributable to more basic individual differences to be controlled for while specific effects are examined, or (c) mediating or moderating variables, which help explain the observed relationship between more specific measures. This type of usage means that the standardized measures chosen tend to be those focused on fundamental parameters such as verbal and nonverbal intelligence, executive function and working memory or language development. It is important to note that, where measures of this kind are used as covariates or potential mediating variables, it is more likely to be the *raw* test scores rather than the standardized ones that are of interest, since the concern will typically be with individual variation relative to others within the same sample, rather than others in the population of the same age.

This use of standardized measures highlights a further point, that contemporary educational psychology makes widespread use of combinations of measures. In part, this simply reflects the objective of investigating the relationship between learning outcomes and factors that predict or constrain these. However, over the past 20 years there has also been increasing recognition of the value of employing multiple measures as a means of cross-validation within studies – observational and test measures may be used to check on relationships between performance and competence indices, for example – and as a basis for cross-referencing data between studies, in order to develop wider theoretical coherence and models of learning with more far-reaching power. Educational neuroscience itself can be seen as a manifestation of this same drive towards coherence and theoretical integration.

## Report measures

Given the fragmented nature of much initial explicit knowledge, report measures of learning, especially self-report indices, present an epistemological contradiction: to be capable of reporting accurately on their own learning requires a level of understanding and metacognitive awareness that would be likely to place an individual at near-ceiling levels of achievement. Unsurprisingly, therefore, report measures are typically used to assess dimensions that impact on learning, rather than learning itself, and in particular to generate data on mediating or moderating variables in similar fashion to standardized tests.

In some instances, self-report measures are used as a direct adjunct to behavioral indices. One common example is the use of confidence measures in competence tests, where learners are asked not just to provide answers to questions but to rate how sure they are that their response is correct, or how easy or difficult they found the question (see, e.g., Tolmie et al., 2006). Data of this kind may provide a more refined measure of knowledge state or a general index of perceived competence. More usually, however, self-report measures are collected separately from behavioral data, using written questionnaires or, less commonly, interviews.

Questionnaire measures have been applied within a number of substantive areas of research within educational psychology, but the most prevalent usage is within work concerning affective influences on educational engagement and outcome. Some research of this kind has focused on direct attitudes to school and to specific areas of the curriculum (e.g., Pell & Jarvis, 2001; Summers & Svinicki, 2007). However, much more extensive work has been undertaken on models of motivational effects on study behavior and attainment, such as self-determination theory (Ryan & Deci, 2000), achievement goal theory (Elliot & Thrash, 2001), academic self-efficacy (Schunk & Pajares, 2002) and academic self-concept (Marsh & O'Mara, 2008). Since the underlying constructs in these models are conceived of as having traitlike characteristics, the constraints of local applicability have typically not been regarded as operating in the same way as they have for measures of competence. In many instances, therefore, the measures employed have acquired the status of standardized instruments without having been through the formal process of standardization. Personality measures have been employed in similar fashion, as have measures of emotional intelligence (see, e.g., Mavroveli, Petrides, Sangareau, & Furnham, 2009).

Third-person report measures are also commonly used in educational psychology research. These usually take the form of parental or teacher reports on individual children, using questionnaires focused on key aspects of behavior. Examples include the Strengths and Difficulties Questionnaire (Goodman, 1997), which is designed to assess the areas in which children appear to be doing well and those where they show problems, and the Academic Self-Regulatory Behavior Questionnaire (Stright, Neitzel, Sears, & Hoke-Sinex, 2001), which assesses how children cope with the challenges posed by academic work (e.g., asking the teacher for help, participating in group discussions, checking for errors).

Interview methods lend themselves to collection of in-depth responses that are not constrained in the same way as those sought by questionnaire items, but which by the same token are not readily amenable to quantification. This is not to say that interview methods are lacking in structure. The general preference is for structured or semistructured interviews, where a fixed series of questions (the interview schedule) is determined in advance and utilized with each interviewee, albeit with a greater degree of individual followup in the case of semistructured approaches. Nevertheless, the greater resource intensiveness tends to restrict the sample size with which interviews can be used, and the flexibility of response permitted makes it easier and more meaningful to apply some form of inductive content or thematic analysis to respondents' answers (see, e.g., Braun & Clarke, 2006). Since this approach is by definition aimed at identifying recurrent regularities *across* individuals, as with Piaget's critical method it does not lend itself well to mapping individual variation. For this reason, the most common usage of interviews in educational psychology is as a supplement to quantitative measures, or as an initial phase of data collection aimed at producing more grounded questionnaires (see, e.g., Lindsay, 2007; Pickering & Howard-Jones, 2007).

## Demographic and environmental measures

Demographic variables such as age and gender have historically been a fundamental focus of interest within educational psychology, and studies that do not collect data on these are an extreme rarity. However, contemporary use of such data is predominantly restricted to ensuring balanced study designs, or as a form of control variable; there are few theories that see age or gender as more than proxies for other forms of neurocognitive or sociocultural difference that are of more substantive relevance to an understanding of process. The same is true of SES or family income variables, and data on these are commonly not even collected: since samples are usually drawn from schools with known catchment areas, the socioeconomic composition can generally be determined from this information, at least in approximate terms. Where environmental influences are the focus of research, as in work on predictors of resilience to adverse life events (see, e.g., Malmberg & Flouri, 2011), the measures used are generally more specific in character. These typically concentrate on particular aspects of parental behavior and home circumstances that, whilst linked to SES and employment, are more likely to have a direct impact on children's learning and development, such as parental mood, quality of parent–child relationships, and time spent in educationally relevant activity such as reading.

The same is true of school environment variables, where interest is likely to focus primarily on measures of school atmosphere, classroom interaction, and peer relationships. Kutnick, Ota, and Berdondini (2008), for instance, made use of classroom mapping measures that recorded the activity of teachers and children at periodic intervals in order to examine the relationship between group work, teacher involvement, and learning outcomes. Pianta (2003) similarly provides a coding scheme for examining the quality of teacher–child interaction and pedagogical approach. More distal variables are used – for instance, the proportion of children within a school or a class receiving free school meals is widely used in UK research as an index of relative deprivation (see, e.g., Howe et al., 2007) – but again as control measures rather than as a predictor.

## Choosing a Study Design

The measurement techniques described in the previous section characterize much of the approach taken to research within educational psychology, but the precise way in which they provide an understanding of process is determined by how they are deployed within different types of study design, and in particular how these are used to identify causal relationships. This section examines quasi-experimental, experimental, and nonexperimental designs, focusing on the rationale for each and some of the issues that they present. It begins, however, with a brief consideration of challenges presented by constructing samples within educational psychology research.

### Sampling issues

Educational psychology is usually concerned with capturing data on learning processes in general, across a range of individuals, and therefore needs to construct representative samples that permit such conclusions to be drawn. Unfortunately, the complexity and contextual sensitivity of educational processes make it hard to claim that convenience sampling is likely to result in representative outcomes, while practical constraints on gaining access to learners – this will almost always have to be arranged through schools or colleges – also make it nearly impossible to adopt any robust form of random sampling.

One solution is to use randomized hierarchical sampling. In this approach, quotas are set for particular types of school or school context and then random instances of these (as far as possible) are sampled to fill the quota. Data are then collected on individual students within the selected targets, without a need to be concerned with representativeness at this level, since it has already been dealt with. The grouping of students within classes or schools creates difficulties with regard to cross-school comparison, since attending the same school produces a degree of between-individual similarity beyond that which would be expected with genuinely random sampling. These problems are far from fatal, though, since they can be dealt with via statistical procedures such as multilevel modeling, which explicitly checks how far different sampling units such as schools exhibit the same pattern of effects (see Tolmie et al., 2010, 2011).

However, hierarchical sampling is only feasible in well-resourced large-scale studies, and most educational psychology research is not of this nature. Smaller-scale work typically depends instead on local sampling, conducted on the basis of the willingness of schools, teachers, and parents to let their children participate. This does not mean that certain principles cannot be applied. For instance, schools with unusual characteristics can be avoided unless there is some specific reason for being interested in these. Similarly, effort can be taken to sample freely from within the participating school, at least among students of a target age range, rather than allowing the sample to be skewed by only having, for example, the most-able or the best-behaved students involved.

Nevertheless, these principles are inherently weak, and only avoid the most obvious aspects of sampling bias. The representativeness of such samples can only be guessed at, certainly at the point of data collection. The task of establishing this is primarily left instead to the stage of data analysis, for instance via comparison with data from other samples – if these have similar characteristics, this provides evidence that each is generally representative – or by checking whether a sample exhibits characteristics that we would expect it to have if it is representative. It is partly for this reason that standardized measures and demographic variables have found a place in school-based research.

## Quasi-experimental designs

Quasi-experimental designs compare the effects on outcomes such as achievement of the participants' level on variables that are not under the researcher's control, such as age or gender. The inability of the researcher to assign cases to specific levels on these variables distinguishes this type of design from true experiments, but quasi-experimental designs are nevertheless akin to experimental research in structure. For instance, they assume an independent–dependent variable relationship, and they tend to be employed to make comparisons under relatively controlled conditions.

The main benefit of quasi-experimental designs is the opportunity they present to capitalize on some naturally occurring variation where actual assignment is either impossible or unethical. Variables of this type include age and gender, but also ethnicity, SES and presence or absence of disease, illness, or deficit. These are sometimes examined in combination, either with each other, or with some other independent variable where genuine assignment is possible (e.g., different task conditions). The weakness of such designs is that any effect associated with a quasi-independent variable may simply reflect the operation of some other variable with which it is correlated. This is particularly true of cross-sectional research comparing the performance of different age groups; even if age differences are found, it is unlikely that these will be attributable directly to age as such. For this reason, cross-sectional designs are now usually employed primarily as a means of ensuring balanced sampling, and direct measures are taken of the proximal source of variation that is hypothesized to be at work (see, e.g., Alloway, Gathercole, & Pickering, 2006, on age-related shifts in working memory and the impact of these on other aspects of performance).

Even if the effects uncovered by quasi-experimental designs need to be interpreted with caution, they may have considerable value in revealing underlying causes of variation that merit further investigation. This is most often the case with case–control designs, in which suitable cases (e.g., those with some specified condition) are identified, and their status on hypothetically important dependent variables is measured. The same variables are also measured in a control sample who are similar to the cases in their general characteristics, but not in terms of their defining features. If the case and control samples differ on the variables of interest, it can be concluded that there is an association between these variables and individuals' case status (see, e.g., Hudson & Farran, 2011, on differences in drawing strategies between individuals with Williams Syndrome and typically developing children).

This approach can be strengthened by finding an actual match for each case, i.e., an individual who shares their characteristics in terms of other influential variables, such as age, gender, social background, and so on. The net result is the creation of matched samples that exhibit identical variation in these respects, which helps rule out the possibility of confounds with case status. Matched-sample designs are commonly used in the context of research on learning difficulties. For instance, children with autism usually have a lower mental age relative to typically developing children. If we wish to identify characteristics that are *specific* to children with autism rather than simply those that are usual amongst children of a given mental age, then the comparison should be with samples of children who are matched in this respect (see, e.g., Farran & Brosnan, 2011). Since children in this sample will usually be substantially younger than the autistic sample, a double-matching procedure is often employed, in which comparison samples of children matched for chronological age and for verbal mental age are both used. By examining performance across these groupings, it becomes possible to determine which characteristics reflect chronological age, which reflect mental age, and which are specific to autism.

## Experimental designs

Experimental designs are specifically intended to identify cause-and-effect relationships in unequivocal fashion, through the use of random assignment of participants to experimental conditions (i.e., levels of the independent variable hypothesized to have a causal influence on the dependent variable). However, isolating causal influences depends on more than random assignment: it is also necessary to ensure that the independent variable is not confounded with other variables that systematically covary with it. Confounding variables are a major hazard for experimental research in educational psychology, since tight control of conditions of the kind common in laboratory research is often impossible. It is important therefore to take specific precautions to guard against their intrusion.

For this reason, experimental research typically focuses on simple competence measures or brief observations, collected in out-of-class settings where some degree of standardization is possible. Where more than one element of data is being collected (for instance, performance on several tasks), it is standard practice to counterbalance these (e.g., with two tasks, half of the participants engage with these in the order A then B, and the other half B then A), or else, with larger numbers of points of data collection, to randomly vary the sequence. This ensures that task order can exert no systematic effect on outcome. There are various other known sources of confounding variables that particularly affect research employing measurement at multiple time points, such as intervention trials, and the possible impact of these should be considered as a matter of course when implementing designs of this kind. These include

- extraneous but related events coinciding with the measurement period (e.g., change in some aspect of school practice)
- the impact of passage of time, which in intervention studies necessitates use of a control condition to assess the change that would have occurred anyway over the period of the intervention
- differential loss of participants across conditions, distorting accurate measurement
- practice effects created by repeated testing using identical instruments, which may be safeguarded against by devising equivalent versions of the measures involved.

There is no strong preference for one type of design over another in educational psychology research, although there are practical constraints on employing some of them, and there is a greater tendency to employ intervention designs than in other branches of psychology, because these present a means of investigating learning processes by directly manipulating them. The characteristics of each of the main types of design are briefly described below.

*Randomized designs* are the most basic form of experimental design, in which a number of experimental conditions are defined by different levels on a single independent variable, and participants are randomly assigned to one or other of these. There are not usually more than four or so conditions, in part because of the practicalities involved in setting these up, but also because of the constraints imposed by analysis of variance, a technique that is applicable to many studies with this kind of design (Tolmie et al., 2011). *Factorial designs* are a simple extension to the basic principle of the randomized design, in which two or more independent variables are manipulated at the same time, by combining or crossing the levels of each. This makes it possible to look not just at the main effects of each independent variable, but also at any interaction effects, and these may often be especially informative (see, e.g., Kerger, Martin, & Brunner, 2011, on the impact of combining science topics with particular types of contextual example for heightening girls' interest in science). Given the exponential increase in the number of interaction effects produced by the inclusion of each additional independent variable, however, three-way designs are generally considered to be the limit of what is desirable both in terms of practicality and interpretation.

*Repeated-measures designs* offer protection against the fact that occasionally extraneous group differences (for instance, between children in different classes) can produce confounds, by employing the same participants in each condition. Since individuals act as their own controls, in principle such designs also provide greater power to detect effects. The difficulty is that repeated-measures designs potentially create extraneous variation of their own, due to the effects of testing participants on more than one occasion – performance may improve because of practice effects, for instance, or deteriorate because of boredom. In general, then, such designs tend to be reserved for circumstances where there is some logical constraint on use of randomized or factorial designs. This is most obviously the case in intervention studies employing pretest and post-test measures to assess the effects of some form of treatment, which is applied in between. Research of this kind usually makes use of a *mixed design* with both between- and within-subjects variables, in fact, since a control condition that receives the testing but not the intervention is normally employed (see, e.g., Howe et al., 2007).

*Microgenetic designs* offer a more specialized form of repeated-measures design, which is becoming increasingly common in educational research. These take advantage of the main weakness of repeated-measures design, the fact that repeated performance of a task leads to changes in that performance, in order to investigate in direct fashion the way in which these changes occur (cf. dynamic assessment). The key characteristic of microgenetic designs is the use of many more repeated observations than would be employed in an ordinary repeated-measures design (perhaps as many as 10 or 12 points of testing may be used), with these being densely distributed over time (every two to three days is not uncommon). These combined features make it possible to examine the trajectory of change in performance under otherwise controlled conditions.

One common extension of this approach is to employ it in conjunction with different forms of intervention. Repeated testing *without* these interventions is then used as a form of control condition. This makes it possible to consider how learning occurs as a result of experience alone, and as a product of coupling that experience with some form of external support or assistance (see, e.g., Philips & Tolmie, 2007, on the effects of initial parental tutoring on changes in children's performance over time on a balance-scale task). A further characteristic feature of these designs is the use of relatively small samples, and data analysis at the level of the individual rather than the group, in order to map both the general effects of different conditions, and also the degree and nature of individual variation in reaction to these. The objective is to provide in-depth data on processes of learning over time, without surrendering the advantages of quantitative, experimental methodologies. The difficulty this approach presents is then triangulating these data with more static measures taken from larger samples, especially since they frequently appear to indicate that there is no such thing as a *general* pattern of learning (see, e.g., Siegler, 1995).

*Randomized control trials* (RCTs) are specialized forms of intervention research employing randomized designs, which are directed at the evaluation of specific programs of activity. In an RCT, no pretest is used to establish a baseline, since the sample is drawn from a population that is known to be homogenous in the sense of being capable of benefiting from the intervention being tested. Once the sample has been identified, participants are randomly allocated to a treatment condition – either alternative forms of intervention, or treatment versus control conditions. The treatment or intervention is then applied, and the outcome monitored, usually for a period of time following the trial, rather than via a one-off post-test, in order to establish whether there are sustained differences between conditions. These data are used to determine whether the treatment has worked, and therefore might be more widely applied. RCTs are usually associated with other safeguards that ensure that extraneous influences cannot intrude. For instance, they typically employ much tighter processes of random assignment to conditions, and care is usually taken to make sure that those making assignments are blind to case characteristics, since knowledge of these might lead to biased allocations. Similarly, those responsible for assessing outcomes are usually kept blind as to the treatment condition to which individual cases were assigned, and in double-blind procedures, where the nature of the intervention permits it, participants are also blind to the treatment condition they are in.

Although RCTs are regarded as the gold standard procedure in medical or health-related research for establishing the best forms of treatment or preventative intervention, they are extremely difficult to implement in education-related research. The blinding procedures require a large enough team to be able to separate out responsibilities, something that is unusual in educational psychology. More crucially, it is rarely possible to implement random assignment at the individual level. This has sometimes been managed in research on the educational impact of nutritional supplements (see, e.g., Richardson & Montgomery, 2005), but, where the intervention involves classroom delivery, assignment to conditions almost always has to be managed at class or even school level.

The closest that most educational research comes to the RCT format is the use of *randomized cluster trials*, which employ a type of hierarchical sampling where schools within a district are randomly assigned to intervention or control conditions (see, e.g., Tymms et al., 2011, on a trial assessing the impact of peer-tutoring schemes). Even these are difficult to conduct to any high standard, since the representativeness of the sample remains restricted; fidelity of implementation of the intervention is threatened where delivery rests on a number of different individuals; blinding procedures are largely impossible; and schools are understandably reluctant to be assigned to the control condition (though this can be managed to some extent by guaranteeing future availability of the intervention if the outcome is positive).

## Nonexperimental designs

The importance attached to detailed measurement, concerns with identifying naturally occurring influences on learning, the relatively slow pace of change, and the difficulties of implementing experimental methods noted above all mean that nonexperimental designs remain a crucial aspect of research within educational psychology. Much sophisticated conceptual work has gone into the development of these designs over the past 20 years, in order to ensure that, despite the lack of direct manipulation of independent variables and random assignment of participants to experimental conditions, they are still capable of playing an important and reliable role in identifying causal processes.

Underpinning this is the distinction between independent and dependent variables, which only depends in part upon the methods used to collect data; in addition, there are certain criteria that variables must meet in order to be classified in this way, which relate to the *logical possibility* of one variable being an influence on another. First and foremost, as a basic principle, causes or influences must *precede* whatever it is they are influencing, and it has to be plausible to at least hypothesize that this is actually the case for *any* variable labeled as "independent".

*Temporal ordering* (i.e., being able to place the operation of variables in a time sequence) is therefore a minimum requirement for potential causality to be inferred. If information on a set of variables is collected at one point in time, assignment of temporal ordering is weakened. Even if there are grounds to hold that one variable was operating at an earlier point in time than another (e.g., the amount of homework school students say they do might be thought to precede their examination grades), if the measurements were taken at the same point in time it is impossible to be sure this is the case. The relationships could be reversed (e.g., students who get better grades are motivated to do more homework). Ultimately then, in order to uncover causal relationships, collection of data on hypothetical independent variables at an earlier time point to that on outcome or dependent variables (i.e., some form of *prospective design*) provides a better basis for classification. However, even with temporal ordering, it remains possible that any identified effect is actually spurious, and attributable to the operation of some further variable or set of variables on both the independent and the dependent.

As a result of these issues, contemporary nonexperimental research has developed a number of key features. First, it typically collects data on a *range* of variables of theoretical importance, so that more complex relationships between variables can be assessed, such as joint dependence on a common cause (the source of spurious associations), *mediation*, where the influence of one variable on another occurs via a third variable (cf. the earlier discussion of the operation of SES), and *moderation*, where the impact of some variable is altered by the operation of another (cf. interaction effects in factorial experiments).

Second, there is growing preference for designs where data collection is time lagged in some fashion. *Longitudinal designs* – studies repeatedly measuring the same characteristics in a single sample at selected time intervals over an extended period (typically a year or more) – are perhaps the most common approach, and provide a means of mapping the profile of individual change and determining how far later characteristics are related to earlier ones (see, e.g., Passolunghi & Lanfranchi, 2012, on the preschool precursors of first-grade mathematics achievement). Longitudinal designs provide unique strengths, but also create particular difficulties. Their principal strength lies in the fact that changes in response pattern over the period of the research can be attributed to real shifts in the participants, since these remain constant. Moreover, if there are three or more points of data collection, it becomes possible to model the trajectory of change on the variables being measured, and determine if it is linear (an even increase or decrease), exponential (an increasingly steep increase or decrease as time goes on), asymptotic (an initially steep increase or decrease that gradually levels off), or displays an intermittent or a U-shaped curve (i.e., increases come in spurts, followed by periods of little or no change, or an increase is followed by a decrease or vice versa). Detail of this type provides crucial evidence to inform theories of the processes involved in generating change (see Siegler, 1996).

However, repeated exposure to the same instruments is likely to lead to practice effects of some kind. As a result, data collection tends to take place at relatively long intervals, but extending the period of data collection exacerbates the problem of losing participants from the initial sample: the longer the time period, the greater the attrition. Moreover, since the primary cause of attrition is loss of contact due to participants moving home or changing school, it differentially affects those whose home circumstances are less stable (characteristically those from lower socioeconomic backgrounds). The net result is that attrition tends to lead to the sample gradually becoming less representative, compounding the fact that it may not have been ideally representative in the first place. Getting families to commit to involvement in a long-term piece of research is not easy, and those who agree are likely to be more persuaded of the value of such work – commonly those from more educated backgrounds.

Problems of attrition and drift in representativeness are likely to be most acute in single-sample longitudinal designs, where one cohort is recruited at the start and maintained as far as possible till the completion of the research. These problems can be addressed to some extent via the use of *longitudinal cohort sequential designs*. In this approach, a number of cohorts are recruited, rather than just one, with these being brought into the research in staggered fashion, and perhaps being followed for different periods of time. For instance, in a study running over a four-year interval, successive cohorts of 5 year olds might be introduced in each year, the first being followed for four years, the second for three years, and so on. This offers advantages over a single-sample longitudinal design because different cohorts can be compared to check on the stability of any emerging patterns. Moreover, since attrition is unlikely to be identical across the different cohorts, this serves to correct for drift in representativeness.

A simpler and less expensive approach, which retains some of the power of longitudinal research, is use of a *prospective survey design*. This employs a two-stage approach, in which data are collected via an initial survey, with a followup restricted to a further survey focused on a small number of variables, with the objective of establishing an element of temporal ordering. One common usage of this type of design is in motivational or attitudinal research, where affective data are collected at one point in time and behavioral or achievement data at a second (see, e.g., Moller, Streblow, & Pohlmann, 2006). This design also suffers from potential problems of attrition and selfselection bias, but if the interval between the two time points for data collection is relatively short and the response load is not large then these should not be as great as for true longitudinal designs.

The third key feature of nonexperimental psychology of education research is its use of statistical modeling, aimed at testing the fit to observed data of hypothesized relationships between variables. The most basic approach involves use of multiple regression to model influences on single continuous dependent variables or logistic regression for dichotomous dependents, but the techniques have become increasingly powerful. Hierarchical methods using sequential entry of predictor variables make it possible to examine mediation and moderation effects, for example (see Baron & Kenny, 1986; Tolmie et al., 2011), by examining how independent–dependent variable relationships change as other variables are included in the model being tested. Multilevel modeling (MLM) techniques extend these approaches to situations where data are nested within sampling units such as classes or schools, and models assuming random sampling cannot be applied (see Tolmie et al., 2011). MLM can also be applied to repeated observations on the same individual, taking him or her as the sampling unit, thus permitting more sensitive growth analyses to be conducted.

These more basic approaches can be extended to simultaneous analyses of the pattern of relationships between a network of variables, in order to test the fit of overall models. Path analysis builds on multiple regression to test models of relationships between observed variables with suitable temporal ordering (see Tolmie et al., 2011), whilst structural equation modeling (SEM) takes this further by making it possible to include latent variables (i.e., underlying factors explaining joint variance between correlated indices) within the same kind of framework (see, e.g., Kaplan, 2000, for an overview of SEM; and see Chen, Hwang, Yeh, & Lin, 2011, for an example of its application). Even problems such as attrition can be dealt with to some extent via the use of multiple imputation techniques, which allow values of missing data to be inferred on the basis of extrapolation from existing data points. If there is a downside to these approaches, it is that they have driven sample sizes upward. MLM and SEM require samples of 200 as a minimum in order to generate reliable estimates of model parameters, and even multiple regression demands similar sample sizes if there are more than a few predictors, since there is a recognized minimum of 15 for the ratio of cases per predictor.

## Conclusion

By way of conclusion to this survey of methods in educational psychology research, I would add a final observation. In reviewing current literature for this chapter, I was struck continually by the fact that, although separate delineation of the measurement methods and study designs we employ is a necessary taxonomic device, it fails to capture the complexity of research currently being conducted in this field. Of the papers published in my own journal, the *British Journal of Educational Psychology*, over the past year, for instance, I could identify none that fell neatly into a single category. This serves to underline the point made earlier regarding the use of combinations of measures, while extending it to methodological approaches more generally. With experimental and nonexperimental techniques often being included within single studies in order to provide points of connection to other work and to do justice to the complexity of the processes that are being examined, there are good grounds for holding that research in the psychology of education is inherently ready to embrace the further complexity entailed by adding in connections to neural data and neuroscience methodologies.

# References

Alloway, T. P., Gathercole, S. E., & Pickering, S. J. (2006). Verbal and visuo-spatial short-term and working memory in children: Are they separable? *Child Development, 77*, 1698–1716.

Baron, R. M., & Kenny, D. A. (1986). The moderator–mediator variable distinction in social psychological research – conceptual, strategic, and statistical considerations. *Journal of Personality and Social Psychology, 51*, 1173–1182.

Blatchford, P., Baines, E., Rubie-Davies, C., Bassett, P., & Chowne, A. (2006). The effect of a new approach to group-work on pupil–pupil and teacher–pupil interaction. *Journal of Educational Psychology, 98*, 750–765.

Braun, V., & Clarke, V. (2006). Using thematic analysis in psychology. *Qualitative Research in Psychology, 3*, 77–101.

Chen, S.-K., Hwang, F.-M., Yeh, Y.-C., & Lin, S. S. J. (2011). Cognitive ability, academic achievement and academic self-concept: Extending the internal/external frame of reference model. *British Journal of Educational Psychology, 82*, 308–326.

Christie, D., Tolmie, A., Thurston, A., Howe, C., & Topping, K. (2009). Supporting group work in Scottish primary classrooms: Improving the quality of collaborative dialogue. *Cambridge Journal of Education, 39*, 141–156.

Croll, P. (1986). *Systematic classroom observation*. Basingstoke, UK: Falmer.

Dowker, A., & Sigley, G. (2010). Targeted interventions for children with arithmetical difficulties. In R. Cowan, M. Saxton, & A. Tolmie (Eds.), Understanding number development and difficulty. *British Journal of Educational Psychology Monograph Series II: Psychological Aspects of Education – Current Trends: Number 7.*

Elliot, A. J., & Thrash, T. M. (2001). Achievement goals and the hierarchical model of achievement motivation. *Educational Psychology Review, 13*, 139–156.

Farran, E. K., & Brosnan, M. (2011). Perceptual grouping abilities in individuals with Autism Spectrum Disorder: The importance of grouping type and of development. *Autism Research, 4*, 283–292.

Goodman, R. (1997). The Strengths and Difficulties Questionnaire: A research note. *Journal of Child Psychology and Psychiatry, 38*, 581–586.

Howe, C. J., Rodgers, C., & Tolmie, A. (1990). Physics in the primary school: Peer inter-action and the understanding of floating and sinking. *European Journal of Psychology of Education, 4,* 459–475.

Howe, C., Tolmie, A., Thurston, A., Topping, K., Christie, D., Livingston, K., Jessiman, E., & Donaldson, C. (2007). Group work in elementary science: Towards organ-isational principles for supporting pupil learning. *Learning and Instruction, 17,* 549–563.

Hudson, K., & Farran, E. K. (2011) Drawing the line: Graphic strategies for simple and complex shapes in Williams Syndrome and typical development. *British Journal of Developmental Psychology, 29,* 687–706.

Huss, M., Verney J. P., Fosker, T., Mead, N., & Goswami, U. (2011). Music, rhythm, rise time perception and developmental dyslexia: Perception of musical meter predicts reading and phonology. *Cortex, 47,* 674–689.

Kaplan, D. (2000). *Structural equation modelling.* London: Sage.

Karmiloff-Smith, A. (1992). *Beyond modularity: A developmental perspective on cognitive science.* Cambridge, MA: MIT Press.

Kerger, S., Martin, R., & Brunner, M. (2011). How can we enhance girls' interest in scientific topics? *British Journal of Educational Psychology, 81,* 606–628.

Kutnick, P., Ota, C., & Berdondini, L. (2008). Improving the effects of classroom group-work with young children; Attainment, attitudes and behaviour. *Learning and Instruction, 18,* 83–95.

Lindsay, G. (2007). Educational psychology and the effectiveness of inclusive education/ mainstreaming. *British Journal of Educational Psychology, 77,* 1–24.

Malmberg, L. E., & Flouri, E. (2011). The comparison and interdependence of maternal and paternal influences on young children's behavior and resilience. *Journal of Clinical Child and Adolescent Psychology, 40,* 434–444.

Marsh, H. W., & O'Mara, A. (2008). Reciprocal effects between academic self-concept, self-esteem, achievement, and attainment over seven adolescent years: Unidimensional and multidimensional perspectives of self-concept. *Personality and Social Psychology Bulletin, 34,* 542–552.

Mavroveli, S., Petrides, K. V., Sangareau, Y., & Furnham, A. (2009). Relating trait emo-tional intelligence to objective socioemotional outcomes in childhood. *British Journal of Educational Psychology, 79,* 259–272.

Meard, J., Bertone, S., & Flavier, E. (2008). How second-grade students internalize rules during teacher–student transactions: A case study. *British Journal of Educational Psychology, 78,* 395–410.

Moller, J., Streblow, L., & Pohlmann, B. (2006). The belief in a negative interdependence of maths and verbal abilities as determinant of academic self-concepts. *British Journal of Educational Psychology, 76,* 57–70.

Nunes, T., Schliemann, A. D., & Carraher, D. W. (1993). *Street mathematics and school mathematics.* Cambridge: Cambridge University Press.

Passolunghi, M. C., & Lanfranchi, S. (2012). Domain-specific and domain-general pre-cursors of mathematical achievement: A longitudinal study from kindergarten to first grade. *British Journal of Educational Psychology, 82,* 42–63.

Pell, T., & Jarvis, T. (2001). Developing attitude to science scales for use with children of ages from five to eleven years. *International Journal of Science Education, 23,* 847–862.

Philips, S., & Tolmie, A. (2007). Children's performance on and understanding of the Balance Scale problem: The effects of parental support. *Infant and Child Development, 16,* 95–117.

Piaget, J. (1929). *The child's conception of the world.* London: Routledge & Kegan Paul.

Pianta, R. C. (2003). *A day in third grade: Classroom quality, teacher and student behaviours.* Charlottesville, VA: NICH Human Development Early Child Care Network, University of Virginia.

Pickering, S. J., & Gathercole, S. E. (2001). *Working memory test battery for children.* London: Psychological Corporation.

Pickering, S. J., & Howard-Jones, P. (2007). Educators' views on the role of neuroscience in education: Findings from a study of UK and international perspectives. *Mind, Brain, and Education, 1,* 109–113.

Pine, K. J., Lufkin, N., & Messer, D. (2004). More gestures than answers: Children learning about balance. *Developmental Psychology, 40,* 159–1067.

Pino-Pasternak, D., Whitebread, D., & Tolmie, A. (2010). A multi-dimensional analysis of parent–child interactions during academic tasks and their relationships with children's self-regulated learning. *Cognition and Instruction, 28,* 219–272.

Richardson, A. J., & Montgomery, P. (2005). The Oxford–Durham study: A randomized controlled study of the effects of supplementation with fatty acids in children with developmental coordination disorder. *Pediatrics, 11,* 1360–1366.

Ryan, R. M., & Deci, E. L. (2000). Self-determination theory and the facilitation of intrinsic motivation, social development, and well-being. *American Psychologist, 55,* 65–78.

Schunk, D. H., & Pajares, F. (2002). The development of academic self-efficacy. In A. Wigfield and J. S. Eccles (Eds.), *Development of achievement motivation* (pp. 15–31). San Diego, CA: Academic Press.

Siegler, R. S. (1995). How does cognitive change occur: A microgenetic study of number conservation. *Cognitive Psychology, 25,* 225–273.

Siegler, R. S. (1996). *Emerging minds: The process of change in children's thinking.* New York: Oxford University Press.

Stright, A. D., Neitzel, C., Sears, K. G., & Hoke-Sinex, L. (2001). Instruction begins in the home: Relations between parental instruction and children's self-regulation in the classroom. *Journal of Educational Psychology, 93,* 456–466.

Summers, J. J., & Svinicki, M. D. (2007). Investigating classroom community in higher education. *Learning and Individual Differences, 17,* 55–67.

Tolmie, A., Muijs, D., & McAteer, E. (2011). *Quantitative methods in educational and social research using SPSS.* Buckingham, UK: Open University Press.

Tolmie, A., Thomson, J. A., O'Connor, R., Foot, H. C. Karagiannidou, E., Banks, M., O'Donnell, C., & Sarvary, P. (2006). *The role of skills, attitudes and perceived behavioural control in the pedestrian decision-making of adolescents aged 11–15 years* (Department for Transport Road Safety Research Report No. 68). London: DfT. Retrieved July 15, 2012, from http://webarchive.nationalarchives.gov.uk/20110509101621/http://www.dft.gov.uk/pgr/roadsafety/research/rsrr/theme1/pedestriandecisionmaking.pdf

Tolmie, A., Topping, K., Christie, D., Donaldson, C., Howe, C., Jessiman, E., Livingston, K., & Thurston, A. (2010). Social effects of collaborative learning in primary schools. *Learning and Instruction, 20,* 177–191.

Tymms, P., Merrell, C., Thurston, A., Andor, J., Topping, K., & Miller, D. (2011). Improving attainment across a whole district: School reform through peer tutoring in a randomized controlled trial. *School Effectiveness and School Improvement, 22,* 265–289.

Tzuriel, D., & Shamir, A. (2010). Mediation strategies and cognitive modifiability in young children as a function of peer mediation with young children program and training in analogies versus math tasks. *Journal of Cognitive Education and Psychology, 9,* 48–72.

Vygotsky, L. S. (1978). *Mind in society: The development of higher psychological processes.* Cambridge, MA: Harvard University Press.

## Further Reading

Breakwell, G. M., Hammond, S., & Fife-Schaw, C. (2006). *Research methods in psychology (3rd ed.).* London: Sage.

Cohen, L., Manion, L., & Morison, K. (2007). *Research methods in education.* Abingdon: Routledge.

Oppenheim, A.N. (1992). *Questionnaire design, interviewing and attitude measurement.* London: Pinter.

Robson, C. (2011). *Real world research: A resource for social cientists and practitioner researchers (3rd ed.).* Blackwell. Oxford.

Rust, J., & Golombok, S. (2008) *Modern psychometrics: The science of psychological assessment (3rd ed.).* Taylor & Francis, London.

# Chapter 6

# Language Development

## Victoria Knowland and Chris Donlan

Educational neuroscience aims to use knowledge of the developing brain to maximize learning outcomes through optimizing the educational environment. Language plays a special role in the realization of this aim, as learning language in turn allows learning across all academic disciplines. Developmental language and communication problems can therefore have a seriously detrimental impact on children's educational outcomes and consequent employability (The Bercow Report; Department of Education, 2008). We will argue here that educational environments have two key roles to play with regard to language learning: the first is to compensate for the effects of early linguistic environments with low quality or quantity input; the second is to help children overcome inherent difficulties in language learning to maximize access to academic and social worlds. The overall aim of this chapter is to show how variability in language systems arises and how enriching the environment can influence developmental trajectories of learning.

The substantial impact of environmental factors on language development has long been acknowledged, with children from backgrounds of lower socioeconomic status (SES) often failing to reach typical benchmarks (Law, McBean, & Rush, 2011; Locke, Ginsborg, & Peers, 2002). We review recent findings concerning the association between SES and language development, and the outcomes of intervention programmes targeting at-risk groups. We consider the ways in which neuroscientific studies exploring the brain-level correlates of the association between SES and language add to our understanding, and ask whether these findings may allow

*Educational Neuroscience*, First Edition. Edited by Denis Mareschal, Brian Butterworth and Andy Tolmie.
© 2014 John Wiley & Sons, Ltd. Published 2014 by John Wiley & Sons, Ltd.

us to refine interventions, for example by distinguishing between language deficits associated with the environmental deprivation and those that are traceable to genetic factors independent of SES.

Language development is also highly dependent on genetic influence, as in part evidenced by the numerous studies showing that genetic factors play an important role in the causation of specific language impairment (SLI) in children, independent of SES. There has been substantial and growing research interest in this area over the last 20 years (Bishop, 1997; Leonard, 1998; Paul & Norbury, 2012). The clinical definition of SLI is based on discrepancy between unimpaired nonverbal cognitive skills and significant impairment(s) in language abilities, which may affect syntax, vocabulary, and phonology. Although the underlying deficits in SLI are the subject of continuing debate (Bishop, 2009), early twin studies demonstrated a significant genetic contribution (Bishop, 2002; and see Chapter 4 of this volume, on genetics), and opened up a fast-moving and expanding area of cross-disciplinary research exploring the complex process of gene expression related to brain systems underlying atypical language development. We aim to show that the educational potential of this research is substantial with regard to enhancing our ability to identify individuals at risk for language difficulties, to identify underlying processing limitations, and to inform the design of specialized educational interventions. Importantly, understanding atypical development can also help us to understand more about the typical developmental process, highlighting aspects of learning that are important but not necessarily obvious in the wider population.

In evaluating evidence of the influence of genetic and environmental factors on language growth, it is important to maintain a developmental perspective. In this chapter we trace the ontogenetic process of language acquisition: from the time infants are first exposed to their native language or languages; through childhood as language develops and begins to impact on academic skills and literacy; and through adolescence as linguistic abilities are solidified but vocabulary continues to develop and extend. We consider the progressive maturation of the language system at the neural level, and the gradual building of language behavior over developmental time. From these data we consider how educational environments might be informed by evidence concerning the developmental process.

Pioneers in language education, such as Conn (1971) and Hutt (1986), have recorded the characteristics of the populations of children they worked with, and the special educational approaches they developed, based on a combination of experience and theoretical insight. These pioneering educational programmes, inspired by the severe and specific language deficits of children identified at the time, correspond in some ways to the neuropsychological advances that followed the discovery and detailed study of classic cases of brain injury of the nineteenth and twentieth centuries. In acknowledgement of the importance of these insights, we include in this chapter a single case study of an individual, TZ, who benefited from the highly specialized educational approaches developed by Hutt and her colleagues. Particularly valuable, we believe, are the reports of the educational principles and the specific materials and intervention strategies that operated so effectively.

## Language in Infancy and Early Childhood 0–5 years

By the time children enter a formal educational setting at age five or six, the majority have achieved levels of receptive and productive language not unlike those of their adult tutors, including a mastery of syntax and the ability to produce complex narrative. Indeed, language at this point is arguably the most developed cognitive skill. However, a substantial degree of variability is also seen at this stage, in terms of both what children can produce and what they can understand (see, e.g., Bates, Bretherton, & Snyder, 1988; Fenson, Dale, Reznick, Bates, & Pethick, 1994). We therefore begin here with a consideration of how individual differences and environmental factors over these early years result in the extent of variability seen by mid-childhood.

### The impact of intrinsic factors on language development

Several recent studies have considered which aspects of the language system in infancy best predict language outcomes in the preschool and school period. Prominent among them are those that consider how infants perceive and make sense of the speech stream, the first requirement of which is to develop categorical representations of phonemes, the smallest meaning-carrying unit of speech (see, e.g., Davenport & Hannahs, 2010, for an introduction). The phonemes that make up any given language are in fact categories of sounds: *phonemic categories*, as the exact acoustic properties of speech sounds vary slightly depending on factors such as speaker and word context. In a continuous acoustic space the same magnitude of difference between speech sounds could either not be encoded if these sounds fall within a category or, by contrast, define a critical linguistic contrast if they cross a category boundary. For example, the acoustic differences between the phonemes "p" and "b" in "pin", "spin" and "bin" are about equal, but in English two fall within the same category space, "p", which is linguistically distinct from the category "b". To be able to establish which contrasts are linguistically relevant and which are not draws on two fundamental properties of auditory processing: the first is sensitivity to the rapid auditory transitions that often define critical contrasts between phonemes (see Rosen, 1992);

the second is to be able to categorize inputs finely, something that is more generally considered to be a fundamental principle of cortical learning. The establishment of phonemic categories is a crucial building block in language learning, and as such is an excellent illustration of the interaction between environmental input and low-level brain mechanisms such as rapid processing or categorization, which here will be referred to as *intrinsic factors*, reflecting their likely genetic basis. This interaction between intrinsic factors and appropriate environmental input is a principle that occurs again and again in the field of educational neuroscience. In the case of early language acquisition we can consider a combination of behavioral and brain measures that together are informative about the nature of emerging language and the brain systems that support this language development over early childhood.

*Phonological development*   Patricia Kuhl has developed an extensive body of work considering the early establishment of phonological representations in the infant brain, and the extent to which these early representations underpin later language success (see Kuhl, 2010, for a review). Over the first year of life, infants move from being able to distinguish between any two phonemes on the basis of acoustic cues to only being able to distinguish between those phonemes that are relevant in their native language (Werker, Gilbert, Humphrey, & Tees, 1981; Werker & Tees, 1984). Kuhl proposes, on the basis of a series of behavioral (Kuhl, Conboy, Padden, Nelson, & Pruitt, 2005) and electrophysiological (Kuhl, Conboy, Padden, Rivera-Gaxiola, & Nelson, 2008) studies, that the speed with which this transition is achieved indicates how much input any given system requires in order to become specialist in processing only environmentally relevant contrasts. Electrophysiological measures, such as event-related potentials (ERPs), are frequently used in infant research, as they are noninvasive, less sensitive than most neuroimaging techniques to movement artefacts, and do not require a behavioral response to be made by the infant; indeed, often ERP measurements do not even require the participant to pay attention (see Chapter 2 of this volume, on neuroimaging methods). A frequently used ERP measure in infancy research is the mismatch response (MMR), where the difference in brain response to an often repeated stimulus (standard) versus a rarely repeated stimulus (deviant) is recorded. The size of the difference then indicates the extent to which the deviant, unexpected, stimulus is perceptually distinguished from the standard stimulus. Kuhl and colleagues (2008) used phonemically contrasting stimulus pairs that were either relevant or irrelevant to a 7.5-month-old's native language. The size of infants' MMR to native contrasts was negatively correlated to the size of the MMR to non-native contrasts; furthermore, positive language outcomes at 24 and 30 months, particularly productive language, correlated with a large MMR to native but a small MMR to non-native contrasts. Such data are taken to support the notion of "neural commitment" (the establishment of representations committed to a specific set of environmentally relevant contrasts), which aids the development of early language skills. This is a strong claim, but it does serve to illustrate the continuity between the low-level representation of speech and the later establishment of abstract language that relies upon such representations. If the neural commitment view is correct, then the rate at which sufficient commitment is established may be determined either by intrinsic factors or by the quantity or quality of data available in the environment. Distinguishing between these possibilities is an important next step for research, as each indicates a different intervention strategy to assist those who show early developmental delay.

*Neurobiological maturation*    Over the first years of life, the enormous behavioral advances made in language acquisition are paralleled at the neurobiological level by substantial changes in processing capacity and speed, and connectivity. Neurobiological changes can be divided into those pertaining to grey matter (predominantly neuronal cell bodies), and to white matter (neuronal axons). Grey matter changes through the processes of synaptogenesis and pruning, that is, the gradual proliferation of synapses (the chemical bridges linking neurons) followed by the removal of those that are not significantly functional, a sequence that varies in onset and rate over different regions of cortex (Huttenlocher & Dabholkar, 1997). This sequence varies in onset and rate over different regions of cortex. White matter changes, including the establishment of myelination (the fatty sheath that aids the rapid transmission of signals) occur in a region-specific manner from early infancy (Deoni et al., 2011), with linear increases in total white matter from early childhood (Giedd et al., 1999). While such changes are not yet well enough understood, and are too temporally expansive, to link clearly to specific changes in language behavior, the substantial individual variability in these neural-level changes (Giedd et al., 2008), and suggestive temporal correlations with behavioral advancement should be noted. One change in particular has been flagged up as a potential basis for the development of environmentally relevant phonemic categories: the maturation of connectivity within the temporal cortex from around six months (Moore, 2002).

Notably though, maturational changes are not necessarily the temporal precedent of functional change. As expounded by the *Interactive Specialization* theory (Johnson, 2010), areas of cortex may become specialist as a result of experience with relevant input; this is distinct from views that suggest that the development of cortex follows a maturational path dependent on chronological age. In the case of language, Interactive Specialization is supported by data showing that vocabulary size rather than age is correlated with functional lateralization (Mills, Coffey-Corina, & Neville, 1993), and at the behavioral level the ability to learn new words based on fine phonological distinctions is more closely correlated with vocabulary than age for infants under 20 months (Werker, Fennell, Corcoran, & Stager, 2002). There is an important lesson for education here, as, if experience promotes the capacity to learn, then early differences in experience, including the quality or quantity of linguistic input, may exacerbate deviations over the course of developmental trajectories.

## The impact of socioeconomic status on language development

It seems that the early emergence of linguistic capacity over even the first months of life is causally relevant to later outcomes, including the variability in competence observed in children by the start of formal education. Learning is in part constrained by variability in intrinsic factors: there is evidence for the impact of not only phonemic categorization but also other skills, including rapid auditory processing (Benasich, Thomas, Choudhury, & Leppanen, 2002) and sensitivity to statistical regularities in the speech stream (Newman, Ratner, Jusczyk, Jusczyk, & Dow, 2006). Variability is evident in typically developing children and may explain later atypicality (Benasich et al., 2006; Benasich & Tallal, 2002, although see Marshall, Snowling & Bailey, 2001; Rosen, 2003). However, early language delay does not necessarily result in persistent problems or atypical learning in other educational domains. For example, while by age five the incidence of SLI is estimated at 7%, based on a representative American sample (Tomblin, Records, Buckwalter, Zhang, & Smith, 1997), a far greater percentage of children, around 15%, are referred for language intervention at around the age of three or four years (Broomfield & Dodd, 2004). It is not clear how language delays resolve in those children who no longer show a deficit by the time they start school, nor is it easy to predict which children will show this resolution and which will show a persistent difficulty. One factor likely to play an important role is the quality and quantity of linguistic input available, something that is associated with SES.

SES is a multidimensional construct generally measured by a combination of parental education, occupation, and income, yet in terms of cognitive development these factors most likely act as a proxy measure for multiple environmental variables. SES affects language development, and children in lower SES groups may have delayed language for environmental reasons. Children with low SES are particularly vulnerable to showing behavioral language deficits (Prathanee et al., 2009; Reilly et al., 2010), and are over-represented in early referrals to clinics (Tomblin, Hardy, & Hein, 1991). Indeed, the UK government recently released figures indicating that around 50% of children from socioeconomically disadvantaged areas enter school with some form of speech or language difficulty (Department of Education, 2008). Both these points are

BRONFENBRENDER.

highly pertinent to our discussion here, as they draw focus away from factors within the child, and start to ask about the early environment and how it might compensate or indeed exacerbate system-level constraints over time.

SES has a larger impact on language development than it does on any other area of cognition, with the possible exception of executive function (Noble, Norman, & Farah, 2005; see Hackman & Farah, 2009, for a review), with SES predicting around 30% of the variance in global language performance at age six (Noble et al., 2005). It is likely that SES explains such a large degree of variability because linguistic input varies to such a great extent across SES (see, e.g., Hart & Risley, 1995; Huttenlocher, Waterfall, Vasilyeva, Vevea, & Hedges, 2010). Exactly how this influence is exerted and how it changes over time is not well understood. Importantly, environmental influence does appear to be causal, rather than mediated via genetic effects, in that the complexity of sentences used by teachers in the classroom has been shown to predict the improvement in children's sentence comprehension skills over the school year (Huttenlocher, Vasilyeva, Cymerman, & Levine, 2002).

SES effects on language are not even across different aspects of language. SES explains more variance in phonological awareness (24%) and receptive vocabulary (24%) than receptive grammar (5%) (Noble et al., 2005), which suggests that different aspects of language development depend to a greater or lesser extent on input quality. Even within the domain of grammar, SES effects have been found for complex but not simple productive syntax for children between 22 and 42 months of age (Vasilyeva, Huttenlocher, & Waterfall, 2006).

Variability in intrinsic factors is likely to act as a constraint on language development for high-SES more than low-SES children. This idea is drawn from data on cognitive ability. The heritability (the relative influence of genetic effects) of cognitive ability is moderated by SES, with heritability at seven years old just 10% in low-SES families, but as much as 72% in high-SES families (Turkheimer, Haley, Waldron, D'Onofrio, & Gottesman, 2003). What this suggests is that a cognitively rich environment allows inherent individual differences to emerge, but when the environment is less enriching the input becomes the dominant constraint on development. Data are available to suggest that the linguistic input differences between high- and low-SES families could be large enough to drive a similar effect with respect to language. A seminal study by Hart and Risley (1995), in which families from varying socioeconomic backgrounds were audiotaped for an hour each month over 2½ years from when the participating children were 7–9 months old, found three main differences between high- and low-SES families: low SES was associated with the use of fewer words, such that by age three children from low-SES households were estimated to have been cumulatively exposed to 30 million fewer words than children from high-SES households; low SES was also associated with parents using a smaller variety of words, more prohibitions and fewer affirmatives. In this study, low SES predicted smaller vocabularies and shallower vocabulary growth curves at age three, which in turn predicted poor receptive and expressive language outcomes at age 10 (Walker, Greenwood, Hart, & Carta, 1994).

Due to the complexity of environmental measures and the interactions between environmental and maturational effects, there are multiple routes by which such SES effects could exert an influence. Emerging data on the influence of SES on hemispheric lateralization may offer some clues. Raizada and colleagues (Raizada, Richards, Meltzoff, & Kuhl, 2008) demonstrated reduced anatomical asymmetry and functional lateralization during a phonological processing task in five-year-old children from low-SES backgrounds. This notion of SES relating to hemispheric lateralization is supported through behavioral data in children and adults (Boles, 2011), and suggests that language measures that vary by SES correlate at the neural level with reduced specialization of language systems. The important questions for educational research are whether early differences in cerebral specialization are amenable to environmental modulation. If we take an Interactive Specialization view of functional development (see Johnson, 2010), then reduced experience with language in early childhood through the reduced quantity of linguistic input in low-SES households may result in less specialization of cortical regions associated with language processing. This hypothesis suggests that long-term deficits are not necessarily determined by early SES effects but rather can be resolved through an enrichment of the environment such that more language input is available to children, allowing specialization of systems at a later age than is maybe seen for children from higher-SES backgrounds.

An additional possibility is that variability in language acquisition results from an interaction between developing systems and input. For example, Stevens and colleagues (Stevens, Lauinger, & Neville, 2009) demonstrated that three- to eight-year-old children from low-SES households were less able than their higher-SES peers to attend selectively to auditory stimuli. Specifically, ERP recordings demonstrated that children with a low-SES background attended to all auditory input, while children from a high-SES background only attended to those stimuli that were currently relevant, suggesting SES-related differences in children's ability to filter irrelevant information. This emphasizes that the term "environment" refers to not just what stimuli are available, but also what is sampled, that is, what is attended to. SES-related differences in attention are thought to be driven by the higher levels of vigilance recorded in children from low-SES households (Chen, Cohen, & Miller, 2010). SES can therefore be seen to relate directly to language development, but also to interact with early variability in language skills to exacerbate or ameliorate differences between children.

*Addressing inequality* What can be done to address the inequalities that emerge in early language ability as a result of SES? This is a key question for the field of educational neuroscience. There have been several attempts to implement programs designed to tackle the issue of cognitive inequality at the start of school as a result of SES gradients, the outcomes of which are encouraging but inconclusive. The good news is that children from low-SES backgrounds benefit most from interventions that enrich their cognitive environments. Interventions such as the Abecerderian and Perry Preschool programs (see Knudsen, Heckman, Cameron, & Shonkoff, 2006, and Raizada & Kishiyama, 2010, for reviews), which tend to provide intensive 1:1 and group work, result in measureable short-term gains across multiple domains (see, e.g., Gramlich, 1986). However, these gains are followed by a fascinating phenomenon where the benefits of programs initially appear to quickly "fade out" after their completion, yet in adulthood those who had been involved have repeatedly been shown to be at an advantage on various life-measures such as going to college and owning a home (Muennig, Schweinhart, Montie, & Neidell, 2009; Reynolds, Temple, Ou, Arteaga, & White, 2011). In the domain of language, a whole-class intervention to boost phonological awareness similarly resulted in rapid fade-out and no measureable benefit on literacy development (O'Connor, Arnott, McIntosh, & Dodd, 2009). However, no long-term followup has yet been conducted on this cohort. Questions about this puzzling postintervention trajectory for children from low-SES backgrounds now need to be addressed through the longitudinal use of neuroimaging techniques, particularly within the domain of language, as the start of school marks the point at which language skills provide the basis for literacy development, learning across domains, and social interaction with peers.

By the age of five, then, the key determinants of variability in language capacity are first variability in intrinsic processing factors such as the fine categorization of inputs, and second the properties of the input provided to shape the system. One key question with regard to education is which causes of atypical, low, or delayed language need to be addressed before formal education begins, and which can be improved or corrected through suitable and enriching educational input.

## Language Development in the Primary-School Years 5–12

Formal teaching in educational settings typically relies on oral language. A learner's linguistic abilities may be put under pressure from the outset, as children are frequently required to assimilate new forms of expression and understanding. In the example that follows we track the conversation between a teacher and a small group of five-year-olds who are struggling to come to terms with simple arithmetic:

| | |
|---|---|
| TEACHER: | What would you do if I asked you to do four add two? What would you do? |
| CHILD A: | Add a one. |
| TEACHER: | Would you? |
| CHILD B: | Add a two. |
| TEACHER: | What would you use to help you? |
| CHILD A: | Plus. |
| TEACHER: | You'd use plus? What does plus mean? |
| CHILD C: | Equals. |
| TEACHER: | Does it? Really? |
| CHILD A: | It's a plus. |
| TEACHER: | Plus means putting things together… putting numbers together. If I put numbers together do I get more, or less? |
| CHILD D: | Yes. Yes. Yes. |
| CHILD A: | More! |

This short extract (Mills, personal communication, 2012) is notable for the misunderstandings it contains. The teacher, who is extremely skilled, is careful to elicit from the children their understanding of key word meanings. As the conversation develops, and in future conversations, she will continue to negotiate these meanings with the children, to demonstrate how these meanings operate within sentences, in the context of actions, and thereby she will enhance learning. Such sensitive linguistic support is exceptional. Most children will meet the challenges of school-based learning without this kind of help. The extent to which they can use and understand language, under the pressure of new formal demands, even in educational domains such as maths, which might seem far removed from traditionally conceived linguistically based subjects, will be of critical importance for their future success in education and in later life.

Neuroscientific insights are starting to throw light on the brain-level developments that support the child's developing linguistic ability. In the sections which follow we look first at typical developmental processes, then focus on the causation and characteristics of SLIs, and the particular educational challenges they present.

## The specialization of neural systems for language

Recent advances in the child-friendly properties of magnetic resonance imaging (MRI) technology have produced the first comprehensive findings concerning the localization of language-related brain activations in childhood

(McNealy, Mazziotta, & Dapretto, 2011). Examining statistical learning of repeated patterns within continuous speech composed of novel sounds, McNealy and colleagues tested a total of 156 participants from five years of age to adulthood. Of particular interest were the differential activations observed over the duration of exposure to speech streams with high statistical regularity. Six-year-olds, 10-year-olds, 13-year-olds, and adults all showed increasing activation strength in temporal cortex, including the superior temporal gyrus; however, the lateralization of these activations varied by age. For six-year-olds, the activation increase was right lateralized, for children aged 10 and 13 there was a bilateral activation increase, while for adults the expected left lateralization was observed. These findings demonstrate the substantial developments that take place in neural systems supporting language learning during mid-childhood. The lateralization of systems responsive to high statistical regularity in speech is protracted and undergoes substantial change during mid-childhood and through puberty.

Auditory and phonetic processing also continues to develop over the primary-school years. Bishop and colleagues (Bishop, Hardiman, & Barry, 2011) have demonstrated this at a neural level using an electrophysiological measure that charts the synchronization of brain responses across trials, in this case in response to simple auditory stimuli. The authors report a significant linear trend of increasing synchronization with age across the three groups tested (7- to 12-year-olds, 13- to 16-year-olds, and adults), which correlated with a behavioral measure of frequency discrimination. Notable here is the need to use appropriate neural measures when testing children, measures that reflect the complexity of the developmental process and that can be interpreted in the light of behavioral data. More traditional electrophysiological measures are often interpreted with reference to adult data, and may therefore be misleading.

In line with the general hypothesis of continuity in language development, observations of infants' and young children's brain-level responses to native language phonemic contrasts have been represented as continuous, with a developmental process that extends to include neural responses indicative of lexico semantic processing and syntactic development (Friederici, 2005). More recent studies are starting to provide insights into the further specialization of neural systems for language in later childhood. Friederici, Oberecker, and Brauer (2012) offer some speculative proposals concerning the possible linkage between the development of fiber-tract connectivity in children in mid- to late childhood and the development of the comprehension of syntax. Research in this area is in very early stages. A central issue to be addressed concerns the differentiation of the neural substrates for syntactic versus semantic processing, and the possibility that the development of these core linguistic systems could be subject to differential influence of maturational and experiential factors.

## Children with specific language impairments

We have already considered evidence for the effects of SES on the development of language systems, and the possibility that these effects are mediated by differences in the quality/quantity of input. We now consider the case of restrictions on language development that are imposed by genetic/maturational factors, and examine the findings that appear to show specific and independent genetic effects on (a) a general measure of phonological memory and (b) a measure of morphosyntactic skill.

SLI is a developmental disorder in which significant deficits in expressive or receptive language, not due to sensory or environmental deprivation, co-occur with nonverbal intelligence within the average range (see, e.g., DSM IV, American Psychiatric Association, 2000). It is the co-occurrence of significantly impaired language and apparently unimpaired intelligence that justifies the use of the term "specific". The cognitive profile of children with SLI is markedly different from that presented by children with other neurodevelopmental disorders such as Williams syndrome (Martens, Wilson, & Reutens, 2008). In Williams syndrome vocabulary levels substantially exceed levels of nonverbal ability, presenting very different challenges to teaching and learning from those presented by SLI. However, it is important to make clear that the ways in which language is affected in SLI vary considerably across individuals and within individuals over time (Bishop, 1997). There may be difficulties with sentence production or comprehension, with grammar or vocabulary, or with language use in context (Chiat, 2000). Furthermore, although research studies tend to focus on language deficits, and to exclude children with speech difficulties, it can be very difficult, or even artificial, to distinguish the two. Educational studies, based on school populations, tend to be more inclusive (Haynes & Naidoo, 1991). Despite these difficulties of definition, there is broad agreement that SLI is common: a widely cited American study by Tomblin and colleagues (1997) found that around 7% of children attending kindergarten were affected. If this figure were constant across populations it would mean that, in every pre-school group of 20 children, one or two would have SLI. Even allowing for substantial error in this estimate, the significance of the educational challenge of SLI is beyond doubt.

*Causes of SLI*  Genetic factors are known to be significant in the causation of SLI. Convergent evidence from twin studies and DNA-based analyses indicates that nonword repetition (a global measure of phonological processing and memory) serves as a phenotypic marker for inherited SLI (Bishop, North, & Donlan, 1995, 1996; SLI Consortium, 2002, 2004). This finding points to a cognitive deficit in phonological processing (the processing of speech sound contrasts critical to a particular language or languages) rather than a perceptual deficit in auditory processing (capturing the acoustic properties of the speech signal). Bishop et al. (1999) used twin data to explore the role of phonological processing versus rapid auditory processing in the etiology of SLI. The results replicated previous findings demonstrating significant differences between children with SLI and typically developing children on both nonword repetition and rapid auditory processing (Gathercole & Baddeley, 1990; Tallal & Piercy, 1974). However, there was no evidence of heritability for rapid auditory processing deficits (fraternal and identical co-twins performed at similar levels, indicating primary environmental causation). Nonword repetition scores, on the other hand, were differentiated in fraternal but not identical twins, replicating previous findings of significant genetic effects (Bishop et al., 1999). In a further and larger-scale twin study Bishop, Adams, and Norbury (2006) found evidence of independent genetic transmission of language impairments linked to nonword repetition scores on the one hand and past-tense production scores (Rice, Wexler, Marquis, & Hershberger, 2000) on the other. Based on this finding, Bishop et al. (2006) proposed that more than one specialized genetically determined system contributes to language development, and that SLI is most likely to occur where genetic variation produces co-occurring deficits in such systems.

The twin-study method (discussed in detail in Chapter 4 of this volume) has proved fruitful in establishing a strong evidence base for genetic causation of SLI, and in moving towards clarification of the etiological importance of particular behavioral measures. Research at the molecular level is now starting to expose the complex neurobiological processes that underlie the genetic transmission of SLI. An important breakthrough relevant to this work came from the study of a single extended family (the KE family), within which numerous individuals have significant speech and language difficulties. Research into the genetic basis of these difficulties provides a lesson in the need for caution in interpretation of findings in new areas of scientific research, and, in this particular case, of the important contribution of experienced education professionals (teachers and speech and language therapists). The first published report of this family (Hurst, Baraitser, Auger, Graham, & Norell, 1990), co-authored by professionals working with family members, emphasized their significant speech difficulties and described their deficit as "severe verbal apraxia" (Hurst et al., 1990, p. 352). This diagnosis was later supported by Vargha-Khadem and colleagues after extensive behavioral testing, based on nonword repetition and orofacial movement, and supported with neuroimaging investigations (Vargha-Khadem et al., 1998). Comparison of affected and unaffected individuals found abnormal activation levels in pre-motor cortex and structural abnormalities in motor-relevant areas. The original report by Hurst and colleagues included a family pedigree demonstrating a striking Mendelian pattern of inheritance, which, years later, was confirmed when molecular genetic investigations found a particular mutation in gene *FOXP2* in the affected family members (Lai, Fisher, Hurst, Vargha-Khadem, & Monaco, 2001). Subsequent research has established that the specific rare genetic mutation that segregates with severe verbal dyspraxia in the KE family is not found in the wider population of children with SLI (Newbury et al., 2002).

It now seems unlikely that a single-gene cause will be found for many of the language deficits found in children with SLI, but rather that complex polygenic interactions are involved (Bishop, 2009), possibly based on combinations of commonly occurring genetic variants rather than rare mutations. Further genetic studies have indicated possible overlap between the pathways of gene expression observed in different developmental disorders. A recent study by Vernes et al. (2008) showed that *FOXP2*, mutated in the KE family but not in SLI, controls the action of a gene (also on chromosome 7) called *CNTNAP2*, known to be important in neural development. Vernes et al. went on to show that variants of *CNTNAP2* are associated with nonword repetition scores in children with SLI. Furthermore, variants in *CNTNAP2* have been found to be linked to autism (Alarcón et al., 2008). Discoveries of this sort bring us closer to the identification of specific causal pathways associated with language and communication deficits, and may eventually lead to a genetically informed redefinition of these developmental disorders, with potential to enhance early identification of affected individuals. However, the current state of knowledge falls short of any such applications. The presence of SLI, unlike some other developmental disorders (e.g., Williams syndrome), is not yet susceptible to genetic testing, but as the extent and pace of research effort in the field expands it is reasonable to expect significant progress in the years ahead. Bishop (2009) poses the following challenge for future research: to enhance phenotypic identification so as to support differentiation between language deficits whose causation is attributable (a) to rare genetic variants (such as *FOXP2*), (b) to complex polygenic factors, and (c) to environmental causation.

While the complex science behind the causation of speech and language impairments may be fascinating, it may also seem distant from the concerns of education policy and from the teacher in the classroom. However, if Bishop's challenge of differential diagnosis is met, then educational practice will be informed from a new perspective. If, as research is starting to indicate, speech and language functions are differentially sensitive to genetic and experiential variation, then, as we begin to understand these differences, we will be better placed to provide optimal intervention, and to monitor at a neural level the changes that result.

*SLI in the early years: screening procedures*   The difficulty of behavioral testing for early identification of children with SLI has been recognized for some considerable time (Law, 1994; Rescorla, 1989). Recent efforts have been directed particularly towards the development of measures of underlying linguistic and cognitive processes. A tool recently developed by van der Lely and colleagues (Gardner, Froud, McClelland, & van der Lely, 2006), was based on the sort of nonword and sentence repetition tasks found to be strongly associated with SLI in studies of older children (Bishop et al., 1996; Conti-Ramsden, 2003; Gathercole & Baddeley, 1990). Despite its plausibility, this measure showed very low sensitivity to cases of SLI in a sample of three- to six-year-olds (Nash, Leavett, & Childs, 2011), identifying only 20% of cases.

A different approach was taken by Benasich, Tallal and colleagues (Benasich & Tallal, 2002; Heim, Friedman, Keil, & Benasich, 2011), based on the theory that a deficit in rapid auditory processing is the underlying cause of SLI (Tallal & Piercy, 1974). In a number of studies, they assessed very young children with a family history of SLI, using a range of habituation and preference tasks. Some consistent differences emerged between groups with a family history and those without. In addition to significant overall correlations between auditory processing in infancy and later language learning, there was evidence of both auditory and visual processing deficits in the family history groups. Studies of this sort may, eventually, lead to the identification and refinement of behavioral measures that contribute to effective screening, but much remains to be done in order to establish that early childhood measurements can produce satisfactory levels of sensitivity and specificity in identifying cases at risk of later language deficits. Recent research by Bishop and colleagues (Bishop, Hardiman, & Barry, 2010) has extended findings with regard to auditory processing in SLI. The authors measured electrophysiological responses to deviant tones and speech sounds in 7- to 16-year-olds with and without SLI and found evidence in a late-appearing MMR of specialist neural processing in the typical but not the SLI group. Furthermore, it is notable that, within the SLI group, the spectral power of the late MMR correlated significantly with behavioral performance on the test of nonword repetition, a candidate phenotypic marker for heritable language impairments (see above). There is some broad correspondence between these findings and the auditory processing deficit proposed by Tallal and colleagues (e.g., Tallal & Piercy, 1974), but it is important to note that the proposals of Bishop and colleagues are more general, in that they are not restricted to brief or rapid stimuli. Such findings may provide new sensitive neural markers of language disorders early in development.

Despite the numerous scientific obstacles to early identification, educationists and clinicians bear the responsibility of assessing the needs of young children referred to them for speech, language, and communication difficulties. Any decision requires the evaluation of relative risk: the risk of wrongly identifying an individual whose language and communication would develop normally without intervention must be weighed against the risk of failing to intervene during any optimal periods for learning. Furthermore, failure to differentiate reliably between children whose language deficits are genetically determined, environmentally determined, or both carries a risk of inappropriate intervention, and itself consequently also presents an obstacle to the scientific evaluation of intervention strategies.

Pioneering work by Chiat and Roy (2008) gives some indication of the complexities entailed in the prediction of outcome. Following a sample of children referred for speech, language, and communication needs at two to three years, they tested the predictive value of (a) functional language assessment, (b) measures of phonological development, and (c) sociocognitive skills (based on theoretical proposals by Tomasello, 1995, and DeLoache, 2004). At four to five years around 50% of the sample performed at age-appropriate levels on language tests. The broad expectation of the study was that the more focused measures of phonological and sociocognitive skills would be most likely to predict later status. However, contrary to prediction, functional receptive language tested at two to three years was the strongest overall predictor of outcome at four to five years, though phonological skill was the best predictor of specific morphosyntactic deficits. Further followup at age 10–11 years (Roy & Chiat, personal communication) replicated the finding that functional language testing was the strongest overall predictor. However, in contrast to the result of the first followup, the strongest prediction of morphosyntactic skill at age 10–11 years came not from early phonological skills, but from early sociocognitive skills. These important findings highlight the complex and interactive nature of processes underlying atypical language development.

*Intervention for auditory processing deficits in SLI*   Educational interventions based on neuroscientific research have been around for many years. Here we take the example of the widely cited Fast ForWord program (http://www.scilearnglobal.com/the-fast-forword-program/) to illustrate the importance of careful research to lead intervention. There are, in theory, two ways to tackle developmental difficulties attributable to atypical perceptual processing through environmental modification: the first is by training aimed at enhancing an individual's perceptual processing capacity; the second is by tailoring inputs to adhere to the constraints of the system, such that those inputs can be successfully processed. Whether or not processing constraints can be directly improved by training is not yet clear. One promising clue is that training on the processing of rapid transitions in children with developmental dyslexia has been shown to result in the normalization of patterns of brain response to such transitions (Gaab, Gabrieli, Deutsch, Tallal, & Temple, 2007). The case of Fast ForWord, however, is a cautionary tale.

Based on the rapid-auditory-processing-deficit account of SLI (Tallal & Piercy, 1974), the Fast ForWord program is a commercially available computer software suite using acoustically modified speech designed to compensate for the student's putative rapid-processing deficit, with gradual reduction of the modification as the student progresses through the material. The program is based on pilot studies published in the prestigious journal *Science* (Merzenich et al., 1996; Tallal et al., 1996). However, a series of evaluative studies culminating in a systematic meta-analytic review (Strong, Torgerson, Torgerson, & Hulme, 2011) has clearly demonstrated that the program is ineffective, though it has been extremely widely used (more than 500 000 children in the United States of America are estimated to have used it; Strong et al., 2011, p. 224). The review by Strong et al. was based on randomized controlled trials, or quasi-experiments with a treatment group taking part in the Fast ForWord intervention and at least one other group receiving either no intervention or an alternative treatment. Meta-analyses were conducted comparing Fast ForWord intervention groups with (a) untreated controls and (b) active controls receiving an alternative intervention. None of the eight comparisons conducted showed a significant difference in outcome between groups; four of the analyses showed negative results (poorer outcome for the Fast ForWord group). The Fast ForWord program provides an object lesson in the need for scientific evaluation in the implementation of superficially plausible interventions; Snowling and Hulme (2011) present a principled approach to this issue and provide a comprehensive review of the existing evidence in this area.

## Alternative developmental pathways: the case of TZ

Education endeavors to allow individuals to achieve functional success in adulthood. In research, behavioral or neural measures in early adulthood (endstates) can be informed by tracing the developmental progression of those measures. Equally though, endstate data can be highly informative about those developmental pathways. In this section we describe the fascinating case study of an individual (TZ), which demonstrates how exceptional endstate achievements can be attained despite highly atypical developmental constraints.

*Background*   TZ is reported to have developed language in line with typical milestones until losing all but single-word communication around age three. If diagnosis were undertaken today consideration might be given to Landau–Kleffner syndrome (Bishop, 1985; Duran, Guimaraes, Medeiros, & Guerreiro, 2009), a disorder in which, after a period of typical development, there is gradual or sudden loss of language. However, in the late 1960s such diagnoses were rare. Instead, TZ received speech and language therapy and attended a mainstream primary school. Despite normal hearing she was described as functioning like a profoundly deaf child. TZ then transferred to a language unit before attending a special school for children with severe and specific speech and language disorders at the age of six years and ten months. Here she benefited from a highly structured curriculum, specialized to deliver language through primarily visual inputs (Conn, 1971; Hutt, 1986), and continued to receive highly specialized education until the age of 16 years. She took secretarial qualifications at a further-education college and pursued a career in office administration. In adulthood she was demonstrated to be a competent communicator and participated in a range of research assessments (Aboagye, 2001; Donlan, Aboagye, Clegg, & Stackhouse, in preparation).

*Nonverbal IQ*　Measurements in childhood and adulthood consistently indicated performance around the average level, with no evidence of significant variation between subtests.

*Verbal/phonological memory*　Massive deficits in phonological memory were recorded throughout childhood and in midlife. In childhood TZ was unable to participate in any assessment of auditory memory. In adulthood she was given the children's nonword repetition test (Gathercole & Baddeley, 1986), but was unable to score. On a test of perception of phoneme sequence based on Bridgeman and Snowling (1988), TZ was at ceiling level (as were six-year-old controls) on discrimination of simple word-final contrasts in monosyllabic word and nonword CVCs (e.g., bus/but; vis/vit), but performed at chance level (significantly worse than six-year-old controls) when attempting to discriminate word and nonword CVCCs (e.g., lost/lots; vust/vuts).

*Lexical knowledge*　Massive deficits were recorded in receptive vocabulary and picture-naming in early childhood. There was substantial improvement in performance between six and eight years, especially when speech was augmented by use of visual methods (manual sign), but significant deficits were still recorded. At age eight years and nine months she performed at age-equivalent three years and nine months on a standardized test of receptive vocabulary delivered without manual sign. In midlife a dramatic improvement was noted, with above average performance on both receptive vocabulary and picture-naming, though word definition was significantly poorer. Of importance here was the tester's note on the receptive vocabulary form, indicating that on several occasions TZ requested that words be spelt out, indicating a preference for orthographic over phonological input.

*Grammar and comprehension*　Massive deficits were observed in grammatical skills and functional language in childhood. Some progress was made by age eight or nine, especially when manual sign supported speech input, but extremely significant deficits were recorded. In midlife, grammatical comprehension still showed deficits. However, the Comprehension subtest of the Wechsler Adult Intelligence Scales (Wechsler, 1997), which includes questions such as "Why should people pay taxes?", engaged TZ's advanced general knowledge so as to produce age-appropriate performance.

*Literacy*   Word reading was an area of relative strength in childhood. Scores fell just below age-appropriate level at seven and eight years, but progress approximated typical rates. High performance was maintained into midlife; reading was within the average range, and spelling was above average (75th centile against adult norms).

TZ's speech processing and phonological memory deficits were extreme and persistent throughout development. Auditory discrimination testing in adulthood revealed that she perceived very simple phoneme contrasts, but that a small increase in complexity produced confusion, even when real-word stimuli were presented. However, by midlife there was a dramatic increase in lexical knowledge. Taken together, this set of findings indicates that the phonological representations associated with TZ's lexical knowledge remained extremely impoverished, despite significant growth in vocabulary size in later childhood or early adulthood. Grammatical skills were extremely limited in childhood and the problems persisted into adulthood. However, further evidence indicated powerful ameliorating factors based on visual inputs. Use of manual sign to support speech in childhood produced substantial advantage in picture-naming and language comprehension. Reading levels were well in advance of spoken language levels throughout development, and orthography appeared to have operated as the preferred medium for lexical development. Thus it appears that an atypical route to development of the semantic system provided TZ with a wide-ranging general knowledge. This may explain age-appropriate performance in midlife on tests of verbal comprehension.

TZ's language skills in adulthood are impressive, especially since she appears to have been continuously unable to process speech sounds with any precision since around the age of three. Her dependence on visual inputs and on the highly specialized educational curriculum devised by Hutt and colleagues (Hutt, 1986) seems to have been absolute. The approach was highly structured, with focused, sequentially organized content, unlike the sorts of enrichment program that have been widely adopted in addressing SES-related linguistic deficits (e.g., Gonzalez et al., 2011). Two key elements in the approach were (a) the comprehensive use of a manual sign system designed to capture lexical and morphological elements of spoken language (Paget Gorman Signed Speech, http://www.pagetgorman.org/) and (b) teaching syntax through written language (Conn, 1971; Lea, 1970).

TZ's difficulties may have resulted from severe persistent neural-level distur-bance of the type associated with Landau–Kleffner Syndrome (Bishop, 1985; Duran et al., 2009); if this is so, then her case is, in a sense, the polar opposite of the case of language deficit associated with restricted input and low SES. The structured visual inputs upon which she seems to have depended constitute an appropriate response to the demands of a neural system whose maturation is systematically and persistently altered from typical expectation (it is worth not-ing here that TZ' s particular strengths in reading distinguish her from the many children with SLI who have persistent literacy difficulties). For TZ, the process of brain development appears to have followed atypical routes, themselves dependent on atypical inputs of the type outlined above, thus illustrating how individuals with vastly atypical systems can achieve success if these atypicalities are understood and environmental and educational needs are met. Such data beg the question of just how flexible developmental pathways to success can be, with respect to either behavioral compensation or neural re-organization.

## Language Development in Adolescence

So far, we have considered early speech and language development, the extraordi-nary establishment of complex language over childhood and how atypical systems or inputs can influence developmental pathways. Given what is already achieved by the time children begin formal education, and the leaps made in literacy and social language over mid-childhood, the prevailing perception is that typical lan-guage development is essentially complete by adolescence, that language systems are well established, and that sensitive periods for language learning are rapidly closing. In this section we challenge the idea that language is static or indeed established by adolescence and emphasize the importance of considering the adolescent brain and language system as part of the dynamic process of development.

The use of language changes dramatically as children enter and progress through adolescence. Secondary school demands the adoption of complex and abstract terms, which must be both learned and integrated into existing schema (Grant-Hennings, 2000). Language, in both written and oral forms, becomes increasingly important as a tool for learning, such that low linguistic competence can have knock-on effects throughout the curriculum. Linguistic demands change not just in the classroom but also with regard to relationships with peers and adults as the adolescent social world expands and becomes more complex. The development of peer-to-peer relationships requires sufficient linguistic competence to exchange knowledge (Turkstra, Williams, Tonks, & Frampton, 2008), along with multiple aspects of pragmatic and metapragmatic abilities including understanding and producing nonliteral language (Nippold, 2000; Nippold & Duthie, 2003), behavioral inhibition, understanding context and inferencing (see Blakemore & Choudhury, 2006). Consequently, the teenage years can be difficult for those with a history of linguistic and pragmatic problems (Botting & Conti-Ramsden, 2010; Wadman, Botting, Durkin, & Conti-Ramsden, 2011). These academic and social changes in the use and importance of language are reflected both in the neural substrates of language production and comprehension, and in the language capacity of children; they also serve to highlight how both the potential and the vulnerability evident in younger children continue to be important through the adolescent years.

## Language behavior in adolescence

Adolescents meet the changing linguistic demands of their environment, not least by showing great changes in pragmatic language, including the understanding of idioms (Nippold & Taylor, 2002), proverbs and figurative language (see Nippold, 2000), which may depend not just on the development of vocabulary knowledge (Nippold, Allen, & Kirsch, 2000), but most likely on fundamental developments in the social brain with respect to theory of mind and perspective taking (Dumontheil, Küster, Apperly, & Blakemore, 2010). It is not just at the level of pragmatics that language function and behavior changes over adolescence. At the most fundamental level, changes have been recorded in rapid auditory processing both over early adolescence and between early adolescence and adulthood, as measured by EEG (Poulsen, Picton, & Paus, 2009), indicating continuing development through mid–late adolescence. Phonemic categorization also continues to mature into adolescence, at least up to age 12 (Hazan & Barrett, 2000), with boundary definitions being inconsistent with those of adults, and boundary precision changing right through to the end of adolescence (Medina, Hoonhorst, Bogliotti, & Seniclaes, 2010). Other measured changes include the motor control of speech, which becomes more precise over this developmental period (Walsh & Smith, 2002), and verbal fluency, which has been shown to improve after age 12 (see Romine & Reynolds, 2005).

## The neural substrates of adolescent language

Adolescence is a time of ongoing change in terms of the anatomical and functional structure of the brain. Of particular note is the maturation of regional and long-range white-matter tracts, permitting changes in local and inter-regional connectivity. Increases in white-matter volume are accompanied by continuing synaptic and neuronal pruning, indexed by reduction in widespread grey-matter volume (Giorgio et al., 2010), with frontal and temporal regions showing the most prolonged reductions in grey matter (Gotgay et al., 2004); lateral temporal lobes are the last to mature physiologically, with grey matter reaching its height at around

16 years of age (Gotgay et al., 2004; and see Blakemore, 2008). Shifts in white matter are important when considering language development, as white matter can be said to represent the interaction and flow of information between systems (Paus, 2010). White matter matures over adolescence in multiple areas throughout the brain, including the arcuate fasciculus (Barnea-Goraly et al., 2005), which connects receptive language areas in posterior temporoparietal cortex with inferior frontal regions associated with motor output (Bernal & Ardila, 2009), and has been shown to correlate with language performance over this age (Ashtari et al., 2007).

White-matter development is also evident through the frontal lobes (Barnea-Goraly et al., 2005); in adult neuropsychology the frontal lobes are strongly associated with the pragmatics of behavior and language (Angeleri et al., 2008; Dardier et al., 2011), including figurative language (Yang, Fuller, Khodaparast, & Krawczyk, 2010) and theory of mind (Martín-Rodríguez & Leon-Carrion, 2010). The developmental correlation between frontal maturation and the establishment of complex pragmatic language is therefore unsurprising.

Vocabulary knowledge is an area that is known to change throughout the lifespan. In adolescence, when vocabulary is still formally taught, but not in adulthood, vocabulary knowledge correlates with grey-matter density in the left posterior supramarginal gyrus (Richardson, Thomas, Filippi, Harth, & Price, 2009). Grey-matter density in adolescence may therefore reflect relating words to lexical or semantic equivalents as learned in formal education. This is a clear indication of the effects of the linguistic environment on adolescent brain-behavior functions.

Neuroimaging techniques have also been utilized to trace the specialization of neural systems, including the lateralization of language, which, although some aspects are strongly lateralized by mid-childhood (see, e.g., Gaillard et al., 2003), continues to change into adolescence over temporal and frontal regions (Everts et al., 2009), right up to age 20 (Szaflarski, Holland, Schmithorst, & Byars, 2006). For example, the arcuate fasciculus lateralizes structurally (Pugliese et al., 2009), and this left lateralization correlates with phonological processing (Lebel & Beaulieu, 2009) and reading (Yeatman et al., 2011) in late childhood and early adolescence. Interestingly, household SES has been shown to predict less frontal asymmetry in resting electrophysiological activity in adolescents (Tomarken, Dichter, Garber & Simien, 2004), possibly supporting a role for the quantity and quality of input in the specialization of function.

## Educational neuroscience in adolescence

Language then is far from static over adolescence, with change evident at the levels of behavior, brain, and brain–behavior relationships. What needs to be considered with respect to the classroom is how best to avoid restricting such changes, and encourage and exploit this time of potential to maximize language gains. We have seen that environmental deprivation may constrain the specialization of language systems. Notably though, very little work has been done on either this phenomenon, or the potential benefits of environmental enrichment at this age. One positive indicator is that work with rats has shown that an enriched environment can reverse the effects of early deprivation on behavior (Zaias, Queeney, Kelley, Zakharova, & Izenwasser, 2008) and even on protein expression in the brain (Laviola et al., 2004), suggesting potentially profound effects at the neural level. Research that has been conducted with humans in this area has focused on the economic implications of intervention (e.g., Doyle, Harmon, Heckman, & Tremblay, 2009), rather than the potential impact on brain systems.

The other source of developmental constraint, as we have seen throughout this review, is at the level of maturing systems. For a minority of children with SLI, language behavior normalizes as they enter adolescence (Conti-Ramsden, 2008); but for the majority, problems in language as well as the social and emotional difficulties associated with these problems persist into adulthood (Clegg, Hollis, Mawhood, & Rutter, 2005), as do the neural correlates of such difficulties, which mark persisting low-level processing problems (Weber-Fox, Leonard, Hampton-Wray, & Tomblin, 2010). The availability of intervention from speech and language therapists reduces as children get older, despite evidence that children with persisting deficits fall further behind over time (Stothard, Snowling, Bishop, Chipchase, & Kaplan, 1998). The challenge for educational neuroscientists with regard to language in adolescence is to provide evidence of the benefit of environmental enrichment with regard to meaningful behavioral and neural-level changes.

## Sensitive Periods in Language Development

Having shown that, far from being established in early childhood, language changes right through adolescence, we finally take a formal look at sensitive periods in language development as a potentially fruitful area for future research into curriculum design.

### Defining sensitive periods

A sensitive period is a point in development when behavioral change can be maximally influenced by environmental input; in neural terms, this means that functional plasticity is at its height and brain structure and function are most malleable, although this does not preclude further change later in development (Knudsen, 2004). Sensitive periods confer considerable advantage to an individual as they ensure that neural processing systems are optimally adapted for the species-typical and individual environment (Knudsen, 2004). Over the course of development, multiple different sensitive periods are thought to occur, relating to functional change in different domains or subdomains; aspects of sensory processing, for example the visual perception of global motion (Lewis & Maurer, 2005), show the earliest and most well-defined sensitive periods. These fluctuations in sensitivity to the nature of the environment are understood to correspond to the course of synaptogenesis and pruning, which, broadly speaking, sweeps over the cortex from low-level sensory processing areas to regions of higher-level integrative or abstract processing (Gogtay et al., 2004; Huttenlocher, 2002). The timecourse and flexibility of sensitive periods for any given domain, and indeed the extent to which such periods can be observed at all, may be determined by three types of datum: the outcome of learning during normal development, the impact of early deprivation, and recovery from damage at different points in development (Lewis & Maurer, 2005; and see Thomas & Knowland, 2009). In terms of sensitive periods for language learning then, we need to consider the effects of age on the acquisition of a second language, the impact of early social or sensory deprivation and the functional outcomes of damage to key neural structures at different points in development. Such data are highly pertinent to our discussion of educational neuroscience, as to optimize learning in any given domain educational input should ideally coincide with maximum sensitivity of relevant neural systems; when related to educational practice, sensitive periods may therefore be referred to as "optimal periods" (Koizumi, 2011, p. 328). With regard to language, to two key issues in education are first when an additional language, or languages, should be introduced, and second to what extent children who arrive at school with lower language competencies due to environmental or sensory factors can catch up with their peers.

## Sensitive periods for foreign language learning

As for many other domains, such as vision (Lewis & Maurer, 2005), multiple sensitive periods for different subdomains can be observed within human language acquisition. Subdomains in this instance refers to different levels of language, from low-level perceptual aspects such as the processing of complex tones and the establishment of native phonology to higher-level aspects such as the establishment of grammatical rules and the learning of vocabulary. As has been stated, sensitive periods are more robustly demonstrated for lower-level perceptual processes (Huttenlocher, 2002) and as such establishing the phonology of a language might be a prime candidate to show a sensitive period. In support of this, the age of arrival in a foreign country correlates with the retention of native phonology, as measured by accent strength, even when controlling for confounding factors such as length of residence and degree of experience (Flege, Yeni-Komshian, & Liu, 1999). The decline in phonological flexibility recorded in this study was shown to be roughly linear, which, the authors propose, may represent ongoing changes in the representation of native phonology, an idea that has subsequently been supported by the suggestion that native and foreign languages compete during second-language learning (Linck, Kroll, & Sunderman, 2009). Such data may be taken as further evidence in support of Kuhl's work on neural commitment (discussed above). However, even in the case of phonology, lost sensitivity to non-native categories in infancy can be reversed given a social learning context (Kuhl, 2007), and the learning of non-native contrasts can be achieved at any age given appropriate learning strategies and manipulation of the input stimuli (McCandliss, Fiez, Protopapas, Conway & McClelland, 2002). So, while the acquisition of phonology does seem to be sensitive to the maturational (and experiential) state of the system, even here there is no clearly defined sensitive period, and indeed given appropriate learning conditions the phonological system remains malleable throughout the lifespan.

With respect to less sensory aspects of language, grammaticality judgments have also been shown to decline with increasing age of arrival in a foreign country (Flege et al., 1999); however, here the relationship does not withstand controlling for confounding factors, suggesting that this effect may reflect not the age of first exposure but rather the degree of experience. A further consideration is the extent to which decline in capacity to learn the syntax and morphology of a new language is dependent first on the acquisition of accurate and stable phonology. In the case of learning new vocabulary, no evidence has been established for constraints on learning as a result of age of first exposure (Slabakova, 2006); in fact, based on behavioral and electrophysiological data from children first exposed to English as a second language between ages 0 and 11, it may be better for semantic development to start second-language learning later, on the condition that level of exposure is high (Ojima, Matsuba-Kurita, Nakamura, Hoshino, & Hagiwara, 2011). Interestingly though, a study of deaf children who received cochlear implants in the first or second year of life found that the greatest effect of a delay in implantation was not phonological development, as might be expected, but rather semantic (Houston, Moberly, Hollich, & Miyamoto, 2012). This study suggests that establishing the link between sound patterns and their real-world referents, typically introduced from the first year of life, may be more stringently subject to a sensitive period than phonological learning.

## The impact of early deprivation

Turning to consider early deprivation, we see that periods of opportunity for learning are also periods of vulnerability. Linguistic deprivation primarily occurs as a result of a sensory deficit, that is, congenital deafness or extreme environmental deprivation. Studies of the linguistic capabilities of children who spent their early childhood in Romanian orphanages have shown substantial language delays by age 30 months (Windsor, Glaze, & Koga, 2007). However, deprivation within the first six months has very little long-term impact, and for those adopted even after 18 months the presence of minimal skills such as imitating speech sounds was a positive indicator (Croft et al., 2007). Therefore, potentially, even acute linguistic deprivation need not have devastating effects on long-term development, so long as that deprivation is short lived. A similar pattern is observed in children who are born severely or profoundly deaf, with the fitting of cochlear implants before the age of around 30 months resulting, after two years of implant use, in age-appropriate vocabulary (Connor, Craig, Raudenbush, Heavner, & Zwolan, 2006), but implantation after 30 months resulting in atypically low vocabularies after two years. Svirsky and colleagues (Svirsky, Teoh, & Neuburger, 2004) show that this benchmark of 30 months does not represent a well-defined sensitive period but rather is part of a gradual decline in ability with increasing age of implantation. A particularly important area for future research with respect to the influences of early sensory deprivation is the role that having at least some experience with complex sounds and linguistic input early in life plays in later language development. In rat pups a well-defined sensitive period for the development of a typical response to complex sounds has been established (Insanally, Kover, Kim, & Bao, 2009). Similarly, with humans, Li and colleagues studied the integrity of white-matter connectivity in the temporal lobe in participants who had acquired profound deafness over the first six years of life and who had not used hearing aids or implants over that time (Li et al., 2012); white-matter connectivity was shown to correlate with the age of onset of deafness when controlling for duration of deafness.

There are several lessons to learn from the literature on sensitive periods in language acquisition with regard to education. When thinking about second-language learning, where declines in behavioral plasticity are seen, they are gradual rather than sharp, and even relatively low-level aspects of language such as phonology are malleable late in life given appropriate learning conditions. There is therefore probably no age by which a second language must be introduced, although the learning environment needs to be manipulated to complement learning styles at different points in development. An important consideration here, however, is the role of establishing skills in the correct order so as not to create bottlenecks in learning. From this point of view, phonology should be established before the vocabulary and syntax of a second language are introduced, thus following the pattern seen during the establishment of a native language over infancy. This principle has also been demonstrated in the case of dyslexia, where children at risk for developing this disorder have been found to be best served by bolstering phonology before tackling literacy directly (Bus & van Ijzendoorn, 1999). With respect to those children who show reduced language capabilities due to environmental deprivation, suitable input can result in substantial progress and normalization of abilities, although the length and extent of the deprivation will modulate the success of such intervention. From the available data on both social and sensory deprivation, it would seem that 30 months is a good rule of thumb for the provision of an informationally rich environment in order to maximize the probability of a good outcome. Again, the issue of the order in which skills need to be established should be considered.

## Summary and Conclusion

Classroom education arguably has two concerns with respect to language development: the first is to level the playing field in terms of providing a rich linguistic environment for all children; the second is to appropriately adapt stimuli in order to optimally engage individuals with variable intrinsic constraints; all with a view to establishing language not just for social communication but as a tool to access the whole curriculum. To that end we have shown that variability in the acquisition of language skills results from variation in the quality and quantity of linguistic input, in the capacity to process that input, and in the interaction between the two. We have shown that language skills, and the underlying neural correlates, continue to change and develop throughout childhood and adolescence, and that the developmental pathways associated with the establishment of mature language can be radically different depending on the constraints of individual systems.

With educational neuroscience in its infancy there are inevitably myriad research directions at this time. Within the field of language we suggest that current priorities should include: (1) Specifying early phenotypes of language atypicalities associated with environmental deprivation on the one hand, and different types of congenitally determined difficulties on the other. (2) Establishing whether intervention is best aimed at the high-level language processes where behavioral difficulties are observed, or whether measurable gains can be made by targeting low-level processing constraints, which then feed up the language hierarchy. (3) Exploring the extent to which the principle of learning skills in a specific order is crucial to expert language and literacy acquisition.

We believe that the key to begin addressing all these questions is to continue focusing on the establishment of an open and mutual dialogue between educationalists and neuroscientists.

## References

Aboagye, S. (2001). *A follow-up study of adults with a childhood history of specific speech and language impairments.* Unpublished MSc thesis, University College London.

Alarcón, M., Abrahams, B. S., Stone, J. L., Duvall, J. A., Perederiy, J. V., Bomar, J. M., Sebat, J., Wigler, M., Martin, C. L., Ledbetter, D. H., Nelson, S. F., Cantor, R. M., & Geshwind, D. H. (2008). Linkage, association, and gene-expression analyses identify *CNTNAP2* as an autism-susceptibility gene. *American Journal of Human Genetics, 82*(1), 150–159.

American Psychiatric Association. (2000). *Diagnostic and statistical manual of mental disorders: DSM-IV-TR* (4th ed.). Washington, DC: Author.

Angeleri, R., Bosco, F. M., Zettin, M., Sacco, K., Colle, L., & Bara, B. G. (2008). Communicative impairment in traumatic brain injury: A complete pragmatic assessment. *Brain and Language, 107*(3), 229–245.

Ashtari, M., Cervellione, K. L., Hasan, K. M., Wu, J., McIlree, C., Kester, H., Ardekani, B. A., Roofeh, D., Philip, R. S., & Kumra, S. (2007). White matter development during late adolescence in healthy males: A cross-sectional diffusion tensor imaging study. *NeuroImage, 35*(2), 501–510.

Barnea-Goraly, N., Menon, V., Eckert, M., Tamm, L., Bammer, R., Karchemskiy, A., Dant, C. D., & Reiss, A. L. (2005). White matter development during childhood and adolescence: A cross-sectional diffusion tensor imaging study. *Cerebral Cortex, 15*, 1848–1854.

Bates, E., Bretherton, I., & Snyder, L. (1988). *From first words to grammar: Individual differences and dissociable mechanisms.* New York: Cambridge University Press.

Benasich, A. A., Choudhury, N., Friedman, J. T., Realpe-Bonilla, T., Chojnowska, C., & Gou, Z. (2006). The infant as a prelinguistic model for language learning impairments: Predicting from event-related potentials to behavior. *Neuropsychologia, 44*(3), 396–411.

Benasich, A. A., & Tallal, P. (2002). Infant discrimination of rapid auditory cues predicts later language impairment. *Behavioural Brain Research, 136*(1), 31–49.

Benasich, A. A., Thomas, J. J., Choudhury, N., & Leppanen, P. H. T. (2002). The importance of rapid auditory processing abilities to early language development: Evidence from converging methodologies. *Developmental Psychobiology, 40*(3), 278–292.

Bernal, B., & Ardila, A. (2009). The role of the arcuate fasciculus in conduction aphasia. *Brain, 132*(9), 2309–2316.

Bishop, D. V. M. (1985). Age of onset and outcome in acquired aphasia with convulsive disorder (Landau–Kleffner syndrome). *Developmental Medicine and Child Neurology, 27*(6), 705–712.

Bishop, D. V. M. (1997). *Uncommon understanding: Development and disorders of language comprehension in children.* Hove, UK: Psychology.

Bishop, D. V. M. (2002). The role of genes in the etiology of specific language impairment. *Journal of Communication Disorders, 35*(4), 311–328.

Bishop, D. (2009). Genes, cognition, and communication insights from neurodevelopmental disorders. *Annals of the New York Academy of Sciences, 1156*, 1–18.

Bishop, D. V. M., Adams, C. V., & Norbury, C. F. (2006). Distinct genetic influences on grammar and phonological short-term memory deficits: Evidence from 6-year-old twins. *Genes Brain and Behavior, 5*(2), 158–169.

Bishop, D. V. M., Bishop, S. J., Bright, P., James, C., Delaney, T., & Tallal, P. (1999). Different origin of auditory and phonological processing problems in children with language impairment: Evidence from a twin study. *Journal of Speech, Language, and Hearing Research, 42*(1), 155–168.

Bishop, D. V. M., Hardiman, M. J., & Barry, J. G. (2010). Lower-frequency event-related desynchronization: A signature of late mismatch responses to sounds, which is reduced or absent in children with specific language impairment. *Journal of Neuroscience, 30*(46), 15578–15584.

Bishop, D. V. M., Hardiman, M. J., & Barry, J. G. (2011). Is auditory discrimination mature by middle childhood? A study using time–frequency analysis of mismatch responses from 7 years to adulthood. *Developmental Science, 14*(2), 402–416.

Bishop, D. V. M., North, T., & Donlan, C. (1995). Genetic basis of specific language impairment: Evidence from a twin study. *Developmental Medicine and Child Neurology, 37*(1), 56–71.

Bishop, D. V. M., North, T., & Donlan, C. (1996). Nonword repetition as a behavioural marker for inherited language impairment: Evidence from a twin study. *Journal of Child Psychology and Psychiatry and Allied Disciplines, 37*(4), 391–403.

Blakemore, S.-J. (2008). The social brain in adolescence. *Nature Reviews: Neuroscience, 9*, 267–277.

Blakemore, S.-J., & Choudhury, S. (2006). Development of the adolescent brain: Implications for executive function and social cognition. *Journal of Child Psychiatry, 47*, 296–312.

Boles, D. (2011). Socioeconomic status, a forgotten variable in lateralization development. *Brain and Cognition, 76*, 52–57.

Botting, N., & Conti-Ramsden, G. (2010). The role of language, social cognition, and social skill in the functional social outcomes of young adolescents with and without a history of SLI. *British Journal of Developmental Psychology, 26*(2), 281–300.

Bridgeman, E., & Snowling, M. (1988). The perception of phoneme sequence: A comparison of dyspraxic and normal children. *British Journal of Disorders of Communication, 23*(3), 245–252.

Broomfield, J., & Dodd, B. (2004). Children with speech and language disability: Caseload characteristics. *International Journal of Language and Communication Disorders, 39*(3), 303–324.

Bus, A. G., & van Ijzendoorn, M. H. (1999). Phonological awareness and early reading: A metaanalysis of experimental training studies. *Journal of Educational Psychology, 91*, 403–414.

Chen, E., Cohen, S., & Miller, G. E. (2010). How low socioeconomic status affects 2-year hormonal trajectories in children. *Psychological Science, 21*(1), 31–37.

Chiat, S. (2000). *Understanding children with language problems.* Oxford: Cambridge University Press.

Chiat, S., & Roy, P. (2008). Early phonological and sociocognitive skills as predictors of later language and social communication outcomes. *Journal of Child Psychology and Psychiatry, 49,* 635–645.

Clegg, J., Hollis, C., Mawhood, L., & Rutter, M. (2005). Developmental language disorders – a follow-up in later adult life: Cognitive, language and psychosocial outcomes. *Journal of Child Psychology and Psychiatry, 46,* 128–149.

Conn, P. (1971). *Remedial syntax.* London: ICAA.

Connor, C., Craig, H. K., Raudenbush, S. W., Heavner, K., & Zwolan, T. A. (2006). The age at which young deaf children receive cochlear implants and their vocabulary and speech-production growth: Is there an added value for early implantation? *Ear and Hearing, 27*(6), 628–644.

Conti-Ramsden, G. (2003). Processing and linguistic markers in young children with specific language impairment (SLI). *Journal of Speech, Language, and Hearing Research, 46*(5), 1029–1037.

Conti-Ramsden, G. (2008). Heterogeneity of specific language impairment in adolescent outcomes. In C. Norbury, B. Tomblin, & D. V. M. Bishop (Eds.), *Understanding developmental language disorders in children: From theory to practice* (pp. 119–133). Hove, UK: Psychology.

Croft, C., Beckett, C., Rutter, M., Castle, J., Colvert, E., Groothues, C., Hawkins, A., Kreppner, J., Stevens, S. E., & Sonuga-Barke, E. J. S. (2007). Early adolescent outcomes of institutionally-deprived and non-deprived adoptees. II: Language as a protective factor and a vulnerable outcome. *Journal of Child Psychology and Psychiatry, 48*(1), 31–44.

Dardier, V., Bernicot, J., Delanoe, A., Vanberten, M., Fayada, C., Chevignard, M., Delaye, C., Laurent-Vannier, A., & Dubois, B. (2011). Severe traumatic brain injury, frontal lesions, and social aspects of language use: A study of French-speaking adults. *Journal of Communication Disorders, 44*(3), 359–378.

Davenport, M., & Hannahs, S. J. (2010). *Introducing phonetics and phonology* (3rd ed.). London: Hodder Education.

DeLoache, J. S. (2004). Becoming symbol-minded. *Trends in Cognitive Sciences, 8*(2), 66–70.

Deoni, S. C. L., Mercure, E., Blasi, A., Gasston, D., Thomson, A., Johnson, M., Williams, S. C. R., & Murphy, D. G. M. (2011). Mapping infant brain myelination with magnetic resonance imaging. *The Journal of Neuroscience, 31*(2), 784–791.

Department of Education. (2008). *The Bercow Report. A review of services for children and young people (0–19) with speech, language and communication needs.* London: Stationery Office.

Donlan, C., Aboagye, S., Clegg, J., & Stackhouse, L. (in preparation). Long term developmental trajectories of three individuals with specific language impairments in childhood.

Doyle, O., Harmon, C. P., Heckman, J. J., & Tremblay, R. E. (2009). Investing in early human development: Timing and economic efficiency. *Economics and Human Biology, 7*(1), 1–6.

Dumontheil, I., Küster, O., Apperly, I. A., & Blakemore, S. J. (2010). Taking perspective into account in a communicative task. *NeuroImage, 52*(4), 1574–1583.

Duran, M. H. C., Guimaraes, C. A., Medeiros, L. L., & Guerreiro, M. M. (2009). Landau–Kleffner syndrome: Long-term follow-up. *Brain and Development, 31*(1), 58–63.

Everts, R., Lidzba, K., Wilke, M., Kiefer, C., Mordasini, M., Schroth, G., Perrig, W., & Steinlin, M. (2009). Strengthening of laterality of verbal and visuospatial functions during childhood and adolescence. *Human Brain Mapping, 30*(2), 473–483.

Fenson, L., Dale, P., Reznick, J. S., Bates, E., & Pethick, S. (1994). Variability in early communicative development. *Monographs of the Society for Research in Child Development, 59*, 5.

Flege, J. E., Yeni-Komshian, G. H., & Liu, S. (1999). Age constraints on second language acquisition. *Journal of Memory and Language, 41*, 78–104.

Friederici, A. D. (2005). Neurophysiological markers of early language acquisition: From syllables to sentences. *Trends in Cognitive Sciences, 9*(10), 481–488.

Friederici, A. D., Oberecker, R., & Brauer, J. (2012). Neurophysiological preconditions of syntax acquisition. *Psychological Research – Psychologische Forschung, 76*(2), 204–211.

Gaab, N., Gabrieli, J. D. E., Deutsch, G. K., Tallal, P., & Temple, E. (2007). Neural correlates of rapid auditory processing are disrupted in children with developmental dyslexia and ameliorated with training: An fMRI study. *Restorative Neurology and Neuroscience, 25*(3/4), 295–310.

Gaillard, W. D., Sachs, B. C., Whitnah, J. R., Ahmad, Z., Balsamo, L. M., Petrella, J. R., Braniecki, S. H., McKinney, C. M., Hunter, K., Xu, B., & Grandin, C. B. (2003). Developmental aspects of language processing: fMRI of verbal fluency in children and adults. *Human Brain Mapping, 18*(3), 176–185.

Gardner, H., Froud, K., McClelland, A., & van der Lely, H. K. J. (2006). Development of the Grammar and Phonology Screening (GAPS) test to assess key markers of specific language and literacy difficulties in young children. *International Journal of Language and Communication Disorders, 41*(5), 513–540.

Gathercole, S. E., & Baddeley, A. D. (1986). *The Children's Non-word Repetition Test.* London: Psychological Corporation.

Gathercole, S. E., & Baddeley, A. D. (1990). Phonological memory deficits in language disordered children: Is there a causal connection? *Journal of Memory and Language, 29*(3), 336–360.

Giedd, J. N., Blumenthal, J., Jeffries, N. O., Castellanos, F. X., Liu, H., Zijdenbos, A., Paus, T., Evans, A. C., & Rapoport, J. L. (1999). Brain development during childhood and adolescence: A longitudinal MRI study. *Nature Neuroscience, 2*, 861–863.

Giedd, J. N., Lenroot, R. K., Shaw, P., Lalonde, F., Celano, M., White, S., Tossell, J., Addington, A., & Gotgay, N. (2008). Trajectories of anatomic brain development as a phenotype. *Novertis Foundation Symposium, 289*, 101–112.

Giorgio, A., Watkins, K. E., Chadwick, M., Winmill, L., Douaud, G., De Stefano, N., Matthews, P. M., Smith, S. M., Johansen-Berg, H., & James, A. C. (2010). Longitudinal changes in grey and white matter during adolescence. *NeuroImage, 49*(1), 94–103.

Gogtay, N., Giedd, J. N, Lusk, L., Hayashi, K. M., Greenstein, D., Vaituzis, A. C., Nugent, T. F. III, Herman, D. H., Clasen, L. S., Toga, A. W., Rapoport, J. L., & Thompson,

P. M. (2004). Dynamic mapping of human cortical development during childhood through early adulthood. *Proceedings of the National Academy of Sciences of the United States of America, 101*(21), 8174–8179.

Gonzalez, J. E., Goetz, E. T., Hall, R. J., Payne, T., Taylor, A. B., Kim, M., et al. (2011). An evaluation of Early Reading First (ERF) preschool enrichment on language and literacy skills. *Reading and Writing, 24*(3), 253–284.

Gramlich, E. M. (1986). Evaluation of education projects: The case of the Perry Preschool Program. *Economics of Education Review, 5*(1), 17–21.

Grant-Hennings, D. (2000). Contextually relevant word study: Adolescent vocabulary development across the curriculum. *Journal of Adolescent and Adult Literacy, 44*(3), 268–279.

Hackman, D. A., & Farah, M. J. (2009). Socioeconomic status and the developing brain. *Trends in Cognitive Sciences, 13*(2), 65–73.

Hart, B., & Risley, T. R. (1995). *Meaningful differences in the everyday experiences of American children*. Baltimore, MD: Brookes.

Haynes, C., & Naidoo, S. (1991). *Children with specific speech and language impairment*. Oxford: Blackwell.

Hazan, V., & Barrett, S. (2000). The development of phonemic categorisation in children aged 6–12. *Journal of Phonetics, 28*(4), 377–396.

Heim, S., Friedman, J. T., Keil, A., & Benasich, A. A. (2011). Reduced sensory oscillatory activity during rapid auditory processing as a correlate of language-learning impairment. *Journal of Neurolinguistics, 24*(5), 538–555.

Houston, D. M., Stewart, J., Moberly, A., Hollich, G., & Miyamoto, R. T. (2012). Word learning in deaf children with cochlear implants: Effects of early auditory experience. *Developmental Science, 15*(3), 448–461.

Hurst, J. A., Baraitser, M., Auger, E., Graham, F., & Norell, S. (1990). An extended family with a dominantly inherited speech disorder. *Developmental Medicine and Child Neurology, 32*(4), 352–355.

Hutt, E. (1986). *Teaching language-disordered children: A structured curriculum*. London: Arnold.

Huttenlocher, P. R. (2002). *Neural plasticity: The effects of the environment on the development of the cerebral cortex*. Cambridge, MA: Harvard University Press.

Huttenlocher, P. R., & Dabholkar, A. S. (1997). Regional differences in synaptogenesis in human cerebral cortex. *The Journal of Comparative Neurology, 387*(2), 167–178.

Huttenlocher, J., Vasilyeva, J., Cymerman, E., & Levine, S. (2002). Language input and child syntax. *Cognitive Psychology, 45*, 337–374.

Huttenlocher, J., Waterfall, H., Vasilyeva, M., Vevea, J., & Hedges, L.V. (2010). Sources of variability in children's language growth. *Cognitive Psychology, 61*(4), 343–365.

Insanally, M. N., Kover, H., Kim, H., & Bao, S. (2009). Feature-dependent sensitive periods in the development of complex sound representation. *Journal of Neuroscience, 29*(17), 5456–5462.

Johnson, M. H. (2010). Interactive Specialization: A domain-general framework for human functional brain development? *Developmental Cognitive Neuroscience, 1*(1), 7–21.

Knudsen, E. I. (2004). Sensitive periods in the development of the brain and behaviour. *Journal of Cognitive Neuroscience, 16*(8), 1412–1425.

Knudsen, E. I., Heckham, J. J., Cameron, J. L., & Shonkoff, J. P. (2006). Economic, neuro-biological, and behavioral perspectives on building America's future workforce. *Proceedings of the National Academy of Sciences of the United States of America, 103*(27), 10155–10162.

Koizumi, H. (2011). Brain science and education in Japan. In S. Della Sala & M. Anderson (Eds.), *Neuroscience in education: The good, the bad, and the ugly* (pp. 319–337). Oxford: Oxford University Press.

Kuhl, P. (2007). Is speech learning "gated" by the social brain? *Developmental Science, 10*(1), 110–120.

Kuhl, P. K. (2010). Brain mechanisms in early language acquisition. *Neuron, 67*, 713–727.

Kuhl, P. K., Conboy, B. T., Padden, D., Nelson, T., & Pruitt, J. (2005). Early speech perception and later language development: implications for the "critical period". *Language Learning and Development, 1*, 237–264.

Kuhl, P. K, Conboy, B. T, Padden, D., Rivera-Gaxiola, M., & Nelson, T. (2008). Phonetic learning as a pathway to language: new data and native language magnet theory expanded (NLM-e). *Philosophical Transactions of the Royal Society B, 363*, 979–1000.

Lai, C. S. L., Fisher, S. E., Hurst, J. A., Vargha-Khadem, F., & Monaco, A. P. (2001). A forkhead-domain gene is mutated in a severe speech and language disorder. *Nature, 413*(6855), 519–523.

Laviola, G., Rea, M., Morley-Fletcher, S., Di Carlo, S., Bacosi, A., De Simone, R., Bertini, M., & Pacifici, R. (2004). Beneficial effects of enriched environment on adolescent rats from stressed pregnancies. *European Journal of Neuroscience, 20*(6), 1655–1664.

Law, J. (1994). Early language screening in City and Hackney: The concurrent validity of a measure designed for use with 2 ½ year olds. *Child Care Health and Development, 20*(5), 295–308.

Law, J., McBean, K., & Rush, R. (2011). Communication skills in a population of primary school-aged children raised in an area of pronounced social disadvantage. *International Journal of Language and Communication Disorders, 46*(6), 657–664.

Lea, J. (1970). *The colour pattern scheme.* Oxted, UK: Moor House School.

Lebel, C., & Beaulieu, C. (2009). Lateralization of the arcuate fasciculus from childhood to adulthood and its relation to cognitive abilities in children. *Human Brain Mapping, 30*(11), 3563–3573.

Leonard, L. (1998). *Children with specific language impairment.* Cambridge, MA: MIT Press.

Lewis, T. L., & Maurer, D. (2005). Multiple sensitive periods in human visual development: Evidence from visually deprived children. *Developmental Psychobiology, 46*, 163–183.

Li, Y., Ding, G., Booth, J. R., Huang, R., Lv, Y., Zang, Y., He, Y., & Peng, D. (2012). Sensitive period for white-matter connectivity of superior temporal cortex in deaf people. *Human Brain Mapping, 33*(2), 349–359.

Linck, J. A., Kroll, J. F., & Sunderman, G. (2009). Losing access to the native language while immersed in a second language: Evidence for the role of inhibition in second language learning. *Psychological Science, 20*(12), 1507–1515.

Locke, A., Ginsborg, J., & Peers, I. (2002). Development and disadvantage: Implications for the early years and beyond. *International Journal of Language and Communication Disorders, 37*(1), 3–15.

Marshall, C. M., Snowling, M. J., & Bailey, P. J. (2001). Rapid auditory processing and phonological ability in normal readers and readers with dyslexia. *Journal of Speech, Language, and Hearing Research, 44,* 925–940.

Martens, M. A., Wilson, S. J., & Reutens, D. C. (2008). Research Review: Williams syndrome: A critical review of the cognitive, behavioral, and neuroanatomical phenotype. *Journal of Child Psychology and Psychiatry, 49*(6), 576–608.

Martín-Rodríguez, J. F., & Leon-Carrion, J. (2010). Theory of mind deficits in patients with acquired brain injury: A quantitative review. *Neuropsychologia, 48*(5), 1181–1191.

McCandliss, B. D., Fiez, J. A., Protopapas, A., Conway, M., & McClelland, J. L. (2002). Success and failure in teaching the [r]-[l] contrast to Japanese adults: Tests of a Hebbian model of plasticity and stabilization in spoken language perception. *Cognitive, Affective, and Behavioural Neuroscience, 2*(2), 89–108.

McNealy, K., Mazziotta, J. C., & Dapretto, M. (2011). Age and experience shape developmental changes in the neural basis of language-related learning. *Developmental Science, 14*(6), 1261–1282.

Medina, V., Hoonhorst, I., Bogliotti, C., & Seniclaes, W. (2010). Development of voicing perception in French: Comparing adults, adolescents and children. *Journal of Phonetics, 38*(4), 493–503.

Merzenich, M. M., Jenkins, W. M., Johnston, P., Schreiner, C., Miller, S. L., & Tallal, P. (1996). Temporal processing deficits of language-learning impaired children ameliorated by training. *Science, 271*(5245), 77–81.

Mills, D. L., Coffey-Corina, S. A., & Neville, H. J. (1993). Language acquisition and cerebral specialization in 20-month-old infants. *Journal of Cognitive Neuroscience, 5,* 317–334.

Moore, J. K. (2002). Maturation of human auditory cortex: Implications for speech perception. *Annals of Otology, Rhinology and Laryngology, 189,* 7–10.

Muennig, P., Schweinhart, L., Montie, J., & Neidell, M. (2009). Effects of a prekindergarten educational intervention on adult health: 37-year follow-up results of a randomized controlled trial. *American Journal of Public Health, 99*(8), 1431–1437.

Nash, H., Leavett, R., & Childs, H. (2011). Evaluating the GAPS test as a screener for language impairment in young children. *International Journal of Language and Communication Disorders, 46*(6), 675–685.

Newbury, D. F., Bonora, E., Lamb, J. A., Fisher, S. E., Lai, C. S. L., Baird, G., Jannoun, L., Slonims, V., Stott, C. M., Merricks, M. J., Bolton, P. F., Bailey, A. J., Monaco, A. P., & the International Molecular Genetic Study of Autism Consortium. (2002). *FOXP2* is not a major susceptibility gene for autism or specific language impairment. *American Journal of Human Genetics, 70*(5), 1318–1327.

Newman, R., Ratner, N. B., Jusczyk, A. M., Jusczyk, P. W., & Dow, K. A. (2006). Infants' early ability to segment the conversational speech signal predicts later language development: A retrospective analysis. *Developmental Psychology, 42*(4), 643–655.

Nippold, M. A. (2000). Language development during the adolescent years: Aspects of pragmatics, syntax and semantics. *Topics in Language Disorders, 20,* 15–28.

Nippold, M. A., Allen, M. M., & Kirsch, D. I. (2000). How adolescents comprehend unfamiliar proverbs: The role of top-down and bottom-up processes. *Journal of Speech, Language, and Hearing Research, 43*, 621–630.

Nippold, M. A., & Duthie, J. K. (2003). Mental imagery and idiom comprehension: A comparison of school-age children and adults. *Journal of Speech, Language, and Hearing Research, 46*, 788–799.

Nippold, M. A., & Taylor, C. L. (2002). Judgments of idiom familiarity and transparency: A comparison of children and adolescents. *Journal of Speech, Language, and Hearing Research, 45*, 384–391.

Noble, K., Norman, M. F., & Farah, M. J. (2005). Neurocognitive correlates of socioeconomic status in kindergarten children. *Developmental Science, 8*(1), 74–87.

O'Connor, M., Arnott, W., McIntosh, B., & Dodd, B. (2009). Phonological awareness and language intervention in preschoolers from low socio-economic backgrounds: A longitudinal investigation. *British Journal of Developmental Psychology, 27*(4), 767–782.

Ojima, S., Matsuba-Kurita, H., Nakamura, N., Hoshino, T., & Hagiwara, H. (2011). Age and amount of exposure to a foreign language during childhood: Behavioral and ERP data on the semantic comprehension of spoken English by Japanese children. *Neuroscience Research, 70*(2), 197–205.

Paul, R., & Norbury C. F. (2012). *Language disorders from infancy through adolescence: listening, speaking, reading, writing, and communicating.* London: Elsevier Mosby.

Paus, T. 2010. Growth of white matter in the adolescent brain: myelin or axon? *Brain and Cognition, 72*(1), 26–35.

Poulsen, C., Picton, T. W., & Paus, T. (2009). Age-related changes in transient and oscillatory brain responses to auditory stimulation during early adolescence. *Developmental Science, 12*(2), 220–235.

Prathanee, B., Purdy, S., Thinkhamrop, B., Chaimay, B., Ruangdaraganon, N., Mo-Suwan, L., & Phuphaibul, R. (2009). Early language delay and predictive factors in children aged 2 years. *Journal of the Medical Association of Thailand, 92*(7): 930–938.

Pugliese, L., Dell'Acqua, F., De Schotten, M., Budisavlievic, S, Williams, S., Murphy, D., & Catani, M. (2009). Lateralization of language pathways during adolescence and early adulthood. In *Proceedings 17th Scientific Meeting, International Society for Magnetic Resonance in Medicine.*

Raizada, R. D. S., & Kishiyama, M. M. (2010). Effects of socioeconomic status on brain development, and how cognitive neuroscience may contribute to levelling the playing field. *Frontiers in Human Neuroscience, 4*(3), 1–11.

Raizada, R., Richards, T. L., Meltzoff, A., & Kuhl, P. (2008). Socioeconomic status predicts hemispheric specialisation of the left inferior frontal gyrus in young children. *NeuroImage 40*, 1392–1401.

Reilly, S., Wake, M., Ukoumunne, O. C., Bavin, E., Prior, M., Cini, E., Conway, L., Eadie, P., & Bretherton, L. (2010). Predicting language outcomes at 4 years of age: Findings from Early Language in Victoria Study. *Pediatrics, 126*(6), e1530–e1537.

Rescorla, L. (1989). The language development survey: A screening tool for delayed language in toddlers. *Journal of Speech and Hearing Disorders, 54*(4), 587–599.

Reynolds, A. J., Temple, J. A., Ou, S.-R., Arteaga, I. A., & White, B. A. B. (2011). School-based early childhood education and age-28 well-being: Effects by timing, dosage and subgroups. *Science, 333*(6040), 360–364.

Rice, M. L., Wexler, K., Marquis, J., & Hershberger, S. (2000). Acquisition of irregular past tense by children with specific language impairment. *Journal of Speech, Language, and Hearing Research, 43*(5), 1126–1145.

Richardson, F. M., Thomas, M. S. C., Filippi, R., Harth, H., & Price, C. (2010). Contrasting effects of vocabulary knowledge on temporal and parietal brain structures across lifespan. *Journal of Cognitive Neuroscience, 22*(5), 943–954.

Romine, C. B., & Reynolds, C. R. (2005). A model of the development of frontal lobe functioning: Findings from a meta-analysis. *Applied Neuropsychology, 12*(4), 190–201.

Rosen, S. (1992) Temporal information in speech: Acoustic, auditory and linguistic aspects. *Philosophical Transactions of the Royal Society of London, Series B, 336*, 367–373.

Rosen, S. (2003). Auditory processing in dyslexia and specific language impairment: Is there a deficit? What is its nature? Does it explain anything? *Journal of Phonetics, 31*(3/4), 509–527.

Slabakova, R. (2006). Is there a critical period for semantics? *Second Language Research, 22*, 302–338.

SLI Consortium. (2002). A genomewide scan identifies two novel loci involved in specific language impairment. *American Journal of Human Genetics, 70*(2), 384–398.

SLI Consortium. (2004). Highly significant linkage to the *SLI1* locus in an expanded sample of individuals affected by specific language impairment. *American Journal of Human Genetics, 74*(6), 1225–1238.

Snowling, M. J., & Hulme, C. (2011). Evidence-based interventions for reading and language difficulties: Creating a virtuous circle. *British Journal of Educational Psychology, 81*(1), 1–23.

Stevens, C., Lauinger, B., & Neville, H. (2009). Differences in the neural mechanisms of selective attention in children from different socioeconomic backgrounds: An event-related brain potential study. *Developmental Science, 12*(4), 634–646.

Stothard, S. E., Snowling, M. J., Bishop, D. V. M., Chipchase, B. B., & Kaplan, C. A. (1998). Language impaired preschoolers: A follow-up into adolescence. *Journal of Speech, Language, and Hearing Research, 41*, 407–418.

Strong, G. K., Torgerson, C. J., Torgerson, D., & Hulme, C. (2011). A systematic meta-analytic review of evidence for the effectiveness of the 'Fast ForWord' language intervention program. *Journal of Child Psychology and Psychiatry, 52*(3), 224–235.

Svirsky, M. A., Teoh, S.-W., & Neuburger, H. (2004). Development of language and speech perception in congenitally, profoundly deaf children as a function of age at cochlear implantation. *Audiology and Neuro-Otology, 9*, 224–233.

Szaflarski, J. P., Holland, S. K., Schmithorst, V. J., & Byars, A. W. (2006). An fMRI study of language lateralisation in children and adults. *Human Brain Mapping, 27*(3), 202–212.

Tallal, P., Miller, S. L., Bedi, G., Byma, G., Wang, X., Nagarajan, S. S., Schreiner, C., Jenkins, W. M., & Merzenich, M. M. (1996). Language comprehension in language-learning impaired children improved with acoustically modified speech. *Science, 271*(5245), 81–84.

Tallal, P., & Piercy, M. (1974). Developmental aphasia: Rate of auditory processing and selective impairment of consonant perception. *Neuropsychologia, 12*(1), 83–93.

Thomas, M. S. C., & Knowland, V. (2009). Sensitive periods in brain development: Implications for education policy. *European Psychiatric Review, 2*(1), 17–20.

Tomarken, A. J., Dichter, G. S., Garber, J., & Simien, C. (2004). Resting frontal brain activity: Linkages to materal depression and socioeconomic status among adolescents. *Biological Psychology, 67*, 77–102.

Tomasello, M. (1995). Joint attention as social cognition. In D. Moore & P. Dunham (Eds.), *Joint attention; Its origins and its role in development*. Hillsdale, NJ: Erlbaum.

Tomblin, J. B., Hardy J. C., & Hein, H. A. (1991). Predicting poor-communication status in preschool children using risk factors present at birth. *Journal of Speech and Hearing Research, 34*, 1096–1105.

Tomblin, J. B., Records, N. L., Buckwalter, P., Zhang, X., & Smith, E. (1997). Prevalence of specific language impairment in kindergarten children. *Journal of Speech, Language, and Hearing Research, 40*, 1245–1260.

Turkheimer, E., Haley, A., Waldron, M., D'Onofrio, B., & Gottesman, I. (2003). Socioeconomic status modifies heritability of IQ in young children. *Psychological Science, 14*, 623–628.

Turkstra, L. S., Williams, W. H., Tonks, J., & Frampton, I. (2008). Measuring social cognition in adolescents: Implications for students with TBI returning to school. *NeuroRehabilitation, 23*(6), 501–509.

Vargha-Khadem, F., Watkins, K. E., Price, C. J., Ashburner, J., Alcock, K. J., Connelly, A., Frackowiak, R. S. J., Friston, K. J., Pembrey, M. E., Mishkin, M., Gadian, D. G., & Passingham, R. E. (1998). Neural basis of an inherited speech and language disorder. *Proceedings of the National Academy of Sciences of the United States of America, 95*(21), 12695–12700.

Vasilyeva, M., Huttenlocher, J., & Waterfall, H. (2006). Effects of language intervention on syntactic skill levels in preschoolers. *Developmental Psychology, 42*(1), 164–174.

Vernes, S. C., Newbury, D. F., Abrahams, B. S., Winchester, L., Nicod, J., Groszer, M., Alarcón, M., Oliver, P. L., Davies, K. E., Geschwind, D. H., Monaco, A. P., & Fisher, S. E. (2008). A functional genetic link between distinct developmental language disorders. *New England Journal of Medicine, 359*(22), 2337–2345.

Wadman, R., Botting, N., Durkin, K., & Conti-Ramsden, G. (2011). Changes in emotional health symptoms in adolescents with specific language impairment. *International Journal of Language and Communication Disorders, 46*(6), 641–656.

Walker, D., Greenwood, C., Hart, B., & Carta, J. (1994). Prediction of school outcomes based on early language production and socioeconomic factors. *Child Development, 65*(2), 606–621.

Walsh, B., & Smith, A. (2002). Articulatory movements in adolescents: Evidence for protracted development of speech motor control processes. *Journal of Speech, Language, and Hearing Research, 45*(6), 1119–1133.

Weber-Fox, C., Leonard, L. B., Hampton-Wray, A., & Tomblin, B. (2010). Electrophysiological correlates of rapid auditory and linguistic processing in adolescents with Specific Language Impairment. *Brain and Language, 115*(3), 162–181.

Wechsler, D. (1997) *The Wechsler Adult Intelligence Scale* (3rd ed.). San Antonio, TX: Psychological Corporation.

Werker, J. F., Fennell, C. T., Corcoran, K. M., & Stager, C. L. (2002). Infants' ability to learn phonetically similar words: Effects of age and vocabulary size. *Infancy*, *3*(1), 1–30.

Werker, J. F., Gilbert, J. H. V., Humphrey, K., & Tees, R. C. (1981). Developmental aspects of cross-language speech perception. *Child Development*, *52*, 349–355.

Werker, J. F., & Tees, R. C. (1984). Cross-language speech perception: Evidence for perceptual reorganisation during the first year of life. *Infant Behaviour and Development*, *7*(1), 49–63.

Windsor, J., Glaze, L. E., & Koga, S. F. (2007). Language acquisition with limited input: Romanian institution and foster care. *Journal of Speech, Language, and Hearing Research*, *50*, 1365–1381.

Yang, F. G., Fuller, J., Khodaparast, N., & Krawczyk, D. C. (2010). Figurative language processing after traumatic brain injury in adults: A preliminary study. *Neuropsychologia*, *48*(7), 1923–1929.

Yeatman, J. D., Dougherty, R. F., Rykhlevskaia, E., Sherbondy, A. J., Deutsch, G. K., Wandell, B. A., & Ben-Shachar, M. (2011). Anatomical properties of the arcuate fasciculus predict phonological and reading skills in children. *Journal of Cognitive Neuroscience*, *23*(11), 3304–3317.

Zaias, J., Queeney, T. J., Kelley, J. B., Zakharova, E. S., & Izenwasser, S. (2008). Social and physical environmental enrichment differentially affect growth and activity of pre-adolescent and adolescent male rats. *Journal of the American Association for Laboratory Animal Science*, *47*(2), 30–34.

## Further Reading

Better Communication Research Programme. Retrieved June 18, 2013, from http://www2.warwick.ac.uk/fac/soc/cedar/better/

Bishop, D. V. M. (2007). Using mismatch negativity to study central auditory processing in developmental language and literacy impairments: Where are we, and where should we be going? *Psychological Bulletin*, *133*(4), 651–672.

Johnson, M. H., & de Haan, M. (2011). Language. In *Developmental Cognitive Neuroscience* (pp. 164–183). London: Wiley.

Snowling, M. J., & Hulme, C. (2011). Evidence-based interventions for reading and language difficulties: Creating a virtuous circle. *British Journal of Educational Psychology*, *81*(1), 1–23.

# Chapter 7

# Literacy Development

## Liory Fern-Pollak and Jackie Masterson

The act of reading may seem straightforward. However, deeper reflection on what is involved when we see a set of printed symbols on a piece of paper, or a computer screen, or a street sign, may lead us to wonder what actually happens in our brain? How does this information that is first perceived by our eyes become information that we can sound out or process internally, to a point where we can understand the underlying *message* behind it? This simple printed information is put together by our brain; we formulate the sound of this information, the meaning, and the context, which enables us to read books with deep philosophical ideas, which fill us with inspiration or indignation, or magazines with idle gossip about our favorite soap stars, which fills us with joy. All through the conversion of little lines, circles, dashes, and points (orthography) into "soundful" (phonology) and "meaningful" (semantics) letters, and words, and sentences, that are perceived by our eyes and put together by our brain to become literature, news, letters, instruction manuals, or Christmas cards. This is far from straightforward, because we do not learn this just by absorbing it from the people around us, as we learn to speak and under- stand spoken language. Learning how to read requires systematic instruction and effortful studying. Children who do not learn how to read remain illiterate until they do. This suggests that our brain, which seems to have hardwired language areas, can utilize these and other areas to extend our ability to speak and under- stand speech to *read* and *write* speech in the process of learning how to read. Understanding the cerebral mechanisms that are at play while we read and write is the basic tenet of cognitive neuroscience. While fascinating in its own right, this

*Educational Neuroscience*, First Edition. Edited by Denis Mareschal, Brian Butterworth and Andy Tolmie.
© 2014 John Wiley & Sons, Ltd. Published 2014 by John Wiley & Sons, Ltd.

is also important for understanding how the brain works, or rather fails to work, when things go wrong.

When children struggle with learning how to read, we try to help them by assessing different aspects of their language abilities. This is in order to diagnose the cause of the problem, and to provide the appropriate (if available) remediation, or techniques to cope with the problem. These techniques were developed from several streams of knowledge, namely educational, developmental, cognitive, and perceptual psychology, and more recently cognitive neuroscience. The merging of all these wonderful streams is the newly emerging field of educational neuroscience.

In this chapter, we review recent studies that have focused on understanding how our brain changes as we learn how to read. Of particular interest are the studies that have set out to investigate how young children learn to make neural connections between brain regions specialized for processing visual information and those that process spoken information (see Chapter 6, "Language Development") through the course of literacy acquisition.

We first present a brief outline of what is known about language processing in the adult brain, including reading and dyslexia, and then go on to describe studies that have focused on reading and reading impairment in the developing brain. Through this knowledge we can develop a deeper understanding of what processes the developing brain goes through to become literate.

## Language in the Brain

The human body has evolved to utilize areas specialized for eating and breathing to produce sounds that constitute verbal language. The human brain, in turn, evolved to manage the motor programming necessary for generating movements of the mouth and tongue in order to speak. Likewise, the body has a specialized organ for hearing sounds, and so the brain has specialized areas that process these sounds and put them together in order to make sense of them and discriminate language-related sounds from other environmental sounds. Current knowledge about these areas has come from a myriad of studies using diverse types of method, from lesion studies to structural and functional neuroimaging.

### Inferring cerebral function through observed dysfunction

While most higher cognitive functions cannot be said to be localized in particular cerebral regions, language processing has been repeatedly associated with a number of regions, predominantly within the left cerebral hemisphere, as first pointed out by the French physician Paul Broca in 1861. Broca noted that damage to the left inferior frontal gyrus (IFG), adjacent to the face area of the motor cortex, led to deficits in speech generation and fluency, coupled with intact comprehension.

In 1874, the German neurologist and psychiatrist Carl Wernicke identified another type of disorder, characterized by impaired comprehension and incoherent, yet fluent speech. This type of impairment, sometimes referred to as fluent, or Wernicke's aphasia, was attributed to lesions in the left superior temporal gyrus (STG), located between the primary auditory cortex and the angular gyrus, within the association cortex. The dissociability between these two types of impairment has led to the notion that, while the IFG may be involved in the mediation of language production, the STG may play a predominant role in language comprehension.

In 1885, German physician Ludwig Lichtheim reported the case of an aphasic patient who exhibited an inability to repeat sentences and a tendency to generate semantically anomalous speech, with otherwise unimpaired comprehension and utterance. Following a post mortem examination, it was discovered that the patient had suffered damage to a bundle of white-matter fibers referred to as the arcuate fasciculus, which connects the IFG and STG. The type of aphasia associated with lesions to this tract is now referred to as "conduction aphasia" (Gazzaniga, Ivry, & Mangun, 1998). Towards the end of the nineteenth century, the French neurologist Joseph Jules Dejerine (1892) identified two major reading impairments: *alexia with agraphia* and *alexia without agraphia*, related to specific cortical lesions. Alexia with agraphia was characterized by acquired deficits in reading (alexia) and writing (agraphia) that were related to lesions in the left angular gyrus (see later, Figure 7.3). By contrast, alexia without agraphia (also referred to as pure alexia), characterized by reading impairment with intact writing ability, was associated with lesions to the left occipital cortex and the splenium of the corpus callosum,[1] and was therefore thought to arise from a disconnection of the left angular gyrus and the visual cortex. The left angular gyrus was thus assumed to be involved in storing memories of visual word forms, an idea that later gave rise to the concept of the mental lexicon: a cerebral "database", which stores concepts of words and visual word forms represented in scattered cortical regions (rather than solely the left angular gyrus). These are connected to areas within the somatosensory junction, which link and integrate visual, auditory, and somatic information from the surrounding environment (see, e.g., Gazzaniga et al., 1998; Geschwind, 1979; see Coltheart, 2004, for a review).

---

[1] The corpus callosum is the fat bundle of white-matter fibres that connects the left and right hemispheres of the brain and facilitates interhemispheric communication. The splenium is the posterior part of the corpus callosum, and as such facilitates the transmission of visual information (among other types of somatosensory information) between the two hemispheres.

Based on the association between cortical lesions and language impairment, Wernicke developed a model for language processing, whose general principles prevail in modern neurolinguistics. According to this model, the underlying structure for language processing is the STG, often referred to as Wernicke's area. For language production, concepts from the mental lexicon are initially processed by the STG, then transferred through the arcuate fasciculus to Broca's area – the IFG, where a detailed and coordinated vocalization "program" is formulated. In turn, this information is transferred to the face area in the primary motor cortex (PMC), where further processing results in speech. Wernicke's account of language comprehension follows a reversed pathway, whereby auditory input is transferred from the primary auditory cortex (PAC) to the STG for coherent decoding, integrated in the IFG to form internal vocalization, and in turn transferred to the mental lexicon for meaning retrieval (Gazzaniga et al., 1998; Price, 2000).

Similarly, nineteenth-century models for the process of reading incorporated largely the same left-lateralized regions as involved in verbal language processing, as well as the visual cortex and regions around the left angular gyrus. Since the time of Broca, Wernicke, and Dejerine, various other types of language impairment have been defined, the majority of which have been associated with damage to left-lateralized cortical regions. For example, damage to the left angular gyrus, the middle portion of the left fusiform gyrus (referred to by some as the visual word form area, e.g., Cohen et al., 2002), and the pathways connecting these regions with the visual cortex, has been associated with various types of alexia (Damasio & Damasio, 1983; Geschwind, 1979). Similarly, damage to the left supramarginal and lingual gyri has been associated with word-finding difficulty, or anomia (Pinker, 1994).

It is remarkable that such a large body of knowledge was gathered in those early years, relying solely on inference of the function of cerebral structures from observed dysfunction, since cortical lesions tend to be extensive and extremely variable across patients, and may thus have differential effects on cognitive processing. Since the late 1980s, the development of neuroimaging techniques, in conjunction with behavioral methods as well as observed deficits, has provided an invaluable opportunity to study language processing in healthy individuals and in those with brain lesions *in vivo*, thus enabling a more controlled and reliable approach to gathering knowledge, particularly on the process of reading, as will be described in the next section.

## To read and read not…

Explained simply, reading begins with visual identification of word forms and culminates in comprehension. However, the processes occurring between the initial and final stages of reading are far from simple. Some words may be read very quickly and easily, while others may involve considerable time and effort. For example, simple, consistently spelled, familiar and short words (e.g., cat, desk, had) can be recognized very quickly and easily, whereas complex, irregular, or rare words (e.g., hymn, cough, hiatus) may take considerably more time and effort, particularly if they are long (e.g., contradistinction, interdenominational)! Similarly, reading words that have not been seen before, or nonexistent words that are not represented in the mental lexicon (nonwords, such as *baft, zode,* or *kench*) may take even longer than complex rare *real* words (Balota & Chumbley, 1984; Forster & Chambers, 1973; Frederiksen & Kroll, 1976; Glushko, 1979; Weekes, Coltheart, & Gordon, 1997). Indeed, accurate reading of long, complex, rare words and nonwords often requires assembly of small linguistic units such as syllables or individual letters, whereas radenig sohrt, siplme, frnqeuet wrdos deos nto nsescealriy reuiqre scuh fnie dteial. This "tolerance to letter position" is often referred to as the "Cambridge effect" (Frost, 2012), and suggests that reading may be achieved by reliance on different strategies: at the two extremes lie whole-word recognition and letter-by-letter reading, respectively.

*To read...*    Several theories and computer-simulated models have been developed to explain how visual identification of word forms culminates in comprehension, in the process of natural reading. Two of the most prominent models are presented herein.

The *dual-route reading model* (Coltheart & Rastle, 1994; Rastle & Coltheart, 1998) postulates the existence of two parallel mechanisms; a lexical route and a sublexical/phonological route (Figure 7.1). The lexical route is thought of as a fast and direct process, whereby the orthographic form of whole words is accessed in the orthographic lexicon, followed either by directly addressing the whole word's sound in the phonological lexicon (e.g., in the case of familiar words), or via the mediation of semantic knowledge of stored concepts (e.g., in the case of rare words).

By contrast, the sublexical/phonological route involves sequential parsing of the letter string, with graphemic information being transformed into phonology by mean of stored grapheme-to-phoneme rules (see Figure 7.1), thus bypassing both orthographic and phonological lexicons. This route is designed for coping with novel words, which do not have a stored lexical entry. The two routes (lexical and sublexical) converge at the "phoneme buffer", where phonological output is prepared for articulation.

According to this model, natural reading involves the parallel activation of the two routes in a competitive manner, such that the preferred route will be the first to generate the correct pronunciation for any given letter string. In the case of high-frequency words, fast and efficient reading is achieved

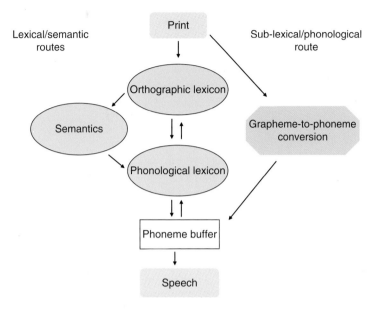

**Figure 7.1**   Schematic representation of the dual-route reading model (after Ziegler, Perry, & Coltheart, 2000).

thanks to the fast activation of the lexical route. However, in the case of low-frequency words, the increased time required for semantic access may allow for the activation of the sublexical phonological route simultaneously, thus creating a conflict between the two routes. In such cases, the preference for either route may be modulated by factors such as spelling consistency and word length.

For example, in the case of low-frequency inconsistent words such as *yacht*, the use of grapheme-to-phoneme conversion would lead to incorrect pronunciation – it would be pronounced as rhyming with *matched*. The correct pronunciation of such words thus requires a "lexical lookup procedure" (Rastle & Coltheart, 2000, p. 343), and the competition between the routes may lead to slower reading than that achieved for high-frequency inconsistent words. By the same token, the correct pronunciation of a new word or a nonword such as *starn* requires sublexical/phonological recoding. Otherwise, "lexical capture" (Funnell & Davidson, 1989) would occur, and lead to its pronunciation as the real word *start*. However, in the case of an irregularly spelled nonword, lexical access may be inevitable. For example, the nonword *jough* requires grapheme-to-phoneme conversion, followed by lexical lookup, that would lead to its pronunciation as rhyming either with *cough*, with *tough*, or with *dough*.

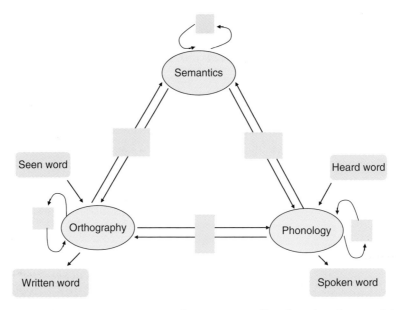

**Figure 7.2**   Schematic representation of connectionist distributed reading model (after Plaut & Kello, 1999). Light-grey circles and ovals represent "hidden units".

An alternative to the dual-route model, the parallel distributed connectionist reading model (Figure 7.2), postulates that words and nonwords are all read by a single mechanism based on the reader's experience (Plaut & Kello, 1999; Plaut, McClelland, Seidenberg & Patterson, 1996; Seidenberg & McClelland, 1989). According to this alternative model, reading requires the orthographic patterns of a word to generate an appropriate phonological pattern, achieved by the cooperative and competitive interactions between three types of unit: orthographic, phonological, and semantic (see Figure 7.2).

Within this theoretical framework, naming words and nonwords alike occurs through a single interactive process relying on a network of weighted connections between orthography, phonology, and semantics, which are sensitive to statistical relationships between "hidden" units (depicted by light-grey oval shapes in the figure), constituting distributed internal representations. These internal representations are modulated by the level of visual exposure to words through reading experience. Orthographic, phonological, and semantic units consist of two layers: a visual input (seeing the word on the page), and an articulatory output (saying it out loud), which are mediated by hidden units. When reading familiar words, the network generates an orthographic representation of the entire word, which with weighted input from semantics is used as input for the sequential articulatory output, much like the lexical route of the DRC model. The weight of the semantic input may vary with exposure as well as with consistency level, such that inconsistent words require a greater semantic input than consistent words (Plaut et al., 1996). By contrast, in the case of new words or nonwords, the network activates a sequence of phonemes, and simultaneously monitors grapheme position. The visual monitoring remains fixed as long as the graphemic and phonemic units are consistent. However, in the case of inconsistent novel words or nonwords, the model relies on multiple visual fixations on the stimulus, virtually grapheme by grapheme, until the correct pronunciation is achieved, much like the phonological route in the DRC model. The main difference between the two models lies in the principle of binarity postulated by the DRC model (two distinct routes), versus the graded nature of the connectionist model.

*To read not...*   Cases of reading impairments, such as developmental and acquired dyslexia, exemplify the complexity of the reading process. Developmental dyslexia refers to reading disability that is apparent in early childhood, whereas acquired dyslexia refers to reading disability that manifests following a stroke or other incident leading to brain damage, in individuals who previously had no apparent reading disability.

Much of the early insight into the different processes that may operate in normal reading has come from the identification of different types of acquired impairment and their dissociability (Marshall & Newcombe, 1973). For example, patients with *surface dyslexia* may read regularly spelled words correctly, but tend to make regularization errors when reading irregularly spelled words (such as reading the word *pint* as rhyming with *hint*). This type of dyslexia may arise as a result of impaired mediation of meaning retrieval (lexical access), and is typically associated with anterolateral temporal lobe atrophy (Patterson & Hodges, 1992). By contrast, patients with *phonological dyslexia* may be able to recognize familiar words regardless of their spelling regularity, but exhibit an inability to correctly pronounce novel words and nonwords. These individuals may read the nonword *motch* as *match* or the nonword *starn* as *start*, suggesting that the impairment may lie in the process of phonological recoding. This type of acquired dyslexia is usually associated with large lesions encompassing left temporoparietal and frontal regions, caused by middle cerebral artery infarcts. Likewise, a third type of impairment, referred to as *deep dyslexia*, is characterized by both lexical and sublexical impairments, in addition to a tendency to make semantic errors, such as reading the word *lemon* as *orange* (reviewed by Gazzaniga et al., 1998; Price, 2000; Price & Mechelli, 2005).

Unlike acquired dyslexia, developmental dyslexia is characterized primarily by reading difficulty in the absence of any neurological damage, or indeed any sensory or intellectual disorders. However, it may co-occur with attention deficit hyperactivity disorder (ADHD), dyscalculia, and dyspraxia, among other developmental disorders. Children diagnosed with dyslexia may therefore also show delays in the onset of language production, and later on difficulties with spelling. The precise incidence of developmental dyslexia is thought to range between 5 and 17.5% among adults and children around the world (Shaywitz, 1998).

Although now widely regarded as a neurobiological disorder with genetic origin, the behavioral symptoms observed in dyslexia may have several different underlying causes, which can affect their manifestation in isolation or in conjunction. Deficits in auditory processing skills (Tallal, 1980), visual processing skills (Stein, 2001), or visual attentional skills (Bosse, Tainturier, & Valdois, 2007) have been associated with poor reading performance observed in dyslexic children and adults, giving rise to a plethora of theories and hypotheses. The most prevalent theory, particularly in the English-speaking world, is the "phonological deficit hypothesis" (Snowling, 2000), which postulates that deficient representation, storage, and/or retrieval of speech sounds lead to difficulties of learning and maintaining awareness of the associations between written letters or letter clusters (graphemes) and their constituent sounds (phonemes). For a detailed review of the different theories of dyslexia please see Ramus (2003). Diagnosis of developmental dyslexia is therefore a complex process, which requires careful consideration of the possible underlying cause(s) in order to provide the most suitable treatment. This is typically provided through educational intervention, which can help dyslexic readers to complete everyday reading and writing tasks through compensatory strategies, but cannot "cure" or eliminate the underlying cause.

## Neuroimaging Studies of Reading

One of the first studies to examine the processes of reading using neuroimaging in healthy participants was conducted by Pugh and colleagues (Pugh et al., 1996). Testing 38 native English speakers using functional magnetic resonance imaging (fMRI), these authors sought to isolate cortical networks associated with orthographic, phonological, and lexical/semantic processes in reading using four types of judgment task: letter-case judgment (orthographic task), nonword rhyme judgment (phonological task), semantic category judgment (semantic task), and line judgment (baseline task).

Results showed that, while orthographic processing was associated with strong activation in lateral middle and inferior occipital cortex bilaterally, phonological processing was strongly related to activation within left lateral orbital, prefrontal dorsolateral, and inferior frontal cortex, though some activation within these regions was also observed during the semantic task. In contrast, semantic processing was specifically associated with activation within the medial occipital cortex and left superior and middle temporal regions.

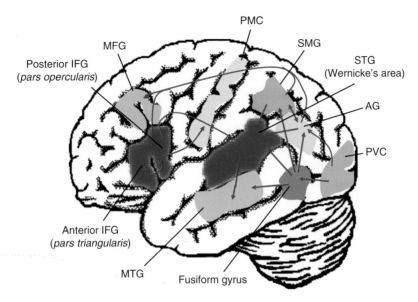

**Figure 7.3** Schematic representation of currently recognized major regions involved in reading. Red arrows represent information flow along white-matter pathways. IFG, inferior frontal gyrus; MFG, middle frontal gyrus; PMC, primary motor cortex; AG, angular gyrus; STG, superior temporal gyrus; SMG, supramarginal gyrus; PVC, primary visual cortex; MTG, middle temporal gyrus.

These findings therefore indicated that functional specialization for the mediation of orthographic, phonological, and semantic processing exists within the language processing network, which led the authors to propose a "sketch" of the possible architecture of some of the anatomical regions associated with reading. According to this model, initial visual processing of print recruits striate and extrastriate occipital regions (Figure 7.3), followed by mapping of featural information onto orthographic representations mediated by lateral and medial extrastriate networks. Then, various inferior frontal and temporal regions contribute to the assembly of phonological representations, and finally, access to and decisions about lexical–semantic information engages the middle and superior temporal gyri bilaterally. In those early days of neuroimaging, the authors noted that some regions known to be involved in the process of reading, such as the angular and supramarginal gyri, could not be visualized under the experimental conditions used at the time. Investigating reading processes within these regions and providing a more detailed account of the neural networks specifically involved in orthographic, phonological, and semantic processing was therefore the task of subsequent studies.

A positron emission tomography study conducted by Fiez, Balota, Raichle, and Petersen (1999) extended these findings by showing significant patterns of activation associated with reading in a number of regions including bilateral inferior and middle frontal gyri, precentral gyrus and medial frontal gyrus, bilateral superior temporal gyrus and bilateral fusiform gyrus. These authors proposed that activation in the left superior temporal gyrus reflected sublexical/phonological processing, and activation in the precentral gyrus and supplementary motor area may be elicited as a result of subvocalization of the stimuli. At the same time, the inferior prefrontal cortex may underlie sublexical/phonological processing such as effortful retrieval, manipulation, or selection of phonological representations.

In another study, McDermott and colleagues (McDermott, Petersen, Watson, & Ojemann, 2003) employed fMRI to examine the role of the left prefrontal cortex in lexical/semantic and sublexical/phonological processing. Results associated semantic processing with activation within the anterior portion of the IFG (triangular part) and in a region near the left superior/middle temporal sulcus. In contrast, phonological processing was associated with activation in a ventral region within the posterior (opercular) part of the gyrus, as well as the left precentral gyrus and left inferior parietal cortex. These authors therefore appeared to successfully distinguish between regions involved in semantic and phonological processing within the network of cortical regions involved in visual word recognition.

Since then, studies using languages other than English, and with other neuroimaging modalities, have produced similar findings. For example, Wydell, Vuorinen, Helenius, and Salmelin (2003) utilized magnetoencephalography (MEG; for a description of this neuroimaging technique see Chapter 2) to examine the neural correlates of printed word length and lexicality effects during reading in Finnish. MEG provides considerably better temporal resolution than hemodynamic imaging techniques such as fMRI, albeit with relatively less accurate spatial information. The authors compared the patterns of activation and their time course, while participants were silently reading short and long words and nonwords. The activation for short words and long nonwords was suggested to maximally reflect lexical/semantic and sublexical/phonological processing, respectively. Results showed that reading led to early activation (within 200 ms of stimulus onset) primarily within the occipital midline, with significantly stronger patterns of activation associated with reading long letter strings (both words and nonwords). After 200 ms, the activation patterns expanded anteriorly, with most significant long-sustained duration of activation predominantly (though not exclusively) located within the left superior temporal cortex. These clusters were detected in response to long nonwords. In contrast, reading short words revealed little activation, detected in the left parietal cortex, in the vicinity of the angular gyrus, and right mid-frontal cortex. Interestingly, effects of letter-string length (short versus long) were predominantly observed during the early course of activation, whereas effects of lexicality (words versus nonwords) were only apparent at the later source clusters. These effects were observed as a systematic increase in duration of activation for each stimulus type, i.e. shortest duration associated with short words, somewhat longer duration for short nonwords, longer yet for long words, and longest duration of activation associated with long nonword stimuli. The authors therefore suggested that the combined length and lexicality effects observed within the left superior temporal region may reflect both types of processing during reading.

More recently, Bick, Goelman, and Frost (2008) examined the neural correlates of reading in Hebrew using fMRI, employing four different types of linguistic task. In a semantic task, participants decided whether two words were semantically related; in an orthographic task, participants decided whether two words were orthographically similar; in a phonological task, participants performed a rhyming decision with two words; and in a morphological task, participants were instructed to decide whether two words were derived from the same root. Results showed that linguistic tasks elicited activation within the same neural circuits as identified previously in reading tasks, namely left-lateralized regions within the middle/inferior frontal cortex, occipitotemporal cortex including fusiform gyrus, inferior parietal cortex, and middle/superior temporal cortex. Importantly, within the middle/inferior frontal cortex, as seen previously, the semantic task was associated with activation in relatively more anterior and inferior regions relative to the other tasks. In addition, this type of processing was associated with activation within the superior temporal cortex, further strengthening the suggestion that this region can be associated with both semantic and phonological processing. The orthographic task also led to activation within this region, as well as the fusiform gyrus, and the border of the superior occipital gyrus and the inferior parietal lobule. The phonological task led to preferential activation in more posterior portions of the inferior frontal gyrus and precentral gyrus, while the morphological task led to preferential activation in the middle frontal gyrus.

Taken together, the data reported by the studies above indicate that early visual analysis of all printed material occurs within the occipital cortex bilaterally, prior to any linguistic processing, gradually engaging left occipital regions for orthographic processing. Subsequently, lexical/semantic processing may be mediated predominantly within the anterior (triangular) portion of the left inferior frontal gyrus and middle frontal gyrus, while sublexical/phonological processing may be subserved predominantly by regions located around the left precentral gyrus and the lateral aspect of the inferior frontal cortex, such as the inferior frontal sulcus and opercular part of the inferior frontal gyrus. Areas that act as mediators between orthographic and phonological information lie within the left association cortex, such as the left inferior parietal lobule, encompassing the angular and supramarginal gyri, as well as regions around the left middle and superior temporal gyrus.

Based on the synthesis of the data reported in the neuroimaging studies described above, Figure 7.1 illustrates a plausible schematic representation of the brain regions involved in reading in the adult brain.

## What is the difference in brain activation between dyslexic readers and skilled readers?

So far we have seen that, in the adult brain, the process of normal reading is mediated by a left-lateralized frontoparietal network, including regions such as the IFG, the angular and supramarginal gyri, and a region of the inferotemporal cortex, commonly referred to as the *visual word form area*. What about abnormal reading? Until the early 2000s only studies of adults existed. Some examined cases of acquired dyslexia following brain injury (as described earlier), while others studied young adults with developmental dyslexia. Among the latter (reviewed by Price & McCrory, 2005), some contradictory findings have emerged due to differences in methodology and sampling. From these early studies, the consensus that emerged was that differences in patterns of activation exist between dyslexic participants and controls within the reading network. Specifically, reduced activation was observed in the left inferior frontal cortex including Broca's area, implicated in output phonology and articulation processes; supramarginal gyrus, implicated in phonological processing; angular gyrus, implicated in the conversion of visual information to phonological information; and inferior temporal cortex, or visual word form area, implicated in encoding of the abstract identity of visual letter strings and rapid recognition of familiar words, which develops with reading experience (see, e.g., Brunswick, McCrory, Price, Frith, & Frith, 1999; Paulesu et al., 2001). These findings have given rise to the notion that the dysfunction of frontoparietal regions required for phonological processing may lead to the poor development of occipitotemporal regions required for fast recognition of words, and thereby impede accurate and fluent reading. In essence, the suggestion has been that the core deficit in dyslexia is phonological in nature (cf. Snowling, 2000).

A more recent line of research has also implicated visual attention span as contributing to poor reading outcome in dyslexia, independently of a phonological deficit (Bosse et al., 2007; Dubois et al., 2010; Valdois et al., 2003). These studies suggest that dysfunction of left-lateralized superior parietal regions, implicated in visual attention, may be an underlying cause of reading difficulty. For example, Peyrin, Lallier, and Valdois (2008) compared the activation patterns of a group of skilled readers with those of a group of dyslexic participants showing visual attention span disorder. The behavioral reading measure in the study was a global report task. This consists of the brief display of sequences of five consonants (e.g., RSHDM). Individuals with a normal visual attention span are able to perceive all five consonants in one visual fixation, whereas those with a reduced span may only perceive two or three consonants (Valdois et al., 2003). In control participants selective activation during performance of the task was observed in the left angular middle occipital gyrus and left superior parietal lobule, whereas in dyslexic participants with a visual attention span deficit no activation was detected within these regions. Subsequent studies by this group (Peyrin et al., 2012; Valdois, Peyrin, & Baciu, 2009) have used more stringent visual attention span tasks, requiring participants to judge whether two visually presented elements belong to the same category (letters and geometrical shapes, described in detail in the next section). These have corroborated previous findings.

All of these adult studies largely show only subtle differences in the neural systems engaged by dyslexic participants and controls during reading. The pattern that has emerged from this research seems to be that dyslexic participants engage largely the same system as normal readers, but the extent or intensity of the activated regions is different. This raises the question of whether the situation is the same at earlier stages of development. Are the patterns of activation observed in dyslexic adults a result of a lifetime of poor reading, or does abnormal neural processing characterize dyslexia in children?

## Educational neuroscience and dyslexia

*Looking inside the brains of dyslexic children*    Shaywitz et al. (2002) used fMRI to compare the patterns of brain activation in 70 dyslexic children and 74 typically developing (TD) readers, aged between 7 and 18 years. The authors used a series of five progressively more demanding tasks, tapping visual, phonological, and semantic processing: first, a line orientation task requiring only visual processing (e.g., do \\V and \\V match?); second, a more complex visual task of letter case judgment (e.g., do bbBb and bbBb match?); third, a simple phonological task of letter rhyme judgment (e.g., do T and V rhyme?), and fourth, a nonword-rhyme task (e.g., do *lete* and *jete* rhyme?). Finally, a semantic categorization task (e.g., are *corn* and *rice* in the same semantic category?) was administered. Dyslexic participants performed significantly more poorly than TD controls on these tasks, and showed reduced activation within left posterior regions associated with reading. Correlating the reading performance with the patterns of activation during the different tasks revealed a positive relationship between reading performance and increased activation within inferior left middle temporal cortex during rhyme judgment and semantic judgment, and a positive relationship between reading performance and activation within temporoparietal regions bilaterally (angular/supramarginal), during the semantic task only. Negative correlation was seen between reading and performance with activation in the right occipitotemporal region. The positive correlations were in keeping with previous findings in adult studies, showing reduced activation in dyslexic participants within inferior left middle temporal cortex (e.g., Brunswick et al., 1999; Paulesu et al., 2001).

Furthermore, correlating the pattern of activation with age showed that older dyslexic children tended to activate the inferior frontal cortex bilaterally more than younger dyslexic participants during the nonword rhyme task, in keeping with previously observed data in adults (Shaywitz et al., 1998). This finding suggests that, with reading experience, dyslexic children learn to compensate for the disruption in posterior regions. Moreover, during the semantic categorization task, older dyslexic children tended to activate the right inferior frontal gyrus, whereas the TD readers activated the left homolog gyrus. This observation therefore suggests that older dyslexic participants compensate for the failure to engage left inferior frontal regions required for semantic processing, by recruiting "an ancillary system" (Shaywitz et al., 2002, p. 106).

This study was one of the first to localize reading impairment in children's brains, and provided insight as to what changes might occur in the brains of dyslexic participants with reading experience. Since then, several other studies have relied on the technological advancement and improvement of neuroimaging techniques to corroborate and extend these findings. For example, van der Mark et al. (2009) examined the activation patterns in dyslexic children specifically within the occipitotemporal region, encompassing the so-called visual word form area. The aim of this study was to assess whether reduced activation in this region could be associated with dyslexic symptoms in children with only a few years of reading experience, under the assumption that this region is associated with two types of processing specific to reading, as previously observed in adult studies: (1) identification of coarse characteristics of letters (as opposed to false fonts), and (2) faster and more efficient processing of familiar words (as opposed to novel words or nonwords). Eighteen children with dyslexia and 24 TD readers, all aged between 10 and 13 years, were scanned while performing a phonological lexical decision task, which required both phonological and orthographic processing. In this task, participants were presented with four types of visual stimulus: (1) real words, (2) pseudohomophones,[2] (3) nonwords, and (4) false fonts, and were asked to indicate whether these sounded like real words or not.

---

[2]  Pseudohomophones are nonwords that, although spelled differently, are pronounced in the same way, e.g., *zode* and *zoad*, *caid* and *kade*.

Outside the scanner, participants were also given an orthographic judgment task, as an additional behavioral measure of performance. In this latter task children were shown either the same words, pseudohomophones, and nonwords from the phonological task, or misspelled versions of these items, and were asked to indicate whether they were correctly spelled or not. This determined children's ability to differentiate between the familiar and the unfamiliar form of the items seen in the scanner.

Dyslexic children were significantly slower than TD controls at judging whether items sounded like real words, and significantly less accurate at rejecting pseudohomophones and nonwords, but were as accurate as controls at accepting real words and rejecting false fonts. In the orthographic judgment task, dyslexic participants were significantly less accurate than controls in identifying familiar forms of the pseudohomophones, but were as accurate as controls at identifying real words and familiar nonwords.

Differences in the patterns of activation within the visual word form system were also observed between dyslexic participants and TD controls. First, when looking for effects of print specificity, the authors found greater activation for real letter strings in more anterior portions of the region, and greater activation for false fonts associated with more posterior portions. The authors termed this a "posterior-to-anterior gradient", which they observed in control children, but not in dyslexic children. Second, TD control children showed an orthographic familiarity effect, reflected in greater activation for unfamiliar printed stimuli compared with familiar words, whereas dyslexic participants did not show this effect. This study therefore indicated that, even at relative early stages of reading acquisition, dyslexic children show evidence of an impaired visual word form system for both the coarse identification of print and word familiarity, compared with TD children.

More recently, Valdois' group (Peyrin, Demonet, N'Guyen-Morel, Le Bas, & Valdois, 2011) scanned 12 dyslexic children with visual attention span disorder and 12 TD readers, aged 10 years on average. Children performed the visual discrimination task previously used in the researchers' adult studies, where they were asked to judge whether two visually presented elements belonged to the same category or not. One element was presented in the center of the screen and the other at three degrees of eccentricity to the left or to the right of the central element. Pairs of elements were either two letters (e.g., E E), or a letter and a geometrical shape (e.g., Δ E). There were two conditions of presentation: an easy condition, in which the visual elements were presented in isolation, and an attentionally more demanding–difficult condition, where the peripheral element was flanked by two "X" letters (e.g., E XEX). The TD control children showed slower reaction times when discriminating whether the peripherally presented flanked elements (difficult condition) were the same as or different to the centrally presented elements than in the easy condition. Concordantly, greater activation was seen within the left superior parietal lobule during this condition. This finding corroborated the adult data, suggesting that the task engaged cerebral regions specifically involved in visual attention, and that the flanked condition was attentionally more demanding than the isolated condition. The dyslexic children were as accurate as controls in the flanked condition, but showed significantly slower responses. The patterns of activation showed that the left superior parietal lobule was significantly less activated during this task, as compared with controls. At the same time, the dyslexic children showed increased activation in medial frontal and occipital regions, associated with perceptual visual processing and general attention, not seen in the control group.

This observation suggests that, in the absence of normal parietal activation, dyslexic children were engaging compensatory neural resources, which may have contributed to performing the task accurately, but still more slowly than control children. These authors therefore suggested that the left superior parietal lobule may play a key role in early reading acquisition, where letter identification elicits great demands on the attentional system. Children who have difficulty attending to letter strings due to a deficient functioning of the left parietal system may therefore miss out on the critical step of establishing strong mental representations of letter strings, which later consolidate as visual word forms, which in turn leads to nonfluent word recognition and the ensuing symptoms of dyslexia.

*Intervention studies*    One of the goals of studying the neural correlates of reading disability is to be able to define the specific type of deficit, in order to tailor specific types of educational remediation. In this section we summarize a few of the studies that have examined the effects of different types of educational remediation on patterns of neural activation and connectivity in children's brains.

Shaywitz et al. (2004) set out to assess the effects of educational remediation on reading fluency, and examine whether this can be linked to changes in patterns of activation in occipitotemporal regions required for skilled reading. The authors administered what they called "evidence-based" phonologically mediated reading intervention to a group of 37 dyslexic children, aged between six and nine years, which aimed to help children develop phonological knowledge and their understanding of the relationship between orthography and phonology. The children were provided with 50 minutes of daily individual tutoring at school for eight months (experimental intervention). This group was compared with a group of 12 dyslexic children of the same age, who received a variety of interventions that were commonly provided within school settings (community intervention), rather than in an experimental setting, such as in a randomized controlled trial, or "evidence based". A third group of children comprised a control group and consisted of 28 children considered good readers (scoring above the 39th percentile on standardized reading tests).

All children were scanned using fMRI immediately before and immediately after the period of intervention. Children in the experimental intervention group were also scanned a year after intervention was completed. In the scanner, children were given a cross-modal letter-identification task, which involved a forced-choice decision as to whether a previously presented spoken letter name (auditory modality) matched a letter presented on the screen (visual modality). The task had two experimental conditions: (1) easy condition, comprising phonologically dissimilar letters (e.g., B and K), and (2) difficult condition, comprising highly confusable letters (e.g., B and T).

Reading ability before intervention began was significantly poorer in both reading-disabled groups compared with control children. After intervention, the experimental intervention group showed a statistically significant improvement in reading ability while the community intervention group did not. At the same time, the pattern of activation associated with the letter identification task differed significantly between the groups, pre- and postintervention. The experimental intervention group showed increased activation in the left hemisphere regions, including inferior frontal gyrus and posterior middle temporal gyrus, previously shown to underlie phonological processing. Interestingly, the patterns were similar for the control group, but not for the community intervention group, who showed increased activation in the left caudate nucleus. It is important to note that there were no group differences in reaction time or accuracy in performance on the letter identification task, an issue that was not addressed by the authors. In addition, the authors could not explain why the community intervention group had shown increased activation in the caudate nucleus postintervention, relative to the other two groups. Despite these limitations, the results of this study provide evidence that targeted "evidence-based" intervention can lead to significant improvement in reading outcome, which appears to be associated with the formation of new neural connections resembling those seen in skilled readers. In other words, the results suggest that, with appropriate guidance, the brain of a dyslexic child can adopt processing systems similar to those used by more skilled readers, thereby reducing the need to resort to compensatory strategies, which are cognitively more demanding.

On the visual attention span front, Vadois' group have begun to explore the effects of remediation exercises designed to increase visual attention span on the patterns of activation within the left superior parietal cortex. In a pilot study with 10 dyslexic children, Peyrin et al. (2006) showed that, following six weeks of intensive training on visual exploration and visual search of targets among distractors, children showed activation in the left superior parietal cortex during the flanked categorization task, which was not present prior to this intervention. These changes were associated with improved performance on this and other visual attention span tasks outside the scanner.

More recently, Richards and Berninger (2008) examined the effects of phonological intervention on the functional connectivity between different regions within the reading network, namely the inferior frontal gyrus, middle frontal gyrus occipital cortex, and cerebellum, in dyslexic children. Unlike conventional fMRI, which identifies all the regions that are associated with a particular cognitive task, functional connectivity MRI allows the examination of the cooperation between different brain regions and the temporal coherence with which these regions are engaged. In this, first connectivity study in children, 18 dyslexic participants were given explicit instruction in linguistic awareness, decoding and spelling, as part of a remedial program to improve their reading ability. The children were scanned before and after the intervention. While in the scanner, children were given a phoneme mapping task and the pattern of activation elicited by the task was compared with that on the same task in 21 nondyslexic control children.

Before the intervention, the dyslexic children showed greater functional connectivity between the left inferior frontal gyrus and the middle frontal gyrus, the SMA and precentral gyrus bilaterally, and the right middle frontal gyrus, relative to the nondyslexic children. Following the program, these differences between dyslexic participants and controls were no longer present. The authors therefore suggested that, prior to intervention, dyslexic children were employing a memory-based strategy to perform the phonological task, evidenced by functional connectivity between left and right frontal regions. After intervention, this overconnectivity between the left and right inferior frontal gyrus, which was previously interfering with efficient phonological processing, decreased, and gave rise to strengthened connectivity within left lateralized frontoparietal regions, which more closely resembles the pattern found for skilled readers. Note that the authors found no differences in connectivity within the occipitotemporal network between the dyslexic participants and control children in this study. This is possibly due to the nature of the task employed.

*Connecting different brain regions*    van der Mark and colleagues (2011) used the data from their earlier study (2009, described above) to assess the functional connectivity between the left occipitotemporal system, implicated in visual word processing, and the rest of the more anterior reading network. The control children showed the typical pattern of connectivity between the region surrounding the left fusiform gyrus and the classical language processing areas in the left frontal and parietal cortex. In contrast, dyslexic children showed disrupted connectivity between the region surrounding the left fusiform gyrus and more anterior areas: on the one hand reduced connectivity with left inferior frontal and inferior parietal regions, and on the other hand increased connectivity with left middle and left superior temporal gyri.

These disrupted connectivity patterns were correlated with phonological processing, which could explain why dyslexic participants were as accurate as controls at accepting real words, albeit slower, while being significantly less accurate at rejecting pseudohomophones and nonwords. Similarly to the previously described intervention studies, this study seems to indicate that children with dyslexia show reduced functional connectivity between brain regions specialized for processing visual information and those regions that are associated with phonological and semantic processing. This reduced connectivity would presumably hinder the development of skills that are essential for efficient reading.

Other researchers have employed imaging methods focused more specifically on imaging the white-matter pathways connecting between the different cortical areas of the reading network. For example, Beaulieu and colleagues (2005) used diffusion tensor MRI (DTI; for a description of this technique see Chapter 2) in order to examine the relationship between white-matter density within the reading network and reading performance in a group of 32 children. Rather than comparing dyslexic participants with skilled readers, this study included normal readers, aged 8–12 years, with varying reading ability. Sixteen of the children were considered average readers, 12 were considered above average, and only four were poor readers. Results showed a strong correlation ($r = 0.54$) between reading ability and index of white-matter connectivity along the left temporoparietal tracts. These tracts connect temporal and parietal regions, which have previously been shown to be associated with phonological processing and to be underactive in dyslexic participants. In other words, above-average readers tended to show a greater connectivity index, while average and poor readers tended to show lower connectivity. Similar results were reported by Deutsch and colleagues (2005), who compared a group of seven dyslexic children with seven skilled readers aged 7–13 years.

So far, we have highlighted studies indicating that dyslexic participants show a different pattern of activation than controls, and that older dyslexic participants tend to compensate for their difficulty by recruiting other and more extensive areas. We have also highlighted that, with adequate intervention, the functional connectivity of dyslexic brains can be "reshaped" to become more efficient at reading by approximating the processing systems used by more skilled readers. Another issue that concerns educational neuroscience is the individual differences that can be seen between dyslexic participants. While some dyslexic individuals seem to be more able to adopt compensatory strategies, and with hard work seem to achieve results the same as, if not better than, those of their skilled reader counterparts, others reach adulthood with persistent reading difficulties, which may hinder their progression in life.

## Individual Differences; Predicting Reading Outcome

Shaywitz et al. (2003) set out to examine whether and how compensated and persistent dyslexic participants differed, and what factors could account for the different outcomes. For this study the authors tested three groups of young adults aged 18–22 years. Nineteen compensated dyslexic participants and 24 persistently poor readers were compared with 27 control participants. Compensated dyslexic participants were those who were identified as poor readers in primary but not secondary school, whereas persistently poor readers had reading difficulties throughout primary and secondary school.

All participants were given the nonword, line orientation, and semantic category matching tasks described earlier (Shaywitz et al., 2002). Behavioral results showed that persistently poor readers were significantly less accurate than compensated dyslexic participants in the nonword matching task, who in turn were slower and less accurate than controls in both nonword and semantic tasks. Concordantly, different activation patterns were observed in the three groups, but these were task dependent. Specifically, during the nonword matching task, both dyslexic groups showed decreased activation in posterior temporal gyri, and increased activation in the right inferior frontal gyrus. In this task, the compensated dyslexic participants also showed increased activation in the right superior frontal, right middle temporal, and left anterior cingulate gyri. The authors interpreted this finding to suggest that compensated readers have come to rely on compensated neural systems to perform this task, which led to better performance, as evidenced by reaction time and accuracy. During the semantic matching task, compensated dyslexic participants showed decreased activation in left occipitotemporal regions, while the persistently poor readers showed preferential activation within right lateralized prefrontal regions coupled by left occipitotemporal activation, similar to the controls. However, the authors note that, in fact, activation in this region was *stronger* in the poor readers compared with the controls, despite their considerably poorer performance. This unexpected finding was taken to indicate abnormal activation in this region by these persistently poor readers, who engage it in a different way to the controls. The authors propose that in skilled readers the occipitotemporal system develops through phonologically based word analysis, achieved via the connection of this area with left inferior frontal regions. By contrast, in the persistently poor readers, activation in this region is coupled by increased activation in right prefrontal cortex: a region that has been associated with working memory and memory retrieval. These findings therefore suggest that the differences between compensated and persistently poor readers lie in the connectivity of the visual system with higher-order cognitive systems, which in the case of compensated dyslexic participants led to overactivation of right lateralized regions, and thus to more efficient reading, whereas in persistently poor dyslexic participants the connections were made with areas that do not normally contribute to reading.

This study was seminal in its ability to distinguish between different types of activation for different types of reading-impaired participant. This knowledge gave rise to a surge of neuroimaging studies aiming to identify activation patterns in young children, which may help predict which children might learn to read easily, and those who do not, which may develop compensatory strategies, and which may have persistent reading difficulties in adulthood. For example, Pihko et al. (1999) and Molfese, Molfese, and Modgline (2001) employed event-related potentials with babies with a family history of dyslexia and compared patterns of activation with those observed in babies with no dyslexic relatives. Evoked responses to speech sounds and phonemes were positively correlated to language and reading ability several years later in both studies. More recently, in a five-year longitudinal study, Maurer et al. (2009) observed that phoneme perception in kindergarten children (aged 6.6 years) evoked bilateral activation in children who by second grade (aged 8.3 years) were classified as poor readers. In contrast, children who showed activation mostly within the left hemisphere were classified as normal readers in second grade. That is, left-lateralized evoked responses observed in kindergarten correlated with higher performance on standardized reading tests at school than bilateral activation.

Hoeft et al. (2010) conducted a prospective longitudinal study with 45 adolescents (aged 14 years), 25 dyslexic participants and 20 controls, using fMRI and DTI. At the start of the study (time 1), children were scanned while performing a word-rhyme judgment task. The patterns of activation were correlated with their reading and language performance, assessed outside the scanner. Then, 2.5 years later (time 2), reading performance was reassessed and compared with that seen at time 1 in dyslexic participants and controls. In addition, the patterns of brain activation and connectivity observed at time 1 were used as predictive measures of reading improvement at time 2. That is, the authors examined whether those children who showed improvement in reading performance between time 1 and time 2 exhibited different patterns of brain activation and connectivity to those children who had not improved in reading performance.

Results of this study showed that, among dyslexic children, those who at time 1 had shown greater activation within the right inferior frontal gyrus and stronger white-matter integrity between right frontal and temporoparietal regions also showed the greatest improvement in reading performance at time 2. The authors noted that typical readers did not show this pattern, similar to Shaywitz et al. (2003), and therefore reasoned that this increased activation and stronger connectivity in the right frontal cortex was related to a compensatory mechanism employed by some dyslexic participants, which promoted relatively successful reading development in the course of time and schooling.

These studies, which have successfully predicted reading performance based on patterns of cortical activation, have brought *neuroprognosis* to education. This term, which is regularly used in clinical settings, refers to the use of neuro-imaging to predict future changes in neurological syndromes. The ability to predict reading gains with observed patterns of cortical activation and white-matter integrity in children may offer the potential to guide professionals in tailoring specific educational intervention to help those children who are not likely to improve reading performance in the course of time and with normal schooling.

## Learning to Read and Failing to Read in Different Languages

As we have seen throughout this chapter, learning to read involves making connections between visual areas in the brain and those that mediate phonological processing. Beginner readers therefore tend to rely primarily on phonological recoding: assembling sounds of small graphemic units (letters and syllables), which gradually gives way to processing of larger linguistic "chunks" (whole words) with increased reading experience. Indeed, as we described in this chapter, this has been shown in languages other than English, such as Finnish, Hebrew, and French, as well as German, Spanish, Italian, Chinese, and Japanese, among others (for detailed reviews see for example Frost, 2005; Ziegler & Goswami, 2006). The rate of literacy development in different languages may vary in keeping with their level of orthographic transparency. This concept refers to the level of correspondence that exists between the written units and their sounds. Languages such as Italian and Spanish may be viewed as extremely transparent, since there is almost a one-to-one correspondence between the letters and their sounds, whereas languages such as Hebrew, and more so Japanese and Chinese, are considered as extremely opaque. Studies looking at the processes of literacy acquisition in different languages have found that native speakers of opaque languages tend to learn how to read more slowly than those whose native language is transparent. Nevertheless, it has also been shown that, once literacy is established, typical readers of transparent and opaque orthographies alike achieve comparable fluency and accuracy levels (see, e.g., Hanley, Masterson, Spencer, & Evans, 2004; Seymour, Aro, & Erksine, 2003).

Similarly, reading disorders such as developmental dyslexia are prevalent worldwide. Indeed, it has been noted that, while showing similar phonological deficits in different countries, children with dyslexia exhibit different manifestations of the condition, depending on the orthographic transparency of the language being learned. In languages with transparent orthographies, reading disabilities become apparent with extremely slow and effortful phonological recoding, coupled by poor spelling. In languages with opaque orthographies it is mainly poor accuracy that helps detection, in addition to slow reading and poor spelling (Ziegler & Goswami, 2005). Moreover, it is plausible that the "give-up" threshold of children with reading difficulties learning to read an opaque orthography may be higher than that of children encountering difficulty in learning to read a transparent orthography (see, e.g., Paulesu, 2006).

An interesting study by Hanley and colleagues (2004) followed up the results of a previous study showing that Welsh-speaking children aged between five and seven years outperformed their English-speaking counterparts at reading words and nonwords (Spencer & Hanley, 2003). The followup study showed that at age 11 both groups had attained comparable word and nonword reading skills. However, among poor readers, group differences remained as observed in the earlier study, whereby the poorest 25% of English readers continued to perform significantly worse on word and nonword accuracy than the lowest-performing 25% of Welsh readers, who showed high accuracy levels, albeit considerably slow reading. Therefore, in the long term, the orthographic opacity of English was shown to be detrimental to poor readers, relative to the transparency of Welsh.

The differences in reading attainment between different languages in typical readers and differential manifestations of reading disability may bear particular importance for bilingual and multilingual children at risk of developing reading disorders. A prevalent problem in the education system faced with bilingual children is that attenuation of reading acquisition in the second language is often attributed to lower language proficiency (Cline & Frederickson, 1999; Geva, 2000; Uno, Wydell, Kato, Itoh, & Yoshino, 2009). This assumption may mask an underlying deficit, which could be overlooked. At the same time, in some cases knowledge of an additional language may actually lead to wrong, or "over"-diagnosis of reading disability (Geva, 2000). Applying the neuroscientific approach to study reading and reading disability in bilingual children may therefore help accurate neuroprognosis in bilingual children at risk of reading disability.

## Conclusion

In this chapter we have highlighted how the seemingly simple process of reading is far from simple indeed, and how learning to read changes the structure of our brains. We have reviewed some of the studies carried out with those experiencing difficulty in acquiring literacy that have shown how the circuitry of the brain can be altered through educational intervention specifically designed to target the underlying deficit. Among these studies, some have shown that individual differences exist between poor readers, whereby those who manage to compensate for their difficulties show patterns of activation and connectivity that are not seen in typical readers or persistently poor readers. The ability to visualize these individual differences is a potentially powerful tool, which we may be able to harness to assist in devising interventions to help all types of struggling reader. Moreover, recent studies have aimed to establish predictive measures in order to anticipate which children may manifest symptoms of reading disability later on in life. While the advent of neuroimaging has given us the opportunity to open a window into the human brain, it is important to remember that any intervention must take into consideration not only the neural substrates of reading but also the affective component. Therefore, the development of teaching strategies must also focus on encouragement and motivation.

We hope that this chapter has helped to highlight the importance of the exciting emerging field of educational neuroscience and its potential to develop new ways of understanding the unique aspects of the central nervous system that make us human.

# References

Balota, D. A., & Chumbley, J. I. (1984). Are lexical decisions a good measure of lexical access? The role of word frequency in the neglected decision stage. *Journal of Experimental Psychology: Human Perception and Performance, 10*(3), 340–357.

Beaulieu, C., Plewes, C., Paulson, L. A., Roy, D., Snook, L., Concha, L., & Phillips, L. (2005) Imaging brain connectivity in children with diverse reading ability, *NeuroImage, 25*(4), 1266–1271.

Bick, A., Goelman, G., & Frost, R. (2008). Neural correlates of morphological processes in Hebrew. *Journal of Cognitive Neuroscience, 20*(3), 1–15.

Bosse, M. L., Tainturier, M. J., & Valdois, S. (2007). Developmental dyslexia: the Visual Attention Span hypothesis. *Cognition, 104*, 198–230.

Broca, P. (1861/1965). Remarques sur le siege de la faculté suivie d'une observation d'aphémie. In R. Herrnstein & E. G. Boring (Eds.), *A source book in the history of psychology* (p. 330). Cambridge, MA: Harvard University Press.

Brunswick, N., McCrory, E., Price, C. J., Frith, C. D., & Frith, U. (1999). Explicit and implicit processing of words and pseudowords by adult developmental dyslexics: A search for Wernicke's Wortschatz? *Brain, 122*, 1901–1917.

Cline, T., & Frederickson, N. (1999). Identification and assessment of dyslexia in bi/multilingual children. *International Journal of Bilingual Education and Bilingualism, 2*(2), 81–93.

Cohen, L., Lehericy, S., Chochon, F., Lemer, C., Rivaud, S., & Dehaene, S. (2002). Language-specific tuning of visual cortex? Functional properties of the visual word form area. *Brain, 125*, 1054–1069.

Coltheart, M. (2004). Are there lexicons? *The Quarterly Journal of Experimental Psychology, 57A*(7), 1153–1171.

Coltheart, M., & Rastle, K. (1994). Serial processing in reading aloud: Evidence for dual-route models of reading. *Journal of Experimental Psychology: Human Perception and Performance, 20*(6), 1197–1211.

Damasio, A. R., & Damasio, H. (1983). The anatomical basis of pure alexia. *Neurology, 33*, 1573–1583.

Dejerine, J. J. (1892). Contribution a l'étudeanatomoclinique el clinique des diferentes variétés de cecite verbal. *Memoires De La Société De Biologie, 4*, 61–90.

Deutsch, G. K., Dougherty, R. F., Bammer, R., Siok, W. T., Gabrieli, J. D. E., & Wandell, B. (2005). Children's reading performance is correlated with white matter structure measured by diffusion tensor imaging. *Cortex, 41*(3), 354–363.

Dubois, M., Kyllingsbaek, S., Prado, C., Musca, S. C., Peoffer, E., Lassus, D., et al. (2010). Fractionating the multi-element processing deficit in developmental dyslexia: Evidence from two case studies. *Cortex, 46*(6), 717–738.

Fiez, J. A., Balota, D. A., Raichle, M. E., & Petersen, S. E. (1999). Effects of lexicality, frequency, and spelling-to-sound consistency on the functional anatomy of reading. *Neuron, 24*(1), 205–218.

Forster, K. I., & Chambers, S. M. (1973). Lexical access and naming time. *Journal of Verbal Learning and Verbal Behavior, 12*(6), 627–635.

Frederiksen, J. R., & Kroll, J. F. (1976). Spelling and sound: Approaches to the internal lexicon. *Journal of Experimental Psychology: Human Perception and Performance, 2*(3), 361–379.

Frost, R. (2005). Orthographic systems and skilled word recognition processes in reading. In M.J. Snowling & C. Hulme (Eds.), *The Science of Reading: A Handbook* (pp. 272–295). Oxford: Blackwell.

Frost, R. (2012). Towards a universal model of reading. *Behavioral and Brain Sciences, 35*(5), 1–67.

Funnell, E., & Davidson, M. (1989). Lexical capture: A developmental disorder of reading and spelling. *Quarterly Journal of Experimental Psychology, 41*(3), 471–487.

Gazzaniga, M. S., Ivry, R. B., & Mangun, G. R. (Eds.). (1998). *Cognitive neuroscience, the biology of the mind.* New York: Norton.

Geschwind, N. (1979/1991). Specializations of the human brain. In W. S. Wang (Ed.), *The emergence of language, development and evolution; readings from Scientific American* (pp. 72–87). New York: Freeman.

Geva, E. (2000). Issues in the assessment of reading disabilities in L2 children – beliefs and research evidence. *Dyslexia, 6*(1), 13–28.

Glushko, R. J. (1979). The organization and activation of orthographic knowledge in reading aloud. *Journal of Experimental Psychology: Human Perception and Performance, 5*(4), 674–691.

Hanley, R., Masterson, J., Spencer, L., & Evans, D. (2004). How long do the advantages of learning to read a transparent orthography last? An investigation of the reading skills and reading impairment of Welsh children at 10 years of age. *Quarterly Journal of Experimental Psychology, 57A*(8), 1393–1410.

Hoeft, F., McCandliss, B. D., Black, J. M., Gantman, A., Zakerani, N., Hulme, C., Lyytinen, H., Whitfield-Gabrieli, S., Glover, G. H., Reiss, A. L., & Gabrieli, J. D. E. (2010).

Neural systems predicting long-term outcome in dyslexia. *Proceedings of the National Academy of Sciences of the United States of America, 108*(1), 361–366.

Marshall, J. C., & Newcombe, F. (1973). Patterns of paralexia: A psycholinguistic approach. *Journal of Psycholinguistic Research, 2*, 175–199.

Maurer, U., Bucher, K., Brem, S., Benz, R., Kranz, F., Schulz, E., van der Mark, S., Steinhausen, H. C., & Brandeis, D. (2009) Neurophysiology in preschool improves behavioral prediction of reading ability throughout primary school. *Biological Psychiatry, 66*(4), 341–348.

McDermott, K. B., Petersen, S. E., Watson, J. M., & Ojemann, J. G. (2003). A procedure for identifying regions preferentially activated by attention to semantic and phonological relations using functional magnetic resonance imaging. *Neuropsychologia, 41*(3), 293–303.

Molfese, V. J., Molfese, D. J., & Modgline, A. A. (2001). Newborn and preschool predictors of second-grade reading scores: An investigation of categorical and continuous scores. *Journal of Learning Disabilities, 34*, 545–554.

Patterson, K., & Hodges, J. R. (1992). Deterioration of word meaning: Implications for reading. *Neuropsychologia, 30*, 1025–1040.

Paulesu, E. (2006). On the advantage of "shallow" orthographies: Number and grain size of the orthographic units or consistency *per se*? *Developmental Science, 9*(5), 443–444.

Paulesu, E., Demonet, J. F., Fazio, F., McCrory, E., Chanoine, V., Brunswick, N., et al. (2001). Dyslexia: Cultural diversity and biological unity. *Science, 291*(5511), 2165–2167.

Peyrin, C., Démonet, J. F., Baciu, M., Lamalle, L., Pichat, C., Troprès, I., Trabanino, M., Lebas, J. F., & Valdois, S. (2006, October). Cerebral reorganization after phonological and visuo-attentional training in dyslexic children: An fMRI study. In *ESN2006*, Toulouse, France

Peyrin, C., Demonet, J. F., N'Guyen-Morel, M. A., Le Bas, J. F., & Valdois, S. (2011). Superior parietal lobule dysfunction in a homogeneous group of dyslexic children with a visual attention span disorder. *Brain and Language, 118*, 128–138.

Peyrin, C., Lallier, M., & Valdois, S. (2008). Visual attention span brain mechanisms in normal and dyslexic readers. In M. Baciu (Ed.), *Neuropsychology and cognition of language; Behavioural, neuropsychological and neuroimaging studies of oral and written language* (pp. 22–40). Trivandrum, India: Research SignPost.

Peyrin, C., Lallier, M., Demonet, J. F., Baciu, M., Pernet, C., Le Bas, J.F., & Valdois, S. (2012). Neural dissociation of phonological and visual attention span disorders in developmental dyslexia: FMRI evidence from two case reports and normal readers. *Brain and Language, 120*(3), 381–394.

Pihko, E., Leppänen, P. H. T., Eklund, K. M., Cheour, M., Guttorm T. K., & Lyytinen, H. (1999). Cortical responses of infants with and without a genetic risk for dyslexia: I. Age effects. *NeuroReport, 10*, 901–905.

Pinker, S. (1994). *The language instinct.* New York: Morrow.

Plaut, D. C., & Kello, C. T. (1999). The emergence of phonology from the interplay of speech comprehension and production: A distributed connectionist approach. In B. MacWhinney (Ed.), *The emergence of language* (pp. 381–415). Mahwah, NJ: Erlbaum.

Plaut, D. C., McClelland, J. L., Seidenberg, M. S., & Patterson, K. (1996). Understanding normal and impaired word reading: Computational principles in quasi-regular domains. *Psychological Review, 103*, 56–115.

Price, C. J. (2000). The anatomy of language: Contributions from functional neuroimaging. *Journal of Anatomy, 197*, 335–359.

Price, C. J., McCrory, R. (2005) Functional brain imaging studies of skilled reading and developmental dyslexia. In M. J. Snowling & C. Hulme (Eds.), *The science of reading: A Handbook* (pp. 473–496). Oxford: Blackwell.

Price, C. J., & Mechelli, A. (2005) Reading and reading disturbance. *Current Opinion in Neurobiology, 15*(2), 231–238.

Pugh, K. R., Shaywitz, B. A., Shaywitz, S. E., Constable, R. T., Skudlarski, P., Fulbright, R. K., Bronen, R. A., Shankweiler, D. P., Katz, L., Fletcher, J. M., & Gore, J. C. (1996). Cerebral organization of component processes in reading. *Brain, 119*(4), 1221–1238.

Ramus, F. (2003). Developmental dyslexia: Specific phonological deficit or general sensorimotor dysfunction? *Current Opinion in Neurobiology, 13*, 212–218.

Rastle, K., & Coltheart, M. (1998). Whammies and double whammies: The effect of length on non-words reading. *Psychonomic Bulletin and Review, 5*, 277–282.

Rastle, K., & Coltheart, M. (2000). Lexical and nonlexical print-to-sound translation of disyllabic words and nonwords. *Journal of Memory and Language, 42*, 342–364.

Richards, T. L., & Berninger, V. W. (2008). Abnormal fMRI connectivity in children with dyslexia during a phoneme task: Before but not after treatment. *Journal of Neurolinguistics, 21*, 294–304.

Seidenberg, M. S., & McClelland, J. L. (1989). A distributed, developmental model of word recognition and naming. *Psychological Review, 96*(4), 523–568.

Seymour, P. H. K., Aro, M., & Erksine, J. M. (2003). Foundation literacy acquisition in European orthographies. *British Journal of Psychology, 94*, 143–174.

Shaywitz, B. A., Shaywitz, S. E., Blachman, B. A., Pugh, K. R., Fulbright, R. K., Skudlarski, P., Mencl, W. E., Constable, R. T., Holahan, J. M., Marchione, K. E., Fletcher, J. M., Lyon, G. R., & Gore, J. C. (2004). Development of left occipitotemporal systems for skilled reading in children after a phonologically-based intervention. *Biological Psychiatry, 55*(9), 926–933.

Shaywitz, B. A., Shaywitz, S. E., Pugh, K. R., Mencl, W. E., Fulbright, R. K., Skudlarski, P., Constable, R. T., Marchione, K. E., Fletcher, J. M., Lyon, G. R., & Gore, J. C. (2002). Disruption of posterior brain systems for reading in children with developmental dyslexia. *Biological Psychiatry, 52*(2), 101–110.

Shaywitz, S. (1998). Current concepts: Dyslexia. *The New England Journal of Medicine, 338*, 307–312.

Shaywitz, S. E., Shaywitz, B. A., Fulbright, R. K., Skudlarski, P., Mencl, W. E., Constable, R. T., Pugh, K. R., Holahan, J. M., Marchione, K. E., Fletcher, J. M., Lyon, G. R., & Gore, J. C. (2003) Neural systems for compensation and persistence: Young adult outcome of childhood reading disability. *Biological Psychiatry, 54*(1), 25–33.

Shaywitz, S. E., Shaywitz, B. A., Pugh, K. R., Fulbright, R. K., Constable, R. T., Mencl, W. E., Shankweiler, D. P., Liberman, A. M., Skudlarski, P., Fletcher, J. M., Katz, L., Marchoine, K. E., Lacadie, C., Gatenby, C., & Gore, J. C.. (1998). Functional disruption in the organisation of the brain for reading in dyslexia. *Proceedings of the National Academy of Sciences of the United States of America, 95,* 2636–2641.

Snowling, M. (2000). *Dyslexia.* Oxford: Blackwell.

Spencer, L. H., & Hanley, J. R. (2003). Effects of orthographic transparency on reading and phoneme awareness in children learning to read in Wales. *British Journal of Psychology, 94,* 1–28.

Stein, J. (2001). The magnocellular theory of developmental dyslexia. *Dyslexia, 7*(1), 12–36.

Tallal, P. (1980). Auditory temporal perception, phonics, and reading disabilities in children. *Brain and Language, 9*(2), 182–198.

Uno, A., Wydell, T. N., Kato, M., Itoh, K., & Yoshino, F. (2009). Cognitive neuropsychological and regional cerebral blood flow study of a Japanese–English bilingual girl with specific language impairment (SLI). *Cortex, 45*(2), 154–163.

Valdois, S., Bosse, M. L., Ans, B., Zorman, M., Carbonnel, S., David, D., & Pellat, J. (2003). Phonological and visual processing deficits are dissociated in developmental dyslexia: Evidence from two case studies. *Reading and Writing, 16,* 543–572.

Valdois, S., Peyrin, C., & Baciu, M. (2009). The neurobiological correlates of developmental dyslexia. In S. Fuchs, H. Loevenbruck, D. Pape, & P. Perrier (Eds.), *Some aspects of speech and the brain* (pp. 141–162). Frankfurt am Main: Lang.

van der Mark, S., Bucher, K., Maurer, U., Schulz, E., Brem, S., Buckelmüller, J., Kronbichler, M., Loenneker, T., Klaver, P., Martin, E., & Brandeis, D. (2009) Children with dyslexia lack multiple specializations along the visual word-form (VWF) system. *NeuroImage, 47*(4), 1940–1949.

van der Mark, S., Klaver, P., Bucher, K., Maurer, U., Schulz, E., Brem, S., Martin, E., & Brandeis, D. (2011) The left occipitotemporal system in reading: Disruption of focal fMRI connectivity to left inferior frontal and inferior parietal language areas in children with dyslexia. *NeuroImage, 54*(3), 2426–2436.

Weekes, B., Coltheart, M., & Gordon, E. (1997). Deep dyslexia and right hemisphere reading – A regional cerebral blood flow study. *Aphasiology, 11,* 1139–1158.

Wernicke, C. (1874). *Der aphasische Symptomencomplex.* Breslau: Kohn and Weigert.

Wydell, T. N., Vuorinen, T., Helenius, P., & Salmelin, R. (2003). Neural correlates of letter-string length and lexicality during reading in a regular orthography. *Journal of Cognitive Neuroscience, 15*(7), 1052–1062.

Ziegler, J. C., & Goswami, U. (2005). Reading acquisition, developmental dyslexia, and skilled reading across languages: A psycholinguistic grain size theory. *Psychological Bulletin, 131*(1), 3–29.

Ziegler, J. C., & Goswami, U. (2006). Becoming literate in different languages: Similar problems, different solutions. *Developmental Science, 9*(5), 429–453.

Ziegler, J. C., Perry, C., & Coltheart, M. (2000). The DRC model of visual word recognition and reading aloud: An extension to German. *European Journal of Cognitive Psychology, 12*(3), 413–430.

# Chapter 8

# Mathematical Development

## Brian Butterworth and Sashank Varma

## Introduction

The importance of mathematics instruction has been stressed, quite rightly, in many official reports in the United Kingdom, the United States, and other nations. Napoleon famously said that mathematics is "intimately connected with the prosperity of the state". In his foreword to the Cockcroft report on math teaching in 1982, Sir Keith Joseph, Secretary of State for Education and Science, wrote "Few subjects are as important to the future of the nation as mathematics" (Cockcroft, 1982). Since Cockcroft, in the United Kingdom alone, there has been Professor Adrian Smith's report on post-14 math (Smith, 2004), and Sir Peter Williams' report on primary math (Williams, 2008). Similarly, the US National Research Council (National Research Council Committee on Early Childhood Mathematics, 2009) noted that "The new demands of international competition in the 21st century require a workforce that is competent in and comfortable with mathematics;" and to that end "The committee [of experts] was charged with examining existing research in order to develop appropriate mathematics learning objectives for preschool children; providing evidence-based insights related to curriculum, instruction, and teacher education for achieving these learning objectives" (p. 1). In 2010, the OECD's report, *The High Cost of Low Educational Performance*, demonstrated that the standard of math drives GDP growth: the standard in 1960 was a good predictor of GDP growth up to 2000; and the improvement in educational standard from 1975 to 2000 was

*Educational Neuroscience*, First Edition. Edited by Denis Mareschal, Brian Butterworth and Andy Tolmie.
© 2014 John Wiley & Sons, Ltd. Published 2014 by John Wiley & Sons, Ltd.

highly correlated with improvement in GDP growth. In particular, the report looked at the potential effects of improving standards in math. So, for example, they found that if the UK improved the standard of the 11% of children who failed to reach the PISA minimum level (which is not very high) to the minimum level, then the effect on GDP growth would be about 0.44%. Not much, you might think, but with an average rate of GDP growth of 1.5%, this would be a massive and cumulative increase of nearly one-third.

Poor math has consequences for the lives of individuals. A UK survey found that learners with poor math are more likely to be unemployed, depressed, and in trouble with the law (Parsons & Bynner, 2005). The accountancy firm, KPMG, estimated that the cost to the United Kingdom of poor math in terms of lost direct and indirect taxes, unemployment benefits, justice costs, and additional educational costs was £2.4 *billion* per year (Gross, Hudson, & Price, 2009).

Can educational neuroscience make a contribution to improving society and the lives of individuals by improving math education?

There is now an extensive psychological and neuroscience literature on mathematical cognition and its development. This chapter focuses on studies of number understanding, as this topic has received the greatest attention in the literature in terms both of cognition and of its neural basis, and is most relevant to the problems of education. As in the other chapters of this book, development is considered across four phases: infancy and childhood (ages 0–5), primary and middle school (5–12), secondary school and adolescence (12–18), and adulthood.

## Neural roadmap

Before beginning, we provide a roadmap of the brain areas of greatest relevance to mathematical thinking, and introduce their putative cognitive functions. We know about their roles from two main sources. The earliest and still influential source is the effect of *brain damage*: how does damage to area A affect different aspects of mathematical processing? Of course, it is vital to compare the effects of damage to area A with damage to other areas of the brain. More recently, it has been possible to induce transient neural malfunctions using *transcranial magnetic stimulation* on normal brains. The other source of information is the map of brain activity when the healthy brain is carrying out a mathematical task. Mapping using *functional magnetic resonance imaging* (fMRI) gives reasonable localization, but not much information about the timecourse of the cognitive processes, since it measures changes in blood flow, which responds slowly to the activity of the brain cells. By contrast, *electroencephalography*, which records changes in electrical potentials across the scalp, gives good temporal resolution, but poor spatial resolution. (See Chapter 2.)

Three brain areas in the parietal lobes are particularly important for numbers and arithmetic (Dehaene, Piazza, Pinel, & Cohen, 2003). (1) *The intraparietal sulcus (IPS)* is the neural correlate of the *magnitude representations* that *number symbols* denote. (Since this sulcus is long, the *horizontal* middle section – hIPS – appears most relevant.) Both left and right IPS are active in most numerical tasks. (2) *The left angular gyrus (AG)* is involved in retrieval of previously learned number facts (see especially Delazer et al., 2005; Ischebeck et al., 2006). When the left AG is damaged, calculation can be severely affected. (3) *The posterior superior parietal lobule (SPL)* is one of the areas involved in relating numbers to space, for example, in counting visible objects.

Other brain areas also play important roles in mathematical cognition and development. For example, the right fusiform gyrus (rFG) is associated with processing the visual form of mathematical symbols (Rykhlevskaia, Uddin, Kondos, & Menon, 2009). The right inferior frontal gyrus (rIFG) is implicated in spatial working memory, and in phenomena that link numbers to space (Rusconi, Bueti, Walsh, & Butterworth, 2011). For more abstract mathematical thinking, the prefrontal cortex is important. When it is damaged, routine or previously learned problems can be solved, but novel problems cannot (Shallice & Evans, 1978).

These various brain areas and their putative roles in mathematical cognition are depicted in Figure 8.1. We refer to this figure later to situate the discussion of individual studies.

## Theoretical roadmap

As noted earlier, most neuroscience research has focused on numbers and arithmetic, which, in terms of the curriculum and everyday life, are the most important aspects of mathematics. It is therefore important to be clear about what numbers are and what we know about how they are represented and processed in the brain.

In our numerate society numbers are used in many different ways. Here our focus is on numbers as abstract properties of sets, for example, to characterize the number of fingers on a hand, the number of dwarves with Snow White, or the number of wishes given by a genie. These are *cardinal* numbers, sometimes called *numerosities*, and are ordered by *magnitude*. So five is larger than four, and a set of five will include a set of four. Two sets have the same numerosity – are exactly equal – when the members of one can be put in one-to-one correspondence with members of the other. This means that adding a number to a set or subtracting a member from a set will affect the numerosity of the set. This is the use or meaning of number that is relevant to arithmetic. There is some disagreement

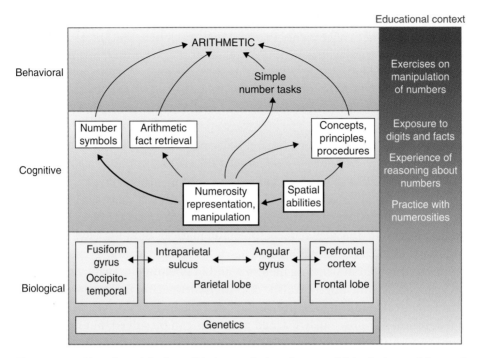

**Figure 8.1**  Causal model of possible inter-relations between biological, cognitive, and simple behavioral levels. Here, the only environmental factors we address are educational. If parietal areas, especially the IPS, fail to develop normally, there will be an impairment at the cognitive level in numerosity representation and consequential impairments for other relevant cognitive systems revealed in behavioral abnormalities. The link between the occipitotemporal and parietal cortex is required for mapping number symbols (digits and number words) to numerosity representations. The prefrontal cortex supports learning new facts and procedures. The multiple levels of the theory suggest the instructional interventions on which educational scientists should focus. (From Butterworth, Varma, and Laurillard (2011) with permission.)

about how magnitudes are represented in the brain, and how we come to have representations of exactly five.

Another familiar use for number is to order things – such as the pages of this book. Page 100 does not have a larger magnitude than page 99 (though the set of pages to 100 will have a larger magnitude than the set to 99, of course). Logicians and mathematicians call these *ordinal* numbers, or *ranks*, and they are sometimes, but not always, referred to by separate vocabulary items: *first, second, third,* 1st, 2nd, 3rd – though usually the same words and symbols are used for ordinals and numerosities, as in page or house numbers. There is now some evidence that the neural representation of ordinals is distinct from that of cardinals (Delazer & Butterworth, 1997).

Still another use of numbers is as *labels*. For example, in bus numbers, telephone numbers, bar codes, TV channels, neither the magnitude of the number nor its order in a sequence is relevant. Thus it makes no sense to say that John's telephone number is larger than Jim's, or that it comes after Jim's.

One of the problems for the learner is to distinguish these uses of number, and ensure that there is the correct mapping between the number symbol – the word or the digit – and its appropriate referent. This is particularly important since understanding the symbol systems is a key to talking and learning about numbers and arithmetic both in school and out of it. Manipulation of symbols is also a mentally efficient way of manipulating and storing arithmetical concepts. As the philosopher A. N. Whitehead observed, an understanding of symbolic notation relieves "the brain of all unnecessary work … and sets it free to concentrate on more advanced problems" (Whitehead, 1948).

## Two important effects

When people are working with symbolic numbers, it is often important to know how they are interpreting them. In particular, when they are engaged in a standard arithmetical task, are representations of numerical magnitude elicited? Two effects are standardly used to test for this.

The first is the *distance effect* – the seminal finding that, when comparing two numbers (i.e., judging which one is greater or lesser), the larger the difference in magnitude, the shorter the response time (Moyer & Landauer, 1967), suggesting that magnitude representations are being compared. The distance effect observed when comparing two symbolic numbers will be referred to as the *symbolic* distance effect, and the one observed when comparing the numerosities of two sets of objects will be referred to as the *nonsymbolic* distance effect (Buckley & Gillman, 1974). It is important to distinguish these two tasks because it is always possible that a learner may be able to do one normally, but not the other. For example, if the learner can do the nonsymbolic task in the normal way, where magnitudes are directly represented in the stimulus, but not the symbolic task, this could imply a problem in linking the symbol to its magnitude representation.

The other diagnostic effect is the *problem size effect*, or really just the size effect. Responses are slower and less accurate when the numbers are larger. This is so reliable, that one famous paper by Zbrodoff and Logan (2005) is titled "What everyone finds: The problem size effect." It may seem surprising that the time it takes to solve even single-digit additions or multiplication table facts depends on the size of the numbers, thus it takes longer to solve $9+8$ and $9\times8$ than $6+7$ and $6\times7$, even though these facts are highly overlearned for

**Box 8.1**   *Approximate numerosities.*

It has been suggested that arithmetical abilities are built on an inherited system for representing numerosities in an approximate way. So instead of representing fiveness exactly, it is represented approximately, and mapped onto an analog magnitude representation, usually with compression. This is represented pictorially here, where the horizontal scale is an arbitrary linear scale, and the vertical scale represents idealized activation, with the peak of activation representing the most probable response. In this model, the representation of each number overlaps with other numbers.

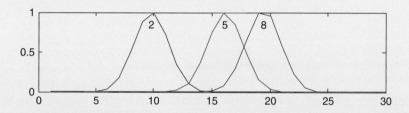

Several studies have found a correlation between arithmetical abilities and measures of the ability to discriminate numerosities greater than about six (Halberda, Mazzocco, & Feigenson, 2008; Piazza et al., 2010), though some have failed to find this (Iuculano, Tang, Hall, & Butterworth, 2008). Notice that the representation for each numerosity overlaps with that of its neighbors. This means that the basic numerical and arithmetical operations cannot be carried out on these representations. For example, the numerical equivalence between two representations cannot be established, whereas between sets it can be established by showing one-to-one correspondence between members of each set. Transformations that affect numerosity, such as adding or subtracting an element, cannot be determined with these analog representations. Children as young as three, who cannot yet count, notice which transformations affect numerosity (Sarnecka & Gelman, 2004). It has been argued by Butterworth (2010) that these representations cannot be foundational for arithmetic: representations of sets are necessary.

most numerate adults. Now, if a learner does not show this effect, it could also be diagnostic of an important individual difference. For example, the learner may be able to recall a fact through rote learning but not really understand it because he or she is not evoking the number magnitudes.

## Mathematical Development

The neural background to all cognitive development is the way the brain changes from conception to old age. Chapter 2 reviewed some of the evidence relevant to the development of mathematics. First, the brain at birth is not the same as the brain later in life. The infant brain has more brain cells (neurons) and more connections (synapses) than the adult brain, and this means that it is more "plastic," that is, more responsive to experience, including formal and informal instruction, than later on. As a consequence, learning new material appears to be easier earlier than later. Nevertheless, the newborn brain is not a blank slate. It comes equipped with structures and biases that support learning, especially learning concepts that evolution has found important. Numerosities are among these concepts.

### Infancy and childhood (0–5)

The inherited capacity to represent and discriminate stimuli on the basis of their numerosity has been observed in infants. This has required developmental psychologists to construct tasks that do not require verbal responses, since one cannot ask infants how many objects they are looking at. Many studies have used a *dishabituation* paradigm, which capitalizes on the fact that young infants will look longer at a stimulus if it differs from prior stimuli in a meaningful way. The first study to show this using a dishabituation paradigm established that at 5 months old babies are sensitive to changes in small numerosities in visual displays of two to six objects (Starkey & Cooper, 1980); subsequent research showed that this sensitivity was present even in the first week of life (Antell & Keating, 1983). Six-month-olds dishabituate to displays of 8 versus 16 objects (a 2.0 ratio) but not 8 versus 12 objects (a 1.5 ratio) (Xu & Spelke, 2000).

    A similar paradigm has been used to establish the neural response to changes in numerosity using event-related potentials (electroencephalography) from three-month-old infants while they were presented with a continuous stream of images, each showing a set of identical objects (Izard, Dehaene-Lambertz, & Dehaene, 2008). These were the habituation images. Within a given run, most sets had the same numerosity ("standard number") and the same object, but occasionally test images that could differ from the habituation images in number and/or object identity. It was thus possible to compare the visual event-related potentials evoked by unforeseen changes (dishabituation) either in the numerosity of a set ("deviant number") or the identity of objects forming the set. Three numerosity contrasts were investigated: two versus three, four versus eight, and four versus 12.

They found that all these numerosity contrasts produced a dishabituation effect – a difference in the pattern of evoked potentials; and the effect for changes in numerosity was different from the effect of change in the object. So it was not just *change* that the infant brain was responding to: there was a specific effect for *change in numerosity*. In particular, there was a significant response in the right parietal lobe, an area that is involved in numerosity processing in adults (see, e.g., Castelli, Glaser, & Butterworth, 2006; Piazza, Mechelli, Price, & Butterworth, 2006; Vetter, Butterworth, & Bahrami, 2011). Thus, not only is the cognitive capacity to discriminate numerosities present in infants, the neural mechanism that grows into adult competence is already in place.

Further evidence for this comes from a study of four-year-olds using a very similar habituation paradigm, but with the neural response measured by fMRI, which can give a more precise localization (Cantlon, Brannon, Carter, & Pelphrey, 2006). (This method is sometimes called "fMRI adaptation;" see Chapter 2). This study had four-year-old children watch sequences of visual stimuli. There were sequences where the same object (e.g., a circle) appeared in the same numerosity (e.g., 16 items), followed by a display with either a different object (e.g., a square) or a different numerosity (e.g., 32 items). The question was which brain areas would show a response, or neurally dishabituate, to numerical deviants versus object deviants. Children showed increasing activation to numerical deviants in right IPS, the same area that Izard et al. found in three-month-olds. The adults in this study showed increased activation in the same area, but also in the left IPS, suggesting that by adulthood these very simple numerosity representations have been connected with left-hemisphere functions, including language.

## Primary and middle childhood (5–12)

The distance effect has been used to investigate the natural number representations of primary and middle school children when comparing sets of objects and digits. For example, in comparing sets of objects, six-, seven-, and eight-year old children show a nonsymbolic distance effect (Ansari & Dhital, 2006). Landerl and Kölle (2009) similarly found a nonsymbolic distance effect in eight-, nine-, and 10-year old children. Developmentally, people become more accurate at comparing numerosities as they get older (Piazza et al., 2010).

Beginning in primary school, it becomes possible to investigate children's understanding of the digits. Sekuler and Mierkiewicz (1977) had kindergarteners, first graders, fourth graders, seventh graders, and adults compare pairs of numbers. They found a symbolic distance effect at all ages. This finding has been replicated and extended with six-, seven-, and eight-year-old children (Holloway & Ansari, 2009) and with eight-, nine-, and 10-year old children (Landerl & Kölle, 2009).

Ansari and Dhital (2006) investigated the neural correlates of numerosity in 10-year-old children and adults. The children displayed a *neural distance effect* – greater activation for near-distance comparisons than far-distance comparisons – in left IPS. The adults also displayed a neural distance effect in left IPS, as well as one in right IPS. These results are further evidence of comparable magnitude representations in young children and adults, with similar neural bases (Cantlon et al., 2006). The neural correlates of the symbolic distance effect have been investigated in 10-year-old children (Ansari, Garcia, Lucas, Hamon, & Dhital, 2005). The adults in this study displayed a neural distance effect in bilateral IPS, a finding that has been replicated in numerous studies. By contrast, the children displayed neural distance effects in a network of right prefrontal areas, including right IFG.

Taken together, these results demonstrate both continuities and discontinuities in the development of number. Young infants and primary- and middle-school children show nonsymbolic distance effects that are comparable to those of adults, both behaviorally and neurally, suggesting a common representation of numerosity in IPS. The story for the symbolic distance effect is different: while both adults and children show this effect behaviorally, the neural correlates are different, with adults showing modulated activation in both the left and right IPS but 10-year-old children showing it in prefrontal cortex. Thus, the neuroscience data reveal a developmental discontinuity in how number symbols are processed.

This is educationally important, since it has been shown that distance effects, both nonsymbolic (Halberda et al., 2008) and symbolic (Holloway & Ansari, 2009) are correlated with arithmetical performance.

## Lifelong learning (adulthood)

Nonsymbolic distance effects are regularly found in adults (Buckley & Gillman, 1974). There is also a symbolic distance effect (Buckley & Gillman, 1974; Moyer & Landauer, 1967). The assumption has been that both effects reflect a common magnitude representation. This assumption has been corroborated by recent studies investigating the neural correlates of these effects. In general, close numbers evoke more activation than distant numbers in the bilateral IPS, whether comparing numerosities (Ansari & Dhital, 2006; Castelli et al., 2006) or number symbols (see, e.g., Fias, Lammertyn, Reynvoet, Dupont, & Orban, 2003; Pinel, Dehaene, Rivière, & Le Bihan, 2001).

There is also an interesting developmental shift from primary and middle school to adulthood in understanding natural number symbols. In children, the neural correlate of the symbolic distance effect is right prefrontal cortex (Ansari et al., 2005), which is associated with executive function and controlled cognition more generally (Shallice & Evans, 1978). For them, mapping number symbols to magnitude referents is an effortful process. By contrast, the neural correlates for adults include bilateral IPS, indicating a more integrated neural representation of number symbols and their magnitude referents.

A strikingly similar anterior-to-posterior shift in the brain is observed in arithmetic development. Rivera, Reiss, Eckert, and Menon (2005) had children aged 8–19 solve addition and subtraction problems. Behaviorally, accuracy rates were high across the age range (greater than 85%), indicating that all of the children were arithmetically competent. Response times decreased linearly with age, from over 2000 ms in the younger children to close to 1000 ms in the older children. It is interesting to consider the neural implications of this behavioral speedup, which has been found in other studies (e.g., Koshmider & Ashcraft, 1991). One possibility is that children across the age range activate the same cortical network, i.e., use similar processing, but that younger children are less efficient than older children. In fact, the fMRI data revealed a very different picture. Younger children activated a network of frontal areas associated with executive function, including bilateral middle frontal gyrus (MFG) and left anterior cingulate cortex (ACC). They also activated frontal and temporal areas associated with controlled retrieval from declarative memory, including left IFG and medial temporal lobe/hippocampus. In other words, younger children activated a cortical network associated with effortful or strategic processing to solve arithmetic problems. Over development, activation in this strategic network decreased and activation in a more posterior and more domain-specific network increased. This included left FG, which is associated with visual symbol processing; left supramarginal gyrus (SMG), an area adjacent to AG, which is also associated with retrieval of verbally coded information; and IPS, which is associated with magnitude processing. Thus, over development, children transitioned from strategic processing to a mixture of symbol processing, automatic (verbal) memory retrieval, and magnitude processing. This qualitative shift, which was opaque given the behavioral data alone, highlights how neuroscience data can provide unique insights into mathematical development.

## Embodied Understanding of Numbers and Arithmetic

In what sense are numbers and arithmetic meaningful? A conventional answer in logic and the philosophy of mathematics is that mathematical symbols and expressions denote sets of objects, and are essentially abstract even when the objects themselves are concrete. An emerging alternative in mathematical cognition is that mathematical symbols and expressions gain meaning through their grounding in the perceptual and motor systems of the body (Lakoff & Núñez, 2000). This view is consistent with the emphasis that mathematics education places on manipulatives such as Cuisenaire rods for building mathematical understanding (Montessori, 1966). It is for this reason that many curricula have children first use manipulatives to help them construct an informal semantics for new mathematical concepts before introducing them to the relevant symbolic formalism.

Although we have emphasized the abstract nature of number – numerosity is a property of a set – humans also think about number in a more embodied way. Many cultures have ways of representing numerosities and counting practices in terms of body parts. We count and show numbers on our fingers because fingers are handy sets to manipulate. These days we use our fingers for numbers up to 10, and you would be forgiven for thinking that we simply hold up as many fingers as the numerosity we wish to convey. However, it is more complicated than that. First, even in presenting numbers to 10, there are cultural conventions. For example, in Northern Europe 1 is presented as the index finger, but in Southern Europe it presented as the thumb, and in Japan as bending the little finger. Even in Europe there existed a traditional method for presenting numbers up to 10 000 on the fingers, which seems to have died out. Illiterate cultures without specialized number words use other body parts in addition to fingers to represent numbers higher than 10. The Yupno of Papua New Guinea count up to 33 using their toes, eyes, ears, nose, nostrils, nipples, belly-button, testicles, and penis (see Butterworth, 1999, Chapter 5, for more details of these practices).

We also think of numbers in a spatial way. This is partly because we see numbers spatially arrayed in everyday life: on clock faces, written out horizontally, and so on. In school, the digits 1 to 10 are almost always written from left to right, and number lines used in teaching similarly put small numbers on the left and large numbers on the right. There is even an unconscious association between small numbers and the left of space, and large numbers and the right side. This was first demonstrated by Dehaene and colleagues. They asked subjects to judge whether a number between 1 and 9 was odd or even, and press a left-hand button for odd, and a right-hand button for even (and vice versa, of course). They found that the response was faster with the left hand for small numbers, and with the right hand for large numbers. They memorably called this the "spatial–numerical association of response codes", or SNARC effect (Dehaene, Bossini, & Giraux, 1993). This effect has been replicated many times. Indeed, the neural basis for the SNARC effect involves the same areas as number processing in the parietal cortex, which is also involved in spatial cognition, suggesting an intrinsic relationship between number and space (Hubbard, Piazza, Pinel, & Dehaene, 2005; Rusconi, Turatto, & Umiltà, 2007). However, there is evidence to suggest that the mental relationship between numbers and space depends on experience and on task. So, for example, in Dehaene's original study, a group of Iranians who write from right to left showed the reverse relationship – a left-hand advantage for large numbers and right-hand advantage for small numbers. Also, if subjects are asked to study a clock face, where the larger numbers are on the left, before the task, this also reverses the SNARC effect (Bächtold, Baumüller, & Brugger, 1998). The SNARC effect seems to depend on the task requiring a lateralized motor response – such as left and right hands.

The close connection between mathematical thinking on one hand and visuo-motor processing on the other – and the neural bases of this connection – have been known to neuropsychologists for years. The *Gerstmann syndrome* is a combination of four impairments, two involving symbol systems (dyscalculia and dysgraphia) and two involving the visuomotor system (left–right disorientation and finger agnosia). It is associated with lesions to left AG. Gerstmann himself thought that the key to the syndrome was an impaired "body schema," that showed up in the left–right disorientation, and particularly in finger agnosia. Rusconi, Walsh, and Butterworth (2005) demonstrated that applying rTMS over left AG disrupts performance on both a number task and a finger gnosia task. Nevertheless, the functional relationship between the neural representation of fingers and calculation has been questioned. Since both involve the left AG, it could be simply that damage that affects the neural representation of fingers, especially hand shapes that could be used to present numbers, is likely to also affect a functionally independent but anatomically neighboring calculation system (Rusconi, Pinel, Dehaene, & Kleinschmidt, 2010).

Nevertheless, there is emerging evidence of an association between visuospatial and motor skills on one hand and mathematical achievement on the other. Fayol, Barrouillet, and Marinthe (1998) found that individual differences in motor ability predict individual differences in mathematical achievement. Using a longitudinal design, measures of finger agnosia, similar to those used with neurological patients, were collected in children at age 5. These included a task in which the children's eyes were closed, and the experimenter touched one finger twice or two fingers. The child, with eyes open, then had to point to the fingers touched. Measures of general intellectual development and mathematical achievement (number and arithmetic concepts) were collected at ages 5 and 6. Finger gnosia measures were a significant predictor of mathematical achievement, even after the effects of general intellectual development and age were partialed out.

Another study was able to refine these results. Noël (2005) tested five-year-olds for finger gnosia and left–right disorientation. Fifteen months later, numerical and reading abilities were assessed. She found that performance in both the finger gnosia and the left–right test were good predictors of numerical skills one year later, but not good predictors of reading skills, which proves their specificity to mathematics. However, because the left–right test was also a pre-dictor, Noël suspected that these tests are just picking up the development of the parietal cortex, not the functional role of fingers.

She further explored this in a training study. If finger representations do aid the development of number concepts and arithmetic, training on finger tasks should improve the acquisition of arithmetical skills in young children. Bafalluy and Noël (2008) trained children in Grade 1 who were found to have poor finger gnosia on finger representation; this improved both their finger gnosia to better-than-average levels, and also their arithmetical performance. "These results indicate that improving finger gnosia in young children is possible and that it can provide a useful support to learning mathematics" (Bafalluy & Noël, 2008).

Bodily activities play other roles in developing arithmetic. In particular, fin-gers are widely used by young children in the early stages acquiring addition skills. For example, Geary, Hoard, Byrd-Craven, and DeSoto (2004) found that American kindergarteners used fingers on 29% of addition trials where the sum was less than 11, and 76% of trials where it was more than 10. In first and second grade, they were still using fingers on 35% of trials. By contrast, Chinese chil-dren of the same age did not use fingers at all (Geary, Bow-Thomas, Liu, & Siegler, 1996). Geary et al. note that "The use of fingers during counting appears to be a working memory aid that allows the child to keep track of the addends physically, rather than mentally, during the process of counting."

In a study on preschoolers, pointing at objects to be counted helps coordinate counting words and objects to be counted, and helps segregate items counted from those to be counted (Alibali & DiRusso, 1999).

## Individual Differences in Mathematical Achievement

Why are some people better at mathematics than others? The question of individual differences is critical for mathematics education. There are of course many causes that could affect all school subjects, such as general intellectual ability, working-memory capacity, socioeconomic status, educational experi-ences, missing school, conduct difficulties, self-esteem, and so on. Here we focus on differences that are specific to learning mathematics.

For example, consider the distance effect, defined as the difference in response times between slower near-distance comparisons (e.g., 8 versus 9) and faster far-distance comparisons (e.g., 1 versus 9). This effect has been replicated hun-dreds of times in the literature. However, not *every* individual shows a distance effect; an average, after all, is typically made up of rather unaverage people. Most people exhibit a distance effect – but some show no effect of distance, and a few even show an *inverse* distance effect, i.e., are faster for near-distance versus far-distance comparisons! Individual differences such as these are proving to be more than statistical noise. Even typically developing people differ quantitatively in their distance effects, and potentially in their neural representations of mathematical concepts. This raises the question of whether individual differences in mathematical cognition are associated with individual differences in mathematical achievement. This question has been addressed in a number of important studies that span the developmental range.

## Primary and middle childhood (5–12)

Holloway and Ansari (2009) used a cross-sectional design to investigate whether individual differences in number representation are associated with individual differences in mathematical achievement. They measured the symbolic and nonsymbolic distance effects in six-, seven-, and eight-year-old children, as well as their mathematical achievement test scores. The size of a child's symbolic distance effect predicted his or her arithmetic fluency (i.e., solving one-digit arithmetic problems in a timed manner), even after controlling for age, raw processing speed, and other general variables. By contrast, the size of the nonsymbolic distance effect did not predict arithmetic fluency. These findings suggest that the fidelity of the mapping between number symbols and magnitude representations – but not necessarily the fidelity of the magnitude representations themselves – is related to mathematics achievement.

De Smedt, Verschaffel, and Ghesquière (2009) used a longitudinal design to sharpen these cross-sectional findings. They measured the symbolic distance effect of children in first grade, and their mathematical achievement in second grade. The size of a child's symbolic distance effect in first grade predicted mathematical achievement in second grade, even after controlling for fluid intelligence, processing speed, and age. The longitudinal nature of this design is stronger evidence that a connection between number symbols and magnitude representations is important for mathematical achievement.

## Secondary school and adolescence (12–18)

We are aware of only one study of students in secondary school investigating whether individual differences in mathematical cognition are associated with individual differences in mathematical achievement. Halberda et al. (2008) had 14-year-olds perform a nonsymbolic comparison task. They found that individual differences in the size of the nonsymbolic distance effect were retroactively associated with individual differences in mathematical achievement in kindergarten through third grade. This association was probably not due to maturational factors: the correlation remained significant even after general intelligence, working memory, visuospatial ability, and other general ability measures in third grade were partialed out. This finding that the fidelity of one's magnitude representations may be important for mathematical achievement is inconsistent with the Holloway and Ansari (2009) findings, demonstrating the need for further research.

## Lifelong learning (adulthood)

Grabner et al. (2007) investigated the neural correlates of individual differences among adults, focusing on arithmetic ability. They included two groups of participants, one low in mathematical competence and one high, who were otherwise comparable in age and general intelligence. Multiplication fluency was measured by having participants solve one-digit problems, and multiplication calculation was measured by having them solve multidigit problems. At the group level, high-competence participants showed greater activation in left AG than low-competence participants. Critically, this was also true at the individual level: mathematical competence was positively correlated with left AG activation, even after overall processing speed was partialed out. Recall that left AG has been implicated in the retrieval of arithmetic facts. Thus, this study suggests that one source of individual differences in mathematical competence is the ability to use relatively fast and effortless memory retrieval when solving arithmetic problems, as opposed to relatively slow and effortful strategic processing.

## Dyscalculia

Developmental dyscalculia is usually and rather broadly defined as a low mathematical achievement in the presence of otherwise normal intelligence and access to educational resources. Current prevalence estimates are between 3% and 6% (Reigosa-Crespo et al., 2011; Shalev, 2007), which is roughly one child in every classroom.

Dyscalculia has been neglected both in research support compared with other neurodevelopmental disorders (Bishop, 2010) and in public recognition, even though its impact on life chances can be at least as damaging as, for example, dyslexia (Parsons & Bynner, 2005). Recent research has revealed that dyscalculia is a congenital condition, often inherited, that can persist into adulthood. It can occur in the presence of normal or superior intelligence and working memory (Landerl, Bevan, & Butterworth, 2004); see Butterworth et al. (2011) for a review.

Thus, it appears to be a deficit specific to learning mathematics, or more particularly to learning arithmetic.

## Dyscalculia as a core deficit in processing numerosities

We have argued that dyscalculia is due to a *core deficit* in representing and processing numerosities (Butterworth, 2005, 2010; Butterworth et al., 2011). People with dyscalculia lack an intuitive sense of the numerosities of sets. This impairs their understanding of the number symbols defined in reference to these numerosities, and ultimately their understanding of arithmetic operations defined over number symbols. The result is low arithmetical achievement beginning in elementary school. This impairment has far-reaching effects, as number and arithmetic are foundational for higher-level mathematics, from algebra to calculus and beyond.

It is important from both a practical and a theoretical perspective to distinguish learners who are bad at math from those who are dyscalculic. As noted above, there are many reasons for poor math, including lack of access to appropriate education. Thus, to be dyscalculic means not just poor at math compared with peers, but to have the core deficit as well. To assess for dyscalculia therefore requires tests of very simple numerosity processing, that depend only minimally on access to appropriate education. For example, Butterworth (2010) and Butterworth et al. (2011) have argued for tests of enumerating small sets and for comparing small numbers.

This distinction is important because different studies of dyscalculia have adopted different inclusion criteria, and this has led to conflicting results. Some studies have adopted overly broad criteria, with dyscalculic groups likely included both real dyscalculics and those who were simply bad at mathematics. For example, Rousselle and Noël (2007) defined their dyscalculic group as children scoring below the 15th percentile on a standardized test of mathematical achievement.

## Dyscalculia in primary and middle childhood (5–12)

The core-deficit hypothesis is consistent with the finding reviewed above that individual differences in elementary-school mathematical achievement are retroactively predicted by the size of the *nonsymbolic* distance effect in adolescence (Halberda et al., 2008; Piazza et al., 2010). Several studies have shown that simple numerosity, such as naming the number of objects in a set or comparing the numerosity of two sets, is defective in dyscalculia (see Butterworth, 2010, for a review).

Another possibility is that dyscalculia is a deficit in *mapping* number symbols onto intact representations of numerical magnitude. This mapping hypothesis is consistent with the findings reviewed above that mathematical achievement in elementary school is predicted by the size of the *symbolic* distance effect (Holloway & Ansari, 2009; De Smedt et al., 2009). Thus, the predictive value of the nonsymbolic versus symbolic distance effect is important for distinguishing between the numerosity and mapping types of deficit. The mapping hypothesis was supported by early studies in the literature, which we review first. However, later studies, which have adopted better inclusion criteria, find evidence for poor discrete magnitude representations – and thus the numerosity hypothesis – at both the behavioral and brain levels.

Rousselle and Noël (2007) compared a group of typically developing second graders and a group with dyscalculia. The dyscalculic group was slower than the control group for symbolic comparison after controlling for age and overall processing speed. By contrast, the two groups were comparable for nonsymbolic comparison. This study supports the hypothesis of a mapping deficit. However, because a rather liberal inclusion criterion for the dyscalculia group was used – mathematical achievement 1.5 standard deviations below the mean – it is possible that these results were driven by typically developing children at the low end of the normal curve rather than by true dyscalculics. More generally, studies that use a liberal inclusion criterion often find conflicting results. Taking just the bottom 5%s dyscalculic, a study of 8- to 10-year-old children found that the dyscalculic group was slower than the control group on both symbolic and nonsymbolic comparison (Landerl & Kölle, 2009).

We can turn to the neuroscience data to more accurately identify the core deficit in dyscalculia. Kucian et al. (2006) conducted the first fMRI study of an neuropathology underlying dyscalculia. A group of 11-year-old children with dyscalculia and a group of age-matched controls performed a nonsymbolic comparison task and an approximate addition task, both of which likely tapped discrete magnitude representations. The largest group differences were observed on an approximate addition task, where the dyscalculic group displayed less activation in a bilateral frontoparietal network including MFG, IFG, and IPS. The finding of a neural difference for an approximate reasoning task supports the hypothesis that the numerosity representations themselves be defective, not just the mapping from symbol to the representations. An additional insight from this study is that there is no qualitative difference between the arithmetic networks of typically developing children and those with dyscalculia – both activated the same network of frontal and parietal area. Rather, there is a quantitative difference in the degree to which the network is activated. In particular, the lower IPS activation in the dyscalculic group implicates a weakened representation of numerosity.

Price et al. (2007) investigated differences between a group of 12-year-old children with dyscalculia and a group of age-matched controls using a nonsymbolic comparison task. (Dyscalculia was defined liberally, as mathematical achievement at least 1.5 standard deviations below the mean.) Behaviorally, the two groups were comparable. However, the fMRI data revealed an important cortical difference: whereas the control group showed the typical neural distance effect in right IPS, the dyscalculia group did not. These results suggest a weakened magnitude representation in people with dyscalculia, consistent with the numerosity proposal. They also demonstrate how neuroscience methods can reveal differences not visible at the behavioral level.

There are also structural differences in the brains of dyscalculics that turn out to be in the left and right IPS, precisely the brain areas implicated in numerosity processing (see Figure 8.2). The first such study was by Isaacs, Edmonds, Lucas,

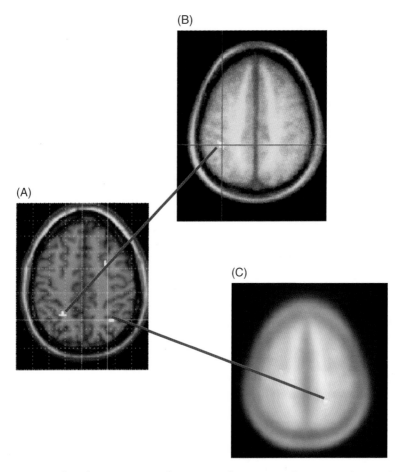

**Figure 8.2** Reduced grey-matter density in the numerosity-processing regions of dyscalculic brains. (A) Brain areas dedicated to numerosity processing (Castelli et al., 2006, with permission). (B) Reduced grey-matter density in left parietal numerosity-processing area in dyscalculic adolescents (Isaacs et al., 2001, with permission). (C) Reduced grey-matter density in right parietal numerosity-processing area in dyscalculic children (Rotzer et al., 2008, with permission).

and Gadian (2001), who found a reduction in grey-matter density in a small region in the left IPS; Rotzer et al. (2008) subsequently found reduced grey matter density in the right IPS in younger subjects, reflecting the developmental trajectory mentioned above, that simple number processing, especially of non-symbolic numerosities, goes from a predominantly right hemisphere locus to a bilateral one.

## Lifelong learning

Developmental dyscalculia can persist into adulthood, though it is unclear what proportion of early dyscalculic learners remains in this condition. One study by Shalev, Manor, and Gross-Tsur (2005) found that some 40% of 11-year-olds were still dyscalculic at age 17, and almost all were in the bottom quartile on a standardized arithmetic task. However, Shalev et al. used a criterion of two years below age norms, but did not test specifically for a core deficit. Certainly, it is not hard to find examples of adults with severe math difficulties and a core deficit, such as "Charles," described by Butterworth (1999). There have been few published functional studies of the brains of adult developmental dyscalculics. One example that used EEG with two-digit addition problems found that older subjects tended to use both hemispheres while younger ones used the left hemisphere predominantly, and suggested that the younger subjects showed more strategic flexibility in how they solved the problems (El Yagoubi, Lemaire, & Besson, 2005). Nevertheless, thorough investigations of the effects of normal aging on the brain systems for mathematics are urgently needed, along with studies of the effects of clinical conditions that are associated with aging, such as mild cognitive impairment and the dementias.

## Educating the Mathematical Brain

One obstacle for bridging from neuroscience to education is that neuroscience methods are not easily portable to the classroom. However, neuroscientists are beginning to isolate elements of mathematical thinking and learning that occur in school, and study them in carefully controlled laboratory settings. The results are pointing the way to new instruction for typical classrooms, and to promising instructional interventions for dyscalculia. It is true that, to date, neuroscience has not had the impact on education – for good or ill – that cognitive and developmental psychology has had. Thorndike's (1922) book, *The Psychology of Arithmetic*, created a focus on drilling simple number bonds. In the 1930s, Brownell, in several important publications, applied psychological ideas about meaningful practice to how math should be taught (Brownell, 1928, 1935, 1938).

In the 1950s and 1960s, Piaget's "constructivist" theories about the nature of cognitive development were very influential. Constructivism emphasizes the child's construction of new schemas (accommodation) when new stimuli cannot be understood using existing schemas (assimilation). Both Montessori in her schools, and Gattegno in the use of Cuisenaire rods, were deeply influenced by Piaget. Many mathematics education researchers continue to advocate constructivist instruction over direct instruction (Bransford, Franks, Vye, & Sherwood, 1989; Duffy & Jonassen, 1992; von Glasersfeld, 1989). Whereas direct instruction assumes that knowledge can be rather directly communicated ("transmitted") from teachers to students, constructivist instruction proposes that students must construct their own knowledge if it is to be meaningful. The emphasis is on particular kinds of activity such as game playing and other hands-on learning.

More recently, Johnson, Karmiloff-Smith, and Mareschal, and their colleagues, have proposed a line of research, based on Piagetian ideas, that they call "neuro-constructivism" (see Westermann, Thomas, & Karmiloff-Smith, 2010, for a recent review). In this, neural specializations in the brain are not directly inherited – the brain does not start out modularized for specific cognitive functions – but rather brain organization is shaped by interaction with the environment, and specializations emerge in a consistent way largely as a result of the common structures of experience and some intrinsic biases in neural receptivity to particular types of information.

Here we focus on two areas where neuroscience can inform education: first, methods of instruction; and, second, individual differences, including new approaches to remediating dyscalculia.

## Methods of instruction

*Practice and transfer*    Direct instruction is the term for a range of traditional classroom activities, including lecture, recitation, reviews, seatwork, home-work, quizzes, and exams (see, e.g., Rosenshine, 1995). In an important early study, Delazer and colleagues investigated the neural consequences of one aspect of direct instruction, practice (Delazer et al., 2005). Adults practiced solving 18 complex multiplication problems, each involving a one-digit operand and a two-digit operand. These arithmetic facts are not normally memorized in school. Participants subsequently verified complex multiplication problems in the scanner, half of which were trained and half of which were untrained. Participants were faster and more accurate on trained versus untrained problems. More importantly, the two classes of problems activated different cortical networks. The network activated by untrained problems included bilateral IPS (associated with magnitude processing) and bilateral IFG (associated with executive function and verbal working memory). This is essentially the same frontoparietal network that Grabner et al. (2009) found when participants self-reported using effortful, strategic processing to solve simple arithmetic problems. By contrast, the trained network included left AG (associated with memory retrieval when solving simple arithmetic problems). These findings demonstrate that following practice – a component of direct instruction – there is a shift from strategy-based processing to memory-based processing, specifically retrieval of verbally/symbolically coded arithmetic facts.

Ischebeck et al. (2006) investigated whether there are different practice effects for multiplication and subtraction. Adults practiced complex multiplication and subtraction problems outside the scanner, and then verified trained and untrained problems in the scanner. Participants were again faster and more accurate on trained versus untrained problems, regardless of the operation, replicating and extending the work of Delazer et al. (2005). At the neural level, the results for multiplication also replicated the work of Delazer et al. (2005), with a training shift from a frontoparietal network (including IPS) to left AG, again suggesting a shift from strategy- to memory-based processing. Critically, the results for subtraction were different: both trained and untrained problems recruited the frontoparietal network associated with strategy-based processing. This suggests that the neural consequences of practice are contingent on the mathematical concept being practiced.

To sum up the results of these two studies, for complex multiplication, the improvement in behavioral performance following practice is a function of a shift from strategic to memory-based processing. This is the analogous to the behavioral patterns and cortical shift that Rivera et al. (2005) documented for simple addition and subtraction over development, where the left inferior parietal lobe becomes increasingly specialized for addition. By contrast, in the case of complex subtraction, the continuous improvement in behavioral performance following practice is a function of increased efficiency in the frontoparietal network associated with strategic processing (Ischebeck et al., 2006). These findings are important, suggesting that if the pedagogical goal is to automatize subtraction, then mathematics educators should look beyond direct instruction methods.

## Individual differences

Neuroscience can help identify cognitive strengths and weakness in individual learners in a way that can inform the design of an educational context appropriate for that learner. This means ensuring that the learning context is adaptive to the learner's current needs and "zone of proximal development" (Vygotsky, 1978). This will include specifying the content that needs to acquired and a pace of progression suitable for the learner.

*Dyscalculia*   This approach is perhaps best exemplified in the learning contexts designed for dyscalculic learners. We have suggested that neuroscience has identified the core deficit, that is, the target for intervention – a deficit in processing numerosities. This does not however specify how dyscalculic learners can be helped.

One needs to turn to *pedagogic principles* and the best practice of special educational needs (SEN) teachers to design appropriate instruction. From a pedagogical perspective, activities that require the manipulation of concrete objects provide tasks that make number concepts meaningful by providing an intrinsic relationship between a *goal*, the *learner's action*, and the *informational feedback* on the action. This kind of feedback provides intrinsic motivation in a task, and this is of greater value to the learner than the extrinsic motives and rewards provided by a supervising teacher (Bruner, 1961; Deci, Koestner, & Ryan, 2001).

Experienced SEN teachers will use Cuisenaire rods, number tracks, and playing cards to give learners experience of the meaning of number. Through playing games with these physical objects, learners can discover from their manipulations, for example, which rod fits with an 8-rod to match a 10-rod, or how many beads to put out on the track to get from the given number to desired number, and so on (Butterworth & Yeo, 2004). These tasks afford discovery learning and the *construction* of solutions, which in turn enable learners to compare their solution with the correct solution, and if necessary adjust their own solution. These are powerful mechanisms for learning with understanding (Papert, 1980; Piaget, 1952).

Ideally, the experienced teacher will adapt the activities to match the learner's current level of understanding, and find ways to push the understanding into the zone of proximal development. However, this may require extensive one-to-one teaching, which may not always be possible, and which, in any case, will be expensive.

Tasks adapted to the learner's current level can now be achieved using software games that embody the pedagogic principles outlined above. The *Number Race* and *Graphogame-Maths* are adaptive games based on neuroscience that target basic numerosity processing, and appear to be effective (Räsänen, Salminen, Wilson, Aunioa, & Dehaene, 2009). However, neither requires learners to manipulate numerical quantities. Manipulation is critical for providing an intrinsic relationship between a task goal, the learner's action, and informational feedback on that action.

An approach that emulates the manipulative tasks used by SEN teachers has been taken in adaptive software that enables the construction of a solution, provides informational feedback, and offers a means to match the learner's solution to the correct solution in the case of error. See Butterworth et al. (2011) for further discussion. Examples can be downloaded from http://www.number-sense.co.uk/.

These games have not been subjected to large-scale evaluation, but one important advantage of adaptive software is that learners can do more practice per unit time than with a teacher. Thus, 12-year-old SEN learners using a number bonds game managed 4–11 trials per minute, while in an SEN class of three supervised learners only 1.4 trials per minute were completed during a 10 min observation. In another SEN group of 11-year-olds, the game elicited on average 173 learner manipulations in 13 min (where a perfect performance, in which every answer is correct, is 88 in 5 min, since the software adapts the timing according to the response) (Butterworth & Laurillard, 2010).

Butterworth et al. (2011) conclude that "At present it is not yet clear whether early and appropriately-targeted intervention can turn a dyscalculic into a typical calculator. Dyscalculia may be like dyslexia in that early intervention can improve practical effectiveness without making the cognitive processing like those of the typically developing."

In dyslexia research, appropriate phonological training can have the effect of making patterns of neural activity more like those in typical readers (Eden et al., 2004). This is important, since it takes the measurement of the effects of an intervention beyond behavior into its underlying mechanisms. Is the same true for dyscalculia? So far, there has only been one study published about the effects of this kind of intervention on patterns of neural activity. In this study, by von Aster's group in Zurich, nine-year-old typical learners and matched nine-year-old dyscalculics (1.5 SD below average) were trained using a specially designed computer game (Kucian et al., 2011). The game required landing a spaceship on a number line from 0 to 100, according to the number on the spaceship, or simple calculation on the spaceship (see Figure 8.3(A)). The game was played for 15 min a day, 5 days a week, for 5 weeks. The effects of the training were assessed behaviorally, and were effective for both dyscalculic and typical learners, with a bigger effect for the dyscalculics, who nevertheless remained worse than the controls (see Figure 8.3(B)). Activation was measured in an fMRI task that required the child to determine whether three numbers were in ascending or descending order, compared with a control task in which they had to determine whether the digit "2" was present. In this situation, dyscalculics showed less parietal activation, but more frontal activation. The authors conclude that the "results lend further support to a deficient number

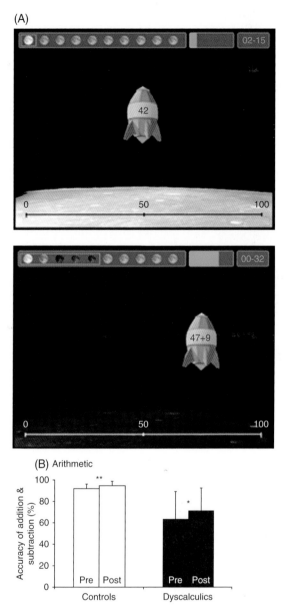

**Figure 8.3**  Effects of training on arithmetical performance and patterns of neural activity. Nine-year-old dyscalculic and typical learners were trained on a simple arithmetical tasks using a computer game for 15 min a day, 5 days a week, for 5 weeks. (A) The game "Rescue Calcularis" required the learner to land the spaceship on the number line below. In the top panel, the task was to land it at 42; in the bottom panel, it was to land at 18, the solution to 27 − 5. (B) Training was effective for both groups, but more for the dyscalculics (black bars). Nevertheless, they still failed to reach typical levels of performance after the training.

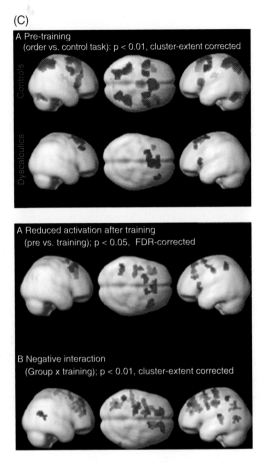

**Figure 8.3** (*continued*)  (C) Top panel: group differences in brain activity in a different number task before training (see text). The dyscalculics showed more frontal activation in the task compared with a control task. Bottom panel: training reduced frontal activity in both groups, but more so in the dyscalculics (negative interaction). (From Kucian et al. (2011) with permission.)

representation in the parietal lobe associated with dyscalculia, causing stronger engagement of supporting frontal lobe functions such as working memory and attentional control to solve a numerical task" (p. 792). The effect of training was striking. In both groups, there was a reduction in frontal activation, suggesting that the training transferred to the fMRI task, making it more automatic and thus dependent on parietal areas, and less strategic and thus dependent on frontal areas. This effect was even more marked in the dyscalculics. The effects of training, therefore, tended to move the dyscalculics to a more typical pattern of both behavior and neural activity, paralleling the shift observed in dyslexia training studies.

## Future Directions

Although neuroscience studies of mathematical thinking are in their infancy, they are already shedding light on topics of great relevance to education, including mathematical development, the spatial basis of mathematical concepts, the nature of individual differences in achievement, the neural correlates of different instructional approaches, the core deficit in dyscalculia, and the design and evaluation of effective remediation. Mathematical thinking is already an important bridge between education and neuroscience, and its importance will only grow. A scientific explanation of the neural bases of mathematics is necessary for an evidence-based education: for understanding why some instructional interventions (but not others) work for some children (but not others), and for informing the design of new instruction. Conversely, mathematics is one of the core symbol systems of human culture, and investigating the neural bases of this symbol system cannot help but generate new empirical paradigms and theoretical explanations that will enrich our understanding of the brain more generally.

Much of the research to date has focused on natural numbers and arithmetic operations defined over them. Comparatively little is known about the psychological and neuroscience underpinnings of more abstract and advanced concepts in mathematics such as negative numbers, place value, and algebra. We briefly review some initial attempts to fill this gap here. We also preview emerging research on the benefits of neural stimulation for mathematics learning.

### Negative numbers

Recent research has illuminated how adults mentally represent negative numbers. Adults show a symbolic distance effect for comparisons of negative numbers that parallels the one for comparisons of natural numbers, for example comparing −1 versus −4 is faster than −1 versus −-9. Some interpret this as evidence that negative numbers are mentally represented as magnitudes (Varma & Schwartz, 2011). Others argue that negative numbers do not have magnitude representations, but are instead mapped to natural numbers via symbolic rules (Tzelgov, Ganor-Stern, & Maymon-Schreiber, 2009). Under this account, when comparing negative numbers (e.g., which of −1 versus −4 is greater?), people first strip the negative signs, then reverse the judgment (e.g., which of 1 versus 4 is lesser?), and finally consult magnitude representations of natural numbers.

Mixed comparisons of negative numbers and natural numbers have the potential to resolve this debate. Tzelgov et al. (2009) found no effect of distance for mixed comparisons, with near comparisons (e.g., −1 versus 2) made as fast as far comparisons (e.g., −1 versus 7). They interpreted this as evidence that people use symbolic rules such as "positives are greater than negatives." However, more recent studies have found distance effects for mixed comparisons (Gullick, Wolford, & Temple, 2011; Krajcsi & Igács, 2010; Varma & Schwartz, 2011). Surprisingly, these effects have been in the inverse direction, with near comparisons faster than far comparisons, suggesting that the magnitude representations of negative numbers are spatially transformed.

Neuroscience data can potentially inform whether negative numbers are understood as magnitudes or using rules. Early studies are finding neural distance effects in bilateral IPS for comparisons of negative numbers and for mixed comparisons of negative numbers and natural numbers, consistent with magnitude representations (Blair, Rosenberg-Lee, Tsang, Schwartz, & Menon, 2010; Gullick et al., 2011). However, these studies also find neural distance effects in prefrontal areas associated with controlled rule processing. Further research is required to untangle the neural correlates of negative number understanding.

Some researchers are beginning to study the cognitive development of integer understanding (Varma & Schwartz, 2011). Others are asking the educational neuroscience question of whether different kinds of instruction – focusing on symbolic rules such as "positive particles cancel negative particles" versus visuomotor movements along number lines – set up different kinds of representation, with correspondingly different neural correlates (Tsang, Blair, Bofferding, Rosenberg-Lee, & Schwartz, 2011). Again, we expect these to be fruitful areas for future research.

## Place value

Place-value notation is a generative system for naming numbers using a small set of symbols. Our base-10 system uses the number symbols 0–9 plus a few extra symbols (".", "–") to name very large and very small numbers using relatively few digits. Place-value notation is important because its structure supports the standard algorithms for "long" arithmetic, for example enabling "borrowing" and "carrying." For this reason, mastering place-value notation is an important goal of early elementary education

Early research on place-value notation focused on how adults and children understand multidigit natural numbers. Consider the task of judging which of 79 versus 17 is greater. Initial studies suggested that, for large numbers such as these, people do not directly consult magnitude representations. Rather, they understand them as composite representations, sequentially comparing the face value of each place from left to right until a judgment is possible (Hinrichs, Berie, & Mosell, 1982; Hinrichs, Yurko, & Hu, 1981). Although some studies have challenged this finding (Dehaene, Dupoux, & Mehler, 1990), the results have largely held up. A particularly diagnostic finding is the *incompatibility effect*: when comparing two-digit numbers, response times are slower when the judgment based on the tens places conflicts with the judgment based on the ones place. For example, people are slower to compare 81 versus 19 than 79 versus 17 (Nuerk, Weger, & Willmes, 2001). Developmental studies of the incompatibility effect indicate that children have the adult composite representation of multidigit numbers as early as second grade (Landerl & Kölle, 2009; Nuerk, Kaufmann, Zoppoth, & Willmes, 2004).

Neuroscientists are identifying the neural correlates of place value in adults. Administering TMS over left AG while adults compare two-digit numbers disrupts number comparison (Göbel, Walsh, & Rushworth, 2001). Recall that this area is associated with the retrieval of symbolically or verbally coded arithmetic facts, and *not* with magnitude processing. This finding suggests that the composite representation of multidigit numbers is accessed and processed using symbolic rules. Further evidence was provided by a study investigating the neural basis of the incompatibility effect, which found greater activation for incompatible versus compatible comparisons in left SMG, an area adjacent to left AG (Liu, Wang, Corbly, Zhang, & Joseph, 2006). However, this study also found neural incompatibility effects in a number of other areas, including bilateral occipitotemporal cortex associated with processing the visual forms of numbers, prefrontal areas associated with controlled symbolic and attentional processing, and IPS, which is associated with magnitude processing. Thus, the neural representation of multidigit numbers remains an open question.

The emerging scientific understanding of how adults and children understand place value promises to inform progress in education. For example, a recent study found larger incompatibility effects in elementary-school-aged children with dyscalculia versus those who were typically developing, indicating that weakened composite representations of very large numbers is associated with low math achievement (Landerl & Kölle, 2009). Further research following up on this tantalizing result is needed.

## Algebra

Anderson and colleagues have conducted a series of fMRI studies of algebra problem solving. These studies have been driven by a theoretical model that assigns to left IFG the function of retrieving information from long-term memory, and to left posterior parietal cortex (PPC; an area posterior to IPS and AG) the function of maintaining and transforming mental representations (Anderson, 2007). These functions are critical for solving simple algebra equations (e.g., $x/3 + 2 = 8$), which requires both retrieving relevant arithmetic facts (e.g., $8 - 2 = 6$) and applying these facts to transform the current equation into a newer, simpler equation (e.g., $x/3 + 2 = 8 \rightarrow x/3 = 6$). As predicted by the model, the greater the number of arithmetic facts that must be retrieved to solve an algebra equation, the greater IFG activation, and the greater the number of transformations that must be performed, the greater PPC activation (Danker & Anderson, 2007; Stocco & Anderson, 2007).

Building on this basic finding, Sohn et al. (2004) investigated the neural processes associated with solving algebra equations versus story problems. They found increased bilateral PPC activation when solving algebra equations, consistent with the sequential transformations. By contrast, they found greater left IFG when solving story problems, consistent with this area's role in verbal working memory and "expressive" language.

Qin et al. (2004) took the next step towards educational relevance, investigating the effect of practice in a sample of children aged 12–15. The children practiced solving multistep algebra equations over the course of 5 days. Behavioral performance improved, of course. More interestingly, both left IFG and left PPC were less active after training, particularly as the number of transformations a problem required increased. This pattern was different from that observed in an earlier study of adults, who only showed a practice effect in left IFG (Qin et al., 2003). Taken together, these studies suggest that practice will have different effects in children versus adults.

The first neuroscience studies of fractions (Schmithorst & Brown, 2004), calculus (Krueger et al., 2008), and other advanced mathematical topics are beginning to appear, although much work remains to be done. Educational neuroscientists are also taking the first tentative steps towards incorporating neural measures of mathematical understanding into computer tutors, which typically depend solely on behavioral measures such as number of problems correct (Anderson, Betts, Ferris, & Fincham, 2010, 2012). We expect rapid progress in understanding the neural bases of abstract mathematical thinking and applying these insights to mathematics education in the future.

## Neural stimulation

One study has looked at the effect transcranial direct current stimulation (TDCS) on learning novel symbols (Cohen Kadosh, Soskic, Iuculano, Kanai, & Walsh, 2010). During TDCS, a weak current is applied constantly over time to enhance (anodal stimulation) or reduce (cathodal stimulation) the excitation of neuronal populations, with maximal effect on the stimulated area beneath the electrodes. Anodal stimulation over the right parietal improved learning of the novel symbols designed to be equivalent to numbers, and this improvement lasted until retesting six months later. This study suggests that more direct intervention in neural processes could help learning, especially for those struggling such as dyscalculics.

# References

Alibali, M. W., & DiRusso, A. A. (1999). The function of gesture in learning to count: More than keeping track. *Cognitive Development, 14*, 37–56.

Anderson, J. R. (2007). *How can the human mind occur in the physical universe?* Oxford: Oxford University Press.

Anderson, J. R., Betts, S. A., Ferris, J. L., & Fincham, J. M. (2010). Neural imaging to track mental states while using an intelligent tutoring system. *Proceedings of the National Academy of Sciences of the United States of America, 107*, 7018–7023.

Anderson, J. R., Betts, S. A., Ferris, J. L., & Fincham, J. M. (2012). Tracking children's mental states while solving algebra equations. *Human Brain Mapping, 33*, 2650–2665.

Ansari, D., & Dhital, B. (2006). Age-related changes in the activation of the intraparietal sulcus during nonsymbolic magnitude processing: An event-related functional magnetic resonance imaging study. *Journal of Cognitive Neuroscience, 18*, 1820–1828.

Ansari, D., Garcia, N., Lucas, E., Hamon, K., & Dhital, B. (2005). Neural correlates of symbolic number processing in children and adults. *NeuroReport, 16*, 1769–1773.

Antell, S. E., & Keating, D. P. (1983). Perception of numerical invariance in neonates. *Child Development, 54*, 695–701.

Bächtold, D., Baumüller, M., & Brugger, P. (1998). Stimulus–response compatibility in representational space. *Neuropsychologia, 36*, 731–735.

Bafalluy, M. G., & Noël, M.-P. (2008). Does finger training increase young children's numerical performance? *Cortex, 44*, 368–375. DOI 10.1016/j.cortex.2007.08.020

Bishop, D. V. M. (2010). Which neurodevelopmental disorders get researched and why? *PLoS ONE, 5*(11), e15112. DOI: 10.1371/journal.pone.0015112

Blair, K. P., Rosenberg-Lee, M., Tsang, J., Schwartz, D. L., & Menon, V. (2010, June). *Representations and rules in negative number processing*. Poster presented at the 16th Annual Meeting of the Organization for Human Brain Mapping, Barcelona, Spain.

Bransford, J. D., Franks, J. J., Vye, N. J., & Sherwood, R. D. (1989). New approaches to instruction: Because wisdom can't be told. In S. Vosniadou & A. Ortony (Eds.), *Similarity and analogical reasoning* (pp. 470–497). Cambridge: Cambridge University Press.

Brownell, W. A. (1928). *The development of children's number ideas in the primary grades.* Chicago, IL: University of Chicago.

Brownell, W. A. (1935). Psychological considerations in the learning and the teaching of arithmetic. *The teaching of arithmetic. The tenth yearbook of the National Council of Teachers of Mathematics.* New York: Teachers College, Columbia University.

Brownell, W. A. (1938). Readiness and the arithmetic curriculum. *The Elementary School Journal, 38*(5), 344–354.

Bruner, J. S. (1961). The act of discovery. *Harvard Educational Review, 31*, 21–32.

Buckley, P. B., & Gillman, C. B. (1974). Comparisons of digits and dot patterns. *Journal of Experimental Psychology, 103*, 1131–1136.

Butterworth, B. (1999). *The mathematical brain*. London: Macmillan.

Butterworth, B. (2005). Developmental dyscalculia. In J. I. D. Campbell (Ed.), *Handbook of mathematical cognition* (pp. 455–467). Hove, UK: Psychology.

Butterworth, B. (2010). Foundational numerical capacities and the origins of dyscalculia. *Trends in Cognitive Sciences, 14*, 534–541. DOI: 10.1016/j.tics.2010.09.007

Butterworth, B., & Laurillard, D. (2010). Low numeracy and dyscalculia: Identification and intervention. *ZDM Mathematics Education, 42*, 527–539. DOI: 10.1007/s11858-010-0267-4

Butterworth, B., Varma, S., & Laurillard, D. (2011). Dyscalculia: From brain to education. *Science, 332*, 1049–1053. DOI: 10.1126/science.1201536

Butterworth, B., & Yeo, D. (2004). *Dyscalculia guidance*. London: nferNelson.

Cantlon, J. F., Brannon, E. M., Carter, E. J., & Pelphrey, K. A. (2006). Functional imaging of numerical processing in adults and 4-y-old children. *Public Library of Science Biology, 4*(5), e125. DOI: 10.1371/journal.pbio.0040125

Castelli, F., Glaser, D. E., & Butterworth, B. (2006). Discrete and analogue quantity processing in the parietal lobe: A functional MRI study. *Proceedings of the National Academy of Sciences of the United States of America, 103*(12), 4693–4698.

Cockcroft, W. H. (1982). *Mathematics counts: Report of the Committee of Inquiry into the Teaching of Mathematics in Schools under the chairmanship of Dr W H Cockcroft*. London: HMSO.

Cohen Kadosh, R., Soskic, S., Iuculano, T., Kanai, R., & Walsh, V. (2010). Modulating neuronal activity produces specific and long-lasting changes in numerical competence. *Current Biology, 20*, 2016–2020. DOI: 10.1016/j.cub.2010.10.007

Danker, J. F., & Anderson, J. R. (2007). The roles of prefrontal and posterior parietal cortex in algebra problem-solving: A case of using cognitive modeling to inform neuroimaging data. *NeuroImage, 35*, 1365–1377.

De Smedt, B., Verschaffel, L., & Ghesquière, P. (2009). The predictive value of numerical magnitude comparison for individual differences in mathematics achievement. *Journal of Experimental Child Psychology, 103*(4), 469–479.

Deci, E. L., Koestner, R., & Ryan, R. M. (2001). Extrinsic rewards and intrinsic motivation in education: Reconsidered once again. *Review of Educational Research, 71*(1), 1–27. DOI: 10.3102/00346543071001001

Dehaene, S., Bossini, S., & Giraux, P. (1993). The mental representation of parity and numerical magnitude. *Journal of Experimental Psychology: General, 122*, 371–396.

Dehaene, S., Dupoux, E., & Mehler, J. (1990). Is numerical comparison digital? Analogical and symbolic effects in two-digit number comparison. *Journal of Experimental Psychology: Human Perception and Performance, 16*, 626–641.

Dehaene, S., Piazza, M., Pinel, P., & Cohen, L. (2003). Three parietal circuits for number processing. *Cognitive Neuropsychology, 20*, 487–506.

Delazer, M., & Butterworth, B. (1997). A dissociation of number meanings. *Cognitive Neuropsychology, 14*, 613–636.

Delazer, M., Ischebeck, A., Domahs, F., Zamarian, L., Koppelstaetter, F., Siedentopf, C. M., Kaufmann, L., & Benke, T. (2005). Learning by strategies and learning by drill – evidence from an fMRI study. *NeuroImage, 25*, 838–849.

Duffy, T. M., & Jonassen, D. (Eds.). (1992). *Constructivism and the technology of instruction: A conversation*. Englewood Cliffs, NJ: Erlbaum.

Eden, G., Jones, K., Cappell, K., Gareau, L., Wood, F., Zeffiro, T., Dietz, N., Agnew, J., & Flowers, D. (2004). Neural changes following remediation in adult developmental dyslexia. *Neuron, 44,* 411-422.

El Yagoubi, R., Lemaire, P., & Besson, M. (2005). Effects of aging on arithmetic problem-solving: An event-related brain potential study. *Journal of Cognitive Neuroscience, 17*(1), 37–50. DOI: 10.1162/0898929052880084

Fayol, M., Barrouillet, P., & Marinthe, C. (1998). Predicting arithmetical achievement from neuro-psychological performance: A longitudinal study. *Cognition, 68,* 63–70.

Fias, W., Lammertyn, J., Reynvoet, B., Dupont, P., & Orban, G. A. (2003). Parietal representation of symbolic and nonsymbolic magnitude. *Journal of Cognitive Neuroscience, 15,* 47–56.

Geary, D. C., Bow-Thomas, C. C., Liu, F., & Siegler, R. S. (1996). Development of arithmetical competencies in Chinese and American children: Influence of age, language, and schooling. *Child Development, 67*(5), 2022–2044.

Geary, D. C., Hoard, M. K., Byrd-Craven, J., & DeSoto, M. C. (2004). Strategy choices in simple and complex addition: Contributions of working memory and counting knowledge for children with mathematical disability. *Journal of Experimental Child Psychology, 88*(2), 121–151. DOI: 10.1016/j.jecp.2004.03.002

Göbel, S., Walsh, V., & Rushworth, F. S. (2001). The mental number line and the human angular gyrus. *NeuroImage, 14,* 1278–1289.

Grabner, R. H., Ansari, D., Koschutnig, K., Reishofer, G., Ebner, F., & Neuper, C. (2009). To retrieve or to calculate? Left angular gyrus mediates the retrieval of arithmetic facts during problem solving. *Neuropsychologia, 47*(2), 604–608.

Grabner, R. H., Ansari, D., Reishofer, G., Stern, E., Ebner, F., & Neuper, C. (2007). Individual differences in mathematical competence predict parietal brain activation during calculation. *NeuroImage, 38,* 346-356.

Gross, J., Hudson, C., & Price, D. (2009). *The long term costs of numeracy difficulties*. London: Every Child a Chance Trust, KPMG.

Gullick, M. M., Wolford, G., & Temple, E. (2011, April) *Understanding less than nothing: An fMRI study of negative number comparisons*. Poster session presented at the annual meeting of the Cognitive Neuroscience Society, San Francisco, CA.

Halberda, J., Mazzocco, M. M. M., & Feigenson, L. (2008). Individual differences in non-verbal number acuity correlate with maths achievement. *Nature, 455,* 665–668. DOI: 10.1038/nature07246

Hinrichs, J. V., Berie, J. L., & Mosell, M. K. (1982). Place information in multidigit number comparison. *Memory and Cognition, 10,* 487–495.

Hinrichs, J. V., Yurko, D. S., & Hu, J. M. (1981). Two-digit number comparison: Use of place information. *Journal of Experimental Psychology: Human Perception and Performance, 7,* 890–901.

Holloway, I. D., & Ansari, D. (2009). Mapping numerical magnitudes onto symbols: The numerical distance effect and individual differences in children's mathematics achievement. *Journal of Experimental Child Psychology, 103*(1), 17–29.

Hubbard, E. M., Piazza, M., Pinel, P., & Dehaene, S. (2005). Interactions between number and space in parietal cortex. *Nature Reviews Neuroscience, 6*(6), 435–448.

Isaacs, E. B., Edmonds, C. J., Lucas, A., & Gadian, D. G. (2001). Calculation difficulties in children of very low birthweight: A neural correlate. *Brain, 124,* 1701–1707.

Ischebeck, A., Zamarian, L., Siedentopf, C., Koppelstatter, F., Benke, T., Felber, S., & Delazer, M. (2006). How specifically do we learn? Imaging the learning of multiplication and subtraction. *NeuroImage, 30*(4), 1365–1375.

Iuculano, T., Tang, J., Hall, C. W. B., & Butterworth, B. (2008). Core information processing deficits in developmental dyscalculia and low numeracy. *Developmental Science, 11*(5), 669–680.

Izard, V., Dehaene-Lambertz, G., & Dehaene, S. (2008). Distinct cerebral pathways for object identity and number in human infants. *PLoS Biology, 6,* e11. DOI: 10.1371/journal.pbio.0060011

Koshmider, J. W., & Ashcraft, M. H. (1991). The development of children's mental multiplication skills. *Journal of Experimental Child Psychology, 51,* 53–89.

Krajcsi, A., & Igács, J. (2010). Processing negative numbers by transforming negatives to positive range and by sign shortcut. *European Journal of Cognitive Psychology, 22,* 1021–1038.

Krueger, F., Spampinato, M. V., Pardini, M., Pajevic, S., Wood, J. N., Weiss, G. H., Landgraf, S., & Grafman, J. (2008). Integral calculus problem solving: An fMRI investigation. *Neuroreport, 19,* 1095–1099.

Kucian, K., Grond, U., Rotzer, S., Henzi, B., Schönmann, C., Plangger, F., Gälli, M., Martin, E., & von Aster, M. (2011). Mental number line training in children with developmental dyscalculia. *NeuroImage, 57*(3), 782–795.

Kucian, K., Loenneker, T., Dietrich, T., Dosch, M., Martin, E., & von Aster, M. (2006). Impaired neural networks for approximate calculation in dyscalculic children: A functional MRI study. *Behavioral and Brain Functions, 2*(31), 1–17.

Lakoff, G., & Núñez, R. E. (2000). *Where mathematics comes from: How the embodied mind brings mathematics into being.* New York: Basic.

Landerl, K., Bevan, A., & Butterworth, B. (2004). Developmental dyscalculia and basic numerical capacities: A study of 8–9 year old students. *Cognition, 93,* 99–125.

Landerl, K., & Kölle, C. (2009). Typical and atypical development of basic numerical skills in elementary school. *Journal of Experimental Child Psychology, 103*(4), 546–565.

Liu, X., Wang, H., Corbly, C. R., Zhang, J., & Joseph, J. E. (2006). The involvement of the inferior parietal cortex in the numerical Stroop effect and the distance effect in a two-digit number comparison task. *Journal of Cognitive Neuroscience, 18,* 1518–1530.

Montessori, M. (1966). *The discovery of the child (M. Johnstone, Trans.).* Madras: Kalakshetra.

Moyer, R. S., & Landauer, T. K. (1967). Time required for judgments of numerical inequality. *Nature, 215,* 1519–1520.

National Research Council Committee on Early Childhood Mathematics. (2009). C. T. Cross, T. A. Woods, & H. Schweingruber (Eds.), *Mathematics learning in early childhood: Paths toward excellence and equity.* Washington, DC: National Academies Press.

Noël, M.-P. (2005). Finger gnosia: A predictor of numerical abilities in children? *Child Neuropsychology, 11*, 413–430.

Nuerk, H.-C., Kaufmann, L., Zoppoth, S., & Willmes, K. (2004). On the development of the mental number line: More, less, or never holistic with increasing age? *Developmental Psychology, 40*, 1199–1211.

Nuerk, H.-C., Weger, U., & Willmes, K. (2001). Decade breaks in the mental number line? Putting the tens and units back in different bins. *Cognition, 82*, B25–B33.

Organization for Economic Cooperation and Development (OECD). (2010). *The high cost of low educational performance: The long-run impact of improving PISA outcomes.* Paris: OECD.

Papert, S. (1980). *Mindstorms: Children, computers, and powerful ideas.* Brighton, UK: Harvester.

Parsons, S., & Bynner, J. (2005). *Does numeracy matter more?* London: National Research and Development Centre for Adult Literacy and Numeracy, Institute of Education.

Piaget, J. (1952). *The child's conception of number.* London: Routledge & Kegan Paul.

Piazza, M., Facoetti, A., Trussardi, A. N., Berteletti, I., Conte, S., Lucangeli, D., Dehaene, S., & Zorzi, M. (2010). Developmental trajectory of number acuity reveals a severe impairment in developmental dyscalculia. *Cognition, 116*(1), 33–41.

Piazza, M., Mechelli, A., Price, C. J., & Butterworth, B. (2006). Exact and approximate judgements of visual and auditory numerosity: An fMRI study. *Brain Research, 1106*, 177–188.

Pinel, P., Dehaene, S., Rivière, D., & Le Bihan, D. (2001). Modulation of parietal activation by semantic distance in a number comparison task. *NeuroImage, 14*, 1013–1026.

Price, G. R., Holloway, I., Räsänen, P., Vesterinen, M., & Ansari, D. (2007). Impaired parietal magnitude processing in developmental dyscalculia. *Current Biology, 17*, 1042–1043.

Qin, Y., Sohn, M.-H., Anderson, J. R., Stenger, V. A., Fissell, K., Goode, A. & Carter, C. S. (2003). Predicting the practice effects on the blood oxygenation level-dependent (BOLD) function of fMRI in a symbolic manipulation task. *Proceedings of the National Academy of Sciences of the United States of America, 100*, 4951–4956.

Qin, Y., Carter, C. S., Silk, E., Stenger, V. A., Fissell, K., Goode, A., & Anderson, J. R. (2004). The change of the brain activation patterns as children learn algebra equation solving. *Proceedings of National Academy of Sciences of the United States of America, 101*, 5686–5691.

Räsänen, P., Salminen, J., Wilson, A. J., Aunioa, P., & Dehaene, S. (2009). Computer-assisted intervention for children with low numeracy skills. *Cognitive Development, 24*, 450–472.

Reigosa-Crespo, V., Valdés-Sosa, M., Butterworth, B., Estévez, N., Rodríguez, M., Santos, E., Torres, P., Suárez, R., & Lage, A. (2011). Basic numerical capacities and prevalence of developmental dyscalculia: The Havana Survey. *Developmental Psychology.* DOI: 10.1037/a0025356

Rivera, S. M., Reiss, S. M., Eckert, M. A., & Menon, V. (2005). Developmental changes in mental arithmetic: Evidence for increased functional specialization in the left inferior parietal cortex. *Cerebral Cortex, 15*, 1779–1790.

Rosenshine, B. (1995). Advances in research on instruction. *The Journal of Educational Research, 88*, 262–268.

Rotzer, S., Kucian, K., Martin, E., von Aster, M., Klaver, P., & Loenneker, T. (2008). Optimized voxel-based morphometry in children with developmental dyscalculia. *NeuroImage, 39*(1), 417–422.

Rousselle, L., & Noël, M.-P. (2007). Basic numerical skills in children with mathematics learning disabilities: A comparison of symbolic vs non-symbolic number magnitude processing. *Cognition, 102*(3), 361–395.

Rusconi, E., Bueti, D., Walsh, V., & Butterworth, B. (2011). Contribution of frontal cortex to the spatial representation of number. *Cortex, 47*(1), 2–13.

Rusconi, E., Pinel, P., Dehaene, S., & Kleinschmidt, A. (2010). The enigma of Gerstmann's syndrome revisited: A telling tale of the vicissitudes of neuropsychology. *Brain, 133*(2), 320–332. DOI: 10.1093/brain/awp281

Rusconi, E., Turatto, M., & Umiltà, C. (2007). Two orienting mechanisms in posterior parietal lobule: An rTMS study of the Simon and SNARC effects. *Cognitive Neuropsychology, 24*(4), 373–392.

Rusconi, E., Walsh, V., & Butterworth, B. (2005). Dexterity with numbers: rTMS over left angular gyrus disrupts finger gnosis and number processing. *Neuropsychologia, 43*(11), 1609–1624.

Rykhlevskaia, E., Uddin, L. Q., Kondos, L., & Menon, V. (2009). Neuroanatomical correlates of developmental dyscalculia: Combined evidence from morphometry and tractography. *Frontiers in Human Neuroscience, 3*(51), 1-13. DOI: 10.3389/neuro.09.051.2009

Sarnecka, B. W., & Gelman, S. A. (2004). Six does not just mean a lot: Preschoolers see number words as specific. *Cognition, 92*(3), 329–352.

Schmithorst, V. J., & Brown, R. D. (2004). Empirical validation of the triple-code model of numerical processing for complex math operations using functional MRI and group Independent Component Analysis of the mental addition and subtraction of fractions. *NeuroImage, 22*, 1414–1420.

Sekuler, R., & Mierkiewicz, D. (1977). Children's judgements of numerical inequality. *Child Development, 48*, 630–633.

Shalev, R. S. (2007). Prevalence of developmental dyscalculia. In D. B. Berch & M. M. M. Mazzocco (Eds.), *Why is math so hard for some children? The nature and origins of mathematical learning difficulties and disabilities* (pp. 49–60). Baltimore, MD: Brookes.

Shalev, R. S., Manor, O., & Gross-Tsur, V. (2005). Developmental dyscalculia: A prospective six year follow up. *Developmental Medicine and Child Psychology, 47*(2), 121–125.

Shallice, T., & Evans, M. E. (1978). The involvement of the frontal lobes in cognitive estimation. *Cortex, 14*, 294–303.

Smith, A. (2004). *Making mathematics count: The report of Professor Adrian Smith's inquiry into post-14 mathematics education.* London: Department for Education and Skills.

Sohn, M.-H., Goode, A., Koedinger, K. R., Stenger, V. A, Fissell, K., Carter, C. S., & Anderson, J. R. (2004). Behavioral equivalence, but not neural equivalence: Neural evidence in mathematical problem solving. *Nature Neuroscience, 7*, 1193–1994.

Starkey, P., & Cooper, R. G., Jr. (1980). Perception of numbers by human infants. *Science, 210*, 1033–1035.

Stocco, A., & Anderson, J. R. (2008). Endogenous control and task representation: An fMRI study in algebraic problem solving. *Journal of Cognitive Neuroscience, 20*, 1300–1314.

Thorndike, E. L. (1922). *The psychology of arithmetic*. New York: Macmillan.

Tsang, J., Blair, K. P., Bofferding, L., Rosenberg-Lee, M., & Schwartz, D. (2011, April). *Educational neuroscience: An example in the context of the integers*. Paper presented at the 2011 Annual Meeting of the American Educational Research Association, New Orleans, LA.

Tzelgov, J., Ganor-Stern, D., & Maymon-Schreiber, K. (2009). The representation of negative numbers: Exploring the effects of mode of processing and notation. *The Quarterly Journal of Experimental Psychology, 62*, 605–624.

Varma, S., & Schwartz, D. L. (2011). The mental representation of integers: A symbolic to perceptual-magnitude shift. *Cognition, 121*, 363–385.

Vetter, P., Butterworth, B., & Bahrami, B. (2011). A candidate for the attentional bottleneck: Set-size specific modulation of the right TPJ during attentive enumeration. *Journal of Cognitive Neuroscience, 23*(3), 728–736. DOI: doi:10.1162/jocn.2010.21472

Von Glasersfeld, E. (1989). Cognition, construction of knowledge, and teaching. *Synthese, 80*, 121–140.

Vygotsky, L. (1978). *Mind in society*. Cambridge, MA: Harvard University Press.

Westermann, G., Thomas, M. S. C., & Karmiloff-Smith, A. (2010). Neuroconstructivism. In *The* Wiley-Blackwell *handbook of childhood cognitive development* (pp. 723–748). Oxford: Wiley-Blackwell.

Whitehead, A. N. (1948). *An introduction to mathematics* . London: Oxford University Press. (Original work published 1911)

Williams, P. (2008). *Independent review of mathematics teaching in early years settings and primary schools (final report)*. London: Department for Children, Schools and Families.

Xu, F., & Spelke, E. (2000). Large number discrimination in 6-month-old infants. *Cognition, 74*, B1–B11.

Zbrodoff, N. J., & Logan, G. D. (2005). What everyone finds: The problem size effect. In J. I. D. Campbell (Ed.), *Handbook of mathematical cognition* (pp. 331–345). New York: Psychology.

# Chapter 9

# The Development and Application of Scientific Reasoning

## Jonathan Fugelsang and Denis Mareschal

### What is Scientific Reasoning?

Scientific reasoning is by definition a broad term, and encompasses the mental activities that are involved when people attempt to make systematic and empirical-based discoveries about the world. The goal of the scientific reasoning process, as highlighted by Zimmerman (2000), is to extend our world knowledge, thus allowing us to gain a more detailed and conceptually richer understanding of the domain of inquiry. Throughout this scientific reasoning process, people make use of several domain-general cognitive processes that are employed across different situations to facilitate the discovery process. It has been argued that these domain-general cognitive processes, such as causal reasoning, deductive reasoning, analogical reasoning, hypothesis testing, and problem solving, are the same cognitive tools that humans use in everyday nonscientific contexts (see Dunbar & Fugelsang, 2005, for broad coverage of these and other domain-general cognitive tools). In the current chapter, we will discuss how these domain-general cognitive processes, together with domain-specific knowledge, are used to support the scientific discovery process. We will focus the majority of this review on the use of causal reasoning, deductive reasoning, and analogical reasoning in scientific thinking, as they have received much empirical attention over the last several decades. In addition, throughout this review, we will concentrate much of our coverage on neuroimaging evidence, as it provides a means of assessing whether the same functional brain systems are active in

*Educational Neuroscience*, First Edition. Edited by Denis Mareschal, Brian Butterworth and Andy Tolmie.

adults and children of different ages, and importantly to establish any links that exist between physiological and behavioral changes with age. Several laboratories over the past decade have begun to explore the neural basis of reasoning, focusing on deductive reasoning, causal reasoning, and relational or analogical reasoning, predominantly in adults. In reviewing some of this work, we will make links between research conducted with children and adults to gain insights into how these competencies develop and change over time.

Before we discuss each of these domain-general reasoning processes, we will first provide a brief description of how domain-general cognitive processes are proposed to work together with conceptual representations (i.e., domain-specific knowledge) to support scientific thinking. In addition, we will briefly discuss how the two types of reasoning process have been examined historically. This overview will be necessarily brief, however, as an in-depth discussion of the historical approaches to such investigations is far beyond the scope of this chapter. The interested reader should refer to the comprehensive reviews and syntheses of this work by Corinne Zimmerman (2000, 2005, 2007), which significantly informed our synopsis below.

## Historical Approaches to the Study of Domain-General and Domain-Specific Scientific Reasoning

As noted above, the process of scientific reasoning makes use of domain-general problem solving and reasoning skills coupled with domain-specific knowledge of the specific area under study. The process of scientific investigation, as exemplified by proficient adults, includes a broad range of procedural and conceptual activities, including, but by no means limited to, formulating hypotheses, designing experiments, making predictions, and collecting data (or making observations) (Klahr, Zimmerman, & Jirout, 2011; Zimmerman, 2005). In addition, once all of the data have been collected, one needs to carefully examine the data (often performing statistical analyses), which then leads to the evaluation and coordination of these new data with pre-existing theory. This latter stage is often complicated by the presence of contradictory data (i.e., data inconsistent with theory). Here, the reasoner may need to revise and update existing theories or models in order to accommodate the new data (Dunbar & Fugelsang, 2005; Fugelsang, Stein, Green, & Dunbar, 2004; Koslowski, 1996), or develop an entirely new theory altogether. These processes rely on a synergist interplay between domain-general reasoning skills (such as those alluded to above) and domain-specific content knowledge. As the coordination of domain-general and domain-specific activities is a highly complex process, researchers studying these processes in children and adults have traditionally attempted to focus their research programs on *either* the conceptual (i.e., domain-specific) *or* the procedural (i.e., domain-general) aspects of the scientific reasoning process in isolation (Zimmerman, 2005). As we will see below, however, this is not always possible.

Concerning the conceptual (i.e., domain-specific) approach, researchers following this research tradition have focused on investigating the nature of the *concepts* that individuals have about various phenomena in a variety of content domains (Zimmerman, 2000). Following this approach, the goal is often to describe and uncover the cognitive mechanisms underlying conceptual development or conceptual *change* as a function of new learning (which may require a radical shift in current ways of thinking) within a specific domain of study (Carey, 1985, 2000). Here, researchers are interested in children's and adults' level of understanding, the nature of their knowledge representations, and how their conceptual understanding (or knowledge representation) develops and changes about specific phenomena in a variety of scientific content areas, such as biology (e.g., Carey, 1985), climatology (Dunbar, Fugelsang, & Stein, 2007), and physics (McCloskey, 1983). Often, the research emphasis is concentrated on indexing the degree to which new conceptual knowledge changes (or overwrites) previously held naïve views, or whether both previously held naïve and new worldviews coexist in the mind (Dunbar et al., 2007; Shtulman & Valcarcel, 2012). These cognitive operations are highly relevant to scientific reasoning, as it is likely very rare that individuals would be faced with a situation that would require them to reason and make decisions in situations where they have no prior knowledge, experience, or conceptual representations. We will see in later sections of this chapter that domain-specific content influences reasoning processes (and subsequent brain recruitment) in significant ways.

Concerning the procedural approach, researchers have focused on understanding the development and application of domain-general skills, which are thought to be applied across multiple content domains in a relatively similar fashion (Zimmerman, 2005). Such empirical investigations have followed from the Piagetian research tradition (see, e.g., Inhelder & Piaget, 1958), whereby children are asked to scientifically reason (i.e., formulate and test hypotheses) while performing tasks that are thought to be relatively free from the influence of any domain-specific content knowledge that could impact performance (e.g., the balance-scale task; Siegler, 1976). The primary objective with this approach is to eliminate (or at least reduce) the potential impact of conceptual knowledge about specific content domains in order to observe how domain-general reasoning strategies are applied in a relatively knowledge-free manner (Zimmerman, 2005). It should be noted, however, that even with these relatively knowledge-free tasks children and adults often possess naïve views about their operation, and these naïve views can be very resilient to change (see, e.g., Pine &

Messer, 2000). Indeed, others have noted that many of the experimental tasks that have been used following this research tradition are arguably quite conceptually rich in nature (Zimmerman, 2005, 2007). Taken together, however, these early empirical approaches laid the foundation for later work looking at the integration of both domain-general and domain-specific reasoning processes.

In the following sections of this chapter, we will mainly focus on the latter scientific reasoning skills that underlie thinking processes in a scientific domain. As discussed above, these are thought to be domain-general skills and should be viewed as interacting with the domain-specific "conceptual" knowledge that is specific to any domain of inquiry. We focus first on causal reasoning, then deductive reasoning, and finally analogical reasoning. The main reason for focusing on these domains is that they are three of the key reasoning areas that underlie much of scientific reasoning (Dunbar & Fugelsang, 2005). In addition, and based on this importance, they are also some of the main domains of reasoning in which the methods of cognitive neuroscience have been applied to elucidate the neural systems and mechanisms that underlie largely adult performance, but also children's performance too. Within our coverage of each of these domain-general reasoning skills, we will discuss work that examines how domain-specific knowledge about problem content impacts these processes behaviorally and neurophysiologically.

## Causal Reasoning

A central goal of many scientific investigations is the discovery of causal relations between key variables. Indeed, isolating causal relations is often the crucial first step in identifying underlying mechanisms governing relations, and eventually being able to control outcomes experimentally. For example, much of scientific theory development involves the construction of comprehensive causal models, which often requires the isolation and modeling of causal relations between variables of interest (Dunbar & Fugelsang, 2005). There are many examples of the primary role of causal reasoning in scientific theory development. For example, scientists have spent decades examining whether there is a causal relation between human activities on earth, greenhouse gases, and global warming (see Figure 9.1), and whether smoking causes cancer. In order to effectively develop causal models, scientists develop techniques that allow them to maximally discriminate between the causal candidates of theoretical interest, and extraneous variables that are also present in the environment.

In this section, we will discuss the types of cognitive operation that govern how one evaluates causal relations. We will begin by discussing evidence for two levels of causal reasoning, one involving perceptually based processes, and one

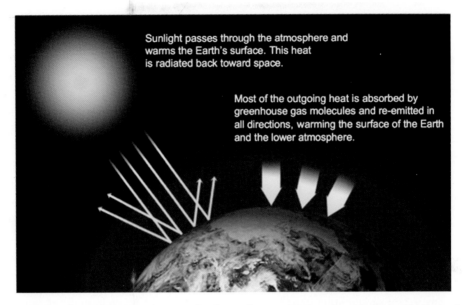

**Figure 9.1**    A contemporary example of causal reasoning in science is the work devoted to studying the possibility of complex causal relations between human activities on Earth and the greenhouse effect, which is thought to be resulting in global warming. Courtesy NASA's Global Climate Change Website.

involving inferential-based processes. We will then focus predominantly on inferential processes in causal reasoning, specifically covering the types of information (i.e., data, evidence, etc.) that children and adults alike use to make causal inferences in probabilistic environments. Finally, we will review experiments that have investigated how people deal with causal evidence that is inconsistent with their conceptual understanding (i.e., their expectations).

Countless studies have examined how people determine the degree to which specific variables are causally related through the use of various causal cues (e.g., covariation information, knowledge of causal mechanisms, temporal and spatial contiguity; for an extensive review of multiple causal cues in adults see Young, 1995, or in children see Shultz, 1982; for a recent Bayesian perspective on causal learning see Pearl, 2009). When thinking about causal reasoning, it is important to differentiate between causal perception, in which the perceptual system "directly" attributes causality to an event such as when viewing physical collision events (see, e.g., Michotte, 1963), and causal inference, which draws on a more "cognitive" level of understanding of cause and effect (e.g., learning that flipping a switch turns a light on). Indeed, there is substantial evidence that different neural systems underlie these two forms of causal competence, with causal perception and causal inference proceeding relatively independently and relying on dissociable

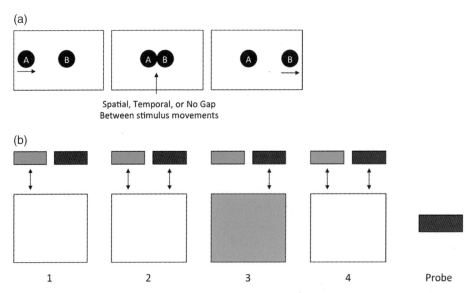

**Figure 9.2** Example stimuli used by Roser et al. (2005). (a) A graphical illustration of the causal collision animations used in the causal-perception task. The three panels depict the motion of a ball A towards a second ball B, and the subsequent motion of ball B. Note that the movement of the second ball (B) was preceded by either a temporal delay, a spatial gap, or no gap. (b) A graphical illustration of the animated causal-inference task. The sequential presentation of four stimulus interactions and a response probe is shown, representing one trial. Arrows indicate the movement of one or both of the colored "switches" on each presentation. Adapted from Roser, M., Fugelsang, J., Dunbar, K., Corballis, P., & Gazzaniga, M. (2005). Dissociating processes supporting causal perception and causal inference in the brain. *Neuropsychology, 19*, pages 593 (a) and 597 (b) with permission from APA.

neural architectures. One of the most striking examples of the independence of these two processes comes from a series of studies led by Matthew Roser (Roser, Fugelsang, Dunbar, Corballis, & Gazzaniga, 2005) with two patients who had undergone callosotomy surgery (J.W. and V.P.): a surgery that severs the corpus callosum, thus severely limiting the communication between the two cerebral hemispheres (see Fugelsang and Dunbar, 2009, for further discussion of this experiment in the context of multiple representations of causality). The two patients were presented with causal collision events (i.e., one object appearing to hit [or not hit] another object, causing it to move) using the standard Michotte paradigm (see Figure 9.2(a); Michotte, 1963), and a task hypothesized to tap into causal inference (adapted from the "blicket detector" task of Gopnik, Sobel, Schulz, & Glymour, 2001). This task consisted of a series of four dynamic stimulus interactions between two "switches" (green or red), and a "lightbox" that changed colors in response to the movement of one of the switches (see Figure 9.2(b)). The participants' task was simply to judge which switch caused the lightbox to change colors. Note here that there was no physical interaction between the stimuli in this condition (i.e., no contact), thus participants would need to *infer* the existence of a causal relation based on the observed patterns of relations in the absence of the ability to directly perceive one. Critically, the stimuli were presented to each hemisphere of the divided brain in isolation using an eye tracker coupled with a mirror deflector system that stabilized the dynamic displays on the retina of the participant.

For the Michotte task, the right hemispheres of J.W. and V.P. performed similarly to control participants with intact corpora callosa; however, the left hemispheres of the same patients performed at chance level on this task. Conversely, for the causal inference task, the left hemispheres of J.W. and V.P. performed similarly to those of control participants, whereas the right hemispheres of the same patients performed at chance level. This clear double dissociation between the causal task (perception versus inference), and cerebral hemisphere supporting that task, lends support to the hypothesis that the ability to draw causal inferences based on statistical associations and the ability to directly "perceive" causality based on physical contact interactions are supported by different hemispheres of the divided brain, and thus anatomically and functionally dissociable. It is important to note here that it is entirely possible that the two tasks noted above may become less independent with time. For example, given experience with colliding events, one may develop theories underlying their interaction, and this may in turn influence the judgment of these events in a top-down manner. Nevertheless, this study provided compelling evidence that humans have independent abilities to directly perceive and to infer causality. The extent to which either process is recruited would depend on the nature of the stimuli being judged.

What cognitive processes might underlie this dissociation? Perhaps the most recognized and empirically supported hemispheric asymmetry in the human brain is that between linguistic and visual–spatial processing. Countless studies of preserved cognitive functioning in patients with focal brain lesions and more recent functional brain imaging studies (using positron emission tomography and functional magnetic resonance imaging, fMRI) have shown that the left hemisphere has a distinct advantage for linguistic processing (Milner, 1962), whereas the right hemisphere has a processing advantage for visual–spatial information (Corballis, 2003; Corballis, Funnell, & Gazzaniga, 2002). Note that this dissociation is true for most (but not all) right-handed individuals, and fewer left-handed individuals. Here, it has been argued (e.g., Roser et al., 2005; Fugelsang, Roser, Corballis, Gazzaniga, & Dunbar, 2005; Fugelsang & Dunbar, 2009) that causal perception may rely on similar underlying neural architectures to those which are involved in visual–spatial processes, whereas causal inference may rely on similar underlying neural architectures to those involved in linguistic processing. These findings are likely to have important developmental implications for understanding the transition from a perceptual to an abstract and productive mind. Here, one may hypothesize that the ability to make causal inferences of the kind described above may be scaffolded onto the same neural architecture that supports linguistic processing. It is also important to note here that the processes described with reference to the causal-inference task may be very different (and rely on different neural architecture) from those that are involved in associative learning of causal relations (see, e.g., Corlett et al., 2004; Fletcher et al., 2001; Turner et al., 2004), which may rely on tacit awareness of associative strength in the absence of any conscious inferential processes.

Fewer studies have focused on the underlying brain correlates of more complex causal reasoning (as opposed to causal perception), which reflects the kind of causal scientific reasoning individuals might undertake in a more ecologically valid context. When we speak of complex causal reasoning in the present context, we are referring to the inferential processes associated with evaluating new observations (i.e., empirical data) to test an existing theory. In an attempt to empirically examine the brain correlates of complex scientific reasoning of this kind, Fugelsang and Dunbar (2005) opted to examine the degree to which individuals reason about covariation-based data that may be consistent or inconsistent with a causal model containing a plausible or implausible mechanism of action. The focus on these two cues (i.e., covariation information and causal mechanisms) is due to the assumption that they nicely map onto the types of cue people use in the real world when making scientific discoveries (see Fugelsang & Dunbar, 2009, for further discussion of this study within the broader context of research on causality). Here, evidence is gathered to test specific hypotheses about the world. These specific hypotheses often involve mechanistic information detailing how certain variables are thought to *produce* changes in other variables. Furthermore, the data collected often come in the form of repeated trial-by-trial observations. Importantly, the data collected (i.e., the cause-and-effect trial observations) may turn out to be either consistent or inconsistent with the theory being tested.

To test these processes in a controlled experimental setting, Fugelsang and Dunbar (2005) presented participants with a reasoning task that required them to reason with covariation-based data that were either consistent or inconsistent with a causal theory. The causal theories could be either plausible or implausible. Theory plausibility was manipulated by presenting participants with introductory cover stories that contained information about a causal mechanism specifying how a specific drug impacted mood in a group of fictitious patients (see Fugelsang & Dunbar, 2005, for a list of the stimuli). For plausible causal theories, the drug cover stories were modeled after known antidepressants (which contained a direct plausible mechanism to affect mood); for implausible theories, the cover stories were modeled after known antibiotics (which did not contain a direct plausible mechanism to affect mood). After participants read over the cover story, covariation-based data were then presented in a sequential trial-by-trial format, where they viewed multiple cause–effect observations that were associated with each causal theory. Importantly, the trials cumulatively contained evidence (i.e., covariation-based data) that was either consistent or inconsistent with the theory provided in the cover story. That is, under some conditions, the theory would set up the participant to believe that a causal relation existed, and the data were consistent with that theory (strong covariation) or inconsistent with that theory (weak covariation). Under other conditions, the theory would set up the participant to believe that a causal relation does *not* exist. Here, strong covariation would be consistent with the theory presented, but inconsistent with what one might expect to observe given that the theory would set one up to believe that no relation should exist. The presence of weak covariation-based data following an implausible theory, however, would be inconsistent with the theory presented, but consistent with what one might expect to observe.

Concerning the behavioral data first, participants' causal responses reflected an interaction between theory plausibility and data strength such that the covariation-based data were weighted more heavily for plausible theories than for implausible theories. This finding was consistent with prior behavioral work (i.e., Fugelsang & Thompson, 2000, 2003; Fugelsang et al., 2004) that has shown that people are biased by their expectations (i.e., beliefs) in their interpretation of covariation-based data when inferring causal relations. That is, there is a bias towards assessing data that are relevant to existing beliefs. Put another way, these findings imply that people may have difficulties with assessing data corresponding to alternative theories – something that both children and adults have been demonstrated to have problems with (see Howe, Tolmie, & Sofroniou, 1999). One could argue that these behavioral findings may reflect a sensible strategy for everyday reasoning, in that they protect individuals from prematurely changing their worldviews based on anomalous observations (i.e., type 1 errors). However, it is obviously not a suitable strategy for scientific thinking in general, as scientists may be inclined to prematurely disregard anomalous observations. Indeed, as an astute reviewer of this chapter noted, paradigm shifts in the history of science often, by definition, involve a radical change in what counts as a plausible theory (see Kuhn, 1962). In addition, it should be noted here that researchers have found that the degree to which prior beliefs impacts the evaluation of covariation-based data also depends on the reliability of that data (Perales, Catena, Maldonado, Cándido, 2007).

Critically, the brain imaging data provided information about a possible neural mechanism underlying this behavioral bias. Here, the consistency between theory plausibility and the covariation-based empirical data (i.e., whether the data were consistent with or conflicted with what one would expect to see given the presented causal theory) influenced the degree to which dissociable neural

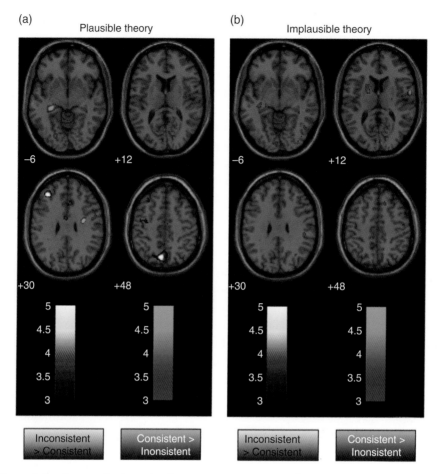

**Figure 9.3**    Average brain activation patterns occurring when participants viewed data *inconsistent* versus *consistent* with a plausible theory (a) and an implausible theory (b). Note that the activations denoted by red to yellow are for the conditions in which the provided theory and data are *inconsistent* and the activations denoted by blue to green are for the conditions in which the theory and data are *consistent*. Adapted from Fugelsang, J. A., & Dunbar, K. N. (2005). Brain-based mechanisms underlying complex causal thinking. *Neuropsychologia, 43,* page 1208, with permission from Elsevier.

networks were recruited. Specifically, when covariation-based data were consistent with what one would expect to see given the causal theory (i.e., strong covariation-based data for plausible theories, and weak covariation-based data for implausible theories), regions in the caudate and parahippocampal gyrus were selectively activated; whereas, when the covariation-based data conflicted with the causal theory, the anterior cingulate (ACC) and precuneus were selectively activated. Fugelsang and Dunbar (2005, 2009) hypothesized that these behavior–brain associations likely reflected the preferential recruitment of learning mechanisms for data that were consistent with what one would expect to observe given the presented theory (see Kelley et al., 1998; McDermott et al., 1999) and conflict monitoring/error detection mechanisms for data inconsistent with what one would expect to observe given the presented theory (see Botvinick, Braver, Barch, Carter, & Cohen, 2001; van Veen & Carter, 2002; Yeung, Botvinick, & Cohen, 2004).

A further interesting finding was discovered when they analyzed the effects of data consistency (i.e., whether the data matched the theory) separately for plausible and implausible theories (see Figure 9.3). Here, when participants evaluated data that were inconsistent (i.e., in conflict) with a *plausible* theory, additional activations were observed in the left dorsal lateral prefrontal cortex (DLPFC) in concert with activations in ACC and precuneus. Of course, there are many possible interpretations of these activation patterns. These interpretations hinge in part on how the presence of conflicting data (i.e., the degree to which theory and data are inconsistent) is presumed to be processed. For example, does this conflict processing result in the active (conscious) inhibition of data inconsistent with one's expectations, or is it more a passive (potentially unconscious) process, where attention is simply shifted to consistent data? Fugelsang and Dunbar (2005) preferred the interpretation that the combined recruitment of the DLPFC and the ACC in this condition may be due to the active *inhibition* of processing the conflicting data. These findings (and interpretation) are consistent with those of Goel and Dolan (2003) and Stollstorff, Vartanian, and Goel (2012) in a deductive reasoning task. Specifically, they found increased recruitment of regions within the DLPFC under conditions in which the believability of a conclusion conflicted with the logical structure of a problem and thus required the *inhibition* of a behavioral response. We will discuss these findings further below when we cover deductive reasoning in more detail.

More recently, others have examined complex causal reasoning in other domains. For example, Parris, Kuhn, Mizon, Bennattayallah, and Hodgson (2009) extended the work of Fugelsang and Dunbar (2005) by teasing apart the neural responses to surprising events, and those that violated well established and "deterministic" causal beliefs. This is in contrast to the work of Fugelsang and Dunbar (2005), who focused on causal events that were probabilistic. To do this, they empirically examined the perception of magic tricks in order to investigate violations of causal relations that are long established. For example, participants viewed videos containing several magic tricks such as disappearing acts and levitation. Note that these types of event are similar in many ways to those of causal perception (e.g., using the standard Michotte paradigm) in that they involve observable physical stimulus interactions. Here, an unexpected finding would presumably violate one's worldview in a similar manner as a temporal or spatial gap would when viewing collision events. When magic-trick perception (which included a violation of a known deterministic causal relation) was contrasted with situations in which expected causal relations are observed, they found that the former recruited greater activations in regions in the left DLPFC and ACC than the latter. The authors also included further control conditions to determine the degree to which these activations were selective to causal events, or common for other surprising events. Critically, the left DLPFC was selectively more active when viewing magic tricks than surprising events. However, the same region in the DLPFC was *not* more active when viewing surprising than nonsurprising causal control events. This latter finding is important, as it provides support for the hypothesis that the DLPFC plays a key role in the higher-order aspects (i.e., causality) of the perception of expectancy violations. These data nicely extend the work of Fugelsang and Dunbar (2005) by showing that information that violates expected causal relations (whether they are probabilistic or deterministic in nature) activates regions in the brain known to be associated with conflict processing (van Veen & Carter, 2002). The degree to which this conflict processing is active or passive is up for debate, and an important avenue for future research.

Taken together, the work of Fugelsang and Dunbar (2005) and Parris et al. (2009) provides insights into the development of causal scientific thinking skills. As noted above, much of scientific thinking involves the testing and establishment of causal relations between variables of interest. Based on the literature reviewed, it appears that the human brain seems to be especially tuned to detect and process information that contradicts and challenges established conceptual knowledge about such relations. As noted by Parris et al., in the context of complex causal thinking, the ACC and DLPFC may play a central role in the establishment of *disbelief*. Here, the development and maturation of this neural architecture may result in a shift from primarily perceptually driven to more inferentially driven reasoning processes, supporting our ability to question and learn from observations that conflict with existing knowledge. As noted above, however, individuals often remain biased when reasoning with causal relations despite this detection of conflict.

The above idea regarding the development of the ability to reason about conflict is also at the heart of Houdé's (2000, 2007) proposal that the *key* cognitive developmental factor across childhood is the improving ability to inhibit pre-potent perceptually based responses, and allow slower reflective processes to act. Consistent with this view, he and his colleagues have found that training on inhibition tasks, but not logical reasoning tasks, led young adolescents to reduce the frequency of logical reasoning errors. This change in behavior was also associated with a shift in activation from posterior cortical regions (involved in early perceptual processing) to anterior cortical regions involved in executive control (Houdé et al., 2000, 2001). The suggestion that such inferential mechanisms tend to exert a dominant influence on judgments once they reach a certain state of organization is also supported by a recent electroencephalography (EEG) study with adults reported by Kallai and Reiner (2010). They employed a trajectory task based on McCloskey's (1983) work on naïve physics, in which participants viewed animations of an object exiting either straight or circular tubes, with either normal parabolic or circular motion. Behavioral judgments (via key press) of whether the displayed motion was accurate or not showed an effect of tube type (more correct responses were made for the straight tube), in line with McCloskey's results. However, event-related potential data gathered from the same trials showed a negative activation peak at 400 ms (associated with semantic violations in previous research) for displays of circular motion from *both* tube types. This suggests that participants held an accurate implicit expectation about the trajectory shape that was overruled by the behavioral judgment in the case of the circular tube. However, a further positive activation peak at 600 ms (associated with syntactic violations) was found in participants incorrectly accepting a circular trajectory from the *straight* tube, but not when correctly accepting a circular trajectory from the circular tube. This suggests that the dominant consideration for decisionmaking was whether trajectories corresponded to rule-based expectations rather than perceptual experience. Importantly, these findings reveal that this ability to detect conflicts between our expectations and our perceptual experience when reasoning can sometimes lead us astray in that they can override an accurate perceptual input. That is, at least some of the time the influence of higher-order inferential processes can impede performance, as the perceptual responses are in fact accurate, and the considered responses are inaccurate (see also Howe, 1998; Howe, Tavares, & Devine, 2012). This point is important given the prevalence of misconceptions of students up to and including the undergraduate level.

## Deductive Reasoning

Alongside causal reasoning, deductive reasoning processes, which are thought to be one of the hallmark processes indexing rational thought (Evans, 2008), underlie much of scientific thinking. This involves reasoning processes that assess the degree to which a conclusion logically follows from stated information (i.e., premises). Deductive reasoning is useful in the scientific enterprise as much of scientific thinking involves reasoning from known (i.e., previously established) information (Dunbar & Fugelsang, 2005). That is, scientists and laypeople alike assume that events in our world unfold due to the operation of stable and predictable rules, and they reason from these known and established rules to draw new conclusions based on new observations, using the tools offered through deductive reasoning.

Deductive reasoning is a key component of scientific thinking, as it underlies much of how scientists make inferences about new discoveries. A contemporary example of deductive reasoning in scientific thinking was provided by Dunbar and Fugelsang (2005), with regard to the discovery of new planets in our solar system, and other solar systems. Here, some scientists speculate that there exists another planet in our solar system (not including Pluto) beyond the orbit of Neptune (referred to as "Planet X"). This is due to the significant orbital perturbations of the planets Uranus and Neptune (note that Neptune was discovered in a similar fashion due to perturbations in the orbit of Uranus). Given that it is generally assumed that only very large objects possessing a strong gravitational pull can cause significant orbital perturbations (discounting Pluto as a possible candidate), and given further that Uranus and Neptune do have notable perturbations in their orbits, it follows logically from these premises that a large planetary body is influencing Uranus and Neptune's orbital patterns. This process of deductive reasoning also extends to the discovery of new planets in other solar systems (see Figure 9.4).

**Figure 9.4**   A famous (and still widely used) example of deductive reasoning is the use of gravitational perturbation theory to predict the presence of new planets in solar systems. A recent example is the discovery of a second planet, "Planet C," orbiting the distant star KOI-872. Based on the discovery of orbital perturbations of "Planet B," and the premise that only large objects possess a strong enough gravitational force to cause such perturbations, the conclusion that there exists a second planet, "Planet C," logically follows. Courtesy Southwest Research Institute.

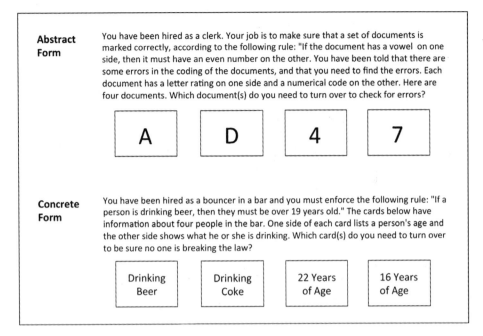

**Abstract Form**

You have been hired as a clerk. Your job is to make sure that a set of documents is marked correctly, according to the following rule: "If the document has a vowel on one side, then it must have an even number on the other. You have been told that there are some errors in the coding of the documents, and that you need to find the errors. Each document has a letter rating on one side and a numerical code on the other. Here are four documents. Which document(s) do you need to turn over to check for errors?

| A | D | 4 | 7 |

**Concrete Form**

You have been hired as a bouncer in a bar and you must enforce the following rule: "If a person is drinking beer, then they must be over 19 years old." The cards below have information about four people in the bar. One side of each card lists a person's age and the other side shows what he or she is drinking. Which card(s) do you need to turn over to be sure no one is breaking the law?

| Drinking Beer | Drinking Coke | 22 Years of Age | 16 Years of Age |

**Figure 9.5**    The Wason four-card selection task in abstract and concrete forms. The logically correct response is the card showing a vowel (or drinking beer in the concrete form), and the card showing a number that is not even (the person 16 years of age in the concrete example).

In this section, we will discuss how both children and adults use deduction to make scientific discoveries. Furthermore, we will look at common errors people make when reasoning deductively. Specifically, we will focus on research looking at the degree to which the content (i.e., reflecting domain-specific conceptual knowledge) of information in the premises and conclusions impact the deductive reasoning process (i.e., the application of the domain-general reasoning process).

Decades of research have shown that adults often fall far short of optimal rational behavior when reasoning with standard deductive reasoning tasks. For example, researchers have consistently found that only around 10% of adult participants correctly solve the abstract version of the Wason selection task (Wason, 1968). However, when abstract content is replaced with thematic content (e.g., the drinking age problem; see Figure 9.5), performance increases dramatically to around 75% correct (Griggs & Cox, 1982). There are several explanations and theoretical accounts of this facilitation in performance, which we will not get into here. For our purposes, it is important simply as an example of how deductive reasoning is profoundly affected by the content with which one is reasoning. That is, the content of a problem greatly influences the degree to which adults reason in a logical manner. This again is an example of how domain-general reasoning processes (in this case

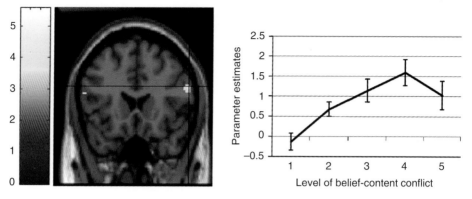

**Figure 9.6** Parametric modulation of lateral prefrontal cortex as a function of conflict between belief and logic. Reprinted from Stollstorff, M., Vartanian, O., & Goel, V. (2012). *Levels of conflict in reasoning modulate right lateral prefrontal cortex. Brain Research, 1428*, page 29, with permission from Elsevier.

deductive reasoning) are significantly influenced by domain-specific knowledge. This is similar to what we discussed above with regard to causal reasoning where participants' beliefs and expectations altered the degree to which they evaluated covariation-based evidence. Related to the content effects discussed above is the "belief-bias effect." Here, people are more likely to judge a conclusion as valid if it is believable, regardless of whether or not the conclusion follows necessarily from the information contained in the premises (Evans, Barston, & Pollard, 1983). Like causal reasoning, one's knowledge can override the acceptance of logically valid conclusions that are unbelievable. Of course, this often results in faulty reasoning whereby valid arguments are prematurely dismissed as invalid.

Research by Vinod Goel and his colleagues has used fMRI extensively to uncover the neural mechanisms underlying how people reason deductively with believable and unbelievable content. In a series of studies (e.g., Goel & Dolan, 2003; Stollstorff et al., 2012), they found that regions within the lateral prefrontal cortex were selectively activated when participants effectively reasoned logically when beliefs conflicted with valid conclusions (i.e., unbelievable but valid conclusions). In addition, they found that the activation in regions in the lateral prefrontal cortex increased parametrically with the amount of conflict present between the believability of the content and the logical structure of the conclusion (see Figure 9.6). This is an important finding, as it demonstrates the sensitivity of this neural region to conflict processing. These findings were taken to support the hypothesis that regions within the lateral prefrontal cortex initiate cognitive control to mediate the successful resolution of belief–logic conflicts during deductive reasoning. This is consistent with the general suggestion that regions of the lateral prefrontal cortex are involved in conflict-resolution tasks that require inhibitory control (see, e.g., Aron, Robbins, & Poldrack, 2004; Carter & van Veen, 2007). In addition, these findings converge with those discussed above regarding causal reasoning (another domain-general cognitive process), in that when reasoning with content (i.e., reflecting domain-specific knowledge) of which the reasoner has personal knowledge, which is often the case in scientific reasoning, effective inhibition of that knowledge is often imperative for successful performance. More generally, this work fits with the growing body of literature on inductive reasoning (e.g., Goel & Dolan, 2000, 2004; Seger et al., 2000) and deductive reasoning (Goel, Gold, Kapur, & Houle, 1998; Osherson et al., 1998; Parsons & Osherson, 2001) that have converged on the dominant role of the DLPFC in high-level reasoning tasks that involve the integration of prior world knowledge with the current logical demands of a given task (Baird & Fugelsang, 2004).

These findings also resonate with the developmental finding of improved reasoning performance in familiar domains by young children. For example, children generally succeed at classic Piagetian tasks if these are contextualized within familiar domains (Donaldson, 1978) or will show evidence of analogical reasoning (to be discussed in the next section) from as early as 3 years of age when tested in familiar domains (Goswami & Brown, 1990). In fact, both unschooled children and unschooled adults will generally succeed on logical reasoning tasks in familiar domains, but do so on the basis of knowledge-based inference rather than applying the rules of formal logic. Only once they have gone to school are they able to overcome this "empirical bias" and reason abstractly and counterfactually (Harris, 2000; Dias, Roazzi, & Harris, 2005). Of course, based on the literature reviewed above, it is clear that this ability to reason abstractly using the rules of logic is not always applied even after much schooling.

More recent research has also provided important new insights into the precise role of multiple brain regions in the prefrontal and parietal cortices, along with the timecourse of their recruitment, during the stages of deductive reasoning. Specifically, using event-related fMRI, Rodriguez-Moreno and Hirsch (2009) have found that areas in the frontal and parietal cortices are differentially recruited at different times in the deductive reasoning process as the participant steps through a syllogistic reasoning problem. Here, by presenting each premise, conclusion, and response phase sequentially, the authors were able to isolate the different brain regions that come online during the three proposed phases of the deductive reasoning process (i.e., premise encoding, premise integration, and conclusion validation). They found evidence for a frontal–parietal–caudate brain network that spanned both the premise integration and conclusion phases of reasoning. Furthermore, they were able to isolate areas of the brain that were primarily engaged during processing of the second premise, where premise integration and conclusion generation is thought to occur, including areas in the left middle and superior frontal gyrus and left superior and inferior parietal cortices. Areas in the medial and left inferior frontal cortex and bilateral inferior parietal and bilateral regions in the caudate nucleus were most active during the conclusion phase, presumably when conclusion validation occurs. Here, the activation of these latter inferior frontal regions suggests that the active conflict-resolution mechanisms associated with deductive reasoning with content likely do not come online until the conclusion-validation phase.

As with all research on higher-level cognition, it is important to be careful when inferring the operation of distinct cognitive processes based on observed patterns of brain activation (see Poldrack, 2006, for a discussion on the "reverse inference" problem, and Shallice and Cooper, 2011, for further discussions on the difficulty of interpreting imaging data in higher-level cognition). In addition, the degree to which these reasoning brain networks are scaffolded onto existing language areas (Hickok & Poeppel, 2004), working memory/executive processing networks, or visual–spatial networks (see Cabeza & Nyberg, 2000, for review of overlapping networks) is an important point of consideration. Indeed, in addition to the work on the impact of domain-specific knowledge (i.e., content) on deductive reasoning, much of the cognitive and neuroscience research on deductive reasoning has been focused on adjudicating between visual–spatial and linguistic theories of reasoning (see Goel, 2003, 2007, for reviews). In general, neuroimaging studies have provided support for the view that both language-based and visual–spatial modes are engaged during logical reasoning. As argued by Goel (2007), rather than having a unitary reasoning system, "the evidence points to a fractionated system that is dynamically configured in response to certain task and environmental cues" (p. 440). Here, the degree to which language-based or visual–spatial modes are recruited can depend on many factors, including, but by no means limited to, the type of logical relation to be reasoned with (e.g., categorical versus conditional), and the content of the problem (e.g., concrete versus abstract).

The findings above are also consistent with the emerging consensus in cognitive neuroscience suggesting that executive control can be separated into "evaluative" and "executive" processing components: one involving the ACC and the other involving the DLPFC (see Carter & van Veen, 2007). Broadly speaking, concerning the respective roles of the ACC and the DLPFC, as noted above, the ACC has been proposed to monitor the presence of conflict in a cognitive task, and the DLPFC is alerted to resolve the conflict. This conclusion mirrors the importance attributed to conflict monitoring in classic theories of reasoning development (e.g., Piaget's reflective abstraction, Karmiloff-Smith, 1992) and the relatively late maturing of the DLPFC across development (Zelazo, Carlson & Kesek, 2008). This could explain the relatively prolonged development of the ability to resolve inconsistencies between prior beliefs and new evidence in scientific learning and discovery. However, it should be noted that these regions have also been associated with a multitude of roles in other reasoning and decisionmaking situations (e.g., executive processing, working memory, attention, etc.). Indeed, converging evidence from a range of neuroscientific methods has implicated the dominant role of the DLPFC in many everyday reasoning tasks (e.g., Shallice & Burgess, 1991; Stuss & Alexander, 2000; Baird & Fugelsang, 2004).

## Analogical Reasoning

Analogical thinking is another central cognitive tool that scientists and laypeople alike use to aid in scientific thinking. Analogies have featured prominently in science (see Holyoak & Thagard, 1995, for a review), enough so to warrant the publication of many academic and popular books, highlighted by Joel Levy's recent book *A Bee in a Cathedral: And 99 Other Scientific Analogies* (Levy, 2011). Indeed, by analyzing the use of analogies in real scientific discoveries, several researchers (e.g., Dunbar & Blanchette, 2001; Gentner & Jeziorski, 1993; Nersessian, 1999; Thagard & Croft, 1999) have shown that analogical reasoning processes play a fundamental role in the scientific discovery process. That is, scientists use information from one relatively known domain ("the source," or earlier situation) and apply it to another domain ("the target," or present problem) (Dunbar & Fugelsang, 2005). Perhaps the most famous example of a scientific analogy is that between the hydrogen atom and the solar system (see Figure 9.7), originally formulated by Ernest Rutherford, where he explained

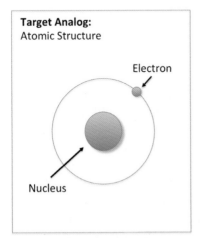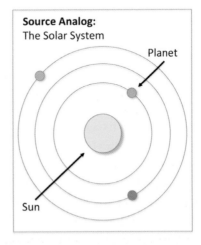

**Figure 9.7**    The "atom is like the solar system" analogy, credited to Ernest Rutherford, is one of the most famous examples of analogies in science. He explained the structure of the atom by picturing the atom as a solar system whereby the electrons orbit the nucleus in a similar way to how the planets orbit the sun. Figure credit: Daniel Brady.

the structure of the atom by picturing the atom as a solar system whereby the electrons orbit the nucleus in a similar way to how the planets orbit the sun (Gentner, 1983). Other examples of the use of analogies in major scientific discoveries (noted by Green, Kraemer, Fugelsang, Gray, and Dunbar, 2012) include William Harvey likening the circulatory system to a water pump, and James Crocker mapping an extendable showerhead to the position control mechanism on the Hubble telescope. Scientific discoveries in psychology are also replete with analogies. For example, researchers have discussed "bottle-neck" (Broadbent, 1958) "filter" (Treisman, 1964), and "spotlight" (Posner, 1980) theories of attention, and computer metaphors of information processing (Neisser, 1967; Atkinson & Shiffrin, 1968). Perhaps not surprisingly, one's ability to draw analogies between two disparate domains has also been linked to fluid intelligence (Ferrer, O'Hare, & Bunge, 2009) and creativity (Sternberg, 1977; Green, Cohen, Kim, & Gray, 2012).

The precise role of analogical thinking in science has been greatly informed by the work of Kevin Dunbar, who has conducted several real-world investigations into how scientists make use of analogies during the scientific discovery process in their respective laboratories. To do this, he immersed himself in several prominent laboratories around the world and recorded, transcribed, and ana-lyzed their laboratory meetings. He also conducted in-depth interviews with the scientists (including the principal investigators, post-docs, and graduate students) in order to get first-hand accounts of the scientific reasoning process. He made several key discoveries. Strikingly, he found that scientists would make use of bet-ween 3 and 15 analogies in a single one-hour laboratory meeting (Dunbar & Blanchette, 2001; see also Dunbar, 1995, 2001, 2002). He also discovered that sci-entists made use of both superficial (focusing on surface similarities between domains) and structural (focusing on deeper relational issues between more dis-tant domains) analogies in their laboratory meetings. The degree to which scien-tists made use of superficial versus structural features, however, depended on the goal of the scientists. Specifically, Dunbar and colleagues found that, if the goal of the scientist was to fix a methodological problem in one of their experiments, the analogies generated were predominantly based on superficial features close to the domain of interest. However, if the goal was to formulate new hypotheses, the sci-entists generated and focused on analogies that were based upon sets of higher-order structural relations. These findings are important as they highlight the critical role of both superficial and structural features of analogical reasoning in scientific thinking (which we will discuss in greater depth below), and also its flexible and goal-driven nature. In the remainder of this section, we will probe further into the operations that guide successful analogical transfer between domains. Furthermore, we will review research that looks at the variables that influence the degree to which one will, or will not draw an analogy between

disparate domains, and cover research revealing the neural mechanisms underlying successful analogical transfer.

Interestingly, research on analogical reasoning has found that participants in the
cognitive laboratory do not easily use analogies when reasoning (Gentner et al.,
1997; Holyoak & Thagard, 1995). For example, consider the classic studies by
Gick and Holyoak (1980, 1983). They found that only about 30% of college student participants spontaneously noticed an analogy between a source (the general problem) and the target (the tumor problem). The percentage of participants
solving the problem increased significantly, however, if they were explicitly told
that the general story would be useful in coming up with a solution to the tumor
problem. The difficulty of spontaneously noticing analogies has also been found
in several other laboratories. For example, Reed, Ernst, and Banerji (1974) found
that participants' reasoning performance was facilitated by exposure to a
previous analogous problem only if the analogy between the two problems was
made explicit to them.

Much headway has been made in recent years towards understanding the
neural underpinnings of analogical or relational reasoning, in both adults and
children. As with causal reasoning, one must be careful to differentiate between
the direct perception of relational similarity (e.g., perceiving the relations
"same" or "different") as opposed to the higher-order processes associated with
analogical inference. These may, in fact be subserved by different neural systems. To this end, Bunge, Wendelken, Badre, and Wagner (2005) evaluated the
contributions of different subregions of the prefrontal cortex (PFC) to different
components of verbal analogical reasoning tasks. To do this, they presented
participants with a pair of semantically related words (e.g., *bouquet* and *flowers*),
followed by an instructional cue that signaled participants to either (a) judge
whether a second word pair was analogous to the first word pair, or (b) judge
whether a second word pair was simply semantically related to the first. In
addition, they manipulated the associative strength of the first word pair in
order to further dissociate the effects of analogical reasoning from those of
semantic relatedness. They found that verbal analogical reasoning depended on
multiple PFC-mediated systems. Specifically, they found that the lateral frontopolar cortex was sensitive to the integration of multiple sources of semantic
information required to complete the analogical equivalence judgments,
whereas the anterior left inferior PFC was modulated by the associative strength
of the first word pair. These results are consistent with the finding that the left
anterior PFC extending to frontopolar cortex is sensitive to the number of elements that need integrating in a nonverbal visual analogy task (Kroger et al.,
2002). Similar "relational-complexity" effects have also been found in bilateral
frontopolar regions when participants are engaged in Raven's progressive
matrices tasks (Christoff et al., 2001).

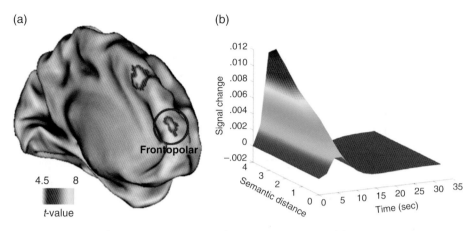

**Figure 9.8**   Neural response to semantic distance in reasoning. (a) Brain activity (orange) shown on an inflated cortical rendering of the left hemisphere; (b) percent signal change in the frontopolar region of interest as a function of increasing semantic distance between anal-ogies. Reprinted from Green, A., Kraemer, D., Fugelsang, J., Gray, J., & Dunbar, K. (2010). Connecting long distance: Semantic distance in analogical reasoning modulates frontopolar cortex activity. *Cerebral Cortex, 20*, page 72, with permission from Oxford University Press.

This prior work was extended in a series of studies by Adam Green and his colleagues (Green, Kraemer, Fugelsang, Gray, & Dunbar, 2010; Green et al., 2012b), who examined the degree to which the *analogical distance* between the two word pairs modulated the recruitment of the frontopolar cortex. Specifically, they parametrically manipulated the "closeness" of the two word pairs to be judged, such that some four word pairs had deep-lying simi-larities between relational representations that are superficially dissimilar (e.g., kitten:cat::spark:fire), referred to as *cross-domain* analogies, whereas other anal-ogies were superficially quite similar (e.g., kitten:cat::puppy:dog), referred to as *within-domain* analogies. They (Green et al., 2010) found a parametric relation between the semantic distance between the analogies and the recruitment of frontopolar cortex, such that activity in frontopolar cortex increased as the semantic distance in the analogies increased (see Figure 9.8). This pattern was found in both a verification (Green et al., 2010) and a production (Green et al., 2012b) version of the task. Taken together, these findings significantly extend previous evidence that the frontopolar cortex plays a central role in analogical mapping (Bunge et al., 2005; Green, Fugelsang, Kraemer, Shamosh, & Dunbar, 2006) by showing that this region of the brain is sensitive to the relational distance of the stimuli that are being reasoned with. It should be noted, how-ever, that the degree to which frontopolar cortex is specifically responsive to the relational integration component of analogical reasoning or more general hypothesis generation is a matter of recent debate (see Shallice & Cooper, 2011).

Several laboratories have now begun to explore the emergence of these functional neural systems in children's relational reasoning. For example, Crone et al. (2009) found that, like adults, 8- to 12-year-olds engaged lateral PFC and parietal cortex during relational matching tasks similar to Raven's matrices. However, they exhibited a different timecourse and overall activation profile. Specifically, while children also engaged rostrolateral PFC (a region just lateral to frontopolar cortex) when relational integration was required for single relations, they failed to do so when required to integrate across two relations. Crone et al. (2009) argued that this key finding suggests that improvements in this ability as a function of development may be dependent on changes in the profile of rostrolateral PFC engagement. Indeed, a more detailed analysis of similar data using age (from 8 to 19 years) as a covariate during a visual–spatial relational reasoning task suggests a gradual shift with age from a more widespread frontal–cingulate–striatal pattern (regions associated with effortful executive processing) in childhood to a predominant occipital–parietal–frontal pattern (regions associated with faster and more efficient visual–spatial processing) in late adolescence (Eslinger et al., 2009).

Finally, Wright, Matlen, Baym, Ferrer, and Bunge (2008) measured the neural responses of 6- to 13-year-olds while they completed visual A:B::C:D proportional analogies. As with the adult work, they found preferential recruitment of the rostrolateral PFC when the task required the integration of semantic relations. However, in contrast to adults, they found that, as a group, the children tended to engage the rostrolateral PFC too late in a trial to impact their behavioral responses, suggesting that critical developments in the function of rostrolateral PFC continue well into adolescence and likely beyond.

## Summary

In the current chapter, we have discussed some of the major domain-general cognitive processes that contribute to scientific reasoning. As noted above, we focused on causal, deductive, and analogical reasoning processes for several reasons. First, these three domains have all been shown to be used frequently by scientists and nonscientists alike when making discoveries about the world. Second, over the last decade there has been much headway in understanding the neural mechanisms that subserve these domain-general processes. Finally, the convergence of research with adults (often university students) and children allow us to gain insights into how these competencies develop. In so doing, a number of key themes regarding the development of the brain and scientific reasoning ability emerge. Here, the brain imaging data are especially informative, particularly as they relate to how domain-specific content influences domain-general reasoning processes (and subsequent brain recruitment). In the current chapter, we have highlighted multiple ways whereby content can influence reasoning processes. For example, content can facilitate reasoning in both children and adults. Here, in a range of tasks it has been shown that the integration of real-world knowledge (which involves recruitment of dorsolateral regions of the PFC) facilitates reasoning in multiple domains. In addition, domain-specific knowledge can also challenge and hinder reasoning performance when such knowledge is in conflict with available evidence. Here, we saw the critical role of conflict processing in multiple domains of reasoning, and the resultant interplay between the anterior cingulate cortex and multiple regions with the prefrontal cortex in the detection of, and subsequent modification of, reasoning behavior in response to conflict. A reasonable hypothesis is that one's ability to suspend belief is highly dependent on the efficiency with which these processes unfold. Finally, when reasoning analogically, the furthest reaches of prefrontal cortex (notably frontopolar) support one's ability to integrate disparate sources of information. Taken together, a clear picture emerges regarding the dependence on multiple regions in the prefrontal cortex for effective scientific reasoning. Considering this, it is not surprising that such abilities take time to develop due to the finding that the DLPFC is relatively late in maturing (Zelazo et al., 2008).

## Future Directions

The majority of neuroimaging results reported above have been obtained with young-adult (most often college students) or adolescent participants. This is because of the technical difficulties associated with testing young children (see Chapter 2) in MRI scanners. While these results are highly informative, they nevertheless remain only suggestive of what might be happening with regards to children's scientific reasoning because many of the changes that occur do so before adolescence, particularly between 4 and 8 years of age (see Zimmerman, 2007, for a review). Consequently, it is vital to extend these sorts of study downwards to younger ages. This would allow us to better understand the modes of reasoning that are most effective in young children (e.g., perceptual versus linguistic presentation of information) and the kind of training that might be most effective at promoting proper scientific reasoning (e.g., training in inhibition). Such findings would also help us to identify *when* and *which* skills are receptive to training, such as that provided in the classroom, and which skills are not developed enough to be receptive to classroom-based science education.

The current adult studies suggest that participants engage different reasoning processes when presented with hypotheses that are consistent with their domain knowledge rather than those not consistent with the current knowledge. If this holds true in children, then it suggests that increasing domain knowledge should be a precursor to teaching children about the domain-general inferential techniques. Thus, when approaching a new topic, early emphasis should be in providing early experiential knowledge of relevant phenomena on which later explicit inferences can be constructed.

Conceptual change also plays an important role in scientific reasoning. What is not clear is how and when this conceptual change takes place in an individual. Neuroimaging, particularly EEG methods, offers the promise of individualized assessment of semantic and conceptual organization (see Gliga & Mareschal, 2008, for further discussion of this). Though currently not practical on a large scale, the promise of low-cost portable EEG systems (see, e.g., Davies, Segalowitz, & Gavin, 2010) may make this a real tool in the schools of the future.

In summary, scientific reasoning is a complex multidimensional activity. Methods in neuroscience provide new windows into the domain-general and domain-specific processes involved and have the potential to help tailor educational practice to the individual needs of individual pupils.

## References

Aron, A. R., Robbins, T. W., & Poldrack, R. A. (2004). Inhibition and the right inferior frontal cortex. *Trends in Cognitive Science, 8*, 170–177.

Atkinson, R. C., & Shiffrin, R. M. (1968). Human memory: A proposed system, and its control processes. In K. W. Spence & J. T. Spence (Eds.), *The psychology of learning and motivation: Advances in research and theory* (Vol. 2, pp. 89–195). New York: Academic.

Baird, A. A., & Fugelsang, J. A. (2004). The emergence of consequential thought: Evidence from neuroscience. *Philosophical Transactions of the Royal Society B, 359*, 1797–1804.

Botvinick, M., Braver, T., Barch, D., Carter, C., & Cohen, J. (2001). Conflict monitoring and cognitive control. *Psychological Review, 108*, 625–652.

Broadbent, D. (1958). *Perception and communication.* London: Pergamon.

Bunge, S. A., Wendelken, C., Badre, D., & Wagner, A. D. (2005). Analogical reasoning and prefrontal cortex: Evidence for separable retrieval and integration mechanisms. *Cerebral Cortex, 15*, 230–249.

Cabeza, R., & Nyberg, L. (2000). Imaging cognition II: An empirical review of 275 PET and fMRI studies. *Journal of Cognitive Neuroscience, 12*, 1–47.

Carey, S. (1985). *Conceptual change in childhood.* Cambridge, MA: MIT Press.

Carey, S. (2000). Science education as conceptual change. *Journal of Applied Developmental Psychology, 21*, 13–19.

Carter, C. S., & van Veen, V. (2007). Anterior cingulate cortex and conflict detection: An update of theory and data. *Cognitive Affective and Behavioral Neuroscience, 7*, 367–379.

Christoff, K., Prabhakaran, V., Dorfman, J., Zhao, Z., Kroger, J. K., Holyoak, K. J., & Gabrieli, J. D. E. (2001). Rostrolateral prefrontal cortex involvement in relational integration during reasoning. *NeuroImage, 14*, 1136–1149.

Corballis, P. M. (2003). Visuospatial processing and the right-hemisphere interpreter. *Brain and Cognition, 53*, 171–176.

Corballis, P. M., Funnell, M. G., & Gazzaniga, M. S. (2002). Hemispheric asymmetries for simple visual judgments in the split brain. *Neuropsychologia, 40*, 401–410.

Corlett, P. R., Aitken, M. R., Dickinson, A., Shanks, D. R., Honey, G. D., Honey, R. A., Robbins, T. W., Bullmore, E. T., & Fletcher, P. C. (2004). Prediction error during retrospective revaluation of causal associations in humans: fMRI evidence in favor of an associative model of learning. *Neuron, 44*, 877–888.

Crone, E. A., Wendelken, C., van Leijenhorst, L., Honomichl, R. D., Christoff, K., & Bunge, S. A. (2009). Neurocognitive development of relational reasoning. *Developmental Science, 12*, 55–66.

Davies, P. L., Segalowitz, S. J., & Gavin, W. J. (2010). Development of response-monitoring ERPs in 7- to 25-year-olds. *Developmental Neuropsychology, 25*, 355–376.

Dias, M., Roazzi, A., & Harris, P. L. (2005). Reasoning from unfamiliar premises: A study with unschooled adults. *Psychological Sciences, 16*, 550–554.

Donaldson, M. (1978). *Children's minds*. London: Fontana.

Dunbar, K. (1995). How scientists really reason: Scientific reasoning in real-world laboratories. In R. J. Sternberg & J. Davidson (Eds.), *Mechanisms of insight* (pp. 365–395). Cambridge MA: MIT Press.

Dunbar, K. (2001). The analogical paradox: Why analogy is so easy in naturalistic settings, yet so difficult in the psychology laboratory. In D. Gentner, K. J. Holyoak, & B. Kokinov (Eds.), *Analogy: Perspectives from cognitive science* (pp. 313–334). Cambridge, MA: MIT Press.

Dunbar, K. (2002). Science as category: Implications of *In Vivo* science for theories of cognitive development, scientific discovery, and the nature of science. In P. Caruthers, S. Stich, & M. Siegel (Eds.), *Cognitive models of science* (pp. 154–170). New York: Cambridge University Press.

Dunbar, K., & Blanchette, I. (2001). The in vivo/in vitro approach to cognition: The case of analogy. *Trends in Cognitive Science, 5*, 335–339.

Dunbar, K., & Fugelsang, J. (2005). Scientific thinking and reasoning. In K. Holyoak & R. Morrison (Eds.), *Cambridge handbook of thinking and reasoning* (pp. 705–725). Cambridge: Cambridge University Press.

Dunbar, K., Fugelsang, J., & Stein, C. (2007). Do naive theories ever go away? Using brain and behavior to understand changes in concepts. In M. Lovett & P. Shah (Eds.), *Thinking with data* (pp. 193–206). New York: Erlbaum.

Eslinger, P. J., Blair, C., Wang, J., Lipovsky, B., Realmuto, J., Baker, D., Thorne, S., Gamson, D., Zimmerman, E., Rohrer, L., & Yang, Q. X. (2009). Developmental shifts in fMRI activations during visuospatial relational reasoning. *Brain and Cognition, 69*, 1–10.

Evans, J. St. B. T. (2008). Dual-processing accounts of reasoning, judgment, and social cognition. *Annual Review of Psychology, 59*, 255–278.

Evans, J. St. B. T., Barston, J. L., & Pollard, P. (1983). On the conflict between logic and belief in syllogistic reasoning. *Memory and Cognition, 11*, 295–306.

Ferrer, E., O'Hare, E. D., & Bunge, S. A. (2009). Fluid reasoning and the developing brain. *Frontiers in Neuroscience, 3*, 46–51.

Fletcher, P. C., Anderson, J. M., Shanks, D. R., Honey, R., Carpenter, T. A., Donovan, T., Papadakis, N., & Bullmore, E. T. (2001). Responses of human frontal cortex to surprising events are predicted by formal associative learning theory. *Nature Neuroscience, 4*, 1043–1048.

Fugelsang, J. A., & Dunbar, K. N. (2005). Brain-based mechanisms underlying complex causal thinking, *Neuropsychologia, 43*, 1204–1213.

Fugelsang, J., & Dunbar, K. (2009). Brain based mechanisms underlying causal reasoning. In E. Kraft, B. Guylas, & E. Poppel (Eds.), *Neural correlates of thinking* (pp. 269–279). Berlin: Springer.

Fugelsang, J., Roser, M., Corballis, P., Gazzaniga, M., & Dunbar, K. (2005). Brain mechanisms underlying perceptual causality. *Cognitive Brain Research, 24*, 41–47.

Fugelsang, J., Stein, C., Green, A., & Dunbar, K. (2004). Theory and data interactions of the scientific mind: Evidence from the molecular and the cognitive laboratory. *Canadian Journal of Experimental Psychology, 58*, 132–141.

Fugelsang. J., & Thompson, V. (2000). Strategy selection in causal reasoning: When beliefs and covariation collide. *Canadian Journal of Experimental Psychology, 54*, 13–32.

Fugelsang, J., & Thompson, V. (2003). A dual-process model of belief and evidence interactions in causal reasoning. *Memory and Cognition, 31*, 800–815.

Gentner, D. (1983). Structure-mapping: A theoretical framework for analogy. *Cognitive Science, 7*, 155–170.

Gentner, D., Brem, S., Ferguson, R. W., Markman, A. B., Levidow, B. B., Wolff, P., & Forbus, K. D. (1997). Analogical reasoning and conceptual change: A case study of Johannes Kepler. *The Journal of the Learning Sciences, 6*, 3–40.

Gentner, D., & Jeziorski, M. (1993). The shift from metaphor to analogy in western science. In A. Ortony (Ed.), *Metaphor and thought* (2nd ed., pp. 447–480). Cambridge: Cambridge University Press.

Gick, M. L., & Holyoak, K. J. (1980). Analogical problem solving. *Cognitive Psychology, 12*, 306–355.

Gick, M. L., & Holyoak, K. J. (1983). Schema induction and analogical transfer. *Cognitive Psychology, 15*, 1–38.

Gliga, T., & Mareschal, D. (2008). What can neuroimaging tell us about the early development of visual categories? *Cogniflie, Creier, Comportament [Cognition, Brain, Behavior], 10*, 757–772.

Goel, V. (2003). Evidence for dual neural pathways for syllogistic reasoning. *Neuropsychologia, 32*, 301–309.

Goel, V. (2007). Anatomy of deductive reasoning. *Trends in Cognitive Sciences, 11*, 435–441.

Goel, V., & Dolan, R. J. (2000). Anatomical segregation of component processes in an inductive inference task. *Journal of Cognitive Neuroscience, 12*, 110–119.

Goel, V., & Dolan, R. J. (2003). Explaining modulation of reasoning by belief. *Cognition, 87*, B11–B22.

Goel, V., & Dolan, R. J. (2004). Differential involvement of left prefrontal cortex in inductive and deductive reasoning. *Cognition, 93*, 109–121.

Goel, V., Gold, B., Kapur, S., & Houle, S. (1998). Neuroanatomical correlates of human reasoning. *Journal of Cognitive Neuroscience, 10*, 293–302.

Gopnik, A., Sobel, D. M., Schulz, L. E., & Glymour, C. (2001). Causal learning mechanisms in very young children: Two-, three-, and four-year-olds infer causal relations from patterns of variation and covariation. *Developmental Psychology, 37*, 620–629.

Goswami, U., & Brown, A. (1990). Melting chocolate and melting snowmen: Analogical reasoning and causal relations. *Cognition, 35*, 69–95.

Green, A., Cohen, M., Kim, J., & Gray, J. R. (2012a). An explicit cue improves creative analogical reasoning. *Intelligence, 40*, 598–603.

Green, A., Fugelsang, J., Kraemer, D., Shamosh, N., & Dunbar, K. (2006). The dynamic role of prefrontal cortex in reasoning and abstract thought. *Brain Research, 1096*, 125–137.

Green, A., Kraemer, D., Fugelsang, J., Gray, J., & Dunbar, K. (2010). Connecting long distance: Semantic distance in analogical reasoning modulates frontopolar cortex activity. *Cerebral Cortex, 20*, 70–76.

Green, A., Kraemer, D., Fugelsang, J., Gray, J., & Dunbar, K. (2012b). Neurocorrelates of creativity in analogical reasoning. *Journal of Experimental Psychology: Learning, Memory, & Cognition, 38*, 264–272.

Griggs, R. A., & Cox, J. R. (1982). The elusive thematics material effect in Wason's selection task. *British Journal of Psychology, 73*, 407–420.

Harris, P. L. (2000) Thinking about the unknown. *Trends in Cognitive Sciences, 5*, 494–498.

Hickok, G., & Poeppel, D. (2004). Dorsal and ventral streams: A framework for understanding aspects of the functional anatomy of language. *Cognition, 92*, 67–99.

Holyoak, K. J., & Thagard, P. (1995). *Mental leaps*. Cambridge, MA: MIT Press.

Houdé, O. (2000). Inhibition and cognitive development: Object, number, categorization and reasoning. *Cognitive Development, 15*, 63–73.

Houdé, O. (2007). First insight on "neuropedagogy of reasoning". *Thinking and Reasoning, 13*, 81–89.

Houdé, O., Zago, L., Crivello, F., Moutier, S., Pinaue, A., Mazoyer, B., & Tzouri-Mazoyer, N. (2001). Access to deductive logic depends on a right ventromedial prefrontal area devoted to emotion and feeling: Evidence from a training paradigm. *NeuroImage, 14*, 1486–1492.

Houdé, O., Zago, L., Mellet, E., Moutier, S., Pinaue, A., Mazoyer, B., & Tzouri-Mazoyer, N. (2000). Shifting from perceptual brain to logical brain: The neural impact of cognitive inhibition training. *Journal of Cognitive Neuroscience, 12*, 721–728.

Howe, C. (1998). *Conceptual structure in childhood and adolescence*. London: Routledge.

Howe, C., Tavares, J. T., & Devine, A. (2012). Everyday conceptions of object fall: Explicit and tacit understanding during middle childhood. *Journal of Experimental Child Psychology, 111*, 351–366.

Howe, C. J., Tolmie, A., & Sofroniou, N. (1999). Experimental appraisal of personal beliefs in science: Constraints on performance in the 9 to 14 age group. *British Journal of Educational Psychology, 69*, 243–274.

Inhelder, B., & Piaget, J. (1958). *The growth of logical thinking from childhood to adolescence.* New York: Basic.

Kallai, A. Y., & Reiner, M. (2010, June). *The source of misconceptions in physics: When event related potential components N400 and P600 disagree.* Poster presented at the 2010 Meeting of the Special Interest Group (SIG) 22 "Neuroscience and Education" of the European Association for Research on Learning and Instruction (EARLI), Zurich.

Karmiloff-Smith, A. (1992). *Beyond modularity: A developmental perspective on cognitive science.* Cambridge, MA: MIT Press.

Kelley, W. M., Miezin, F. M., McDermott, K. B., Buckner, R. L., Raichle, M. E., Cohen, N. J., Ollinger, J. O., Akbudak, E., Conturo, T. E., Snyder, A. Z., & Petersen, S. E. (1998). Hemispheric specialization in human dorsal frontal cortex and medial temporal lobe for verbal and nonverbal memory encoding. *Neuron, 20,* 927–936.

Klahr, D., Zimmerman, C., & Jirout, J. (2011). Educational interventions to advance children's scientific thinking. *Science, 333,* 971–975.

Koslowski, B. (1996). *Theory and evidence: The development of scientific reasoning.* Cambridge: MA: MIT Press.

Kroger, J. K., Sabb, F. W., Fales, C. L., Bookheimer, S. Y., Cohen, M. S., & Holyoak, K. J. (2002). Recruitment of anterior dorsolateral prefrontal cortex in human reasoning: A parametric study of relational complexity. *Cerebral Cortex, 12,* 477–485.

Kuhn, T. (1962). *The structure of scientific revolutions.* Chicago, IL: University of Chicago Press.

Levy, J. (2011). *A bee in a cathedral: And 99 other scientific analogies.* New York: Firefly.

McCloskey, M. (1983). Naive theories of motion. In D. Gentner & A. L. Stevens (Eds.), *Mental models* (pp. 299–324). Hillsdale, NJ: Erlbaum.

McDermott, K. B., Ojemann, J. G., Petersen, S. E., Ollinger, J. M., Snyder, A. Z., Akbudak, E., Conturo, T. E., & Raichle, M. E., (1999). Direct comparison of episodic encoding and retrieval of words: An event-related fMRI study. *Memory, 7,* 661–678.

Michotte, A. (1963). *The perception of causality.* New York: Basic.

Milner, B. (1962). Laterality effects in audition. In V. B. Mountcastle (Ed.), *Interhemispheric relations and cerebral dominance* (pp. 177–198). Baltimore, MD: Johns Hopkins Press.

Neisser, U. (1967). *Cognitive psychology.* New York: Appleton-Century-Crofts.

Nersessian, N. (1999). Models, mental models, and representations: Model-based reasoning in conceptual change. In L. Magnani, N. Nersessian, & P. Thagard (Eds.), *Model-based reasoning in scientific discovery* (pp. 5–22). New York: Plenum.

Osherson, D., Perani, D., Cappa, S., Schnur, T., Grassi, F., & Fazio, F. (1998). Distinct brain loci in deductive versus probabilistic reasoning. *Neuropsychologia, 36,* 369–376.

Parris, B. A., Kuhn, G., Mizon, G. A., Benattayallah, A., & Hodgson, T. L. (2009) Imaging the impossible: An fMRI study of impossible causal relationships in magic tricks. *NeuroImage, 45,* 1033–1039.

Parsons, L. M., & Osherson, D. N. (2001). New evidence for distinct right and left brain systems for deductive versus probabilistic reasoning. *Cerebral Cortex, 11,* 954–965.

Pearl, J. (2009). *Causality: models, reasoning, and inference* (2nd ed.). New York: Cambridge University Press.

Perales, J. C., Catena, A., Maldonado, A., & Cándido, A. (2007). The role of mechanism and covariation information in causal belief updating. *Cognition, 105,* 704-714.

Pine, K. J., & Messer, D. J. (2000). The effect of explaining another's actions on children's implicit theories of balance. *Cognition and Instruction, 18,* 35–51.

Poldrack, R. A. (2006). Can cognitive processes be inferred from neuroimaging data? *Trends in Cognitive Sciences, 10,* 59–63.

Posner, M. I. (1980). Orienting of attention. *Quarterly Journal of Experimental Psychology, 32,* 3–25.

Reed, S. K., Ernst, G. W., & Banerji, R. (1974). The role of analogy in transfer between similar problem states. *Cognitive Psychology, 6,* 437–450.

Rodriguez-Moreno, D., & Hirsch, J. (2009). The dynamics of deductive reasoning. *Neuropsychologia, 47,* 949–961.

Roser, M., Fugelsang, J., Dunbar, K., Corballis, P., & Gazzaniga, M. (2005). Dissociating processes supporting causal perception and causal inference in the brain. *Neuropsychology, 19,* 591–602.

Seger, C., Poldrack, R., Prabhakaran, V., Zhao, M., Glover, G., & Gabrieli, J. (2000). Hemispheric asymmetries and individual differences in visual concept learning as measured by functional MRI. *Neuropsychologia, 38,* 1316–1324.

Shallice, T., & Burgess, P. W. (1991). Deficits in strategy application following frontal lobe damage in man. *Brain, 114,* 727–741.

Shallice, T., & Cooper, R. P. (2011). *The organisation of mind.* Oxford: Oxford University Press.

Shtulman, A., & Valcarcel, J. (2012). Scientific knowledge suppresses but does not supplant earlier intuitions. *Cognition, 124,* 210–215.

Shultz, T. R. (1982). Rules of causal attribution. *Monographs of the Society of Research in Child Development, 47*(whole No. 194).

Siegler, R. S. (1976). Three aspects of cognitive development. *Cognitive Psychology, 8,* 481–520.

Sternberg, R. (1977). *Intelligence, information processing, and analogical reasoning.* Hillsdale, NJ: Erlbaum.

Stollstorff, M., Vartanian, O., & Goel, V. (2012). Levels of conflict in reasoning modulate right lateral prefrontal cortex. *Brain Research, 1428,* 24–32.

Stuss, D. T., & Alexander, M. P. (2000). Executive functions and the frontal lobes: A conceptual view. *Psychological Research, 63,* 289–298.

Thagard, P., & Croft, D. (1999). Scientific discovery and technological innovation: Ulcers, dinosaur extinction, and the programming language Java. In L. Magnani, N. Nersessian, & P. Thagard (Eds.), *Model-based reasoning in scientific discovery* (pp. 125–137). New York: Plenum.

Treisman, A. (1964). Selective attention in man. *British Medical Bulletin, 20,* 12–16.

Turner, D. C., Aitken. M. R., Shanks, D. R., Sahakian, B. J., Robbins, T. W., Schwarzbauer C., & Fletcher, P. C. (2004). The role of the lateral frontal cortex in causal associative learning: Exploring preventative and super-learning. *Cerebral Cortex, 14,* 872–880.

van Veen, V., & Carter, C. S. (2002). The anterior cingulate as a conflict monitor: fMRI and ERP studies. *Physiology and Behavior, 77,* 477–482.

Wason, P. (1968). Reasoning about a rule. *Quarterly Journal of Experimental Psychology*, *20*, 273–281.

Wright, S. B., Matlen, B. J., Baym, C. L., Ferrer, E., & Bunge, S. A. (2008). Neural correlates of fluid reasoning in children and adults. *Frontiers in Human Neuroscience*, *1*, 1–8.

Yeung, N., Botvinick, M. M., & Cohen, J. D. (2004). The neural basis of error-detection: Conflict monitoring and the error-related negativity. *Psychological Review*, *111*, 931–959.

Young, M. E. (1995). On the origin of personal causal theories. *Psychonomic Bulletin and Review*, *2*, 83–104.

Zelazo, P. D., Carlson, S. M., & Kesek, A. (2008). The development of executive function in childhood. In C. A. Nelson & M. Luciana (Eds.), *Handbook of developmental cognitive neuroscience* (2nd ed., pp. 553–574). Cambridge, MA: MIT Press.

Zimmerman, C. (2000). The development of scientific reasoning skills. *Developmental Review*, *20*, 99–149.

Zimmerman, C. (2005). *The development of scientific reasoning: What psychologists contribute to an understanding of elementary science learning.* Paper commissioned by the National Academies of Science (National Research Council's Board of Science Education, Consensus Study on Learning Science, Kindergarten through Eighth Grade).

Zimmerman, C. (2007). The development of scientific thinking skills in elementary and middle school. *Developmental Review*, *27*, 172–223.

## Further Reading

Shallice, T., & Cooper, R. M. (2011). Chapter 12: Thinking. In T. Shallice and R. Cooper (Eds.), *The organisation of mind* (pp. 463–504). Oxford: Oxford University Press.

Zimmerman, C. (2007). The development of scientific reasoning skills in elementary and middle school. *Developmental Review*, *27*, 172–223.

# Chapter 10

# Social Development

## Sarah-Jayne Blakemore, Kathrin Cohen Kadosh, Catherine L. Sebastian, Tobias Grossmann, and Mark H. Johnson

## Introduction

Humans are an exquisitely social species. We are constantly reading each other's actions, gestures, and faces in terms of underlying mental states and emotions, in an attempt to figure out what other people are thinking and feeling, and what they are about to do next (Blakemore, Winston, & Frith, 2004). Social and emotional functioning is a critical component of educational attainment. There is a rapidly expanding literature on social cognitive development during the first two years of life, and it is here that we start our review. Much less is known about the neurodevelopment of social skills in mid-childhood and adolescence. Nevertheless, the second half of this chapter focuses on the development of social understanding during this period of life and on possible contributions of an improved understanding for education.

## Early Development of the Social Brain

The earliest stage of postnatal development, infancy (0–2 years), is a time of life during which enormous changes take place – the "helpless" newborn seems almost a different creature from the active, inquisitive two-year-old. During this period, human infants develop in a world filled with other people, and developing an understanding of other people and their actions is one of the

*Educational Neuroscience*, First Edition. Edited by Denis Mareschal, Brian Butterworth and Andy Tolmie.
© 2014 John Wiley & Sons, Ltd. Published 2014 by John Wiley & Sons, Ltd.

most fundamental tasks infants face in learning about the world. In this section, we present empirical findings from several areas of social information processing in early development: (1) face and gaze processing, (2) joint attention, (3) biological motion, and (4) understanding human action. The findings discussed are mainly based on electroencephalography (EEG)/ event-related potential (ERP) methods, which are the most commonly used methods with this age group. These EEG/ERP methods, which provide precise information on the timing of brain and cognitive processes, have more recently been complemented by functional near-infrared spectroscopy (fNIRS) (see Chapter 2), which enables us to better localize cortical activation in infants (see Lloyd-Fox, Blasi, & Elwell, 2010, for a review).

## Face Processing

Human faces in particular provide a plethora of social information, including the identity, the emotional state, and the attentional focus of a conspecific (via the direction of eye gaze). Behavioral work with newborn infants has revealed that newborns attend preferentially to facelike patterns within hours of being born (Morton & Johnson, 1991; Johnson, 2005), providing evidence for a mechanism to bias the input that is processed by the newborn's brain. The face preference observed in newborns is thought to be guided largely by subcortical brain structures, while it has been proposed that the maturation of visual cortical areas is necessary for the emergence of the more sophisticated competencies underlying identity recognition from faces (for a discussion, see Johnson, 2005). Newborns first recognize their mother's face on the basis of information from the outer contour of the head, hairline, and the internal configuration of eyes, nose, and mouth (Bushnell, Sai, & Mullin, 1989), but it is not until after six weeks of life that they become able to make this recognition solely on the face's internal configuration (de Schonen & Mathivet, 1990).

Investigations of brain areas involved in face processing in infants have been limited mainly by technical issues (de Haan & Thomas, 2002; Grossmann, 2008). One exception has been a study by Tzourio-Mazoyer and colleagues, who took advantage of the opportunity to perform positron emission tomography (PET) on infants in an intensive care unit as part of a clinical followup (Tzourio-Mazoyer et al., 2002). In this small-scale study, a group of six 2-month-olds were imaged while they watched a face or an array of coloured diodes used as a control stimulus. The results revealed that faces activated a network of areas in 2-month-old infants' brains similar to that described as the core system for face processing in adults (Gauthier, Tarr, Anderson, Skudlarski, & Gore, 2000; Haxby, Hoffman, & Gobbini, 2000; Kanwisher, 2000). It is interesting to note that a cortical region that at the age of 2 months is neuroanatomically immature (Huttenlocher, 2002; Huttenlocher & Dabholkar, 1997) and has only a low level of resting metabolic activity (Chugani & Phelps, 1986; Chugani, Phelps, & Mazziotta, 1987) can be functionally activated. In addition, viewing faces activated bilateral inferior occipital and right inferior parietal areas in infants. The former has been implicated in early perceptual analysis of facial features, whereas the latter is thought to support spatially directed attention in adults (Haxby et al., 2000). In contrast to what is known from adults, face processing in 2-month-olds also recruited areas in the inferior frontal and superior temporal gyrus, which have been identified as a part of the adult language network. One possible interpretation of this is that the co-activation of face and future language networks has a facilitatory effect on social interactions guiding language learning by attention toward the speaker's face and mouth (Tzourio-Mazoyer et al., 2002).

    However, most studies of infant face perception rely on the more readily applicable recording of EEG measures. We now discuss briefly the empirical evidence available on infants' face processing using event-related brain potentials (ERPs; for a more detailed review, see de Haan, Johnson, & Halit, 2003). In adults, human faces elicit an N170 response (a negative component, which occurs at around 170 ms post stimulus presentation), which is most prominent over posterior temporal sites and is larger in amplitude and longer in latency in response to inverted than to upright faces (Bentin, Allison, Puce, Perez, & McCarthy, 1996; de Haan, Pascalis, & Johnson, 2002). This component is not modulated by the inversion of monkey faces (de Haan et al., 2002), or when upright objects are compared with inverted objects (Bentin et al., 1996). This selective inversion effect for human faces has been taken as evidence for a face-related processing mechanism generating the N170.

    On the basis of waveform morphology and some of its response properties, it has been suggested that the infant N290 is a precursor to the adult N170, in that it shows similar stimulus sensitivities and scalp distribution patterns. In these studies, infants' and adults' ERPs were measured in response to upright and inverted human and monkey faces (de Haan et al., 2002; Halit, de Haan, & Johnson, 2003). Similarly to the adult N170, the infant N290 is a negative-going deflection observed over posterior electrodes, whose peak latency decreases from 350 ms at 3 months to 290 ms at 12 months of age (Halit et al., 2003). This is consistent with the latency of many prominent ERP components reducing with increasing age during childhood. The results of these studies indicate that at 12 months of age the amplitude of the infant N290, like the adult N170, increases in response to inverted human but not inverted monkey faces when compared with the upright faces. However, the amplitude of the N290 was not affected by stimulus inversion at an earlier age (3 and 6 months).

The development of the face-related brain processes reflected in the N170/N290 continues well beyond infancy (for a review, see Taylor, Batty, & Itier, 2004). While latency of the adult N170 is delayed by face inversion, no such effect is observed for the latency of the infant N290 at any age (de Haan et al., 2002; Halit et al., 2003). There is evidence that suggests that this latency effect is not apparent until 8–11 years of age (Taylor et al., 2004). Furthermore, while the amplitude of the adult N170 is larger in response to monkey faces, infants' N290 shows the opposite pattern. A completely adult-like modulation of the amplitude of the N170 has not been reported until 13–14 years of age (Taylor et al., 2004).

In summary, evidence available from PET and EEG/ERP studies suggests that most of the brain areas and mechanisms implicated in adult face processing can be activated within the first few months of postnatal life. However, this should not be interpreted as meaning that these cortical areas are specialized for processing faces at this stage, nor that they function in the same way as they do in adulthood, as considerable further tuning of these areas continues into childhood (Johnson, 2011, see later sections).

## Gaze Processing

An important social signal encoded in faces is eye gaze. The detection and monitoring of eye gaze direction is essential for effective social learning and communication among humans (Csibra & Gergely, 2009). Eye gaze provides information about the target of another person's attention and expression, and it also conveys information about communicative intentions and future behavior. Eye contact is considered to be one of the most powerful modes of establishing a communicative link between humans (Kampe, Frith, & Frith, 2003). From birth, human infants are sensitive to another person's gaze as reflected in their preference to look at faces that have their eyes opened rather than closed (Batki, Baron-Cohen, Wheelwright, Connellan, & Ahluwalia, 2000). Furthermore, newborns look longer at faces with direct/mutual gaze as compared with faces with averted gaze (Farroni, Csibra, Simion, & Johnson, 2002). Eye gaze has also been shown to effectively cue newborn infants' attention to spatial locations, suggesting a rudimentary form of gaze following (Farroni, Pividori, Simion, Massaccesi, & Johnson, 2004). The question that arises is how the behaviorally expressed preference for direct gaze and the capacity to follow gaze are implemented in the infant brain.

By 4 months, the infant brain manifests enhanced processing of faces with direct gaze as indexed by an increased amplitude of the N290 when compared with averted gaze (Farroni et al., 2002). This finding is obtained even when the head is averted but direct mutual gaze is maintained (Farroni, Johnson, &

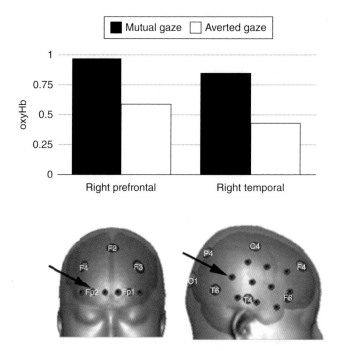

**Figure 10.1**   This figure shows 4-month-olds' hemodynamic responses (oxygenated hemoglobin) to mutual gaze and averted gaze as measured with fNIRS from the right prefrontal and right temporal cortical regions (marked by arrows in the bottom panel). This figure was adapted from Grossmann et al. (2008).

Csibra, 2004). However, enhanced neural processing of faces with direct gaze is only found when eyes are presented in the context of an upright face. Moreover, 4-month-old infants watched two kinds of dynamic scenario in which a face either established mutual gaze or averted its gaze (Grossmann et al., 2008). Hemodynamic responses were measured by NIRS, permitting spatial localization of brain activation. The results revealed that processing mutual gaze social interactions activates areas in the infant right superior temporal cortex (STS) and prefrontal cortex (PFC) that correspond to the brain regions implicated in these processes in adults (Kampe et al., 2003; Pelphrey, Viola, & McCarthy, 2004) (see Figure 10.1). The ERP and NIRS results reviewed above support the notion the mutual gaze is processed in the brain from early in development.

Another communicative function of eye gaze is to direct attention to certain locations, events, and objects. In an ERP study, 9-month-old infants and adults watched a face whose gaze shifted either towards (object congruent) or away from (object incongruent) the location of a previously presented object (Senju, Johnson, & Csibra, 2006). This paradigm was based on that used in an earlier fMRI study (Pelphrey, Singerman, Allison, & McCarthy, 2003), and was designed to reveal the neural basis of "referential" gaze perception. When the ERPs elicited by object-incongruent gaze shifts were compared with the object-congruent gaze shifts, an enhanced negativity around 300 ms over occipitotemporal electrodes was observed in both infants and adults. This suggests that infants encode referential information of gaze using similar neural mechanisms to those engaged in adults. However, only infants showed a frontocentral negative component that was larger in amplitude for object-congruent gaze shifts. It is thus possible that in the infant brain the referential information about gaze is encoded in more widespread cortical circuits than in the more specialized adult brain. We return to this interesting finding on referential gaze in the next section, in which the neural basis of a very closely related social–cognitive phenomenon called joint attention will be discussed.

## Joint Attention

The process by which two people share attention towards the same object or event is called joint attention. Joint attention is considered to be one of the most fundamental social cognitive skills that develop during infancy. Besides attending to an external object or event herself, the ability to jointly attend with another person requires the infant to monitor (a) the other person's attention in relation to the self and (b) the other person's attention toward the same object or event. Behavioral studies suggest that triadic representations between two minds and a shared object of attention emerge around 9 months of age. They are also thought to be uniquely human representations supporting shared attention and collaborative goals (Tomasello, Carpenter, Call, Behne, & Moll, 2005). The dorsal part of the medial prefrontal cortex (mPFC) has been identified as a critical region to support joint attention in the adult brain (Frith & Frith, 2006; Saxe, 2006; Schilbach et al., 2010; Williams et al., 2005).

Striano, Reid, and Hoehl (2006) examined the ERP correlates of joint attention in 9-month-old infants by having an adult interact live with the infant in two contexts. In the joint-attention context the adult looked at the infant and then at the computer screen displaying a novel object, whereas in the non-joint-attention context the adult only looked at the chest of the infant and then at the novel object presented on the screen. Objects presented in the joint-attention context compared with objects in the non-joint-attention context were found to elicit a greater negative component (Nc) peaking around 500 ms with a maximum amplitude over frontal and central channels. The Nc is thought to be generated within the prefrontal cortex and may indicate the allocation of attention to a visual stimulus (Reynolds &

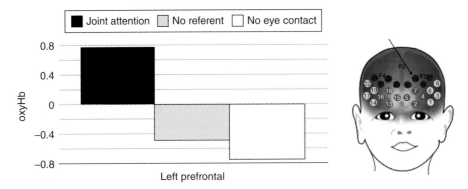

**Figure 10.2**  This figure shows 5-month-olds' hemodynamic responses (oxygenated hemoglobin) to joint-attention, no-referent, and no-eye-contact conditions as measured with fNIRS from a left dorsal prefrontal cortical region (marked by an arrow in the right panel). This figure was adapted from Grossmann and Johnson (2010).

Richards, 2005). Therefore, Striano et al. (2006) suggested that infants benefit from the joint-attention interaction and thus devote more attentional resources to those objects presented in this context. This ERP paradigm has also been used to examine joint attention in younger infants (see Parise, Reid, Stets, & Striano, 2008). This study found that by 5 months infants show an increased allocation of attention to the cued object in a joint-attention condition.

Despite these insights from using ERP methods, it still remains unclear which brain regions are involved in engaging in triadic interactions. However, in a recent another study, NIRS was used to localize infant brain responses during triadic interactions (Grossmann & Johnson, 2010). In this study, 5-month-old infants showed increased left prefrontal cortical responses when engaged in joint triadic interactions compared with two (nontriadic) control conditions, in which either no eye contact was established or the person looked away from the object (see Figure 10.2). These findings are in line with previous fMRI work with adults implicating left prefrontal regions in joint attention (Schilbach et al., 2010). Thus, 5-month-old infants seem to engage similar prefrontal regions during triadic social interactions to adults.

Further support for the notion that left prefrontal cortex plays a critical role in joint attention comes from a clinical study in which cortical metabolism in infants was measured using PET (Caplan et al., 1993). In this study, higher rates of preoperative glucose metabolism in frontal cortical regions, especially the left frontal region, were a positive predictor of the postoperatively assessed tendency to initiate joint-attention bids. To further assess the role of the frontal cortex, resting EEG coherence and its relation to joint-attention skills in typically developing infants was examined (Mundy, Card, & Fox, 2000). EEG coherence is a measure of phase synchrony between spatially separated EEG generators, which provides an index of aspects of neural network integration (Thatcher, Krause, & Hrybyk, 1986). EEG coherence measures of left frontal cortical activity were found to be associated with the infants' tendency to initiate joint attention at 14 and 18 months. Furthermore, in a followup study, it was shown that behavioral measures of joint attention and EEG coherence at 14 months were both related to language development at 24 months (Mundy, Fox, & Card, 2003).

In summary, ERP and NIRS data suggest that, as early as 5 months, infants are sensitive to triadic social interactions. This early sensitivity to joint attention appears to depend on left prefrontal brain areas. This early emergence of joint-attention skills is also supported by behavioral data showing that, by the age of 3 months, infants already discriminate between dyadic and triadic interactions (Striano & Stahl, 2005). Despite the early evidence for joint attention, it is important to keep in mind that it develops continuously throughout the first decade of life, and early indicators of deficits in joint attention are central to most developmental disorders.

## Action Observation

Human actions are an exceedingly complex set of visual stimuli providing dynamic and continuous information about the behavior of other humans. The capacity to parse ongoing actions into meaningful segments is critical for the interpretation of others' behavior. There is evidence to suggest that, in adults and infants, this parsing of action sequences is partly based upon understanding the goal of an action (Baldwin, Baird, Saylor, & Clark, 2001; Blakemore & Decety, 2001). For example, when 8-month-old infants were presented with complete and incomplete goal-directed actions they looked for longer at the incomplete than at the complete action (Reid, Csibra, Belsky, & Johnson, 2007). It is possible that the infants detected a mismatch between anticipated and perceived actions, which resulted in increased looking time in the case where an action is terminated before a goal is achieved. This detection might be based on a process called forward-mapping, which involves the continuous prediction of possible motion trajectories and future actions based on their own motor representations (see, e.g., Falck-Ytter, Gredebäck, & von Hofsten, 2006).

Researchers have also asked the question of whether infants come to understand other people's actions through a mirror-neuron system (Rizzolatti & Craighero, 2004) that maps an observed action onto infants' own motor representation of that action. According to the mirror-neuron system view, infants are not expected to predict others' action goals before they can perform the action themselves. In a behavioral study (Falck-Ytter et al., 2006),

12-month-olds but not 6-month-olds were found to show proactive (anticipatory) goal-directed eye movements during observation of an action (putting objects into a box). Because it is known that infants do not master this kind of motor task until 7–9 months of age (Bruner, 1973), this finding was taken as evidence for the mirror-neuron system view of action understanding. Furthermore, based on the finding that proactive eye movements were only found when a human agent produced the action and not when the objects were self-propelled (Falck-Ytter et al., 2006), it was argued that a human agent is required to activate the mirror-neuron system. These findings are also interesting in light of evidence showing that good motor skills in 8-month-old infants correlate with their sensitivity to discriminate biologically possible from impossible arm movements (Reid, Belsky, & Johnson, 2005). Despite the value of these interesting behavioral findings, a shortcoming is that they provide only indirect evidence for a neural mechanistic explanation.

A candidate neural signature that has been shown to be useful for the study of action perception in adults is the mu wave (oscillatory bursts at 9–11 Hz), which can be measured with EEG. This wave activity appears to be associated with the motor cortex, and is diminished with movement or an intent to move, or when others are observed performing actions (Oberman et al., 2005). Therefore, EEG oscillations in the mu-wave range recorded over sensorimotor cortex are thought to reflect mirror-neuron activity and have been associated with enabling an adult observer to understand an action through motor simulation.

Southgate, Johnson, Osborne, and Csibra (2009) investigated 9-month-olds' mu-wave activity over the sensorimotor cortex during elicited reaching for objects. Critically, they also examined whether mu activity was modulated when observing a grasping action performed by someone else. The results obtained in this study revealed that, like adults, 9-month-old infants display a reduction in mu activity during performing and observing a grasping action. Another interesting finding in this study was that motor activation (mu suppression) was measured before the actual onset of the observed action. Infants must have learned to anticipate the occurrence of the action because they were presented with repeated trials and no mu suppression was evident during the first three trials. This finding of predictive motor activation during action observation supports accounts according to which the mirror-neuron system plays an important role in action prediction (Csibra, 2007).

In a followup study, 9-month-old infants watched an action (a hand grasping behind an occluder) that could only be interpreted as goal directed if they are able to predict a hidden outcome (Southgate, Johnson, El Karoui, & Csibra, 2010). As in the previous study, motor activity was measured as indexed by mu activity over sensorimotor cortex. Motor activity during this goal prediction condition was compared with three control conditions, which consisted of (1) a turned hand, unable to reach, going behind an occluder, (2) an open grasping hand being placed on the table in front of an occluder, and (3) a turned hand, unable to reach, being placed on the table in front of an occluder. Only when infants watched the grasping hand going behind the occluder was mu activity suppressed, and no such suppression was observed during any of the control conditions. This finding provides further evidence for 9-month-olds infants' ability to predict the goal of an action, and strengthens the notion that the motor system plays a critical role in action understanding. In addition, it shows that already by the age of 9 months motor activity is influenced by top-down processes such as goal prediction rather than being simply being driven by observing any kind of action.

However, in both studies (Southgate et al., 2009, 2010) the grasping actions presented to the infants in the action-observation conditions were in their action repertoire. Thus, in another study (van Elk, van Schie, Hunnius, Vesper, & Bekkering, 2008), the role of motor experience with an action was investigated with 14- to 16-month-old infants. As predicted on the basis of infants' limited motor experience with walking at this age, infants exhibited stronger mu suppression during the observation of crawling than during the observation of walking. Furthermore, the size of this suppression effect was strongly correlated with the infants' own crawling experience, such that infants who had longer crawling experience showed a stronger mu suppression. These findings provide some first evidence that motor activity during action observation in infants depends on motor experience with an action.

All the studies concerning action understanding presented up to here relied on EEG scalp recordings placed over sensorimotor cortex. However, these scalp recordings cannot be localized to motor-cortex activation with certainty during these tasks. Therefore, Shimada and Hiraki (2006) used NIRS to examine whether motor cortex is activated during action execution and action observation. They found that 6- to 7-month-old infants and adults activated motor cortex during the execution and observation of an action. Interestingly, at both ages, the activation of the motor system during action observation was only evoked when the action was presented live, and not when it was presented on video (see Shimada & Hiraki, 2006, for a discussion). However, the mu-suppression effects reported using EEG were obtained under live (Southgate et al., 2009, 2010) and video conditions (van Elk et al., 2008) alike. It therefore seems critical to co-register EEG and NIRS in infants in order to clarify this issue. In any case, the findings of Shimada and Hiraki (2006) further support the notion that there is an intricate link between observing and executing an action in the motor system.

In summary, the findings reviewed show that at least by the age of 9 months the brain processes that underlie motor cognition seem to emerge. There is also some initial evidence that experience with a motor skill influences motor-cortex activation during action observation, suggesting that with development, as new motor skills and action patterns are integrated into the developing child's repertoire, a better perceptual understanding of these actions as performed by others may be acquired.

This review of the early development of the social brain has revealed that newborns enter the world with biases that help them to direct increased processing resources to their social world. Newborns show strong preferences for faces, eye contact, and biological motion. These biases, which may be based on subcortical processes, pave the way for the development and gradual specialization of cortical processes that help infants to interact with, and learn about and from, social agents.

Perhaps the most surprising insight from this literature is that some of the brain regions implicated in the adult social brain network are already sensitive to social interaction and cognition during the first year of life. Faces specifically activate the right fusiform gyrus of 2-month-olds, eye contact cues activate the posterior STS (pSTS) and PFC in 4-month-olds, watching biological motion results in functional activation in pSTS in 5-month-olds, joint triadic interaction appears to be processed in regions in the left PFC in 5-month-olds, and finally, observing and executing actions result in specific brain activation in the motor system in 6- to 7-month-olds. However, from these early activation patterns there is a still a long way to go to reach the highly specialized and specific patterns of responses observed in adults.

## Social Brain Development in Childhood and Adolescence

In the first half of this chapter, we reviewed evidence for the emerging social brain network in early infancy. In the rest of the chapter, we focus on social brain development in adolescence. Most researchers define adolescence as starting with the hormonal and physical changes of puberty. The end of adolescence is harder to define and there are significant cultural variations. However, the end of the teenage years represents a working consensus in Western countries. Adolescence is characterized by psychological changes in terms of identity, self-consciousness, and relationships with others. Compared with children, adolescents are more sociable, form more complex and hierarchical peer relationships, and are more sensitive to acceptance and rejection by peers (Steinberg & Morris, 2001). Although the factors underlying these social changes are likely to be multifaceted, one possible cause is the development of the social brain. In this section, we describe research on the development of face processing, theory of mind, and social rejection during adolescence.

## Face Processing

In view of the early face preferences reviewed in the earlier sections of this chapter, it has been a surprising discovery that both the behavioral and neural bases of face-processing abilities continue to develop throughout the first two decades of life. Whether this continuous development is due to the fact that the information that is extracted from faces becomes increasingly complex with age (during adolescence, for example, new face aspects, such as attractiveness, social status, or trustworthiness, become increasingly important; Scherf, Behrmann, & Dahl, 2012), or whether this is simply the result of protracted training with basic face-processing strategies together with underlying brain development (see also below), still remains to be determined. It has therefore been suggested that adolescent face processing holds important insights for our understanding of the emerging bases for cognitive and neural face processing from childhood through adulthood (Scherf et al., 2012).

An early study (Carey, Diamond, & Wood, 1980) showed improvement in facial-identity recognition across the first decade of life, followed by a brief dip in performance at age 12. In a later study by Mondloch and colleagues (Mondloch, Geldart, Maurer, & Le Grand, 2003), 6-, 8-, and 10-year-old children and adults had to compare faces on the basis of identity (with facial expression and head orientation varying), facial expression, gaze direction, and sound being spoken. Results showed that, in comparison to adults, the 6-year-olds made more errors on every task, and the 8-year-olds made more errors on three of the five tasks, namely when matching the direction of gaze and on the two identity tasks. The 10-year-olds made more errors than did adults on the identity task in which head orientation varied. This suggests that basic face-processing abilities, here the ability to recognize identity in a context-invariant manner, continue to develop until at least the end of the first decade of life. Last, it would have been interesting to assess how a sample of adolescents performed on the tasks used by Mondloch and colleagues.

Another study investigated the developmental trajectories of emotional expression processing in children (7–13 years), adolescents (14–18 years), and adults (Thomas, De Bellis, Graham, & LaBar, 2007) and found that emotion processing develops continuously beyond early childhood, with specific expressions following distinct trajectories. More specifically, adults were more accurate at identifying the emotion shown than were children and adolescents. However, whereas recognition accuracy for fear showed a linear improvement across the three age groups, anger showed a quadratic trend, with sharp improvement between adolescence and adulthood. This suggests that adolescence is characterized by continuing improvement in facial emotion recognition, but that the shape of the developmental trajectory may differ between emotions.

With the recent advent of pediatric neuroimaging methods (see Chapter 2), new vistas have been opened to study the implementation of cognitive functions in the developing brain (Blakemore, Dahl, Frith, & Pine, 2011). With regards to face-processing abilities, developmental neuroimaging studies have shown that the protracted development at the behavioral level is mirrored at the brain level by pro-longed cortical specialization within the regions of the face network (Cohen Kadosh & Johnson, 2007). In one fMRI study, children (7–11 years), adolescents (12–16 years), and adults passively viewed photographic images of faces versus objects, places, or abstract patterns (Golarai et al., 2007). Results showed an age-related increase in the activation within right fusiform cortex, with adults showing a significantly larger activation than child groups and the adolescent group exhibiting an intermediate pattern. In addition, the expansion of the fusiform face area (FFA) into surrounding cortex was correlated with a behavioral improvement in recogni-tion memory for facial identity. In a different study, Scherf and colleagues (Scherf, Behrmann, Humphreys, & Luna, 2007) showed children (5–8 years), adolescents (11–14 years), and adults short movie clips of faces, places, and objects. They observed an age-related increase in face-selective FFA activation between childhood and adolescence, as well as an increase in face-selective activation in the STS.

More recent evidence from two developmental fMRI studies contrasts sharply with the studies reviewed above, in that they did not find developmental differ-ences in face processing between children and adults (Cantlon, Pinel, Dehaene, & Pelphrey, 2011; Pelphrey, Lopez, & Morris, 2009). In the first study, Pelphrey and colleagues (2009) compared neural responses to faces, flowers, objects, and bodies in the core face areas in children (7–11 years) and adults. They found no developmental changes in face-selectivity in the FFA from mid-childhood to adulthood when contrasting face-specific responses with those to flower stimuli, suggesting that face processing is adult-like from mid-childhood. It is less clear, however, whether similar results would have been obtained in this study upon contrasting face responses with neural responses to the other stimulus categories (i.e., objects, bodies), a question that is particularly relevant as both categories are preferentially processed in adjacent cortical areas in the mature brain.

In the second study, Cantlon et al. (2011) observed a robust FFA response in children as young as 4 years for faces in comparison with other categories, such as shoes, letters, numbers, or scrambled images. A particularly interesting find-ing with regard to the question of cortical specialization was the observation that responses for the nonpreferred stimulus categories (e.g., shoes in the FFA) decreased with age. This led the authors to suggest that cortical specialization might reflect category-selective "pruning" in a given brain region, Moreover, this finding speaks to current theoretical frameworks of cortical specialization, such as the *interactive specialization* approach to human brain development (Johnson, 2011), which predicts that postnatal functional brain development relies less on the slow maturation of particular core areas, and rather more on significant specialization and fine-tuning of these areas (Johnson, Grossmann, & Cohen Kadosh, 2009), both as a result of environmental experience and brain development. In addition, it has been suggested that this specialization process may reflect a continuous reorganization process during which systematic connections between cortical areas are strengthened and core areas become increasingly specialized (Cohen Kadosh, 2011).

Last, a developmental fMRI study used dynamic causal modeling analysis (Friston, Harrison, & Penny, 2003) to examine task-dependent interactions among cortical face-processing regions in three face-processing tasks (Cohen Kadosh, Cohen Kadosh, Dick, & Johnson, 2011). Dynamic causal modeling (DCM) approaches can be used to assess not only functional connectivity patterns (correlations in activation between different brain regions), but also to determine how experimental input influences these connectivity patterns (effective connectivity) (Friston et al., 2003). This allows one to test the influence of top-down modulation via different cognitive processes. For example, DCM assesses experimental input in two ways: the first step tests the direct influence on specific anatomical nodes in the network, an influence that could be compared to direct, stimulus-driven sensory inputs. The second input is largely stimulus independent and modulates the coupling between nodes: comparable to the different attentional states induced by a task instruction and when participants use a different cognitive strategy for each task. A better understanding of the influence of top-down cognitive task strategies on brain activation is particularly important for developmental neuroimaging studies, which assess how developmental changes in cognitive abilities are reflected in differential brain activation (Cohen Kadosh, 2011). In the study by Cohen Kadosh and colleagues, this DCM analysis enabled investigation of age group differences (in children (7–8 years), preadolescents (10–11 years), and adults) and the impact of differing task demands (matching based on identity, emotion, or gaze) on effective connectivity between regions (Cohen Kadosh et al., 2011) (Figure 10.3). They found that the same basic cortical network, comprising FFA, STS, and inferior occipital gyrus, was present in all age groups. However, there was an age-related increase in the extent of top-down cognitive strategy modulation of network connections for the three tasks, with only adults showing task-specific strengthening of specific network paths. This finding was interpreted as a cumulative effect of exposure and training, such that the cortical network for face processing becomes increasingly fine-tuned with age.

In sum, evidence has suggested that the observed developmental trajectory for face-processing abilities is also mirrored by protracted development at the brain level (Cohen Kadosh & Johnson, 2007). It remains to be determined whether both behavioral and neural face processing continues to develop during adolescence, as some studies suggest (Carey et al., 1980; Scherf et al., 2012), or

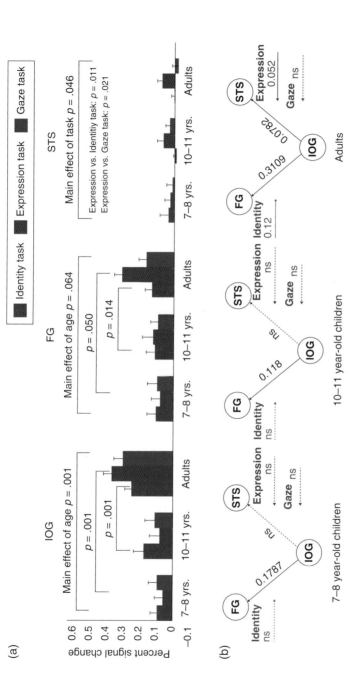

**Figure 10.3** Developmental changes in cortical response patterns in the core face network in children aged 7–11 years and adults. While the overall network configuration was confirmed for all three age groups, a continuous increase in functional response was observed in the two child groups, along with changing patterns of effective connectivity in the network. Most notably, the two child groups did not exhibit any task-dependent changes in network connectivity, a finding that has been attributed to lower levels of processing proficiency. (A) Percent signal change in brain activation in three core face network regions as a function of age and task. (B) Dynamic causal modeling analysis of the developmental changes in the core face network in three age groups. Solid arrows indicate significant changes in effective connectivity between two network regions; dotted arrows indicate nonsignificant effects. Black arrows indicate the intrinsic connection between the areas of interest. Colored arrows indicate modulatory effects of each task on the connection between the areas. Abbreviations: IOG, inferior occipital gyrus; FG, fusiform gyrus; STS, superior temporal sulcus. Adapted from Cohen Kadosh et al. (2011).

whether the observed findings of lower face-processing abilities during this developmental period reflect a general shift in social information processing (Scherf et al., 2012).

## Theory of Mind Development

The ability to attribute mental states to other people is known as theory of mind or mentalizing. An understanding of others' mental states plays a critical role in social interaction because it enables us to work out what other people want and what they are about to do next, and to modify our own behavior accordingly. There is a rich literature on the development of social cognition in infancy and childhood, pointing to stepwise changes in social cognitive abilities during the first five years of life. While certain aspects of theory of mind are present in infancy (Baillargeon, Scott, & Hea, 2010), it is not until around the age of four years that children begin explicitly to understand that someone else can hold a belief that differs from one's own, and which can be false (Barresi & Moore, 1996).

There has been surprisingly little empirical research on social cognitive development beyond childhood. Only recently have studies focused on development of the social brain beyond early childhood, and these support evidence from social psychology that adolescence represents a period of significant social development. A number of fMRI studies have investigated the development of the functional brain correlates of mentalizing during adolescence. These studies have used a wide variety of mentalizing tasks – involving the spontaneous attribution of mental states to animated shapes, reflecting on one's intentions to carry out certain actions, thinking about the preferences and dispositions of oneself or a fictitious story character, and judging the sincerity or sarcasm of another person's communicative intentions (see Blakemore, 2008). Despite the variety of mentalizing tasks used, these studies of mental-state attribution have consistently shown that dorsal medial prefrontal cortex (mPFC) activity during mentalizing tasks *decreases* between adolescence and adulthood (Figure 10.4). Each of these studies compared brain activity in young adolescents and adults while they were performing a task that involved thinking about mental states (see Figure 10.4 for details of studies). In each of these studies, mPFC activity was greater in the adolescent group than in the adult group during the mentalizing task compared with the control task. In addition, there is evidence for differential functional connectivity between mPFC and other parts of the mentalizing network across age (Burnett & Blakemore, 2009).

To summarize, a number of developmental neuroimaging studies of social cognition have been carried out by different research groups around the world, and there is striking consistency with respect to the direction of change in mPFC activity. It is not yet understood why mPFC activity decreases between adolescence

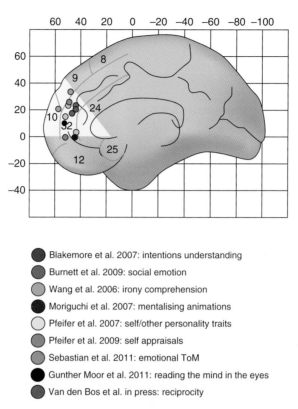

**Figure 10.4**  A section of the dorsal mPFC that is activated in studies of mentalizing: Montreal Neurological Institute (MNI) *y* coordinates range from 30 to 60, and *z* coordinates range from 0 to 40. Dots indicate voxels of decreased activity during seven mentalizing tasks between late childhood and adulthood. The mentalizing tasks ranged from understanding irony, which requires separating the literal from the intended meaning of a comment, thinking about one's own intentions, thinking about whether character traits describe oneself or another familiar other, watching animations in which characters appear to have intentions and emotions, and thinking about social emotions such as guilt and embarrassment.

and adulthood during mentalizing tasks, but two non-mutually-exclusive explanations have been put forward (see Blakemore, 2008, for details). One possibility is that the cognitive strategy for mentalizing changes between adolescence and adulthood. A second possibility is that the functional change with age is due to neuroanatomical changes that occur during this period. Decreases in activity are frequently interpreted as being due to developmental reductions in grey matter volume, presumably related to synaptic pruning. However, there is currently no direct way to test the relationship between number of synapses, synaptic activity, and neural activity as measured by fMRI in humans (see Blakemore, 2008, for discussion). If the neural substrates for social cognition change during adolescence, what are the consequences for social cognitive behavior?

## Online Mentalizing Usage is Still Developing in Mid-adolescence

Most developmental studies of social cognition focus on early childhood, possibly because children perform adequately in even quite complex mentalizing tasks at around age four. This can be attributed to a lack of suitable paradigms: generally, in order to create a mentalizing task that does not elicit ceiling performance in children aged five and older, the linguistic and executive demands of the task must be increased. This renders any age-associated improvement in performance difficult to attribute solely to improved mentalizing ability. However, the protracted structural and functional development in adolescence and early adulthood of the brain regions involved in theory of mind might be expected to affect mental-state understanding. In addition, evidence from social psychology studies shows substantial changes in social competence and social behavior during adolescence, and this is hypothesized to rely on a more sophisticated manner of thinking about and relating to other people – including understanding their mental states (Steinberg, 2005).

We adapted a task that requires the online use of theory of mind information when making decisions in a communication game, and which produces large numbers of errors even in adults (Keysar, Lin, & Barr, 2003). In our computerized version of the task, participants view a set of shelves containing objects, which they are instructed to move by a "Director," who can see some but not all of the objects (Dumontheil, Apperly, & Blakemore, 2010; Figure 10.5). Correct interpretation of critical instructions requires participants to use the director's perspective and only move objects that the director can see (the director condition). We tested participants aged between 7 and 27 years and found that, while performance in the director and a control condition followed the same trajectory (improved accuracy) from mid-childhood until mid-adolescence, the mid-adolescent group made more errors than the adults in the director condition only. These results suggest that the ability to take another person's perspective to direct appropriate behavior is still undergoing development at this relatively late stage.

## Social Evaluation: Acceptance and Rejection

Social-psychology studies have shown that adolescents, and by some accounts particularly female adolescents, are more sensitive to being excluded from a social interaction by peers, relative to adults or younger children (Kloep, 1999; O'Brien & Bierman, 1988). In cases where risky behavior is a group norm, this effect could contribute to the impact of peer influence on risky behavior. A behavioural study (Sebastian, Viding, Williams, & Blakemore, 2010b) investigated social rejection experimentally, using a computerized ball-passing paradigm

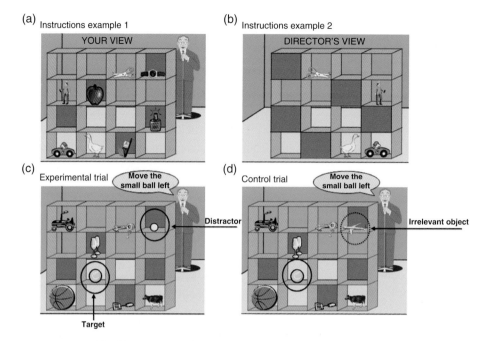

**Figure 10.5** (a), (b) Images used to explain the Director condition: participants were shown an example of their view (a) and the corresponding director's view (b) for a typical stimulus with four objects in occluded slots that the director cannot see (e.g., the apple). (c), (d) Example of an Experimental (c) and a Control (d) trial in the Director condition. The participant hears the verbal instruction "Move the small ball left" from the director. In the Experimental trial (c), if the participant ignored the director's perspective, she would choose to move the distractor ball (golf ball), which is the smallest ball in the shelves but which cannot be seen by the director, instead of the larger ball (tennis ball) shared by both the participant's and the instructor's perspective (target). In the Control trial (d), an irrelevant object (plane) replaces the distractor item.

known as Cyberball (Williams, Cheung, & Choi, 2000). In Cyberball, participants are told that they are playing a ball-passing game over the internet with two other players, represented by cartoon drawings. In reality, the players are preprogrammed computer algorithms, which systematically include (by passing the ball to) or exclude participants. In this study, female adolescents (young adolescents, 11–13 years; mid-adolescents, 14–16 years) showed significantly reduced self-reported positive mood following episodes of exclusion (social rejection) than did female adults (22–47 years). Additionally, levels of anxiety were disproportionately increased following social rejection in younger adolescents (11–13 years) relative to adults, while anxiety was sustainedly high in older adolescents (14–15 years). Thus, female adolescents show heightened sensitivity to social rejection in an experimental context.

Neuroimaging studies are beginning to explore the neural basis of this effect. One study used the Cyberball paradigm, combined with fMRI, in a group of adolescents (12–13 years) (Masten et al., 2009). The results showed patterns of brain activity that were similar to those in a previous study in adults (Eisenberger, Lieberman, & Williams, 2003): positive correlations were found between self-reported distress and activity within visceral pain and negative-affect-related regions (e.g., insula) during social exclusion versus inclusion; and negative correlations were found between self-reported distress and activity in regions associated with emotion regulation, including ventrolateral prefrontal cortex (VLPFC).

One study (Sebastian et al., 2011) directly compared female adolescents (14–16 years) and female adults (23–28 years) during a modified version of the Cyberball task, and found that adults activated VLPFC to a greater extent during exclusion than inclusion conditions, while adolescents exhibited the reverse pattern. Since right VLPFC has previously been associated with the regulation of distress during social exclusion (Eisenberger et al., 2003), it is possible that a reduced engagement of this region in adolescents in response to rejection-related stimuli underlies the increased affective response seen in adolescents in behavioral studies. A similar result was found in an fMRI study exploring neural responses to the automatic processing of rejection-related information (Sebastian et al., 2010a). This study compared female adolescents ($N=19$, 14–16 years) and adults (23–28 years) on a rejection-themed emotional Stroop task in which participants were asked to indicate the ink color in which rejection, acceptance, and neutral words were written. In adults, rejection-themed words activated the right VLPFC to a greater extent than acceptance or neutral words, while this pattern of responding was not seen in the adolescent group. These studies are consistent with theories suggesting that prefrontal regulatory mechanisms continue to develop between mid-adolescence and adulthood (see, e.g., Nelson, Leibenluft, McClure, & Pine, 2005), and this may be one factor underlying observed adolescent hypersensitivity to rejection.

Rejection by peers is an extreme form of peer evaluation. This was the subject of an fMRI study that used an internet chat-room paradigm with male and female participants aged 9–17 years (Guyer, McClure-Tone, Shiffrin, Pine, & Nelson, 2009). Results showed that, in females only, there was an age-related increase in activity during expectation of peer evaluation within brain regions involved in affective processing (nucleus accumbens, hypothalamus, hippocampus, and insula), but no differences within the anterior cingulate cortex (ACC) or other social brain regions. The finding of gender differences in the neural response to social evaluation is in line with reports of greater social anxiety in female adolescents than in males in response to negative social evaluations in everyday life (La Greca & Lopez, 1998). However, the possibility that female adolescents are more sensitive to social rejection than are males has not been tested empirically. Guyer et al. (2009), for example, did not find gender differences in behavior on their task.

An fMRI study investigated peer evaluation and rejection across age, in groups of preadolescent (8–10 years), adolescent (12–14, 16–17 years), and adult (19–25 years) participants (Gunther Moor, van Leijenhorst, Rombouts, Crone, & Van der Molen, 2010). In this experiment, participants supplied photos of their faces in advance and were told that these would be rated by a panel of peers. Then, during fMRI scanning, participants viewed a sequence of photographs of same-age individuals who they were led to believe comprised the panel of peers, and for each photo answered the yes/no question "Do you believe this person liked you?" This was followed by fictitious yes/no feedback response indicating whether the individual depicted in the photo liked the participant or not. Results showed an age-related increase in activity within ventral mPFC, ACC, and striatum when participants predicted they would be liked by a peer, while predicted social rejection resulted in increasing activity with age in affect-regulation regions such as orbitofrontal cortex and lateral PFC. An interesting point to note in this study is the age-related increase in ventral mPFC activity, while mentalizing studies show age-related decreases in the more dorsally situated anterior rostral mPFC (see also Moriguchi et al., 2007). This difference could relate to possible functional subdivisions within mPFC, a large and incompletely functionally characterized brain area (Gilbert, Henson, & Simons, 2010).

## Implications for Education

A Royal Society policy report stated that common ground between education and neuroscience "suggests a future in which educational practice can be transformed by science, just as medical practice was transformed by science about a century ago" (Royal Society, 2011). The evidence reviewed above shows that infants enter the world with biases that allow them to quickly develop skills that help them interact with and learn from others. Very early in ontogeny the human brain becomes tuned to processing social information, thus paving the way to benefit from others' knowledge and instruction. This has important implications for education, because it demonstrates that the fundamental social capacities, which facilitate and profit from teaching and instruction, are laid down early in development. In fact, it has been proposed that social communication among humans is adapted to facilitate the transmission of generalizable knowledge between individuals. This communication system has been termed "natural pedagogy," and it is thought to enable fast and efficient social learning of cultural knowledge (Csibra & Gergely, 2009). There is now accumulating evidence that human infants are equipped to benefit from "natural pedagogy". This new understanding of the infant as a competent and prepared social learner is likely to impact our early education practices before entering school. In particular, future research will allow us to further specify the conditions under which infants learn from others most efficiently and thus help us improve infants' learning environments.

The evidence reviewed above suggests continuing development across adolescence in the neural correlates of key social cognitive processes including face processing, mentalizing, peer influence, and the emotional response to social evaluation (acceptance and rejection). These data could have particular relevance for pastoral provision in schools, particularly at secondary level.

There is an increasing realization that schools play a critical role in pupils' social and emotional development. In the UK, the "Social and Emotional Aspects of Learning" (SEAL) program (2007) is now implemented in 70% of secondary schools (Humphrey, Lendrum, & Wigelsworth, 2010). However, this report also found considerable variability in SEAL's effectiveness in promoting socioemotional skills and mental health among pupils, with few schemes subscribing to evidence-based interventions. Cognitive neuroscience is well placed to provide an evidence base that can inform educational policy on this issue (Viding, McCrory, Blakemore, & Frederickson, 2011), via its characterization of key cognitive and neural processes underlying social and emotional development. For example, managing social relationships is a significant challenge for adolescents. Relational or social forms of bullying are common within school peer groups; for example, one study (Wang, Iannotti, & Nansel, 2009) found that 27.4% of adolescent girls (mean age 14.3 years) reported being excluded or ignored by a group of peers while at school. Being bullied (including relational aggression) is associated with decreased school achievement and psychological wellbeing (Boulton, Trueman, & Murray, 2008; Hawker & Boulton, 2000); thus, a greater understanding of adolescent responses to phenomena such as social rejection (such as that provided by the above studies) may contribute to greater understanding of the factors contributing to schooling success and failure (Blakemore, 2010). The next major challenge for educational neuroscience is to work out how the potential for cognitive neuroscience evidence to influence school-based interventions may be best realized. This will likely require the training of "brokers" between education and neuroscience, who can build bridges between these two currently disparate fields (Viding et al., 2011).

If early childhood is seen as a major opportunity – or a "sensitive period" - for teaching, so too should be the teenage years. Sensitive periods can be thought of as periods of development in which the brain is particularly susceptible to certain environmental stimuli and particularly efficient at processing and assimilating new information – at learning. It is possible that certain skills might be particularly amenable to learning during adolescence, while for other skills it might be too late – or even too early. Understanding the brain mechanisms that underlie learning and memory, and the effects of genetics, the environment, emotion, and age on learning, could transform educational strategies and enable us to design programs that optimize learning for people of all ages and of all needs. Neuroscience can now offer some understanding of how the brain learns new information and processes this information throughout life (Blakemore & Frith, 2005). Understanding the brain basis of social functioning and social development is crucial to the fostering of social competence inside and outside the classroom. Social functioning plays a role in shaping learning and academic performance (and vice versa), and understanding the neural basis of social behavior can contribute to understanding the origins and process of schooling success and failure. The finding that changes in brain structure continue into adolescence (and beyond) has challenged accepted views, and has given rise to a spate of investigations into the way cognition (including social cognition) might change as a consequence. Research suggests that adolescence is a key time for the development of regions of the brain involved in social cognition and self-awareness. This is likely to be due to the interplay between a number of factors, including changes in the social environment and in puberty hormones, as well as structural and functional brain development and improvements in social cognition.

Adolescence is a time of opportunity for learning new skills and forging an adult identity. However, it is also a time of vulnerability, as adolescents begin to face adult challenges whilst still developing physically, socially, and cognitively (Steinberg, 2005). The idea that teenagers should still go to school and be educated is relatively new. Yet, the research on brain development suggests that education during the teenage years is vital, with the brain needing to be molded and shaped during this period of relative plasticity. Perhaps the aims of education for adolescents might change based on these neuroscientific findings to include abilities that are controlled by the parts of the brain that undergo most change during adolescence. These abilities include cognitive control, multitasking, and planning – but also self-awareness and social cognitive skills such as extracting social information from faces, regulating emotional responses during peer interactions, perspective taking, and the understanding of other people's minds.

## Acknowledgments

S.-J. B. is supported by a Royal Society University Research Fellowship. T. G. was supported by the Max Planck Society and the Wellcome Trust (082659/Z/07/Z). M. H. J. is primarily supported by the Medical Research Council (currently PG0701484).

# References

Baillargeon, R., Scott, R. M., & Hea, Z. (2010). False-belief understanding in infants. *Trends in Cognitive Sciences, 14*(3), 110–118.

Baldwin, D. A., Baird, J. A., Saylor, M. M., & Clark, M. A. (2001). Infants parse dynamic action. *Child Development, 72,* 708–717.

Barresi, J., & Moore, C. (1996). Intentional relations and social understanding. *Behavioral and Brain Sciences, 19,* 107–154.

Batki, A., Baron-Cohen, S., Wheelwright, S., Connellan, J., & Ahluwalia, J. (2000). Is there an innate gaze module? Evidence from human neonates. *Infant Behaviour and Development, 23,* 223–229.

Bentin, S., Allison, T., Puce, A., Perez, A., & McCarthy, A. (1996). Electrophysiological studies of face perception in humans. *Journal of Cognitive Neuroscience, 8,* 551–565.

Blakemore, S. J. (2008). The social brain in adolescence. *Nature Reviews Neuroscience, 9*(4), 267–277.

Blakemore, S. J. (2010). The developing social brain: Implications for education. *Neuron, 65*(6), 744–747.

Blakemore, S-J., Dahl, R. D., Frith, U., & Pine, D. S. (2011). Editorial. *Developmental Cognitive Neuroscience, 1*(1), 3–6.

Blakemore, S. J., & Decety, J. (2001). From the perception of action to the understanding of intention. *Nature Reviews Neuroscience, 2,* 561–567.

Blakemore, S. J., & Frith, U. (2005). *The learning brain: Lessons for education.* Oxford: Blackwell.

Blakemore, S-J., Winston, J., & Frith, U. (2004). Social cognitive neuroscience: Where are we heading? *Trends in Cognitive Sciences, 8*(5), 216–222.

Boulton, M. J., Trueman, M., & Murray, L. (2008). Associations between peer victimization, fear of future victimization and disrupted concentration on class work among junior school pupils. *British Journal of Educational Psychology, 78,* 473–489.

Bruner, J. S. (1973). Organization of early skilled action. *Child Development, 44,* 1–11.

Burnett, S., & Blakemore, S. J. (2009). Functional connectivity during a social emotion task in adolescents and in adults. *European Journal of Neuroscience, 29*(6), 1294–1301.

Bushnell, I. W. R., Sai, F., & Mullin, J. T. (1989). Neonatal recognition of the mothers face. *British Journal of Development Psychology, 7,* 3–15.

Cantlon, J. F., Pinel, P., Dehaene, S., & Pelphrey, K. A. (2011). Cortical representations of symbols, objects, and faces are pruned back during early childhood. *Cerebral Cortex, 21*(1), 191–199.

Caplan, R., Chugani, H. T., Messa, C., Guthrie, D., Sigman, M., de Traversay, J., & Mundy, P. (1993). Hemispherectomy for intractable seizures: Presurgical cerebral glucose metabolism and post-surgical non-verbal communication. *Developmental Medicine and Child Neurology, 35,* 582–592.

Carey, S., Diamond, R., & Wood, B. (1980). Development of face recognition – A maturational component. *Developmental Psychology, 16*(4), 257–269.

Chugani, H. T., & Phelps, M. E. (1986). Maturational changes in cerebral function in infants determined by 18FDG positron emission tomography. *Science, 231,* 840–843.

Chugani, H. T., Phelps, M. E., & Mazziotta, J. C. (1987). Positron emission tomography study of human brain functional development. *Annals of Neurology, 22*, 487–497.

Cohen Kadosh, K. (2011). What can emerging cortical face networks tell us about mature brain organisation? *Developmental Cognitive Neuroscience, 1*(3), 246–255.

Cohen Kadosh, K., Cohen Kadosh, R., Dick, F., & Johnson, M. H. (2011). Developmental changes in effective connectivity in the emerging core face network. *Cerebral Cortex, 21*, 1389–1394.

Cohen Kadosh, K., & Johnson, M. H. (2007). Developing a cortex specialized for face perception. *Trends in Cognitive Sciences, 11*(9), 267–269.

Csibra, G. (2007). Action mirroring and action interpretation: An alternative account. In P. Haggard, Y. Rosetti, & M. Kawato (Eds.), *Sensorimotor foundations of higher cognition. Attention and performance XXII* (pp. 435–459). Oxford: Oxford University Press.

Csibra, G., & Gergely, G. (2009). Natural pedagogy. *Trends in Cognitive Sciences, 13*, 148–153.

de Haan, M., Johnson, M. H., & Halit, H. (2003). Development of face-sensitive event-related potentials during infancy: A review. *International Journal of Psychophysiology, 51*, 45–58.

de Haan, M., Pascalis, O., & Johnson, M. H. (2002). Specialization of neural mechanisms underlying face recognition in human infants. *Journal of Cognitive Neuroscience, 14*, 199–209.

de Haan, M., & Thomas, K. M. (2002). Applications of ERP and fMRI techniques to developmental science. *Developmental Science, 5*, 335–343.

de Schonen, S., & Mathivet, E. (1990). Hemispheric asymmetry in a face discrimination task in infants. *Child Development, 61*, 1192–1205.

Dumontheil, I., Apperly, I. A., & Blakemore, S-J. (2010). Online usage of theory of mind continues to develop in late adolescence. *Developmental Science, 13*(2), 331–338.

Eisenberger, N. I., Lieberman, M. D., & Williams, K. D. (2003). Does rejection hurt? An fMRI study of social exclusion. *Science, 302*, 290–292.

Falck-Ytter, T., Gredebäck, G., & von Hofsten, C. (2006). Infants predict other people's action goals. *Nature Neuroscience, 9*, 878–879.

Farroni, T., Csibra, G., Simion, F., & Johnson, M. H. (2002). Eye contact detection in humans from birth. *Proceedings of the National Academy of Sciences of the United States of America, 99*(14), 9602–9605.

Farroni, T., Johnson, M. H., & Csibra, G. (2004a). Mechanisms of eye gaze perception during infancy. *Journal of Cognitive Neuroscience, 16*, 1320–1326.

Farroni, T., Pividori D., Simion F., Massaccesi, S., & Johnson, M. H. (2004b). Eye gaze cueing of attention in newborns. *Infancy, 5*, 39–60.

Friston, K. J., Harrison, L., & Penny, W. (2003). Dynamic causal modelling. *NeuroImage, 19*(4), 1273–1302.

Frith, C. D., & Frith, U. (2006). The neural basis of mentalizing. *Neuron, 50*(4), 531–534.

Gauthier, I., Tarr, M. J., Moylan, J., Skudlarski, P., Gore, J. C., & Anderson, A. W. (2000). The fusiform "face area" is part of a network that processes faces at the individual level. *Journal of Cognitive Neuroscience, 12*(3), 495–504.

Gilbert, S. J., Henson, R. N., & Simons, J. S. (2010). The scale of functional specialization within human prefrontal cortex. *Journal of Neuroscience, 30*(4), 1233–1237.

Golarai, G., Gharemani, D. G., Whitfield-Gabrieli, S., Reiss, A., Eberhardt, J. L., Gabrieli, J. D., & Grill-Spector, K. (2007). Differential development of high-level visual cortex correlates with category-specific recognition memory. *Nature Neuroscience, 10*(4), 512–522.

Grossmann, T. (2008). Shedding light on infant brain function: The use of near-infrared spectroscopy (NIRS) in the study of face perception. *Acta Paediatrica, 97,* 1156–1158.

Grossmann, T., & Johnson, M. H. (2010). Selective prefrontal cortex responses to joint attention. *Biology Letters, 6,* 540–543.

Grossmann, T., Johnson, M. H., Lloyd-Fox, S., Blasi, A., Deligianni, F., Elwell, C., & Csibra, G. (2008). Early cortical specialization for face-to-face communication in human infants. *Proceedings of the Royal Society B, 275,* 2803–2811.

Gunther Moor, B., van Leijenhorst, L., Rombouts, S. A., Crone, E. A., & Van der Molen, M. W. (2010). Do you like me? Neural correlates of social evaluation and developmental trajectories. *Social Neuroscience, 5*(5/6), 461–482.

Guyer, A. E., McClure-Tone, E. B., Shiffrin, N. D., Pine, D. S., & Nelson, E. E. (2009). Probing the neural correlates of anticipated peer evaluation in adolescence. *Child Development, 80*(4), 1000–1015.

Halit, H., de Haan, M., & Johnson, M. H. (2003). Cortical specialisation for face processing: Face-sensitive event-related potential components in 3- and 12-month-old infants. *NeuroImage, 19,* 1180–1193.

Hawker, D. S., & Boulton, M. J. (2000). Twenty years' research on peer victimization and psychosocial maladjustment: A meta-analytic review of cross-sectional studies. *Journal of Child Psychology and Psychiatry, 41,* 441–455.

Haxby, J. V., Hoffman, E. A., & Gobbini, M. I. (2000). The distributed human neural system for face perception. *Trends in Cognitive Sciences, 4,* 223–233.

Humphrey, N., Lendrum, A., & Wigelsworth, M. (2010). *Social and emotional aspects of learning (SEAL) programme in secondary schools: National evaluation* (Research Rep. No. DFE-RR049). London: Department for Education, UK Government. Retrieved July 4, 2013, from http://dera.ioe.ac.uk/11567/1/DFE-RR049.pdf

Huttenlocher, P. R. (2002). *Neural plasticity.* Cambridge: Harvard University Press.

Huttenlocher, P. R., & Dabholkar, A. S. (1997). Regional differences in synaptogenesis in human cerebral cortex. *Journal of Comparative Neurology, 387,* 167–178.

Johnson, M. H. (2005). Subcortical face processing. *Nature Reviews Neuroscience, 6,* 766–774.

Johnson, M. H. (2011). Interactive specialization: A domain-general framework for human functional brain development? *Developmental Cognitive Neuroscience, 1*(1), 7–21.

Johnson, M. H., Grossmann, T., & Cohen Kadosh, K. (2009). Mapping functional brain development: Building a social brain through interactive specialization. *Developmental Psychology, 45,* 151–159.

Kampe, K., Frith, C. D., & Frith, U. (2003). "Hey John": Signals conveying communicative intention toward self activate brain regions associated with "mentalizing," regardless of modality. *Journal of Neuroscience, 12,* 5258–5263.

Kanwisher, N. (2000). Domain specificity in face processing. *Nature Neuroscience, 3,* 759–763.

Keysar, B., Lin, S., & Barr, D. J. (2003) Limits on theory of mind use in adults. *Cognition*, *89*(1), 25–41.

Kloep, M. (1999). Love is all you need? Focusing on adolescents' life concerns from an ecological point of view. *Journal of Adolescence*, *22*, 49–63.

La Greca, A. M., & Lopez, N. (1998). Social anxiety among adolescents: Linkages with peer relations and friendships. *Journal of Abnormal Child Psychology*, *26*(2), 83–94.

Lloyd-Fox, S., Blasi, A., & Elwell, C. E. (2010). Illuminating the developing brain: The past, present and future of functional near infrared spectroscopy. *Neuroscience and Biobehavioural Reviews*, *34*, 269–284.

Masten, C. L., Eisenberger, N.I ., Borofsky, L. A., Pfeifer, J. H., McNealy, K., Mazziotta, J. C., & Dapretto, M. (2009). Neural correlates of social exclusion during adolescence: Understanding the distress of peer rejection. *Social Cognitive and Affective Neuroscience*, *4*, 143–157.

Mondloch, C. J., Geldart, S., Maurer, D., & Le Grand, R. (2003). Developmental changes in face processing skills. *Journal of Experimental Child Psychology*, *86*, 67–84.

Moriguchi, Y., Ohnishi, T., Mori, T., Matsuda, H., & Komaki, G. (2007). Changes of brain activity in the neural substrates for theory of mind during childhood and adolescence. *Psychiatry and Clinical Neurosciences*, *61*(4), 355–363.

Morton, J., & Johnson, M. H. (1991). CONSPEC and CONLERN: A two-process theory of infant face recognition. *Psychological Review*, *98*, 164–181.

Mundy, P., Card, J., & Fox, N. (2000). Fourteen month cortical activity and different infant joint attention skills. *Developmental Psychobiology*, *36*, 325–338.

Mundy, P., Fox, N., & Card, J. (2003). EEG coherence, joint attention and language development in the second year. *Developmental Science*, *6*, 48–54.

Nelson, E. E., Leibenluft, E., McClure, E. B., & Pine, D. S. (2005). The social re-orientation of adolescence: A neuroscience perspective on the process and its relation to psychopathology. *Psychological Medicine*, *35*, 163–174.

Oberman, L. M., Hubbard, E. M., McCleery, J. P., Altschuler, E. L., Ramachandran, V. S., & Pineda, J. A. (2005). EEG evidence for mirror neuron dysfunction in autism spectrum disorders. *Brain Research*, *24*, 190–198.

O'Brien, S. F., & Bierman, K. L. (1988). Conceptions and perceived influence of peer groups – Interviews with preadolescents and adolescents. *Child Development*, *59*, 1360–1365.

Parise, E., Reid, V. M., Stets, M., & Striano, T. (2008). Direct eye contact influences the neural processing of objects in 5-month-old infants. *Social Neuroscience*, *3*, 141–150.

Pelphrey, K. A., Lopez, J., & Morris, J. P. (2009). Developmental continuity and change in responses to social and nonsocial categories in human extrastriate visual cortex. *Frontiers in Human Neuroscience*, *3*, 25.

Pelphrey, K. A., Singerman, J. D., Allison, T., & McCarthy, G. (2003). Brain activation evoked by perception of gaze shifts: the influence of context. *Neuropsychologia*, *41*, 156–170.

Pelphrey, K. A., Viola, R. J., & McCarthy, G. (2004). When strangers pass: Processing of mutual and averted gaze in the superior temporal sulcus. *Psychological Science*, *15*, 598–603.

Reid, V. M., Belsky, J., & Johnson, M. H. (2005). Infant perception of human action: Toward a developmental cognitive neuroscience of individual differences. *Cognition, Brain and Behaviour, 9*, 35–52.

Reid, V. M., Csibra, G., Belsky, J., & Johnson, M. H. (2007). Neural correlates of the perception of goal-directed action in infants. *Acta Psychologica, 124*, 129–138.

Reynolds, G. D., & Richards, J. E. (2005). Familiarization, attention, and recognition memory in infancy: An ERP and cortical source analysis study. *Developmental Psychology, 41*, 598–615.

Rizzolatti, G., & Craighero, L. (2004). The mirror-neuron system. *Annual Review of Neuroscience, 27*, 169–192.

Royal Society, UK. (2011). *Brain Waves 2: Neuroscience: Implications for education and lifelong learning.* Retrieved July 2, 2013, from http://royalsociety.org/policy/projects/brain-waves/education-lifelong-learning/

Saxe, R. (2006). Uniquely human social cognition. *Current Opinion in Neurobiology, 16*(2), 235–239.

Scherf, K. S., Behrmann, M., Humphreys, K., & Luna, B. (2007). Visual category-selectivity for faces, places and objects emerges along different developmental trajectories. *Developmental Science, 10*(4), F15–F31.

Scherf, K. S., Behrmann, M., & Dahl, R. (2012). Facing changes & changing faces in adolescence: investigating the neural basis of key developmental shifts in social-information processing. *Developmental Cognitive Neuroscience, 2*(2), 199–219.

Schilbach, L., Wilms, M., Eickhoff, S. B., Romanzetti, S., Tepest, R., Bente, G., Shah, N. J., Fink, G. R., & Vogeley, K. (2010). Minds made for sharing: Initiating joint attention recruits reward-related neurocircuitry. *Journal of Cognitive Neuroscience, 22*, 2702–2715.

Sebastian, C. L., Roiser, J. P., Tan, G. C., Viding, E., Wood, N. W., & Blakemore, S. J. (2010a). Effects of age and MAOA genotype on the neural processing of social rejection. *Genes, Brain and Behavior, 9*, 628–637.

Sebastian, C. L., Tan, G. C. Y., Roiser, J. P., Viding, E., Dumontheil, I., & Blakemore, S.-J. (2011). Developmental influences on the neural bases of responses to social rejection: Implications of social neuroscience for education. *NeuroImage, 57*(3), 686–694.

Sebastian, C., Viding, E., Williams, K. D., & Blakemore, S. J. (2010b). Social brain development and the affective consequences of ostracism in adolescence. *Brain and Cognition, 72*, 134–145.

Senju, A., Johnson, M. H., & Csibra, G. (2006). The development and neural basis of referential gaze perception. *Social Neuroscience, 1*, 220–234.

Shimada, S., & Hiraki, K. (2006). Infant's brain responses to live and televised action. *NeuroImage, 32*, 930–939.

Southgate, V., Johnson, M. H., El Karoui, I., & Csibra, G. (2010). Motor system activation reveals infants' online prediction of others' goals. *Psychological Science, 21*, 355–359.

Southgate, V., Johnson, M. H., Osborne, T., & Csibra, G. (2009). Predictive motor activation during action observation in human infants. *Biology Letters, 5*, 769–772.

Steinberg, L. (2005). Cognitive and affective development in adolescence. *Trends in Cognitive Sciences, 9*, 69–74.

Steinberg, L., & Morris, A. S. (2001). Adolescent development. *Annual Review of Psychology, 52*, 83–110.

Striano, T., Reid, V. M., & Hoehl, S. (2006). Neural mechanisms of joint attention in infancy. *European Journal of Neuroscience, 23*, 2819–2823.

Striano, T., & Stahl, D. (2005). Sensitivity to triadic attention in early infancy. *Developmental Science, 4*, 333–343.

Taylor, M. J., Batty, M., & Itier, R. J. (2004). The faces of development: A review of early face processing over childhood. *Journal of Cognitive Neuroscience, 16*, 1426–1442.

Thatcher, R. W., Krause, P. J., & Hrybyk, M. (1986). Cortico-cortical associations and EEG coherence: A two-compartmental model. *Electroencephalography and Clinical Neurophysiology, 64*, 123–143.

Thomas, L. A., De Bellis, M. D., Graham, R., & LaBar, K. S. (2007). Development of emotional facial recognition in late childhood and adolescence. *Developmental Science, 10*(5), 547–558.

Tomasello, M., Carpenter, M., Call, J., Behne, T., & Moll, H. (2005). Understanding and sharing intentions: The origins of cultural cognition. *Behavioural and Brain Sciences, 28*, 675–691.

Tzourio-Mazoyer, N., de Schonen, S., Crivello, F., Reutter, B., Aujard, Y., & Mazoyer, B. (2002). Neural correlates of woman face processing by 2-month-old infants. *NeuroImage, 15*, 454–461.

van Elk, M., van Schie, H. T., Hunnius, S., Vesper, C., & Bekkering, H. (2008). You'll never crawl alone: Neurophysiological evidence for experience-dependent motor resonance in infancy. *NeuroImage, 43*, 808–814.

Viding, E., McCrory, E. J., Blakemore, S. J., & Frederickson, N. (2011). Behavioural problems and bullying at school: Can cognitive neuroscience shed new light on an old problem? *Trends in Cognitive Sciences, 15*(7):289–291.

Wang, J., Iannotti, R. J., & Nansel, T. R. (2009). School bullying among adolescents in the United States: Physical, verbal, relational, and cyber. *Journal of Adolescent Health, 45*, 368–375.

Williams, J. H. G., Waiter, G. D., Perro, O., Perrett, D. I., & Whiten, A. (2005). An fMRI study of joint attention experience. *NeuroImage, 25*, 133–140.

Williams, K. D., Cheung, C. K., & Choi, W. (2000). Cyberostracism: Effects of being ignored over the Internet. *Journal of Personality and Social Psychology, 79*, 748–762.

## Further Reading

Blakemore, S. J. (2008). The social brain in adolescence. Nature Reviews Neuroscience, *9,* 267–277.

Johnson, M. H., Grossmann, T., & Cohen Kadosh, K. (2009). Mapping functional brain development: Building a social brain through interactive specialization. Developmental Psychology, *45,* 151–159.

Lieberman, M.D. (2013). Social: Why our brains are wired to connect. New York: Crown.

# Chapter 11

# Emotional Development

## Alice Jones

*All learning has an emotional base*

*Plato*

## Introduction

One of the key aims of education is for children to develop and reach their potential. Consequently, much educational research has focused on identifying those factors that may place a child at risk for poor outcome, or may protect and promote a child's development and school success. Although for many children school is a place of learning, development, and safety, school can nevertheless provide a child with many challenges, including academic learning, peer-groups, and teachers. Research has consistently demonstrated that emotional development is key to equipping children with the skills that they need to manage many of these challenges, and thus plays a vital role in providing a sound basis for children to learn and reach their potential. This chapter will examine neurobiological accounts of emotional development, and the effect that normal and atypical emotional functioning might have on a child's school life. It will cover temperament, emotion regulation, emotional understanding and empathy, motivation, psychological well-being, and mental health, and place these within the appropriate contexts of preschool, primary, and secondary education and lifelong learning.

*Educational Neuroscience*, First Edition. Edited by Denis Mareschal, Brian Butterworth and Andy Tolmie.

## Emotion and education

The importance of considering the interface between emotion and learning has been argued and demonstrated for some time (Emde et al., 1992; Izard et al., 2001). Knowledge about own and others' emotions, and the ability to regulate emotions, can have an important influence on children's classroom experience and on their capacity to access the curriculum in a full and developmentally appropriate manner.

The brain-imaging literature also strongly argues for a dynamic relationship between cognition and emotion at the neural level. For example, Davidson (2003) claimed that it is one of "seven deadly sins of cognitive neuroscience" to assume that emotions are independent from cognition. The same can certainly also be argued to be true for educational neuroscience. Complex cognitive–emotional behaviors, many of which are relevant to learning, are believed to have their basis in networks of brain areas not normally conceptualized as specifically affective or cognitive in nature. Pessoa's (2008) review of emotion and cognition in the brain presents evidence that brain regions typically described as being involved in "emotion processing" are often also involved in "cognition" and vice versa. For example, although the amygdala is part of the limbic system, a primitive part of the brain long perceived to be central to emotion processing, it also plays a role in directing attention – traditionally considered to be a cognitive task. There is also a wealth of evidence to suggest that the amygdala mediates the processing advantage of emotional items (Anderson & Phelps, 2001), and that attention is, at least in part, directed via information from the amygdala. Pessoa suggests that those brain areas with a high degree of efferent and afferent connections to other brain regions play an important role in regulating the flow and integration of information, and so are central to cognition–emotion interactions. It is also important to keep in mind that the relationship between cognition and emotion is a dynamic one. Much of human behavior shows us that cognitions can affect emotions, just as emotional state can influence cognitions. At the level of the brain, anatomical evidence for connections between dorsolateral, anterior cingulate, and orbital areas of the prefrontal cortex (areas typically associated with working memory, attention, and sensitivity to reward) and subcortical limbic structures typically associated with emotion processing, including the amygdala, suggests a functional link between the prefrontal executive processes and the emotional–motivational processes of the limbic system. Brain-imaging studies have been instrumental in demonstrating the dynamic nature of cognition and emotion processing, and this chapter will further demonstrate the importance of emotion in learning across the lifespan.

## Preschool Years

The nursery and preschool years are an important transition period for children. In their ecological and dynamic model of transition, Rimm-Kaufman and Pianta (2000) make the point that the nursery environment is qualitatively different from school and home environments. In nursery and preschool, children must learn to adapt to a new system that expects them to accomplish numerous goals such as literacy, numeracy, and socialization skills. Moreover, these goals must be accomplished under less supervision than the child is used to, due to increased emphasis on autonomy and decreased amounts of direct adult supervision (Bronson, Tivnan, & Seppanen, 1995). The novel demands of learning new academic and interpersonal skills, in combination with encouragement toward independence, present many young children with a challenge. Consequently, these novel demands coupled with a new academic environment likely elicit various arousing emotions such as excitement, anxiety, and fear. Emotion regulation refers to the processes by which we influence which emotions we have, when we have them, and how we experience and express them (Gross, 1998). Children's ability to regulate these emotions efficiently may facilitate their transition to preschool and consequently their ability to get along with an academic curriculum.

## Temperament

It is also important for educationalists to consider those characteristics inherent to the child that may have an influence on children's capacity to regulate their own emotion and engage with learning. Temperament can be considered as the "constitutional differences in reactivity and self-regulation," where "constitutional" refers to the relatively stable makeup of individuals influenced by their genes and life experience (Rothbart & Derryberry, 1981). The model of temperament developed and posited by Hans Eysenck (1991) is relevant to this chapter's topic: placing emotion within the context of cortical arousal. Eysenck suggested that individuals differ in their baseline level of arousal, and so therefore also vary in their optimal level of stimulation (with individuals who have relatively high base levels of arousal requiring less stimulation to reach their point of optimal functioning). This model has been linked to personality research, for example with extraverts being suggested to have relatively low base arousal, and so seek out more novel and stimulating experiences than do their introvert peers. While this model of temperament has certainly proved to be a useful theoretical jumping-off point, and has generated a considerable amount of research in fields such as psychophysiology, neuroimaging, behavioral genetics, and cognitive behavioral learning, more recent work has challenged some of its core notions.

Psychophysiological and neuroimaging evidence indicates that the processes of arousal and emotion are not quite as straightforward as may have been suggested by Eysenck and other early theorists. It is not necessarily the case that emotion derives from arousal; rather, it has been consistently demonstrated that arousal, cognition, and behavior can be influenced by emotional stimuli. For example, induction of negative mood has been associated with a greater number of behavioral lapses and "mind-wandering" (Smallwood, Fitzgerald, Miles, & Phillips, 2009), and positive mood has been associated with greater creativity (Baas, De Dreu, & Nijstad, 2008). Further, some brain areas have been reported to show enhanced reactivity to sad images in participants who had been subject to negative mood induction prior to imaging (Wang, LaBar, & McCarthy, 2006). These areas include amygdala, anterior cingulate, ventromedial and orbital prefrontal cortex, and insula. A negative relationship was also reported between the degree of amygdala activation to sad stimuli and reaction times in responding to attentional targets (i.e., greater amygdala activation was associated with slower reaction times), which occurred only in the sad-mood condition. These findings suggest specific brain areas that are involved in the integration of emotional input and current mood state, which may help us to better understand the nature of cognitive distractibility in those individuals experiencing low mood or depression.

Suggested to be a precursor to personality, temperament has been consistently demonstrated to be highly heritable, suggesting a strong biological basis (Plomin et al., 1993; Plomin & Rowe, 1977; Robinson, Kagan, Reznick, & Corley, 2004). Although estimates of heritability tend to differ between studies, these estimates generally fall within the range of 0.20–0.60, suggesting that genetic differences among individuals account for approximately 20–60% of the variability of temperament within a population (Saudino, 2005). Work has also begun to look at the brain areas associated with temperament differences in young children, and what effects different temperament styles might have on brain development. One such study has linked temperament style at four months of age with cortical thickness in those same individuals as adults (Schwartz et al., 2010). This study reported regional differences in the thickness of adult orbitofrontal and ventromedial prefrontal cerebral cortex that were predicted by temperamental differences observed at 4 months of age. Specifically, "low-reactives" were characterized by greater cortical thickness in the left orbitofrontal cortex, a brain region suggested to be involved in the suppression of unpleasant feelings, and the reappraisal of negative emotion into a more positive direction (Goldin, McRae, Ramel, & Gross, 2008).

Schwartz and colleagues link this finding to individuals who are diagnosed with depression, and show abnormal reward processing with altered brain activation in a region of left orbitofrontal cortex that overlaps substantially with the temperament-related cluster (Tremblay et al., 2005). It may be the case that a thicker left-sided orbitofrontal cortex, conferring a great number of efferent and afferent pathways, could facilitate the development of low-reactive infants into children who are able to adapt easily to change, are not easily afraid, and are characterized by a relatively stable mood during adolescence (Schwartz et al., 2010). In contrast, thinner cortex in this region might identify those individuals at increased risk for depression later in life. Conversely, those infants who were characterized by "high reactivity" demonstrated greater cortical thickness in the right ventromedial prefrontal cortex. Schwartz et al. suggest that thickness in these brain regions indicates robust connectivity with structures that mediate the observable characteristics of high-reactive infants. For example, this subregion has connections with regions of the periaqueductal gray that have been linked to defensive and withdrawal responses (see, e.g., Bandler, Keay, Floyd, & Price, 2000). This includes a response known as arching of the back, observed almost exclusively in high-reactive young infants. Direct projections to the hypothalamus from this subregion of ventromedial prefrontal cortex can also activate the medulla and sympathetic chain (Ongür, An, & Price, 1998), resulting in the increases in blood pressure and heart rate seen in inhibited children in response to the unfamiliar (Schwartz et al., 2010).

Having some knowledge about how early temperament might influence later brain development, and the vulnerabilities and protective factors that may be conferred by such brain development, are of clear interest and importance to those working with young children. Indeed, it is particularly important to be aware of how the biological underpinnings of temperament styles may be shaping a child's preferences and behaviors in the nursery.

## Emotion regulation

Arguably, the ability to regulate one's own emotions and behaviors is also fundamental to learning. Teachers themselves rate these regulatory aspects of a child's behavior as being the most important for nursery preparedness. Communication needs, curiosity, and the ability to follow directions and take note of others' feelings are rated as the most important nursery skills – far outweighing knowing how to hold a pencil, or knowing how to count to 20 (Lewit & Baker, 1995). However, there are suggestions that many children are arriving at nursery and preschool with considerable variance in their ability to self-regulate. While emotion regulation continues to develop across early childhood (Bariola, Gullone, & Hughes, 2011), such variability has been a cause for concern for some educationalists. Rimm-Kaufman, Pianta, and Cox (2000) report that almost half of kindergarten teachers surveyed said that at least half of their children lacked the kinds of ability and experience that would allow them to function productively in a classroom. Moreover, regulation has also been consistently associated with academic success. In one preschool sample, positive associations were reported between parental reports of young children's emotion regulation and children's scores on a standardized achievement test (Howse, Calkins, Anastopoulos, Keane, & Shelton, 2003). Further, this relation was mediated by children's behavioral regulation in the classroom (i.e., their ability to refrain from disruptive behavior in the classroom).

Another potential mechanism by which emotion regulation skills impact on children's early academic success is by affecting the quality of the student–teacher relationship. The quality of children's relationships with their teachers has increasingly been recognized as an important contributor to children's early school adaptation (Birch & Ladd, 1997; Pianta, Steinberg, & Rollins, 1995; Pianta & Stuhlman, 2004). The modulation of arousal required by emotion regulation has been hypothesized to affect children's social relationships by facilitating an organism's ability to engage and disengage with the environment (Porges, 2003). This ability can be thought of as a core aspect of developmentally appropriate social skills, as children must know when to appropriately engage with others (i.e., talk to or play with them) and when to disengage with them (i.e., ignore them). This constant shift between communication, behavioral engagement, and disengagement during social interactions is likely to be more straightforward for children who are able to regulate their emotions. Unsurprisingly, children who appropriately regulate emotions have been found to display greater social competence, better social skills, and greater popularity amongst peers (Dunn & Brown, 1994; Eisenberg et al., 1995; Fabes et al., 1999; Graziano, Keane, & Calkins, 2007). Conversely, students who are not able to appropriately regulate their own emotions are more likely to show poor interpersonal skills and greater externalizing problems, such as oppositional behavior, hyperactivity, and aggression (Dunn & Brown, 1994; Rydell, Berlin, & Bohlin, 2003). Given these findings, it seems reasonable to expect that children's emotion-regulation skills might impact on the quality of the student–teacher relationship (Eisenhower, Baker, & Blacher, 2007).

Developmental neuroscience has indicated that early infancy is a time of rapid growth and modification of those brain areas subserving self-regulation (including emotion, memory, and attention). It is evident that, as children develop, their methods of emotion regulation become more complex; from gaze aversion, self-soothing, and gross motor activities, children progress to being able to regulate their own emotions through cognitive reappraisal, verbalizing feelings, and disengaging attention from negative stimuli (Kopp, 1989; McCabe, Cunnington, & Brooks-Gunn, 2004; Cole, Dennis, Smith-Simon, & Cohen,

2009; Gullone, Hughes, King, & Tonge, 2010). The development of more sophisticated emotion-regulation strategies can be attributed to developments in a network of anterior cortical brain regions including parts of the prefrontal cortex and the anterior cingulate cortex. The anterior cingulate has been suggested to be of particular importance here, as it provides a point of integration of information about bodily sensations and attentional and emotional information. This region has also been postulated to be involved in the rapid increase in use of "effortful control" (Posner & Rothbart, 1998, 2000) that occurs at around four years of age. This rise in regulation is attributed to the child's developing capacity to use the anterior cingulate to moderate behavior via deliberate selection of appropriate strategies (Lewis & Sieben, 2004). In infants, by age two, the anterior cingulate shows a proliferation of connections to frontal areas and to lateral parietal areas, but connectivity continues to increase during childhood, alongside the increasing sophistication of emotion-regulation strategies available to developing children (Fair et al., 2009; Gao et al., 2009). This understanding of the brain development can allow us to better understand a child's increasing capacity for self-regulation, and also allow us to consider what happens in the brain when children have particular difficulties in regulating their own emotions and behavior.

## Middle Years

### Social, emotional, and behavioral difficulties

Neuroimaging work with children in middle childhood has allowed us to better understand the neural substrates for emotional processing in children who might be characterized as having social, emotional, and/or behavioral difficulties (SEBD) in the classroom. The SEBD label covers a heterogeneous group of children who may be characterized by learning disabilities, autistic spectrum disorder traits, conduct problems, particularly difficult home environments or life experiences, and/or difficulties with communication. There are many other difficulties faced by teachers who work with such children, and one main difficulty facing all children with SEBD is that they are at great risk of difficulty in engaging with the national curriculum in a regular classroom environment.

### Autistic spectrum disorders

Not only has there been a large increase in the number of children diagnosed with an autism spectrum disorder (ASD), but there has also been an increase in the number of children with an ASD who are being educated in a mainstream classroom (Humphrey & Lewis, 2008). As such, understanding some of the possible neural underpinnings of the behaviors observed in students with ASD may prove useful to teachers in planning individual learning programs, and to learning support assistants, who often work one on one or in small groups with such students. One recent avenue of research has been to examine the mirror-neuron system in individuals with ASD. The mirror-neuron hypothesis of autism has proposed that early dysfunction in this system may lead to the cascade of impairments characteristic of ASD including deficits in imitation, theory of mind, and social communication (Dapretto et al., 2006). However, this area is not without considerable controversy. While some studies have reported decreased, or an absence of, activity in the inferior frontal gyrus, a brain area suggested to be central to the mirror neuron system (Dapretto et al., 2006), others have reported no differences in brain activity during observation of another's actions (Yang-Teng, Decety, Chia-Yen, Ji-Lin, & Yawei, 2010); see Southgate and Hamilton (2008) for a more thorough examination. It is certainly the case that educationalists often feel overwhelmed by the amount of conflicting research; however, in the case of the mirror-neuron hypothesis, although the theory has been the subject of a lot of media coverage, it is premature to consider it a central theory of autism.

## Behavioral problems

Conduct problems are one of the most common reasons for referral to child mental-health services; 26% of children on "school action plus" programs have been diagnosed with conduct disorder, as have 14% of children receiving a statement of special educational needs. Recent neuroimaging work has sought to better understand the neural underpinnings of such behavioral difficulties.

Related to this, work by Seth Pollak's group has sought to understand the outcomes for children who have experienced harsh discipline and physical abuse in their early years. Such children are often at risk for developing SEBD (as described above). These children appear to process emotions in a different way from their peers, showing increased attention to "angry face" stimuli, and a delayed disengagement phase from angry faces when they were not relevant (Pollak & Tolley-Schell, 2003). Results from an event-related potential study (ERP, a non-invasive psychophysiological method of measuring cortical activity during a task – see Chapter 2 on Neuroimaging Methods) showed that children who had been abused demonstrated a selective increase in P3b during trials that required a shift in attention from a location previously cued by an angry face. The P3b ERP is robustly associated with attention, and also with subsequent memory processing (Polich, 2007). The increase in P3b observed by Pollak and

Tolley-Schell is suggested to reflect an increase in resources required to disengage from the previously cued location. The findings that children who have experienced disadvantageous early parenting experiences may be more likely to make attributions of anger in others, and be less able to disengage themselves from signs of anger in their environment, are likely to be of use to those educationalists working directly with children who seem to be quick to respond in an angry way to seemingly nonthreatening situations. It should also be possible to work with these children to train their understanding of social signals, and to reduce emotional outbursts in the classroom and playground.

Other children with chronic and severe behavioral problems have also been the subject of neuroimaging studies. Several structural MRI studies on children have reported differences in grey-matter volume between children with conduct disorder (CD) and typically developing comparison children. CD is one of the most common reasons for referral to child and adolescent mental health services, and is characterized by a repetitive and persistent pattern of behavior that violates the rights of others (e.g., through aggression, vandalism, or theft) or major age-appropriate societal norms (e.g., truancy, deceitfulness, or running away from home) (APA, 2013). One group reported significant right-temporal decreased grey-matter volumes in children with CD compared with matched controls. Unfortunately, further analysis of small structures (e.g., amygdala) was precluded by the poor spatial resolution of the scans collected (Kruesi, Casanova, Mannheim, & Johnson-Bilder, 2004). More recently, several groups have reported reduced grey-matter volume in amygdala in children with CD relative to comparison children. Sterzer, Stadler, Poustka, and Kleinschmidt (2007) reported reduced grey-matter volume in left amygdala and bilateral anterior insula cortex in a group of children with CD relative to matched comparison children. Grey matter is made up of densely packed neuronal cell bodies that transfer information throughout the brain. Grey-matter development follows a largely inverted U-shaped trajectory, with a proliferation in childhood followed by a marked decrease over adolescence (Giedd et al., 1999). In boys with CD, one further study reported significant reduction in global grey-matter volume and regional reduced grey matter in the temporal lobes bilaterally, as well as left amygdala, left hippocampus, and left OFC between boys with a diagnosis of CD and matched controls (Huebner et al., 2008). Reduced grey-matter volume has also been reported in early- and adolescent-onset CD groups compared with typically developing comparisons, and grey-matter volume of right insula was related to severity of conduct problems (Fairchild et al., 2011). Sterzer's group also reported a link between bilateral insula grey-matter volume and empathy scores.

One group of children who may be better understood through knowledge of their neural processing styles is those children characterized by the presence of elevated levels of callous–unemotional (CU) traits. These CU traits index a particularly serious form of behavioral disturbance and include such characteristics as lack of guilt and empathy, which are also considered primary in clinical descriptions of adult psychopathy (Frick, O'Brien, Wootton, & McBurnett, 1994). Recent data from studies of twins suggest that conduct problems in CU children are under strong genetic influence (Viding, Blair, Moffitt, & Plomin, 2005; Viding, Jones, Frick, Moffitt, & Plomin, 2008). It is likely that children with CU traits cause some of the greatest and most prolonged disruptions in a classroom, and consequently to the learning of others. Furthermore, these traits have also been suggested to play a role in bullying behaviors (Muñoz, Qualter, & Padgett, 2011; Viding, Simmonds, Petrides, & Frederickson, 2009). CU traits are now considered under DSM-V's description of Conduct Disorder as part of the qualifier 'limited prosocial emotions' (APA, 2013; Kahn, Frick, Youngstrom, Findling & Youngstrom, 2012). It is therefore extremely timely to consider the impact of such traits on behaviour as it relates to education.

Previous behavioral and neuroimaging work has demonstrated that both adult psychopaths and children with conduct problems and CU traits are poor at processing visual and auditory displays of emotions commonly associated with distress (e.g., fear and sadness; Blair, Budhani, Colledge, & Scott, 2005; Blair, Colledge, Murray, & Mitchell, 2001; Muñoz, 2009). Both groups also experience difficulties in aversive learning paradigms (Budhani, Richell, & Blair, 2006). This profile is also reported in patients with damage to the amygdala (Feinstein, Adolphs, Damasio, & Tranel, 2011; Gupta, Koscik, Bechara, & Tranel, 2011; Scott et al., 1997). These associations have led to the hypothesis that CU traits may be associated with lessened amygdala response to distress stimuli. In support of this idea, functional neuroimaging studies with children with conduct problems and elevated levels of CU traits have demonstrated reduced amygdala reactivity to fearful face stimuli compared with typically developing comparisons and with children with a diagnosis of ADHD (Jones, Laurens, Herba, Barker, & Viding, 2009; Marsh et al., 2008; see Figure 11.1). However, in

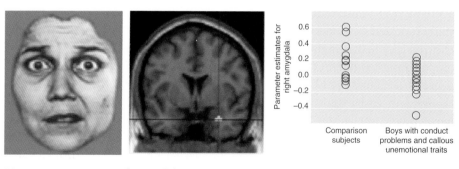

**Figure 11.1**   Decreased amygdala response to fearful facial expression in children with conduct problems and elevated levels of callous–unemotional traits (from Jones et al., 2009; *American Journal of Psychiatry*).

contrast to the literature on structural differences between children with CD and matched-comparison children, no structural differences in amygdala in some children with CU traits have been reported (De Brito et al., 2009). However, De Brito et al. did report some interesting increases in grey-matter volume for boys with CU traits compared with typically developing boys. Increased grey-matter volume was reported in the medial orbitofrontal and anterior cingulate cortices, as well as increased grey-matter volume and concentration in the temporal lobes bilaterally. Grey matter is usually observed to decrease in volume across adolescence, thus it has been suggested that a larger grey-matter volume may result in poorer cognitive performance and may indicate a delay in cortical maturation in these brain areas, all of which have been previously implicated in decision-making, morality, and the development of empathy.

Further to the role of amygdala reactivity to distress emotions, recent work has reported on a deficit in orienting toward the eyes, and eye contact, in children with elevated levels of CU. This was first reported using an eye-tracking method and presenting faces depicting basic emotions to typically developing boys (average age 12 years) (Dadds, El Masry, Wimalaweera, & Guastella, 2008). In line with the literature above, poor fear recognition was associated with CU traits. CU traits were also negatively associated with the number and duration of fixations to the eye region of the faces, as well as fewer first orientations to the eyes for all emotions. There were no differences in gaze indices to the mouth region. Looking to the eye region was positively correlated with accurate recognition of fear for the boys with elevated CU traits, particularly the number of times that subjects looked at the eyes first. This study suggests that the deficit in fear recognition typically characteristic of CU and psychopathy may be related to a deficit in orienting toward the eye region of faces.

In another study, children assessed with early behavioral problems (aged between four and eight years of age) and their mothers, and typically developing comparison children and their mothers, were observed during an interaction following some activities where they had been working in partnership (Dadds et al., 2012). Here, mothers were requested to look at their children, to engage in eye contact, and to tell them that they were really pleased with how they had been doing in the activities and that they loved them. There were no group differences in affection and eye contact expressed by the mothers, and low levels of eye contact were not correlated with maternal coercive parenting or feelings toward the child. However, children with behavioral problems expressed lower levels of affection back towards their mothers as compared with the typically developing control children. Moreover, those with elevated CU traits showed lower levels of affection than the children without these traits, and demonstrated lower levels of eye contact toward their mothers. A similar finding was reported in a different sample of children with elevated levels of CU traits with both mothers and fathers (Dadds, Jambrak, Pasalich, Hawes, & Brennan, 2011). Here, levels of eye contact were also associated with independent measures of fear recognition, and general empathy in the boys. These studies add further weight to the theory that a deficit in orientation to the eyes of others, and a subsequent reduction in eye contact during communication, may be a deficit that underpins the emotional and social difficulties seen in children with CU traits.

This deficit in relating to the eyes also draws comparisons with individuals who have amygdala damage. One such patient has been reported to show a deficit in the number of first fixations on the eye region of a face (similarly to the high-CU group in the study above). These findings suggest that the saliency of the eyes normally attracts our gaze in an amygdala-dependent manner, and knowledge of this may provide scope for intervention training, not only for children with elevated CU traits, but also for other conditions that are likely to be associated with amygdala dysfunction, including autism (Kennedy & Adolphs, 2010).

Taken all together, it may be suggested that the brain correlates of early CU traits may be associated with a vulnerability to be less reactive to distress in other people. This (very) low reactivity and a predisposition to not orient to eyes may have an influence on the development of empathy and other moral emotions (Shirtcliff et al., 2009). Dadds et al. (2011) suggest that a predisposition to attend to other people's emotions is crucial for the development of empathy, and much of the information about feelings relating to distress is communicated via the eyes. Studies have demonstrated a deficit in affective empathy in children with conduct problems and CU traits, but not necessarily in the understanding of others' emotions (Jones, Happé, Gilbert, Burnett, & Viding, 2010). Broadly speaking, it seems to be the case that while individuals with CU traits are able to understand the thoughts and feelings of others, they are less likely to be emotionally moved by them in an appropriately empathic manner. Most of the research on socialization and the development of moral emotions has traditionally pointed to an important role for parents. However, in this small minority of children, it may be the case that parents and educationalists need to think differently about how to develop the emotional skills of these children. Some intervention work focusing on CU traits is starting to be reported. For example, Hawes and Dadds (2007) have reported on a parent-training program that showed that CU traits were associated with a decreased emotional response to time-out, but that some children showed an "unstable" CU profile, and improved in behavior and CU traits after their parents took part in the program. Haas et al. (2011) reported on an intensive summer treatment program designed for children with conduct problems, which demonstrated an association between CU traits and poorer improvement in social and problem-solving skill development. White, Frick, Lawing, and Bauer

(2013) report that adolescents with elevated CU traits on a functional family therapy program were associated with poorer adjustment prior to treatment, but greater improvements in adjustment over the course of treatment. One school-based intervention study shows similar results, with a whole-school program designed to address the socioaffective profile of CU children showing improvements in behavior for both elevated CU and non-CU pupils (Frederickson, Jones, Warren, Deakes, & Allen, 2013). Although these intervention studies are currently modest in their size and require replication, it is reasonable to expect that there will be a proliferation of targeted intervention work over the coming years.

## Secondary School and Adolescence

### Motivation

Adolescence can be a time of conflict, and schoolwork and achievement can slide as a result. Carol Dweck's innovative work on student motivation has yielded a number of possible intervention ideas, and has tested these strategies using neuroscience methods. One of the core theories of Dweck's work focuses on individuals' own "theories of intelligence". This framework has been useful in addressing not only how these beliefs about own intelligence affect overall performance, but also how they affect rebound following failure. Previous behavioral studies have shown that students who believe that intelligence is a fixed quantity ("entity theorists") are particularly vulnerable to decreased performance when they realize they are at risk of failing, whereas students who view intelligence as acquirable ("incremental theorists") appear better able to remain effective learners (Dweck & Leggett, 1988). Consider the student who has never really needed to work hard to do well. He passes his GCSEs adequately, but is then disappointed with his relatively poor grades at the start of his A level study. The entity theorist student decides that she's just not clever enough to cope with A level and that she's destined to do badly. She sets her sights low, and her parents become concerned to find that she frequently misses classes at college. On the other hand, the "incremental theorist" views these initial poor grades as a warning. He realizes that his success and ability to go on to higher education is contingent on him engaging with the work and putting in the effort.

These outcomes may be rooted in the different goals that follow from holding either a fixed or an acquirable view of intelligence (Dweck & Leggett, 1988; Mangels, Butterfield, Lamb, Good, & Dweck, 2006). Individuals who are considered "entity theorists" tend to be concerned with competing with, and winning over, their peers in order to prove their intelligence ("performance goals"), leaving them highly vulnerable to negative feedback. As a result, these individuals are more likely to avoid learning opportunities where they anticipate a high risk of errors, or to disengage from these situations when errors occur (Chiu, Hong, & Dweck, 1997). In contrast, incremental theorists are more likely to endorse the goal of increasing ability through effort and are more likely to gravitate toward tasks that offer real challenges ("learning goals"). For the latter individuals, in line with their view that there is always potential for intellectual growth, they are more willing to pursue remedial activities when they experience academic difficulty.

In order to better understand what mechanisms might underlie these differences in learning types, Dweck and colleagues have attempted to address the questions of how motivation influences attention and processing in tough academic situations. Dweck's model proposes that entity and incremental theorists will respond to negative feedback in different ways. Entity theorists, who are concerned with doing well relative to others, should find negative feedback to be a threat to their goal of proving ability. These individuals might also then engage their attention in self-critical thinking about their ability and performance, which may interfere with their ability to pay attention to the learning-relevant information (thus increasing the likelihood of error repetition). Incremental theorists, on the other hand, should be more likely to be interested in encoding the correct answer in order to increase their ability to answer this question correctly in the future.

Working from the hypothesis that self-beliefs about ability and their allied goals would influence direction of attention and mode of processing would be moderated by the type of belief system held by the student, Butterfield and Mangels (2003) used ERP methods to examine the influences of beliefs about intelligence. The study aimed to investigate both how students respond to negative performance feedback (e.g., participant response error), and how participants might be subsequently engaged toward feedback that could assist in learning new information that could correct that error. Participants were asked to provide answers to general-knowledge questions and to indicate their confidence in the accuracy of their response. ERP responses were recorded during two pieces of feedback: the first provided information about response accuracy, while the second provided the correct answer. This study demonstrated greater frontal P3 response to situations where the participants' views about their accuracy (i.e., that they were correct) did not match their actual accuracy (i.e., that their answer had been incorrect). This finding was in line with previous work that had implicated a similar waveform occurring in response to novel or unexpected stimuli (e.g., Courchesne, Hillyard, & Galambos, 1975). This frontal P3 potential has been hypothesized to index the interruption of ongoing processes and reorienting of attention to the unexpected event, subserved by an anterior attentional system that includes both anterior cingulate and lateral prefrontal regions (Bledowski, Prvulovic, Goebel, Zanella, & Linden, 2004; Crottaz-Herbette & Menon, 2006).

Mangels et al. (2006) used a similar paradigm to examine the differences in neural response to negative feedback between entity and incremental theorists. They reported that entity theorists were characterized by an enhanced anterior frontal P3, which was positively correlated with concerns about proving ability relative to others. However, following negative feedback, entity theorists also demonstrated less sustained memory-related activity (left temporal negativity) to the corrective information. Mangels et al. suggest that this finding is evidence for reduced effortful encoding of this material, which may have contributed to reduced error correction on a subsequent surprise retest. These results suggest that beliefs can influence learning success through top-down biasing of attention and conceptual processing toward goal-congruent information. It is encouraging that interventions based on this theory have demonstrated that a more incremental model of intelligence can be acquired (Blackwell, Trzesniewski, & Dweck, 2007), but no research to date has examined the effect that this might have on brain function.

## Psychological well-being and mental-health concerns

Adolescence is undoubtedly a time of great change in behavior, body, and brain. Many teenagers navigate their way through the years with only the odd minor difficulty; others experience an adolescence that marks the onset of difficulties that can last for a long time. It is clearly not sensible to think that psychiatric difficulties just "appear" at age 18, and so we can look to adolescence for clues as to how mental health and psychological well-being might be represented before the formal diagnosis of a psychiatric disorder in adulthood. The peak age of onset for many psychiatric disorders is, in fact, during adolescence (Kessler et al., 2005). It is sensible to suggest that the onset of many psychiatric problems during adolescence comes as a result of anomalies in, or exaggerations of, adolescent brain maturation and psychosocial factors (which may include peer and family relationships, risky behavior, or substance use). Affective disorders (such as anxiety and depression) and substance abuse are two classes of psychiatric disorder that are relatively common amongst teenagers, and can have a significant effect on a student's capacity to succeed in school.

Risk-taking and novelty-seeking are considered a relatively normative part of adolescence. Many teenagers become involved in trying, or experimenting with, drugs and alcohol. An earlier onset of drug use is often associated with a greater severity of addiction problems, and other poor mental-health outcomes, later down the line, and might serve as a "gateway" to the use of multiple substances later in life (Kandel, Yamaguchi, & Chen, 1992; Vida et al., 2009). The neural correlates of substance abuse in adolescents present with a somewhat complex picture. There appear to be some brain regions that are smaller before the onset of substance problems, for example the amygdala is smaller in adolescents who come from a family with a history of alcohol problems (Brown & Tapert, 2004), while other brain areas are clearly deleteriously affected by substance use (Medina, Schweinsburg, Cohen-Zion, Nagel, & Tapert, 2007; Nagel, Schweinsburg, Phan, & Tapert, 2005). Decreases in hippocampal volume have been reported to be correlated with the age of onset and duration of the alcohol abuse, lending further support to the notion that adolescent alcohol problems may be exerting neurotoxic effects on the brain (De Bellis et al., 2000; Nagel et al., 2005). One possible mechanism for this brain-volume decrease is that alcohol has been found to have an inhibitory effect on N-methyl-D-aspartate (NMDA) receptors in such a way that excitatory glutamate neurotransmission is impaired (Smith, 2003). The role of the NMDA receptor in learning and memory is attributed to its role in brain plasticity. The receptor plays an essential role in both the strengthening and weakening of synapses. By acting to strengthen neighboring connections of similar activity patterns, the NMDA receptor enforces the principle that "cells that fire together, wire together" (Shatz, 1992). Following alcohol withdrawal, the hippocampus has also been shown to exhibit enhanced NMDA-mediated neurotoxicity (Davidson, Shanley, & Wilce, 1995). Animal studies also suggest that this effect may be more severe in less mature brains (Swartzwelder, Wilson, & Tayyeb, 1995).

The adolescent brain is characterized by maturation of the limbic system with heightened reward sensitivity in conjunction with the protracted development of the prefrontal cortex and developing cognitive control. It is this disparity between the development of these two systems which may be underpinning the risk-taking behaviors often observed in adolescents. Rutherford, Mayes, and Potenza (2010) make the sensible point that intervention initiatives might do well to identify those adolescents who are more likely to engage in risky behaviors, and thus may also be more vulnerable to negative behaviors such as alcohol and substance use.

Neuroimaging studies of children and adolescents with psychiatric disorders represent a fast-developing field. However, it is important to note that, although neuroimaging is beginning to establish correlations between brain structure/physiology and behavior, the link between typical behavioral changes and psychopathology has not been firmly established. Paus, Keshavan, and Giedd (2008) make the point that the neural circuitry that underlies "moodiness" in an adolescent might not be the same as that which is involved in depression or bipolar disorder. Neuroimaging is able to help develop neuroanatomical models of cognitive, affective, and social processes that are based on findings from developmental psychology (Ernst & Mueller, 2008). These differences in adolescent brain structure and function help to indicate when and how normal development takes an alternative course, and should allow interventions to be appropriately targeted. In clinical practice this information can be used to consider appropriate cognitive and chemical intervention strategies, but for educationalists better understanding the brain differences that affect students with psychiatric difficulties allows insight into the problems being faced by a student who may be presenting as a challenging, disruptive, or maybe even absent student.

## Lifelong Learning

### The emotional experiences of undergraduates

It is important to understand that brain changes persist past the "teenage" years, and that brain development and maturation is not complete until well beyond the classic adolescent years (Aimone, Deng, & Gage, 2010; Lebel & Beaulieu, 2011; Raznahan et al., 2011). Behaviorally, there is much evidence for maturation between the adolescent and early adult years, which are typically characterized by developments in romantic relationships, risk-taking, and worldview (Arnett, 2004). Recent neuroimaging studies suggest that these behavioral changes and developments are also accompanied by development in the central nervous system and the brain. In fact, postmortem studies have demonstrated that changes in the central nervous system go on into an individual's third decade of life (e.g., Benes, Turtle, Khan, & Farol, 1994). Neuroimaging studies using positron emission tomography (PET; see Chapter 2 for more on neuroimaging methods) have also demonstrated that adult-like levels of glucose metabolism do not stabilize until the mid-20s (Van Bogaert, Wikler, Damhaut, Szliwowski, & Goldman, 1998). MRI studies have also demonstrated changes in white matter (proliferation; Giedd et al., 1999) and grey matter (decreasing through late adolescence and early adulthood; Gogtay et al., 2004). Morphological differences have also been linked to changes in behavior over the period of early adulthood. For example, Bennett and Baird (2006) suggest that observed increases in voxel intensity in insula cortex, cingulate, and caudate nucleus during fMRI scans are linked with functional changes in self-awareness and awareness of one's own emotions.

The insula has been associated with processing information from the body about physical sensations and emotional feelings, otherwise known as interoception (Craig, 2011), and interoception has been suggested to be central to self-awareness. Other studies have demonstrated a relationship between prefrontal brain activity and age in a sample of adolescents, during a task where they viewed a series of fearful faces (Yurgelun-Todd & Killgore, 2006). These studies lend credence to the suggestion that emotional processing capacity during adolescence and early adulthood are related to the development of prefrontal cortex during this time. However, the study by Bennett and Baird (2006) provides us with another thought to consider. Their sample of young adults were all young first-year undergraduates, thus it is possible that these increases in voxel intensity may have come about as a reaction to the transition to university, suggesting that brain structures may be reacting to the environmental demands of the situations in which new undergraduates find themselves. While these results are certainly interesting and should stimulate discussion about how normative life-transitions might affect brain structure, future studies offering replication of this work will be important before definitive conclusions can be drawn.

## Stress as an obstacle in lifelong learning

Daily life is full of emotionally laden experiences, causing everything from happiness and excitement to minor annoyances and trauma. Although we might not think it at the time, all of these experiences are collectively referred to as "stressors". These stressors take many forms. They can be tangible or mentally evoked, and of a physical or psychological nature (Joëls, Pu, Wiegert, Oitzl, & Krugers, 2006). For adults in education, there are many stressors that are similar to those of child and adolescent students, including work deadlines, examinations, and relationships with teachers and peers; but also many new stressors, including managing family and work life alongside education. University students, particularly first-year undergraduates, are at particular risk for stress. As discussed with respect to preschool entry, university education is also a major point of transition for many young (and older) adults. Students are required to adapt to a new environment, make new peer relationships, become more self-directed and autonomous in their learning, and maintain a high level of academic achievement, all with the thought of a future career in mind (Robotham & Julian, 2006; Ross, Niebling, & Heckert, 1999).

Students' responses to stress can take a number of forms, including emotional (e.g., fear, anxiety, depression), cognitive (e.g., faulty appraisals of situations), behavioral (e.g., drinking, substance use, irritability), and physiological reactions (e.g., insomnia, lack of appetite, physical pains) (Misra, McKean, West, & Russo, 2000). However, stress also has the potential to affect students' capacity to learn, and neuroscience research has contributed some important knowledge to this field of learning. Stress in the environment triggers the activation of the hypothalamus–pituitary–adrenal or HPA axis, resulting in the production of glucocorticoids by the adrenal glands. During stress, the HPA axis mediates physiological functioning by stimulating behavioral arousal and increasing heart rate, blood pressure, and metabolism. There are receptors for these glucocorticoids throughout the brain, and these steroid hormones have the capacity to regulate gene expression – which means possible long-lasting effects on the functioning of brain regions that regulate their release (Lupien, McEwen, Gunnar,

& Heim, 2009). At first examination, the literature on stress and learning may appear to be contradictory, with some stress being a facilitative influence on learning and memory and other stressful situations causing difficulties in these areas (Shors, 2006).

Most studies suggest an inverted U-shaped relationship between stress and functioning, where cognitive performance typically increases with mild stress until a point where stress becomes too overwhelming and begins to interfere with cognitive performance. Enhanced memory for emotionally charged events definitely can be an adaptive outcome. Emotionally arousing events may be instructive, or it may be otherwise advantageous for us to remember them (McGaugh, 2006). McGaugh considers three possible routes for enhanced memory for emotional events. First is an initial enhancement of attention, where emotional arousal might increase the attention given to experiences during their encoding (Anderson, 2005). Second, emotional experiences may be more likely to be strengthened by rehearsal (Guy & Cahill, 1999). Third, a perseveration–consolidation process has been proposed, which suggests that emotional arousal may activate those neurobiological processes involved in the consolidation of event memories (Lechner, Squire, & Byrne, 1999).

This third hypothesis has received a wealth of support in its 100-plus years, including evidence from the psychophysiological and neuroscience literature. McGaugh's work on the role that stress hormones (i.e., adrenaline and cortisol) play in memory has been demonstrated in rats and mice, by showing enhanced memory for events after administering stress hormones after rodent training (McGaugh & Roozendaal, 2002), and in humans by exposing participants to a stressor that raised levels of cortisol. Typically, the U-shaped relationship between glucocorticoid levels and performance mirrors that of environmental stress and functioning; however, differential effects of glucocorticoids on the type of information remembered have been demonstrated. Most studies have demonstrated an association between increases in glucocorticoids and disrupted long-term memory for neutral events, but facilitated long-term memory for an equivalent emotional event (Lupien et al., 2004; Payne et al., 2007). These stress hormones modulate hormone activation in amygdala, and modulated memory processing in other brain regions, including the hippocampus and prefrontal regions (Cahill & McGaugh, 1998; Lupien & Lepage, 2001; Porcelli et al., 2008).

Feelings of negative stress arise when individuals feel that they do not have the resources to cope with a situation. Although there are clear individual differences in the ability of students to respond to stress, knowledge about how the human brain responds to stressful situations might help to develop programs of study that reduce periods of intense stress, or to develop methods of helping students to better understand and manage their own stressful situations.

# Conclusion

This chapter set out to demonstrate that learning and emotions do not occur side by side, but are interactive processes with the potential to influence each other dynamically. Understanding the neural correlates of emotion in the brain, and knowledge about how these areas develop over time, allows us to best understand how an individual might cope with the social and cognitive demands of the learning environment. This information is also useful to those educationalists wanting to develop targeted interventions for children or adolescents who are showing symptoms of emotional and behavioral difficulties.

# References

Aimone, J. B., Deng, W., & Gage, F. H. (2010). Adult neurogenesis: Integrating theories and separating functions. *Trends in Cognitive Sciences, 14*, 325–337.

American Psychiatric Association (APA). (2013). *Diagnostic and statistical manual of mental disorders.* Washington, DC: Author.

Anderson, A. K. (2005). Affective influences on the attentional dynamics supporting awareness. *Journal of Experimental Psychology: General, 134*, 258–281.

Anderson, A. K., & Phelps, E. A. (2001). Lesions of the human amygdala impair enhanced perception of emotionally salient events. *Nature, 411*, 305–309.

Arnett, J. J. (2004). *Emerging adulthood: The winding road from the late teens through the twenties.* New York: Oxford University Press.

Baas, M., De Dreu, C. K. W., & Nijstad, B. A. (2008). A meta-analysis of 25 years of mood–creativity research: Hedonic tone, activation or reglatory focus? *Psychological Bulletin, 134*, 779–806.

Bandler, R., Keay, K. A., Floyd, N., & Price, J. (2000). Central circuits mediating patterned autonomic activity during active vs. passive emotional coping. *Brain Research Bulletin, 53*, 95–104.

Bariola, E., Gullone, E., & Hughes, E. K. (2011). Child and adolescent emotion regulation: The role of parental emotion regulation and expression. *Clinical and Child and Family Psychology Review, 14*, 198–212.

Benes, F. M., Turtle, M., Khan, Y., & Farol, P. (1994). Myelination of a key relay zone in the hippocampal formation occurs in the human brain occurs during childhood, adolescence and adulthood. *Archives of General Psychiatry, 51*, 477–484.

Bennett, C. M., & Baird, A. A. (2006). Anatomical changes in the emerging adult brain: A voxel-based morphometry study. *Human Brain Mapping, 27*, 766–777.

Birch, S., & Ladd, G. (1997). The teacher–child relationship and children's early school adjustment. *Journal of School Psychology, 35*, 61–79.

Blackwell, L. S., Trzesniewski, K. H., & Dweck, C. S. (2007). Implicit theories of intelligence predict achievement across an adolescent transition: a longitudinal study and an intervention. *Child Development, 78*, 246–263.

Blair, R. J., Budhani, S., Colledge, E., & Scott, S. (2005). Deafness to fear in boys with psychopathic tendencies. *Journal of Child Psychology and Psychiatry, 46,* 327–336.

Blair, R. J., Colledge, E., Murray, L., & Mitchell, D. G. (2001). A selective impairment in the processing of sad and fearful expressions in children with psychopathic tendencies. *Journal of Abnormal Child Psychology, 29,* 491–498.

Bledowski, C., Prvulovic, D., Goebel, R., Zanella, F. E., & Linden, D. E. (2004). Attentional systems in target and distractor processing: A combined ERP and fMRI study. *NeuroImage, 22,* 530–540.

Bronson, M. B., Tivnan, T., & Seppanen, P. S. (1995). Relations between teacher and classroom activity variables and the classroom behaviors of prekindergarten children in Chapter 1 funded programs. *Journal of Applied Developmental Psychology, 16,* 253–282.

Brown, S. A., & Tapert, S. F. (2004). Adolescence and the trajectory of alcohol use: Basic to clinical studies. *Annals of the New York Academy of Sciences, 1021,* 234–244.

Budhani, S., Richell, R. A., & Blair, R. J. (2006). Impaired reversal but intact acquisition: Probabilistic response reversal deficits in adult individuals with psychopathy. *Journal of Abnormal Psychology, 115,* 552–558.

Butterfield, B., & Mangels, J. A. (2003). Neural correlates of metamemory mismatch and error correction in a semantic retrieval task. *Cognitive Brain Research, 17,* 793–817.

Cahill, L., & McGaugh, J. L. (1998). Mechanisms of emotional arousal and lasting declarative memory. *Trends in Neuroscience, 21,* 294–299.

Chiu, C. Y., Hong, Y., & Dweck, C. S. (1997). Lay dispositionism and implicit theories of personality. *Journal of Personality and Social Psychology, 73,* 19–30.

Cole, P. M., Dennis, T. A., Smith-Simon, K. E., & Cohen, L. H. (2009). Preschoolers' emotion regulation strategy understanding: Relations with emotion socialization and child self-regulation. *Social Development, 18,* 324–352.

Courchesne, E., Hillyard, S. A., & Galambos, R. (1975). Stimulus novelty, task relevance, and the visual evoked potential in man. *Electroencephalography and Clinical Neurophysiology, 39,* 131–143.

Craig, A. D. (2011). Significance of the insula for the evolution of human awareness of feelings from the body. *Annals of the New York Academy of Sciences, 1225,* 72–82.

Crottaz-Herbette, S., & Menon, V. (2006). Where and when the anterior cingulate cortex modulates attentional response: Combined fMRI and ERP evidence. *Journal of Cognitive Neuroscience, 18,* 766–780.

Dadds, M. R., Allen, J. L., Oliver, B. R., Faulkner, N., Legge, K., Moul, C., Woolgar, M., & Scott, S. (2012). Love, eye contact and the developmental origins of empathy v. psychopathy. *British Journal of Psychiatry, 200,* 191–196.

Dadds, M. R., El Masry, Y., Wimalaweera, S., & Guastella, A. J. (2008). Reduced eye gaze explains "fear blindness" in childhood psychopathic traits. *Journal of the American Academy of Child and Adolesentc Psychiatry, 47,* 455–463.

Dadds, M. R., Jambrak, J., Pasalich, D., Hawes, D. J., & Brennan, J. (2011). Impaired attention to the eyes of attachment figures and the developmental origins of psychopathy. *Journal of Child Psychology and Psychiatry, 52,* 238–245.

Dapretto, M., Davies, M. S., Pfeifer, J. H., Scott, A. A., Sigman, M., Bookheimer, S. Y., & Iacaboni, M. (2006). Understanding emotions in others: Mirror neurons in children with autism spectrum disorders. *Nature Neuroscience, 9,* 28–30.

Davidson, R. J. (2003). Seven sins in the study of emotion: Correctives from affective neuroscience. *Brain and Cognition, 52,* 129–132.

Davidson, M., Shanley, B., & Wilce, P. (1995). Increased NMDA-induced excitability during ethanol withdrawal: A behavioral and histologic study. *Brain Research, 674,* 91–96.

De Bellis, M. D., Clark, D. B., Beers, S. R., Soloff, P. H., Boring, A. M., Hall, J., Kersh, A., & Keshavan, M. S. (2000). Hippocampal volume in adolescent-onset alcohol use disorders. *American Journal of Psychiatry, 157,* 737–744.

De Brito, S. A., Mechelli, A., Wilke, M., Laurens, K. R., Jones, A. P., Barker, G. J., Hodgins, S., & Viding, E. (2009). Size matters: Increased grey matter in boys with conduct problems and callous–unemotional traits. *Brain, 132,* 843–852.

Dunn, J., & Brown, J. (1994). Affect expression in the family, children's understanding of emotions, and their interactions with others. *Merrill-Palmer Quarterly, 40,* 120–137.

Dweck, C. S., & Leggett, E. L. (1988). A social–cognitive approach to motivation and personality. *Psychological Review, 95,* 256–273.

Eisenberg, N., Fabes, R., Murphy, B., Maszk, P., Smith, M., & Karbon, M. (1995). The role of emotionality and regulation in children's social functioning: a longitudinal study. *Child Development, 66,* 1360–1384.

Eisenhower, A. S., Baker, B. L., & Blacher, J. (2007). Early student–teacher relationships of children with and without intellectual disability: Contributions of behavioral, social, and self-regulatory competence. *Journal of School Psychology, 45,* 363–383.

Emde, R. N., Plomin, R., Robinson, J., Corley, R., DeFries, J., Fulker, D. W., Resnick, S., Campos, J., Kagan, J., & Zahn-Waxler, C. (1992). Temperament, emotion, and cognition at fourteen months: The MacArthur longitudinal twin study. *Child Development, 63,* 1437–1455.

Ernst, M., & Mueller, S. C. (2008). The adolescent brain: Insights from functional neuroimaging research. *Developmental Neurobiology, 68,* 729–743.

Eysenck, H. J. (1991). Dimensions of personality: The biosocial approach to personality. Explorations in temperament: International perspectives on theory and measurement. In J. Strelau & A. Angleitner (Eds.), *Explorations in temperament: International perspectives on theory and measurement (perspectives on individual differences)* (pp. 87–103). New York: Plenum.

Fabes, R., Eisenberg, N., Jones, S., Smith, M., Guthrie, I., Poulin, R.,Shepard, S., & Friedman, J. (1999). Regulation, emotionality, and preschoolers' socially competent peer interactions. *Child Development, 70,* 432–442.

Fair, D. A., Cohen, A. L., Power, J. D., Dosenbach, N. U. F., Church, J. A., Meizin, F. M., Schlaggar, B. L., & Petersen, S. E. (2009). Functional brain networks develop from a "local to distributed" organization. *PLoS Computational Biology, 5,* e1000381.

Fairchild, G., Passamonti, L., Hurford, G., Hagan, C. C., von dem Hagen, E. A., van Goozen, S. H., Goodyer, I. M., & Calder, A. J. (2011). Brain structure abnormalities in early-onset and adolescent-onset conduct disorder. *American Journal of Psychiatry, 168,* 624–633.

Feinstein, J. S., Adolphs, R., Damasio, A., & Tranel, D. (2011). The human amygdala and the induction and experience of fear. *Current Biology, 21,* 34–38.

Frederickson, N., Jones, A. P., Warren, L., Deakes, T., & Allen, G. (2013). Can developmental cognitive neuroscience inform intervention for social, emotional and behavioural difficulties (SEBD)? *Emotional and Behavioural Difficulties, 18,* 135–154.

Frick, P., O'Brien, B., Wootton, J., & McBurnett, K. (1994). Psychopathy and conduct problems in children. *Journal of Abnormal Psychology, 103,* 700–707.

Gao, W., Zhu, H., Giovanello, K. S., Smith, J. K., Shen, D., Gilmore, J. H., & Lin, W. (2009). Evidence on the emergence of the brain's default network from 2-week-old to 2-year-old healthy pediatric subjects. *Proceedings of the National Academy of Sciences, 106,* 6790–6795.

Giedd, J. N., Blumenthal, J., Jeffries, N. O., Castellanos, F. X., Liu, H., Zijdenbos, A., Paus, T., Evans, A. C., & Rapoport, J. L. (1999). Brain development during childhood and adolescence: A longitudinal MRI study. *Nature Neuroscience, 2,* 861–863.

Gogtay, N., Giedd, J. N., Lusk, L., Hayashi, K. M., Greenstein, D., Vaituzis, A. C., Nugent, T. F., Herman, D. H., Clasen, L. S., Toga, A. W., Rapoport, J. L., & Thompson, P. M. (2004). Dynamic mapping of human cortical development during childhood through early adulthood. *Proceedings of the National Academy of the Sciences, 101,* 8174–8179.

Goldin, P. R., McRae, K., Ramel, W., & Gross, J. J. (2008). The neural bases of emotion regulation: Reappraisal and suppression of negative emotion. *Biological Psychiatry, 63,* 577–586.

Graziano, P., Keane, S., & Calkins, S. (2007). Cardiac vagal regulation and early peer status. *Child Development, 78,* 264–278.

Gross, J. J. (1998). Antecedent- and response-focused emotion regulation: Divergent consequences for experience, expression, and physiology. *Journal of Personality and Social Psychology, 74,* 224–237.

Gullone, E., Hughes, E. K., King, N. J., & Tonge, B. (2010). The normative development of emotion regulation strategy use in children and adolescents: A 2-year follow-up study. *Journal of Child Psychology and Psychiatry, 51,* 567–574.

Gupta, R., Koscik, T. R., Bechara, A., & Tranel, D. (2011). The amygdala and decision-making. *Neuropsychologia, 49,* 760–766.

Guy, S. C., & Cahill, L. (1999). The role of overt rehearsal in enhanced conscious memory for emotional events. *Consicousness and Cognition, 8,* 14–122.

Haas, S. M., Waschbusch, D. A., Pelham, W. E., King, S., Andrade, B. F., & Carrey, N. J. (2011). Treatment response in CP/ADHD children with callous–unemotional traits. *Journal of Abnormal Psychology, 39,* 541–552.

Hawes, D. J., & Dadds, M. R. (2007). Stability and malleability of callous–unemotional traits during treatment for childhood conduct problems. *Journal of Clinical Child and Adolescent Psychology, 35,* 347–355.

Howse, R., Calkins, S., Anastopoulos, A., Keane, S., & Shelton, T. (2003). Regulatory contributors to children's academic achievement. *Early Education and Development, 14,* 101–119.

Huebner, T., Vloet, T. D., Marx, I., Konrad, K., Fink, G. R., Herpertz, S. C., & Herpertz-Dahlmann, B. (2008). Morphometric brain abnormalities in boys with conduct disorder. *Journal of the American Academy of Child and Adolescent Psychiatry, 47*, 540–547.

Humphrey, N., & Lewis, S. (2008). What does "inclusion" mean for pupils on the autistic spectrum in mainstream secondary schools? *Journal of Research in Special Educational Needs, 8*, 132–140.

Izard, C., Fine, S., Schultz, D., Mostow, A., Ackerman, B., & Youngstrom, E. (2001). Emotion knowledge as a predictor of social behavior and academic competence in children at risk. *Psychological Science, 12*, 18–23.

Joëls, M., Pu, Z., Wiegert, O., Oitzl, M. S., & Krugers, H. J. (2006). Learning under stress: How does it work? *Trends in Cognitive Sciences, 10*, 152–158.

Jones, A. P., Happé, F. G., Gilbert, F., Burnett, S., & Viding, E. (2010). Feeling, caring, knowing: Different types of empathy deficit in boys with psychopathic tendencies and autism spectrum disorder. *Journal of Child Psychology and Psychiatry, 51*, 1188–1197.

Jones, A. P., Laurens, K. R., Herba, C., Barker, G., & Viding, E. (2009). Amygdala hypo-reactivity to fearful faces in boys with conduct problems and callous–unemotional traits. *American Journal of Psychiatry, 166*, 95–102.

Kahn, R. E., Frick, P. J., Youngstrom, E., Findling, R. L., & Youngstrom, J. K. (2012). The effects of including a callous–unemotional specifier for the diagnosis of conduct disorder. *Journal of Child Psychology and Psychiatry, 53*, 271–282.

Kandel, D. B., Yamaguchi, K., & Chen, K. (1992). Stages of progression in drug involvement from adolescence to adulthood: Further evidence for the gateway theory. *Journal of Studies on Alcohol, 53*, 447–457.

Kennedy, D. P., & Adolphs, R. (2010). Impaired fixation to eyes following amygdala damage arises from abnormal bottom-up attention. *Neuropsychologia, 48*, 3392–3398.

Kessler, R. C., Berglund, P., Demier, O., Jin, R., Merikangas, K. R., & Walters, E. E. (2005). Lifetime prevalence and age-of-onset distributions of DSM-IV disorders in the National Comorbidity Survey Replication. *Archives of General Psychiatry, 62*, 593–602.

Kopp, C. B. (1989). Regulation of distress and negative emotions: A developmental view. *Developmental Psychology, 25*, 343–354.

Kruesi, M. J., Casanova, M. F., Mannheim, G., & Johnson-Bilder, A. (2004). Reduced temporal lobe volume in early onset conduct disorder. *Psychiatry Research, 15*, 1–11.

Lebel, C., & Beaulieu, C. (2011). Longitudinal development of human brain wiring continues from childhood into adulthood. *Journal of Neuroscience, 31*, 10937–10947.

Lechner, H. A., Squire, L. R., & Byrne, L. H. (1999). 100 years of consolidation – remembering Müller and Pilzecker. *Learning and Memory, 6*, 77–87.

Lewis, M. D., & Sieben, J. (2004). Emotion regulation in the brain: Conceptual issues and directions for developmental research. *Child Development, 75*, 371–376.

Lewit, E. M., & Baker, L. S. (1995). School readiness. *Future of Children, 5*, 128–139.

Lupien, S. J., Fiocco, A., Wan, N., Maheu, F., Lord, C., Schramek, T., & Tu, M. T. (2004). Stress hormones and human memory function across the lifespan. *Psychoneuroendocrinology, 30*, 225–242.

Lupien, S. J., & Lepage, M. (2001). Stress, memory, and the hippocampus: Can't live with it, can't live without it. *Behavioural Brain Research, 127*, 137–158.

Lupien, S. J., McEwen, B. S., Gunnar, M. R., & Heim, C. (2009). Effects of stress throughout the lifespan on the brain, behaviour and cognition. *Nature Reviews Neuroscience, 10*, 434–445.

Mangels, J. A., Butterfield, B., Lamb, J., Good, C. D., & Dweck, C. S. (2006). Why do beliefs about intelligence influence learning success? A social-cognitive-neuroscience model. *Social, Cognitive, and Affective Neuroscience, 1*, 75–86.

Marsh, A., Finger, E., Mitchell, D., Reid, M., Sims, C., Kosson, D., & Blair, R. J. R. (2008). Reduced amygdala response to fearful expressions in children and adolescents with callous–unemotional traits and disruptive behavior disorders. *American Journal of Psychiatry, 165*, 712–720.

McCabe, L. A., Cunnington, M., & Brooks-Gunn, J. (2004). The development of self-regulation in young children: Individual characteristics and environmental contexts. In R. F. Baumeister & K. D. Vohs (Eds.), *Handbook of self-regulation: Research, theory and applications* (pp. 340–356). New York: Guilford.

McGaugh, J. L. (2006). Make mild moments memorable: Add a little arousal. *Trends in Cognitive Sciences, 10*, 345–347.

McGaugh, J. L., & Roozendaal, B. (2002). Role of adrenal stress hormones in forming lasting memories in the brain. *Current Opinions in Neurobiology, 12*, 205–210.

Medina, K. L., Schweinsburg, A. D., Cohen-Zion, M. C., Nagel, N. J., & Tapert, S. F. (2007). Effects of alcohol and combined marijuana and alcohol use during adolescence on hippocampal volume and asymmetry. *Neurotoxicology and Teratology, 29*, 141–152.

Misra, R., McKean, M., West, S., & Russo, T. (2000). Academic stress of college students: Comparison of student and faculty perceptions. *College Student Journal, 34*, 236–245.

Muñoz, L. C. (2009). Callous–unemotional traits are related to combined deficits in recognizing afraid faces and body poses. *Journal of the American Academy of Child and Adolescent Psychiatry, 48*, 554–562.

Muñoz, L. C., Qualter, P., & Padgett, G. (2011). Empathy and bullying: Exploring the influence of callous–unemotional traits. *Child Psychiatry and Human Development, 42*, 183–196.

Nagel, B. J., Schweinsburg, A. D., Phan, V., & Tapert, S. F. (2005). Reduced hippocampal volume among adolescents with alcohol use disorders without psychiatric comorbidity. *Psychiatry Research, 139*, 181–190.

Ongür, D., An, X., & Price, J. L. (1998). Prefrontal cortical projections to the hypothalamus in macaque monkeys. *Journal of Comparative Neurology, 401*, 480–505.

Paus, T., Keshavan, M., & Giedd, J. N. (2008). Why do many psychiatric disorders emerge during adolescence? *Nature Reviews Neuroscience, 9*, 947–957.

Payne, J. D., Jackson, E. D., Hoscheidt, S., Ryan, L., Jacobs, W. J., & Nadel, L. (2007). Stress administered prior to encoding impairs neutral but enhances emotional long-term episodic memories. *Learning and Memory, 14*, 861–868.

Pessoa, L. (2008). On the relationship between emotion and cognition. *Nature Reviews Neuroscience, 9*, 148–158.

Pianta, R. C., Steinberg, M. S., & Rollins, K. B. (1995). The first two years of school: Teacher–child relationships and deflections in children's classroom adjustment. *Development and Psychopathology, 7*, 295–312.

Pianta, R. C., & Stuhlman, M. W. (2004). Teacher–child relationships and children's success in the first years of school. *School Psychology Review, 33*, 444–458.

Plomin, R., Kagan, J., Emde, R. N., Reznick, J. S., Braungart, J. M., Robinson, J., Zahn-Waxler, C., & De Fries, J. C. (1993). Genetic change and continuity from fourteen to twenty months: The MacArthur Longitudinal Twin Study. *Child Development, 64*, 1354–1376.

Plomin, R., & Rowe, D. C. (1977). A twin study of temperament in young children. *Journal of Psychology: Interdisciplinary and Applied, 97*, 107–113.

Polich, J. (2007). Updating P300: An integrative theory of P3a and P3b. *Clinical Neurophysiology, 118*, 2128–2148.

Pollak, S. D., & Tolley-Schell, S. A. (2003). Selective attention to facial emotion in physically abused children. *Journal of Abnormal Psychology, 112*, 323–338.

Porcelli, A. J., Cruz, D., Wenberg, K., Patterson, M. D., Biswal, B. B., & Rypma, B. (2008). The effects of acute stress on human prefrontal working memory systems. *Physiology and Behavior, 95*, 282–289.

Porges, S. (2003). The polyvagal theory: Phylogenetic contributions to social behavior. *Physiology and Behavior, 79*, 503–513.

Posner, M. I., & Rothbart, M. K. (1998). Attention, self-regulation and consciousness. *Philosophical Transactions of the Royal Society of London, B, 353*, 1915–1927.

Posner, M. I., & Rothbart, M. K. (2000). Developing mechanisms of self-regulation. *Development and Psychopathology, 12*, 427–441.

Raznahan, A., Shaw, P., Lalonde, F., Stockman, M., Wallace, G. L., Greenstein, D., Clasen, L., Gogtay, N., & Giedd, J. N. (2011). How does your cortex grow? *Journal of Neuroscience, 31*, 7174–7177.

Rimm-Kaufman, S. E., & Pianta, R. C. (2000). An ecological perspective on the transition to kindergarten: A theoretical framework to guide empirical research. *Journal of Applied Developmental Psychology, 21*, 491–511.

Rimm-Kaufman, S. E., Pianta, R. C., & Cox, M. J. (2000). Teachers' judgments of problems in the transition to kindergarten. *Early Childhood Research Quarterly, 15*, 147–166.

Robinson, J. L., Kagan, J., Reznick, J. S., & Corley, R. (2004). The heritability of inhibited and uninhibited behavior: A twin study. *Developmental Psychology, 28*, 1030–1037.

Robotham, D., & Julian, C. (2006). Stress and the higher education student: A critical review of the literature. *Journal of Further and Higher Education, 30*, 107–117.

Ross, S. E., Niebling, B. C., & Heckert, T. M. (1999). Sources of stress among college students. *College Student Journal, 33*, 312–317.

Rothbart, M. K., & Derryberry, D. (1981). Development of individual differences in temperament. In M. E. Lamb & A. N. Brown (Eds.), *Advances in developmental psychology* (pp. 38–85). Hillsdale, NJ: Erlbaum.

Rutherford, H. J. V., Mayes, L. C., & Potenza, M. N. (2010). Neurobiology of adolescent substance use disorders: Implications for prevention and treatment. *Child and Adolescent Psychiatry Clinics of North America, 19*, 479–492.

Rydell, A., Berlin, L., & Bohlin, G. (2003). Emotionality, emotion regulation, and adaptation among 5- to 8-year-old children. *Emotion, 3*, 30–47.

Saudino, K. J. (2005). Behavioral genetics and child temperament. *Journal of Developmental Behavior and Pediatrics, 26*, 214–223.

Schwartz, C. E., Kunwar, P. S., Greve, D. N., Moran, L. R., Viner, J. C., Covino, J. M., Kagan, J., Stewart, S. E., Snidman, N. C., Vangel, M. G., & Wallace, S. R. (2010). Structural differences in adult orbital and ventromedial prefrontal cortex are predicted by 4-month infant temperament. *Archives in General Psychiatry, 67*, 78–84.

Scott, S. K., Young, A. W., Calder, A. J., Hellawell, D. J., Aggleton, J. P., & Johnson, M. (1997). Impaired auditory recognition of fear and anger following bilateral amygdala lesions. *Nature, 385*, 254–257.

Shatz, C. J. (1992). The developing brain. *Scientific American, 267*, 61–67.

Shirtcliff, E. A., Vitacco, M. J., Graf, A. R., Gostisha, A. J., Merz, J. L., & Zahn-Waxler, C. (2009). Neurobiology of empathy and callousness: Implications for the development of antisocial behavior. *Behavioral Science and the Law, 27*, 137–171.

Shors, T. J. (2006). Stressful experience and learning across the lifespan. *Annual Review of Psychology, 57*, 55–85.

Smallwood, J., Fitzgerald, A., Miles, L. K., & Phillips, L. H. (2009). Shifting moods, wandering minds: Negative moods lead the mind to wander. *Emotion, 9*, 271–276.

Smith, R. F. (2003). Animal models of periadolescent substance abuse. *Neurotoxicology and Teratology, 25*, 291–301.

Southgate, V., & Hamilton, A. F. (2008). Unbroken mirrors: Challenging a theory of autism. *Trends in Cognitive Sciences, 12*, 225–229.

Sterzer, P., Stadler, C., Poustka, F., & Kleinschmidt, A. (2007). A structural neural deficit in adolescents with conduct disorder and its association with lack of empathy. *NeuroImage, 37*, 335–342.

Swartzwelder, H. S., Wilson, W. A., & Tayyeb, M. Y. (1995). Age-dependent inhibition of long-term potentiation by ethanol in immature vs mature hippocampus. *Alcoholism Clinical and Experimental Research, 19*, 1480–1485.

Tremblay, L. K., Naranjo, C. A., Graham, S. J., Herrmann, N., Mayberg, H. S., Hevenor, S., & Busto, U. E. (2005). Functional neuroanatomical substrates of altered reward processing in major depressive disorder revealed by a dopaminergic probe. *Archives of General Psychiatry, 62*, 1228–1236.

Van Bogaert, P., Wikler, D., Damhaut, P., Szliwowski, H. B., & Goldman, S. (1998). Regional changes in glucose metabolism during brain development from the age of 6 years. *NeuroImage, 8*, 62–68.

Vida, R., Brownlie, E. B., Beitchman, J. H., Adlaf, E. M., Atkinson, L., Escobar, M., Johnson, C. J., Jiang, H., Koyama, E., & Bender, D. (2009). Emerging adult outcomes of adolescent psychiatric and substance use disorders. *Research Advances in Comorbidity of Substance Misuse and Mental Disorders, 34*, 800–805.

Viding, E., Blair, R. J., Moffitt, T. E., & Plomin, R. (2005). Evidence for substantial genetic risk for psychopathy in 7-year-olds. *Journal of Child Psychology and Psychiatry, 46*, 592–597.

Viding, E., Jones, A. P., Frick, P., Moffitt, T. E., & Plomin, R. (2008). Heritability of antisocial behaviour at 9: Do callous–unemotional traits matter? *Developmental Science, 11*, 17–22.

Viding, E., Simmonds, E., Petrides, K. V., & Frederickson, N. (2009). The contribution of callous–unemotional traits and conduct problems to bullying in early adolescence. *Journal of Child Psychology and Psychiatry, 50*, 471–481.

Wang, L., LaBar, K. S., & McCarthy, G. (2006). Mood alters amygdala activation to sad distractors during an attentional task. *Biological Psychiatry, 60*, 1139–1146.

White, S. F., Frick, P. J., Lawing, S. K., & Bauer, D. (2013). Callous–unemotional traits and response to functional family therapy in adolescent offenders. *Behavioral Sciences and the Law, 31*, 271–285.

Yang-Teng, F., Decety, J., Chia-Yen, Y., Ji-Lin, L., & Yawei, C. (2010). Unbroken mirror neurons in autism spectrum disorders. *Journal of Child Psychology and Psychiatry, 51*, 981–988.

Yurgelun-Todd, D. A., & Killgore, W. D. (2006). Fear-related activity in the prefrontal cortex increases with age during adolescence: A preliminary fMRI study. *Neuroscience Letters, 406*, 194–199.

# Further Reading

Immordino-Yang, M.H., & Damasio, A.R. (2007). We feel, therefore we learn: The relevance of affective and social neuroscience to education. Mind, Brain and Education, 1, 3–10.

McCrae, K., Gross, J.J., Weber, J., Robertson, E.R., Sokol-Hessner, P., & Ochsner, K.N. (2012). The development of emotion regulation: An fMRI study of cognitive reappraisal in children, adolescents and young adults. Social, Cognitive and Affective Neuroscience, 7, 11–22.

Pfeifer, J.H., & Blakemore S. J. (2012). Adolescent social cognitive and affective neuroscience: Past, present, and future. Social, Cognitive and Affective Neuroscience, 7, 1–10.

# Chapter 12

# Attention and Executive Control

## Michelle de Haan

Executive functions include a range of skills that help us to control and regulate our thoughts and behaviors in order to attain goals. Basic executive functions, such as the ability to inhibit an inappropriate response, emerge early in life and subsequently contribute to the development of more complex executive functions, such as reasoning, planning, and problem solving. In adults, executive functions depend on a network of brain regions including the prefrontal cortex, a part of the brain that develops slowly and is not yet fully mature even in adolescence. Measures of executive function correlate with academic abilities such as reading and mathematical skills, and measures of executive function in preschoolers can predict subsequent gains in these skills. This collection of findings suggest that measures of executive functions may be useful in the early identification of children at risk for poor academic progress, and that training executive functions might be an effective means of facilitating the acquisition of numeracy and literacy. This chapter will review evidence regarding the development of executive functions, their role in acquisition of academic abilities, and how information about their neural underpinnings provides insight into the mutual development of executive function and academic skills.

## Defining Prefrontal Executive Functions in Children

Executive functions allow us to interact with the world in a purposive, goal-directed manner. They are abilities that we call on when faced with situations where routine behaviors or automatic thoughts are not sufficient. Different

*Educational Neuroscience*, First Edition. Edited by Denis Mareschal, Brian Butterworth and Andy Tolmie.

views regarding the structure of executive functions and their neural correlates during development will be overviewed in this section to provide a background for a more detailed discussion of basic executive skills, their neural bases and their relation to academic achievement in the next sections.

## Structure of executive function

Executive function has been conceptualized both as a unitary, supervisory function and as a set of component skills. One influential example of the latter view argues that executive function consists of a set of distinct, yet inter-related, components (Miyake et al., 2000). This work used confirmatory factor analysis to test whether data from a larger number of studies of executive function fit with a component model. In young adults they identified three basic components of executive function: (a) *working memory*, the ability to temporarily maintain and manipulate information in a mental workspace, (b) *inhibitory control*, the ability to stop an inappropriate prepotent response and ignore distractions, and (c) *switching*, the ability to shift between mental states, rule sets, or tasks. Studies with children have generally supported this model, and indicate that at least from 7 years of age the structure of executive function is relatively stable (Huizinga, Dolan, & van der Molen, 2006; Rose, Feldman, & Jankowski, 2011; see Best & Miller, 2010, for a review). Studies with children younger than 7 years provide more mixed results, with some studies finding distinct components of executive function (Senn, Espy, & Kaufman, 2004) but others finding evidence for a unitary skill (Hughes, Ensor, Wilson & Graham, 2009; Wiebe et al., 2011). The latter findings raise the possibility that executive functions begin as a unitary skill that becomes differentiated into distinct components over development.

## Neural bases

Executive functions involve a brain network including prefrontal cortex, parietal cortex, and subcortical structures. Postnatal development of the cortex involves both progressive changes, such as synapse formation and myelination, as well as regressive changes, such as synapse elimination. For example, post-mortem studies show that the density of synapses in the human prefrontal cortex is highest at about three and a half years of age, when it reaches a level 50% greater than that seen in adults, and then gradually decreases throughout adolescence (Huttenlocher & Dabholkar, 1997). These studies also show that the course of development of the prefrontal cortex is protracted relative to other areas of cortex, a conclusion supported by neuroimaging studies of brain development. For example, diffusion-tensor imaging measures of white-matter tracts show that many association tracts are mature by adolescence, but the frontostriatal tract, known to be important for top-down executive control of behavior, does not mature until after adolescence (Asato, Terwilliger, Woo, & Luna, 2010). These types of result have led to the view that the slow development of the prefrontal cortex is a limiting factor in the development of executive function.

The debate mentioned above regarding the cognitive structure of executive function during development is also relevant to understanding the brain underpinnings of executive function. If executive function is a unitary skill, a common neural signature may dominate across a range of tasks. In contrast, if it consists of a set of distinct components, these may in turn map on to distinct neural networks. Studies with adults generally support the latter view of a differentiated system. The main lines of evidence in favor of this view are (a) the low correlations between scores on tasks measuring different executive components, (b) the double dissociations in performance on different executive components following brain injury, and (c) the different patterns of brain activation measured by functional magnetic resonance imaging (fMRI) or other neuroimaging methods during performance of tasks tapping different executive components (discussed by Shallice & Burgess, 1996; see Chapter 2 on Neuroimaging Methods in the current volume).

Is the same differentiation seen in children? As discussed above, evidence from behavioral studies suggests that there are separable components of executive functions by 7 years of age, but results are less clearcut in younger children. Studies that have examined the neural underpinnings of children's executive functions also suggest that these may not be as differentiated or localized as they are in adults. For example, in one study of over 100 children aged 7–16 years, children with extrafrontal lobe pathology were as likely as those with frontal lobe pathology to show deficits in executive function (Jacobs, Harvey, & Anderson, 2011). This suggests that extrafrontal regions play a more prominent role in executive functions during childhood than adulthood. Thus, the pattern of brain regions linked to executive functions in children may be broader than in adults, becoming more differentiated with age.

## Academic achievement

Learning to read, write, and carry out mathematics can in part be seen as a process whereby simple skills (e.g., letter recognition) lead on to more complex ones (e.g., word reading; see Chapter 7 on literacy and Chapter 8 on mathematics, this volume, for more detailed discussion of these specific skills). These precursor skills can be described as part of a crystallized knowledge base, built up based on past experiences at home, nursery, school, and so on. In addition to this crystallized knowledge, it has been argued that there is a basic capacity for learning that is less dependent on experience and prior knowledge, and represents a more fluid, biologically based capacity for acquiring new information across the lifespan (Gathercole, Pickering, Knight, & Stegman, 2004). These fluid skills are often described as some of the basic executive-function skills that rely on prefrontal cortex, including working memory, inhibitory control, and switching. From this perspective, it might be predicted that brain regions involved in executive functions would overlap with brain activation seen during tasks like reading and math, particularly during acquiring these skills, when they are less routine and automatic. Brain regions involved in executive function may become less involved as the knowledge becomes crystallized and/or aspects of these skills become more routine and automatic.

In summary, executive functions consist of a set of differentiated yet interrelated skills that rely on brain regions including the prefrontal cortex. This organization seems to emerge over development from a system that is initially more multipurpose in function and diffusely distributed in the brain. Since executive functions are particularly important in situations where routine, automatic processes are insufficient, the specific links between executive function and academic attainment are also likely to change over time, as some skills become automatic and other new skills are being acquired. The next section will summarize the development and neural bases of each of the three basic components of executive function and examine in more detail how they may related to academic progress.

## Basic Components of Executive Function: Development, Brain Bases, and Links to Academic Achievement

There is general agreement that working memory, inhibitory control, and switching are basic executive skills that are measurable in children and contribute to the emergence of more complex executive skills such as problem solving, planning, and reasoning (reviewed by Best & Miller, 2010; Diamond, 2011). It is easy to imagine how children who begin school with difficulties in these basic areas may struggle. For example they may have problems remembering and carrying out instructions, inhibiting irrelevant information and staying focused on task, or planning and monitoring progress of individual steps of a task as it progresses. The resulting missed opportunities for learning and practicing skills may then have a negative impact on the ability to achieve normal incremental progress in complex skill domains such as reading and mathematics

(Gathercole & Alloway, 2006). In this section, each of the three basic components of executive function will be discussed in turn with respect to developmental emergence, brain correlates, and links to school progress, with a focus on attainments in literacy and numeracy.

## Inhibition

Inhibition is the ability to stop an inappropriate response or thought. Many tasks of executive function involve inhibition, though a challenge for researchers is that few tasks are "pure" measures of inhibition that do not involve other executive skills. To partially address this issue, tasks of inhibition are often classed as either tapping "simple inhibition", when memory or shifting demands are minimized, or "complex inhibition", when inhibition must be used along with working memory and/or shifting skills for successful performance.

Commonly used tasks of complex inhibition in young children are the day–night task, where the child must inhibit the prepotent response and say "Day" for a picture of the moon and "Night" for a picture of the sun (Gerstadt, Hong, & Diamond, 2004), and the Dimensional Change Card Sort (Zelazo, 2006), where the child must inhibit a practiced response (e.g., sort cards according to color) in order to follow a new rule (e.g., sort according to shape). In older children, more commonly used tasks are the antisaccade task (reviewed by Luna, Velanova, & Geier, 2008), where participants must move their eyes in the direction opposite to a peripheral cue, and Go–No-Go or Stop Signal tasks (see, e.g., Johnstone et al., 2007), where participants are required over a series of trials to respond consistently to one cue but withhold response to another.

*Development in infancy and preschool-aged children* The ability to exert inhibitory control during a single instance exists even in infancy. For example, at around 7 months infants become able to inhibit the prepotent response of searching for a hidden object in the location where it was successfully found on several previous occasions in order to search in the new, correct location (Diamond, 1985, 2001). This suggests that the circuitry supporting transient inhibitory control is available early in development. However, there are dramatic improvements in children's performance on complex inhibition tasks over the period of 3–5 years, which some researchers have argued represent a qualitative change in abilities. For example, one study of 93 children aged 3–5 years using the Dimensional Change Card Sort task found that, while most 3-year-olds perseverated on the first trial after a rule switch and most 5-year-olds correctly followed the new rule, a large proportion of 3–4-year-olds showed instabilities in performance. This pattern was best modeled as a discontinuous pattern of development rather than a continuous or stepwise trajectory (van Bers, Visser, van Schijndel, Mandell, & Raijmakers, 2011).

*Development in school-aged children* Performance on tasks such as the Dimensional Change Card Sort or Day–Night task tends to stabilize around 5–6 years, which has led some researchers to conclude that inhibitory control is largely mature by this age. However, the lack of further improvement on these types of task might be due to ceiling effects (the task becomes too easy). Studies that have looked at children's ability to consistently show inhibitory control over tasks involving multiple trials and using more subtle measures (e.g., reaction times) have provided evidence for continued development of inhibitory control over middle childhood and adolescence. For example, performance on the anti-saccade task continues to improve from 8 to years to adolescence and from adolescence to adulthood (Velanova, Wheeler, & Luna, 2009). Similarly, in Go–No-Go tasks, there is a decrease in commission errors (mistakenly responding to the No-Go signal) from 9 years to adulthood (Casey et al., 1997; Jonkman, Lansbergen, & Stauder, 2003; but see Johnstone et al., 2007). These results suggest that there is further quantitative improvement in inhibitory-control abilities during middle childhood and adolescence.

*Neural bases in preschool- and school-aged children* The brain network involved in inhibitory control in adults includes the dorsolateral prefrontal cortex, inferior frontal gyrus, anterior cingulate cortex, posterior parietal cortex, striatum, and cerebellum (Curtis, Cole, Rao, & D'Esposito, 2005; Rubia, Smith, Brammer, & Taylor, 2003).

There is evidence that the inferior frontal region is involved in developmental improvements in inhibition skills from 3–5 years. One study using near-infrared spectroscopy (NIRS) showed that adults and 5-year-old children successfully performed the Dimensional Change Card Sort task and showed bilateral inferior frontal activation in pre- and postswitch trials. By contrast, 3-year-olds were more likely to show perseverative responses, and those who did failed to show inferior frontal activation (Moriguchi & Hiraki, 2009). This suggests that successful performance on the task activates the same inferior frontal regions in preschoolers and adults, and that the improvement in performance from age 3–5 might be related to development of this region. A limitation of the study is that brain activity was only measured over the frontal region of interest and not the whole brain, thus task-related activations in other brain areas that might have contribute to the difference in behavioral performance with age could not be evaluated. An fMRI study with 7- to 8-year-olds and adults suggests that the pattern of brain regions involved in inhibition does change with age. During a task similar to the Dimensional Change Card Sort task, both children and adults showed activation related to making errors after a rule change in the right inferior frontal, superior frontal sulcus, premotor cortex, superior parietal cortex, and intraparietal sulcus. However, this effect was greater for children than adults in the right frontal region and greater for adults than children in the left parietal region (Morton, Bosma, & Ansari, 2009). This might reflect a less efficient parietal region in children that is compensated for by increased effort from prefrontal processes.

Other research has used the antisaccade task to examine inhibition in older children. One such study examined how connections among the regions involved in inhibitory control develop over middle childhood and adolescence. Results from 78 participants aged 8–27 years suggested that adults' abilities to inhibit automatically moving their eyes to a peripheral target is supported by top-down control from frontal regions to downstream cortical and subcortical effector regions (regions involved in oculomotor control). Developmental improvements in inhibitory control were supported by enhances in this top-down connectivity from frontal cognitive control regions to downstream effector regions as well as by decreases in short-range connectivity within parietal and frontal regions (Hwang, Velanova, & Luna, 2010).

In summary, the ability to inhibit an incorrect response emerges in infancy, with dramatic improvements over the preschool period and further quantitative changes continuing in adolescence. Increased inferior frontal involvement in inhibition may underlie improvements in seen in preschoolers, while changes in frontal connectivity and more efficient parietal processing may underlie changes seen in middle childhood and adolescence.

## Relation to academic skills

Several studies with preschoolers have found links between inhibitory control and mathematical skills, even when potential confounders such as age, vocabulary, and mother's education are controlled for (Espy et al., 2004; but see, e.g., Monette, Bigras, & Guay, 2011, for negative results). With respect to reading, links have also been reported, but these may be indirect. For example, one study examining whether kindergarten executive function predicted Grade 1 reading abilities found that, once confounding variables were controlled for, inhibition did not a have a direct effect on reading, but did have an indirect effect on reading and writing via anger and aggression (Monette et al., 2011).

In middle-school-aged children, those who are poor at reading comprehension or at solving mathematical word problems have been found to have poorer inhibition, shown by poorer recall of critical task information and better recall of irrelevant information compared with their more able peers (DeBeni, Palladino, Pazzaglia, & Cornoldi, 1998; Passolunghi, Cornoldi, & De Liberto, 1999). In 11-year-olds inhibition predicts curriculum attainment in mathematics and English, indicating that these skills support general academic learning rather than acquisition of skills and knowledge in specific domains (St. Clair-Thompson & Gathercole, 2006).

Generally, the results of studies examining relations between inhibition and academic skills are consistent with the view that there is a more specific link between inhibitory control and math in the preschool years, but that in older children there is a more general effect on learning. The early link with math may reflect the fact that there are fewer automated processes for this skill during the initial learning stages; with skill acquisition, the classic intraparietal area implicated in numeracy in adults becomes increasingly active.

## Working memory

Working memory provides temporary storage and manipulation of information, skills that are necessary for complex cognitive tasks including reading comprehension, learning, reasoning, and mathematics (Baddeley, 1992). Working-memory tasks can be divided into simpler tasks, where information must only be maintained over a delay (e.g., digit span), and more complex tasks, where information must be mentally manipulated (e.g., reverse digit span). In a common model of working memory, slave systems including the phonological loop for verbal material and the visuospatial sketchpad for visuospatial material are involved in maintaining information and a central executive plays a role in manipulating the contents (Baddeley, 1992).

*Development in school-aged children*   Working-memory abilities improve continuously over childhood. For example, one study found that when participants from 4 to 12 years old were tested using the CANTAB (Cambridge Neuropsychological Testing Automated Battery), a well-established and validated battery of tests previously used with adult human and animal lesion populations (Fray, Robbins, & Sahakian, 1996), measures of working memory improved with age but had not yet reached adult levels even by age 12 (Luciana & Nelson, 2002). Most studies find a linear increase in working memory skills from age 4 years to 14–15 years (Conklin, Luciana, Hooper, & Yarger, 2007; Gathercole, Pickering, Ambridge, & Wearing, 2004; Luciana & Nelson, 2002; Westerberg, Hirvikoski, Forssberg, & Klingberg, 2004), when improvements begin to level off (Gathercole et al., 2004a), with the age of mastery sometimes being later for more complex tasks (Conklin et al., 2007; Luciana & Nelson, 2002).

*Neural bases in school-aged children* Working memory in adults is mediated by a brain network involving the dorsolateral prefrontal cortex (in particular, the superior frontal sulcus) and the parietal cortex (intra- and inferior parietal cortex; reviewed by Klingberg, 2006). This same basic network is active in 8–18-year-olds, with stronger activation of the frontoparietal network being related to greater working-memory capacity (Klingberg, Forssberg, & Westerberg, 2002; Olesen, Nagy, Westerberg, & Klingberg, 2003). Activation of the network also increases with age independent of performance (Klingberg et al., 2002). Development of white-matter tracts connecting the frontal and parietal regions seems to play a role in this process: maturation of these tracts relates to working-memory (but not reading) performance, and to the degree of cortical activation in the frontal and parietal grey matter (Nagy, Westerberg, & Klingberg, 2004; Olesen et al., 2003). At a cellular level, computational modeling indicates that stronger synaptic connectivity between the prefrontal and parietal regions, and not faster transmission of neural signals or stronger connections within each region, can by itself account for observed changes in brain activity associated with the development of working memory in childhood (Edin, Macoveneau, Olesen, Tegnér, & Klingberg, 2007).

This body of evidence might suggest that maturation of the frontoparietal network drives development of working-memory capacity. However, training studies provide one challenge to this view. Traditionally working-memory capacity was thought to be a fixed, heritable unchangeable trait in adults, but more recent studies show greater flexibility in working-memory capacity. For example, one study showed that, after 5 weeks of training on a working-memory task, adults showed both an increased working-memory capacity and increased working-memory-related brain activity in the frontoparietal network (Olesen, Westerberg, & Klingberg, 2004). This suggests that experience using working memory and/or the increased demands on working memory as children develop might drive changes in brain network underlying this ability.

Other lines of evidence also suggest that the neural bases of working memory may be more broadly based early in life than in adults. For example, electroencephalography studies have reported that in 6-month-old infants there is a burst of high-frequency electroencephalography activity over right temporal regions during the period of maintenance of the representation of the object, after it disappears and before it reappears (Kaufman, Csibra, & Johnson, 2003, 2005). A recent study of the development of working memory in infants born preterm showed that neonatal hippocampal volumes correlated with working memory ability at 2 years of age, but cortical volumes, even from the dorsolateral prefrontal region, did not (Beauchamp et al., 2008). This result is consistent with findings of a neuroimaging study in adolescents and adults, which found a role of the hippocampus in working memory that diminished with age (Finn,

Sheridan, Kam, Hinshaw, & D'Esposito, 2010). Findings such as these hint that the neural network underlying working memory may be different, possibly more diffuse, and become increasingly focused on the frontoparietal network with development (Kaldy & Sigala, 2004).

## Links to academic skills in school-aged children

Working memory is our mental workspace, and as such is involved in a number of other cognitive skills. There have been several studies that have examined the relation of working-memory skills to development of reading and math abilities. This section will use example studies to highlight the general findings from the larger literature (for further review see Holmes, Gathercole, & Dunning, 2010).

*Math* Visuospatial working memory is correlated to mathematical abilities, in children with (see, e.g., Henry & MacLean, 2003) and without (see, e.g., Jarvis & Gathercole, 2003; Kyttälä, Aunio, Lehto, & Luit, 2003) learning disabilities. This link has been interpreted as reflecting the numerous instances where visuospatial skills are needed in mathematics, from aligning columns of numbers to manipulating mental number lines. Holmes and Adams (2006) showed that visual spatial working memory in a maze task uniquely predicted all aspects of 8-year-olds' math achievements even after controlling for variance associated with age, phonological memory, and other measures of executive functioning. By contrast, for 10-year-olds visual spatial working memory only predicted performance on more difficult math questions. It may be that older children can use other strategies, such as direct retrieval, for simpler questions, but must revert to using visual–spatial strategies for more complex questions. This might suggest that as children become older the relations between working memory and math skills change, though other studies have reported a more consistent link over an even wider age span from 6 to 16 years (Dumontheil & Klingberg, 2012). Measures of working memory can also predict future gains in mathematical skills. For example, one study of children aged 6–16 years found that visuospatial working memory provided unique prediction of math skills 2 years later, even when age, verbal working memory, and nonverbal IQ were taken into account (Dumontheil & Klingberg, 2012).

Some studies have found that verbal working memory is related to mathematical skills (Monette et al., 2011) and can predict future math performance (Dumontheil & Klingberg, 2012). However, not all studies have found this link (Gathercole, Brown, & Pickering, 2003), and there is evidence that the link between verbal working memory and math may diminish with age

(Bull, Espy, & Wiebe, 2008; Dumontheil & Klingberg, 2012). The link has been interpreted as being due to the need to use verbal codes for counting or retaining interim solutions.

*Reading*   Most studies of the relation between working memory and reading have focused on verbal working memory. Verbal working-memory skills at age 4 have been found to predict reading comprehension, writing, and spelling skills 2.5 years later (Gathercole et al., 2003). One study found that the relation between verbal working memory and reading in preschoolers was indirect and mediated by effects on anger–aggression (Monette et al., 2011). Generally, the most consistent links have been found with reading comprehension (Cain, Oakhill, & Lemmon, 2004; Swanson, Howard, & Saez, 2006). In adults, mind wandering is a significant mediator in the relationship between working memory and reading comprehension, suggesting that the working-memory–comprehension correlation is driven, in part, by attention control over intruding thoughts (McVay & Kane, 2011).

In summary, links have been found between working memory and math and reading skills, even when controlling for associated variables such as age or IQ. Studies examining math have found more consistent links with visuospatial than verbal working memory; and studies examining reading comprehension the opposite. However, there is variation among studies, which might relate to the different tests of math and reading used and/or the ages at which participants are tested.

## Shifting

Shifting refers to the ability to switch between mental states, rule sets, or tasks. Shifting tasks are often distinguished from inhibition tasks in that rule changes in the latter are made explicit, whereas rule changes in shifting tasks must be figured out based on feedback (Best & Miller, 2010). For example, in the Wisconsin Card Sorting Task, participants must discover the rule and recognize when the rule has changed through trial and error rather than explicit statement of the rule. Successful shifting typically does also call on inhibition and working memory skills, since previously active mental states or response sets must be inhibited and feedback must be processed via working memory.

*Development in preschool-aged children*   Preschoolers are capable of shifting in age-appropriate tasks. For example, in a child-friendly adaptation of the Wisconsin Card Sort Task, preschoolers can figure out what a teddy bear's favorite shape is and then switch to determine what his favorite color is based on feedback (Hughes, 1998). Shifting abilities, like other executive skills, continue to improve throughout childhood (Luciana & Nelson, 1998: reviewed by Best & Miller, 2010).

*Development in school-aged children*   Measures of accuracy in shifting tasks tend to improve over childhood and become adult-like in early to mid-adolescence (Davidson, Amso, Anderson, & Diamond, 2006; Huizinga et al., 2006). Interestingly, measures of reaction times to switch trials increase until adulthood, suggesting that adolescents learn to slow down on switch trials to ensure a correct response (Huizinga et al., 2006).

*Neural bases in school-aged children*   A frontoparietal network is involved in switching, and stronger activation for rule-switch than repeat trials in this network is usually interpreted as reflecting an active reconfiguration process in switch trials, to tune the system for proper response execution.

Studies have found evidence of decreases in prefrontal involvement in shifting with age. One study using a regression analysis that tested all areas of the brain found that switch-related activity in dorsolateral and medial prefrontal cortex was negatively correlated with age (Rubia et al., 2006) and another study found robust switch-related activity in the inferior frontal gyrus, dorsolateral prefrontal cortex, and presupplementary motor area, but age differences in the magnitude of these effects were confined to the superior frontal sulcus, with an effect of switching evident in children but not adults (Morton et al., 2009).

There is evidence of emerging functional specialization in medial and ventrolateral prefrontal cortex (VLPFC) over development (Crone, Donohue, Honomichi, Wendelken, & Bunge, 2006). The medial prefrontal cortex is active for both rule representation and rule switching in children, but only rule switching in adults. Moreover, VLPFC is active for rule representation in adults, but not adolescents or children.

## Links to academic skills

Shifting has been less often linked to reading and math skills than have inhibition or working memory. For example, Bull et al. (2008) did not find links between preschoolers' switching abilities and gains in math over the first years in school, though there were links to math performance at each timepoint. This is consistent with other studies not finding strong relations between shifting abilities and math or reading gains in children (e.g., Monette et al., 2011). It might be that switching becomes more important later for more complex math or reading skills.

## Are Links Between Academic Skills, Executive Functions, and Attention Related to Overlapping Brain Systems?

Are the links between development of executive functions and academic skills due to common neural correlates, whereby brain development mutually benefits both domains? The intraparietal sulcus is an area of convergence for both mathematical skills and visuospatial working memory, suggesting that maturation of this brain area could underlie links between these skills during development. One recent study found that greater activation of the left intraparietal sulcus relative to the rest of the brain during a visuospatial working memory task is associated with poorer performance in math 2 years later (Dumontheil & Klingberg, 2012). Left intraparietal sulcus activity was still a significant predictor of math abilities when working memory and reasoning abilities were taken into account.

In a meta-analysis of 52 studies involving over 800 children aged 4–17 years, Houdé, Rossi, Lubin, and Joliot (2010) found both overlap and distinction when examining neural regions activated during math, reading, and executive function (see Figure 12.1). Math tasks were related to the right inferior frontal gyrus, left superior frontal gyrus, and upper part of the left middle occipital gyrus near the junction with the parietal cortex; reading tasks were related to the left frontal, temporoparietal and occiptiotemporal (visual word-form area) regions, and executive functions were related to bilateral dorsolateral and inferior prefrontal cortex, extending to the insular cortex, as well as posterior areas. Only for executive functions was the age contrast between children and adolescents significant. This was due to a greater involvement of the right anterior insula in adolescents compared with children. Generally, these findings were interpreted as suggesting that the brain network related to reading was relatively stable over age and similar to that of adults, whereas the brain network related to number skills showed more prefrontal and less parietal involvement compared with that typically observed in adults. The main regions of overlap in the networks for reading and numeracy with executive skills were the middle and inferior frontal gyri. Unfortunately, this study did not look at the components of different executive skills separately to examine any unique relations.

## Effects of Training

There is a large and growing literature examining the influence of training executive-function skills on cognitive development. Training studies can provide information as to whether executive functions play a causal role in academic achievement by examining whether training-induced improvements

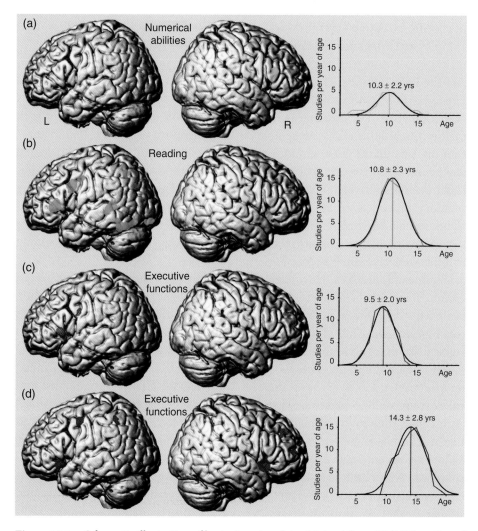

**Figure 12.1** Schematic illustration of brain-imaging data obtained from 52 fMRI studies of 842 healthy children and adolescents. On the left side of the figure, colors indicate locations of cognitive functions (numerical abilities [A], reading [B], and executive functions [C and D]) in each hemisphere (L, left; R, right) rendered onto a 3D view of the Montreal Neurological Institute standard brain (for illustrative purposes, the four ALE activation likelihood estimation maps were thresholded to $p = .001$). On the right side, the corresponding distributions showing the number of studies per year of age are drawn (A, B, and C for children, and D for adolescents). These were computed for all studies of each meta-analysis set, and modeled using a Gaussian distribution (solid black lines). Reprinted with permission from Houdé et al. (2010).

in executive function lead to improvements in academic progress. Investigators have examined effects of training on trained tasks, on new tasks in similar domains, and on tasks in other domains. Two approaches to training programs have emerged from this literature and will be discussed in turn below: (a) training of specific executive function, and (b) training via engagement in more general complex activities such as dance or martial arts.

## Training specific executive skills

Of the three basic executive functions studied in this chapter, the effects of training have been most well studied for working memory. Thus this component will be discussed in more detail below, with broader studies or those examining other skills included only where relevant for particular arguments.

As mentioned above, the capacity of working memory has long been thought to be limited and unchangeable (Cowan, 2001). However, more recent studies have demonstrated that this might not be the case, and that practice/training can increase the capacity of working memory (reviewed by Klingberg, 2010; Morrison & Chein, 2011). Since working memory is a mental workspace used in service of ongoing cognition, enhancing working-memory capacity might have an effect on other tasks, including academic skills. Programs aimed at improving working memory can be aimed at improving strategies in order to better remember certain types of information, and as such these types of program can be seen as domain specific, and less likely to generalize to a range of other tasks (reviewed by Morrison & Chein, 2011). For example, training might be targeted at strategies to remember the steps involved to complete a math problem. Programs aimed at improving working memory can also be aimed at more general, core processes (reviewed by Morrison & Chein, 2011). These types of program tend to involve repeated practice of demanding working-memory tasks, for example presenting information in rapidly multiple modalities in tasks involving interference that minimize use of automated processes. The aim here is to improve general processes involved in working memory, with the aim that training will generalize to other skills. Examples here include Robo-Memo and CogMed, computerized working-memory training programs for children where working memory is practiced at the limits of a child's capacity (Klingberg et al., 2002).

Studies with children show that, following working-memory training, children with attention deficit–hyperactivity disorder show improvement in these skills and also generalize these new skills (Klingberg et al., 2005). However, a randomized control trial using CogMed to train working memory and reasoning in 4-year-olds showed benefits to the practiced domains but not generalization to nonpracticed domains (Bergman Nutley et al., 2011). Less promising findings came from a study training inhibition in 4- to 6-year-olds, where training resulted in improvement on only two out of three training tasks and did not generalize to nontrained inhibition tasks (Thorell, Lindqvist, Bergman Nutley, Bohlin, & Klingberg, 2009). It might be that benefits are seen most clearly in groups of children who have low skills to begin with, as in ADHD.

Studies which have more specifically looked at benefits to academic skills have reported some positive findings. One study showed that working-memory training can improve both working memory itself and mathematical reasoning, in at least the short term, though it had no impact on IQ or literacy abilities (Holmes, Gathercole, & Dunning, 2009). This is supported by the results of another study, in which a school-based working-memory training program was found to lead to gains in the trained task, an untrained visuospatial working memory task, and in mathematical skills (Witt, 2011). Another study did find benefits of working-memory training using the CogMed program daily for 5 weeks on reading comprehension but not word reading in 9–12-year-olds with special needs (Dahlin, 2010). Other researchers have cautioned that the link between executive functions and academic skills may be spurious, as most studies have not adequately controlled for possible confounds (e.g., caregiver's executive function, or many other potential unmeasured confounds, see Willoughby, Kupersmidt & Voegler-Lee, 2011). Still others have pointed out the importance of considering individual differences in response to training. For example, one study examining the effects of a video-game-like working-memory training program on untrained measures of fluid intelligence showed that only those who improved with training showed improvement on the measure of fluid intelligence that was retained 3 months later (Jaeggi, Buschkeuhl, Jonides, & Shah, 2011). These additional considerations can be evaluated in future planned studies for randomized control trials of the effects of working-memory training on academic progress (Roberts et al., 2011).

Functional imaging of the effects of working-memory training has showed increased brain activation in the fronto-parietal network (Olesen et al., 2004; Westerberg & Klingberg, 2007). The pattern indicated that changes in activity were not due to activation of additional brain areas not involved pre-training, but rather that they were due to small increases in the area of activation in the core regions (Westerberg & Klingberg, 2007). The neural bases of generalized training effects have not yet been well studied, thus the brain mechanisms whereby working-memory training affects math or reading skills are unclear.

## Complex activity-based training

A different approach to training executive functions argues that it is not necessary to directly train particular executive skills (Diamond, 2011) as in the approach described above. In this view executive functions can improve following involvement in a range of skills that engage executive functions, and particularly if they combine this with physical activity, as in activities such as dance or martial arts. A recent randomized control study of the effects of exercise on sedentary, overweight

7–11-year-olds showed dose–response benefits of exercise on executive function and mathematics achievement as well as preliminary evidence of increased bilateral prefrontal cortex activity and reduced bilateral posterior parietal cortex activity attributable to exercise (Davis et al., 2011).

## Summary and Conclusions

Executive functions include the basic skills of inhibition, working memory, and switching ability, and in adults are mediated by a brain network including prefrontal cortex, parietal cortex, and subcortical structures. There is improvement in all of these basic skills over childhood and into adolescence, with a possible qualitative change in inhibition over the period of 3–5 years and steady improvement thereafter. While most evidence suggests that the same basic brain networks as implicated in adults are also activated in children, brain networks involved in these skills still show numerous changes over development. One change is that they become less diffuse and more localized, an example being the diminishing role of the medial temporal lobe in working memory with age. Another change is that the core areas involved in the skill become more differentiated, an example being the differentiation of the representation of rules and rule switching in the ventromedial prefrontal cortex with age. In addition, several studies observed a shift in which prefrontal areas became less active with age and posterior areas played a greater role, a finding that may reflect that, even for the same level of behavioral performance, a given task may require more effort in younger participants and may require less effort and be performed more automatically in older participants.

It is easy to imagine how inhibition, working memory, and switching might all be important for successful progress in school. Studies examining links between these abilities and reading and math have found the strongest links with working memory, and some links with inhibition, but fewer links with switching. This might be because most studies focus on preschool or middle-school age, and switching abilities may be more important later in schooling for more complex math and other higher-level skills. Recent analyses have suggested that executive function might be a unitary skill in children less than 7 years, but the observation of unique prediction of reading and math by the components of executive function even in preschoolers might suggest that these skills are in fact already differentiated to some degree by this age.

Studies examining links with working memory and inhibition have found evidence both for general relations to learning, and for specific links to math and/or reading. Perhaps the strongest link observed has been that of visuospatial working memory and inhibition skills with math abilities. Most studies examining links between executive functions and reading math have focused on preadolescent children. However, frontal regions underlying executive functions continue to develop during adolescents. It has been argued that adolescence reflects a unique period in that performance can approach adult-like, and important aspects of brain circuitry are in place, but there are still immaturities that limited the flexible use of cognitive control supported by frontal areas such as error processing (reviewed by Luna, Padmanabhan, & O'Hearn, 2010). Studying links between executive function and academic skills into adolescence will thus provide a more complete picture of how this relation develops.

Interestingly, the meta-analysis of brain areas underlying children's math, reading, and executive-function abilities indicated that frontal regions are particularly important for math abilities, a finding that contrasts with studies of adults, which have focused on the intraparietal sulcus. Whether links between executive functions and math are in part mediated by common brain regions being involved in these processes remains a question for future research. Findings that activation during a visuospatial working-memory task in the intraparietal sulcus, an area also associated with both visuospatial working memory and math, uniquely predicts math skills 2 years later suggests that neuroimaging measures may be useful in identifying those at risk for slow academic progress.

Training studies suggest that executive-function skills can be trained, but there are some mixed findings as to whether training generalizes beyond trained tasks or domains. The existing work suggests that working memory may be more amenable to training than inhibitory control, though it may be that an effective program for the latter has simply not been identified. Studies showing that working-memory training is related to gains in math and reading skills are promising, and future large-scale randomized control trials will help to more robustly test this link. A better understanding of the mutual influence of these skills will be informative. The role of working-memory skills in reading and math has been described, but the finding that training affects working memory suggests that reading and math practice may in turn have an effect on working memory. There is as yet little information about the brain and cognitive mechanisms underlying such training effects, and this is a further important area for future study.

## References

Asato, M. R., Terwilliiger, R., Woo, J., & Luna, B. (2010). White matter development in adolescence: A DTI study. *Cerebral Cortex*, *20*, 2122–2131.

Baddeley, A. (1992). Working memory. *Science*, *255*, 556–559.

Beauchamp, M. H., Thompson, D. K., Howard, K., Doyle, L. W., Egan, G. F., Inder, T. E., & Anderson, P. J. (2008). Preterm infant hippocampal volumes correlate with later working memory deficits. *Brain*, *131*, 2986–2994.

Bergman Nutley, S., Soderqvist, S., Bryde, S., Thorell, B., Humphreys, K., & Klingberg, T. (2011). Gains in fluid intelligence after training non-verbal reasoning in 4-year-old children: A controlled randomized study. *Developmental Science, 14,* 591–601.

Best, J. R., & Miller, P. H. (2010). A developmental perspective on executive function. *Child Development, 81,* 1641–1660.

Bull, R., Espy, K. A., & Wiebe, S. A. (2008). Short-term memory, working memory and executive functioning in preschoolers: Longitudinal predictors of mathematical achievement at age 7 years. *Developmental Neuropsychology, 33,* 205–228.

Cain, K., Oakhill, J., & Lemmon, K. (2004). Individual differences in the inference of word meanings from context: The influence of reading comprehension, vocabulary knowledge, and memory capacity. *Journal of Educational Psychology, 96,* 671–681.

Casey, B. J., Castellanos, F. X., Giedd, J. N., Marsh, W. L., Hamburger, S. D., Schubert, A. B., Vauss, Y. C., Vaituzis, A. C., Dickstein, D. P., Sarfatti, S. E., & Rapporot, J. E. (1997). Implication of right frontostriatal circuitry in response inhibition and attention-deficit/hyperactivity disorder. *Journal of the American Academy of Child and Adolescent Psychiatry, 36,* 374–383.

Conklin, H. M., Luciana, M., Hooper, C. J., & Yarger, R. S. (2007). Working memory performance in typically developing children and adolescents: Behavioral evidence of protracted frontal lobe development. *Developmental Neuropsychology, 31,* 103–128.

Cowan, N. (2001). HYPERLINK "http://www.ncbi.nlm.nih.gov/pubmed/11515286" \t "_blank" The magical number 4 in short-term memory: a reconsideration of mental storage capacity. *Behavioral and Brain Sciences, 24*(1), 87–114; discussion 114–185.

Crone, E., Donohue, S. E., Honomichi, R., Wendelken, C., & Bunge, S. A. (2006). Brain regions mediating flexible rule use during development. *Journal of Neuroscience, 26,* 11239–11247.

Curtis, C. E., Cole, M. W., Rao, V. Y., & D'Esposito, M. (2005). Canceling planned action: An fMRI study of countermanding saccades. *Cerebral Cortex, 15,* 1281–1289.

Dahlin, K. I. E. (2010). Effects of working memory traiing on reading in children with special needs. *Reading and Writing, 24,* 479–-491.

Davidson, M. C., Amso, D., Anderson, L. C., & Diamond, A. (2006). Development of cognitive control and executive functions from 4 to 13 years: Evidence from manipulations of memory, inhibition and task switching. *Neuropsychologia, 44,* 2037–2078.

Davis, C. L., Tomporowski, P. D., McDowell, J. E., Austin, B. P., Miller, P. H., Yanasak, N. E., Allison, J. D., & Naglieri, J. A. (2011). Exercise improves executive function and achievement and alters brain activation in overweight children: A randomized controlled trial. *Health Psychology, 30,* 91–98.

DeBeni, R., Palladino, P., Pazzaglia, F., & Cornoldi, C. (1998). Increases in intrusion errors and working memory deficits of poor comprehenders. *Quarterly Journal of Experimental Psychology, 51,* 305–320.

Diamond, A. (1985). The development of the ability to use recall to guide action, as indicated by infants' performance on A-not-B. *Child Development, 56,* 868–883.

Diamond, A. (2001). Looking closely at infants' performance, and experimental procedures, in the A-not-B task. *The Behavioral and Brain Sciences, 24,* 38–41.

Diamond, A. (2011). Biological and social influences on cognitive control processes dependent on prefrontal cortex. In O. Braddick, J. Atkinson, & G. Innocenti (Eds.), *Progress in brain research* (Vol. 189, pp. 319–339). Amsterdam: Elsevier.

Dumontheil, I., & Klingberg, T. (2012). Brian activity during a visuospatial working memory task predicts arithmetical performance 2 years later. *Cerebral Cortex, 22,* 1078–1085.

Edin, F., Macoveanu, J., Olesen, P., Tegnér, J., & Klingberg, T. (2007). Stronger synaptic connectivity as a mechanism behind development of working memory-related brain activity during childhood. *Journal of Cognitive Neuroscience, 21,* 21–29.

Espy, K. A., McDiarmid, M. M., Cwik, M. F., Stalets, M. M., Hamby, A., & Senn, T. E. (2004). The contribution of executive functions to emergent mathematic skills in preschool children. *Developmental Neuropsychology, 26,* 445–464.

Finn, A. S., Sheridan, M. A., Kam, C. L., Hinshaw, S., & D'Esposito, M. (2010). Longitudinal evidence for functional specialization of the neural circuit supporting working memory in the human brain. *Journal of Neuroscience, 30,* 11062–11067.

Fray, P. J., Robbins, T. W., & Sahakian, B. J. (1996). Neuropsychiatric applications of CANTAB. *International Journal of Geriatric Psychiatry, 11,* 329–336.

Gathercole, S. J., & Alloway, T. P. (2006). Short-term and working memory impairments in neurodevelopmental disorders: A diagnosis and remedial support. *Journal of Child Psychology and Psychiatry, 47,* 4–15.

Gathercole, S. E., Brown, L., & Pickering, S. J. (2003). Working memory assessments at school entry as longitudinal predictors of National Curriculum attainment levels. *Educational and Child Psychology, 20,* 109–122.

Gathercole, S. E., Pickering, S. J., Ambridge, B., & Wearing, H. (2004a). The structure of working memory from 4 to 15 years of age. *Developmental Psychology, 40,* 177–190.

Gathercole, S. E., Pickering, S. J., Knight, C., & Stegman, Z. (2004b).Working memory skills and educational attainment: Evidence from National Curriculum assessments at 7 and 14 years of age. *Applied Cognitive Psychology, 18,* 1–16.

Gerstadt, C. L., Hong, Y. J., & Diamond, A. (2004). The relationship between cognition and action: Performance of children 3½ to 7 years old on a Stroop-like day–night test. *Cognition, 53,* 129–153.

Henry, L. A., & MacLean, M. (2003). Relationships between working memory, expressive vocabulary and arithmetical reasoning in children with and without intellectual disabilities. *Educational and Child Psychology, 20,* 51–64.

Holmes, J., & Adams, J. W. (2006). Working memory and children's mathematical skills: Implications for mathematical development and mathematics curricula. *Educational Psychology, 26,* 339–366.

Holmes, J., Gathercole, S. E., & Dunning, D. L. (2009). Adaptive training leads to sustained enhancement of poor working memory in children. *Developmental Science, 12,* F9–15.

Holmes, J., Gathercole, S. E., & Dunning, D. L. (2010). Poor working memory: Impact and interventions. *Advances in Child Development and Behavior, 39,* 1–43.

Houdé, O., Rossi, S., Lubin, A., & Joliot, M. (2010). Mapping numerical processing, reading and executive functions in the developing brain: An fMRI meta-analysis of 52 studies including 842 children. *Developmental Science, 13,* 876–885.

Hughes, C. (1998). Executive function in preschoolers: Links with theory of mind and verbal ability. *British Journal of Developmental Psychology, 16,* 233–253.

Hughes, C., Ensor, R., Wilson, A., & Graham, A. (2009). Tracking executive function across the transition to school: A latent variable approach. *Developmental Neuropsychology, 35,* 20–36.

Huizinga, M., Dolan, C. V., & van der Molen, M. W. (2006). Age-related change in executive function: Developmental trends and a latent variable analysis. *Neuropsychologia, 44,* 2017–2036.

Huttenlocher, P. R., & Dabholkar, A. S. (1997). Regional differences in synaptogenesis in human cerebral cortex. *Journal of Comparative Neurology, 387,* 167–178.

Hwang, K., Velanova, K., & Luna, B. (2010). Strengthening of top-down frontal cognitive control networks underlying the development of inhibitory control: A functional magnetic resonance imaging effective connectivity study. *Journal of Neuroscience, 30,* 15535–15545.

Jacobs, R., Harvey, A. S., & Anderson, V. (2011). Are executive skills primarily mediated by the prefrontal cortex in childhood? Examination of focal brain lesions in childhood. *Cortex, 47,* 808–824.

Jaeggi, S. M., Buschkuehl, M., Jonides, J., & Shah, P. (2011). Short- and long term benefits of cognitive training. *Proceedings of the National Academy of Sciences of the United States of America, 108,* 10081–10086.

Jarvis, H. L., & Gathercole, S. J. (2003). Verbal and non-verbal working memory achievements on National Curriculum tests at 11 and 14 years of age. *Educational and Child Psychology, 20,* 123–140.

Johnstone, S. J., Dimoska, A., Smith, J. L., Barry, R. J., Pleffer, C. B., Chiswick, D., & Clarke, A. R. (2007). The development of stop signal and Go/Nogo response inhibition in children aged 7–12 years: Performance and event-related potential indices. *International Journal of Psychophysiology, 63,* 25–38.

Jonkmans, L. M., Lansbergen, M., & Stauder, J. E. (2003). Developmental differences in behavioral and event-related brain responses associated with response preparation and inhibition in a go/nogo task. *Psychophysiology, 40,* 752–761.

Kaldy, Z., & Sigala, N. (2004). The neural mechanisms of object working memory: What is where in the infant brain? *Neuroscience and Biobehavioral Reviews, 28,* 113–121.

Kaufman, J., Csibra, G., & Johnson, M. H. (2003). Representing occluded objects in the human infant brain. *Proceedings of the Royal Society B: Biological Sciences, 270*(Suppl. 2), S140–143.

Kaufman, J., Csibra, G., & Johnson, M. H. (2005). Oscillatory activity in the infant brain reflects object maintenance. *Proceedings of the National Academy of Sciences of the United States of America, 102,* 15271–15274.

Klingberg, T. (2006) Development of a superior frontal–intraparietal network for visuospatial working memory. *Neuropsychologia, 44,* 2171–2177.

Klingberg, T. (2010). Training and plasticity of working memory. *Trends in Cognitive Sciences, 14,* 317–324.

Klingberg, T., Fernell, E., Olesen, P. J., Johnson, M., Gustafsson, P., Dahlstrom, K., Gillberg, C. G., Forssberg, H., & Westerberg, H. (2005). Computerized training of working memory in children with ADHD – a randomized controlled trial. *Journal of the American Academy of Child and Adolescent Psychiatry, 44*, 177–186.

Klingberg, T., Forssberg, H., & Westerberg, H. (2002). Increased brain activity in frontal and parietal cortex underlies the development of visuospatial working memory capacity during childhood. *Journal of Cognitive Neuroscience, 14*, 1–10.

Kyttälä, M., Aunio, P., Lehto, J. E., & Luit, J. V. (2003). Visuospatial working memory and early numeracy. *Educational and Child Psychology, 20*, 65–76.

Luciana, M., & Nelson, C. A. (1998). The functional emergence of prefrontally-guided working memory systems in four-to-eight-year-old children. *Neuropsychologia, 36*, 273–293.

Luciana, M., & Nelson, C. A. (2002). Assessment of neuropsychological function through the use of the Cambridge Neuropsychological Testing Automated Battery: Performance in 4- to 12 year old children. *Developmental Neuropsychology, 22*, 595–624.

Luna, B., Padmanabhan, A., & O'Hearn, K. (2010). What has fMRI told us about the development of cognitive control through adolescence? *Brain and Cognition, 72*, 101–113.

Luna, B., Velanova, K., & Geier, C. F. (2008). Development of eye movement control. *Brain and Cognition, 68*, 293–308.

McVay, J. C., & Kane, M. J. (2011). Why does working memory capacity predict variation in reading comprehension? On the influence of mind wandering and executive attention. *Journal of Experimental Psychology – General, 141*, 302–320.

Miyake, A., Friedman, N., Emerson, M., Witazki, A., Howerter, A., & Wager, T. (2000). The unity and diversity of executive functions and their contributions to complex "frontal lobe" tasks: A latent variable analysis. *Cognitive Psychology, 41*, 49–100.

Monette, S., Bigras, M., & Guay, M.-C. (2011). The role of executive functions in school achievement at the end of Grade 1. *Journal of Experimental Child Psychology, 109*, 158–173.

Moriguchi, Y., & Hiraki, K. (2009). Neural origin of cognitive shifting in young children. *Proceedings of the National Academy of Sciences of the United States of America, 106*, 6017–6021.

Morrison, A., & Chein, M. H. (2011). Does working memory training work? The promise and challenges of enhancing cognition by training working memory. *Psychonomic Bulletin and Review, 18*, 46–60.

Morton, J. B., Bosma, R., & Ansari, D. (2009). Age-related changes in brain activation associated with dimensional shifts of attention: An fMRI study. *NeuroImage, 46*, 249–256.

Nagy, Z., Westerberg, J., & Klingberg, T. (2004). Maturation of white matter is associated with development of cognitive functions during childhood. *Journal of Cognitive Neuroscience, 16*, 1227–1233.

Olesen, P. J., Nagy, Z., Westerberg, H., & Klingberg, T. (2003). Combined analysis of DTI and fMRI data reveals a joint maturation of white and grey matter in a fronto-parietal network. *Brain Research. Cognitive Brain Research, 18*, 48–57.

Olesen, P. J., Westerberg, H., & Klingberg, T. (2004). Increased prefrontal and parietal activity after training of working memory. *Nature Neuroscience, 7*, 75–79.

Passolunghi, M. C., Cornoldi, C., & De Liberto, S. (1999). Working memory and intrusions of irrelevant information in a group of specific poor problem solvers. *Memory and Cognition, 27*, 779–790.

Roberts, G.,, Quach,, J., Gold, L., Anderson, P., Rickards, F.,Mensah, F., Ainley, J.,Gathercole, S., & Wake,, M. (2011). HYPERLINK "http://www.ncbi.nlm.nih.gov/pubmed/21682929" \t "_blank" Can improving working memory prevent academic difficulties? A school based randomised controlled trial. . BMC Pediatrics, 57. DOI: 10.1186/1471-2431-11-57

Rose, S. A., Feldman, J. F., & Jankowski, J. J. (2011). Modeling a cascade of effects: The role of speed and executive functioning on preterm/fullterm differences in academic achievement. *Developmental Science, 14*, 1161–1175.

Rubia, K., Smith, A. B., Brammer, M. J., & Taylor, E. (2003). Right inferior prefrontal cortex mediates response inhibition while mesial prefrontal cortex is responsible for error detection. *NeuroImage, 20*, 351–358.

Rubia, K., Smith A. B., Woolley, J., Nosarti, C., Heyman, I., Taylor, E., & Brammer, M. (2006). Progressive increase of frontostriatal brain activation from childhood to adulthood during event-related tasks of cognitive control. *Human Brain Mapping, 27*, 973–993.

Senn, T. E., Espy, K. A., & Kaufmann, P. M. (2004). Using path analysis to understand executive function organization in preschool children. *Developmental Neuropsychology, 26*, 445–464.

Shallice, T., & Burgess, P. (1996). The domain of supervisory processes and temporal organization of behaviour. *Philosophical Transactions of the Royal Society B: Biological Sciences, 351*, 1405–1411.

St. Clair-Thompson, H. L., & Gathercole, S. E. (2006). Executive functions and achievements in school: Shifting updating inhibition and working memory. *Quarterly Journal of Experimental Psychology, 59*, 745–759.

Swanson, H. L., Howard, C., & Saez, L. (2006). Do different components of working memory underlie different subgroups of reading disabilities? *Journal of Learning Disabilities, 39*, 252–268.

Thorell, L. B., Lindqvist, S., Bergman Nutley, S., Bohlin, G., & Klingberg, T. (2009). Training and transfer of executive functions in preschool children. *Developmental Science, 12*, 106–113.

Van Bers, B. M., Visser, I., van Schijndel, T. J., Mandell, D. J., & Raijmakers, M. E. (2011). The dynamics of development on the Dimensional Change Card Sorting Task. *Developmental Science, 14*, 960–971.

Velanova, K., Wheeler, M. E., & Luna, B. (2009). The maturation of task set-related activation supports late developmental improvements in inhibitory control. *Journal of Neuroscience, 29*, 12558–12567.

Westerberg, H., Hirvikoski, T., Forssberg, H., & Klingberg, T. (2004). Visuo-spatial working memory span: A sensitive measure of cognitive deficits in children with ADHD. *Child Neuropsychology, 10*, 155–161.

Westerberg, H., & Klingberg, T. (2007). Changes in cortical activity after working memory training – a single subject analysis. *Physiology and Behavior, 92*, 186–192.

Wiebe, S. A., Sheffield, T., Nelson, J. M., Clark, C. A., Chevalier, N., & Espy, K. A. (2011). The structure of executive function in 3-year-olds. *Journal of Experimental Child Psychology, 108,* 436–452.

Willoughby, M. T., Kupersmidt, J. B., & Voegler-Lee, M. E. (2011). Is preschool executive function causally related to academic achievement? *Child Neuropsychology, 18*(1), 79–91.

Witt, M. (2011). School based working memory training: Preliminary finding of improvement in children's mathematical performance. *Advances in Cognitive Psychology, 7,* 7–15.

Zelazo, P. D. (2006). The Dimensional Change Card Sort (DCCS): A method of assessing executive function in children. *Nature Protocols, 1,* 297–301.

## Further Reading

Best, J. R., & Miller, P. H. (2010). A developmental perspective on executive function. *Child Development, 81,* 1641–1660.

Diamond, A., & Lee, K. (2011). Interventions shown to aid executive function development in children 4 to 12 years old. *Science, 333,* 959–964.

Dumontheil, I., & Klingberg, T. (2012). Brain activity during a visuospatial working memory task predicts arithmetical performance 2 years later. *Cerebral Cortex, 22,* 1078–1085.

Houdé, O., Rossi, S., Lubin, A., & Joilot, M. (2010). Mapping numerical processing, reading and executive function in the developing brain: An fMRI meta-analysis of 52 studies including 842 children. *Developmental Science, 13,* 876–885.

# Afterword

## John T. Bruer

### Introduction

In 1997 I wrote "Education and the brain: A bridge too far" (Bruer, 1997, hereafter "Bridge"). The article was highly critical of then current claims about the relevance of neuroscience to education. Since then I have often been asked if subsequent developments in areas such as educational neuroscience have caused me to modify the conclusions expressed in "Bridge". The editors of this book suggested that I reflect on my earlier views in light of the research reviewed in this volume. Although there has been progress in the field of developmental cognitive neuroscience, developments over the past 15 years give me no reason to modify my earlier conclusions. In particular, I remain skeptical of the claim that educational neuroscience is now capable of building a direct bridge from neuroscience to education.

First, let us be clear about what I claimed in "Bridge". The article was a response to misconceptions spawned by a public relations effort to encourage United States Government support for early childhood education programs. The campaign's message derived its appeal from oversimplifying and misappropriating well-known results from developmental neurophysiology: the phenomenon of developmental synaptogenesis and pruning, the existence of critical periods in development (especially critical periods in the development of the visual system), and the effects of enriched environments on synaptic density in rodent brain. The distilled message of this campaign was that birth to three, the period of rapid developmental synaptogenesis, was *the* critical period for brain development, during which learning was

*Educational Neuroscience*, First Edition. Edited by Denis Mareschal, Brian Butterworth and Andy Tolmie.
© 2014 John Wiley & Sons, Ltd. Published 2014 by John Wiley & Sons, Ltd.

easiest and during which enrichment would have permanent, irreversible effects. "Bridge" and, at much greater length, *The Myth of the First Three Years* (Bruer, 1999) argued that the neuroscience did not support such strong conclusions about the importance of early childhood education. This critique has been well received and endorsed by most neuroscientists and psychologists, although psychiatrists in the attachment theory tradition tend to remain unconvinced (Bruer, 2011). So, the first claim I made in "Bridge" was that neuroscience, understood as developmental neurophysiology, had little, if any, relevance to education. This remains true today. However, that is not to say that there might be paths, direct or indirect, from other areas of neuroscience to education.

In fact, I suggested that cognitive neuroscience was the most likely area of brain research to contribute to improved education and instruction. Cognitive neuroscience attempts to map cognitive functions onto their neural correlates. When cognitive neuroscience first emerged in the early 1980s, one rationale for pursuing this work was the conviction that behavioral data and neural data together might mutually constrain theory development on both the cognitive and systems neuroscience levels. Cognitive psychology has a long history of using behavioral data to develop functional models of mental processes. For example, 40 years of research resulted in models of word recognition, selective attention, number comparison, and mental arithmetic. These models provide insights for developing successful research-based educational interventions (Bruer, 1993; McGilly, 1994). The promise of cognitive neuroscience, that is, using neural data in combination with behavioral data in hypothesis testing, was that brain-based data could contribute to the development and refinement of cognitive models, which in turn could serve as a basis for instructional design. I still believe that this two-bridge solution is the most likely one. The majority of work reviewed in this volume is basic developmental cognitive neuroscience. It is only by down-playing the importance of functional models and experimental tasks based on these functional models that it appears at all plausible that neuroimaging will allow the construction of a direct connection from neuroscience to education.

## What Has Changed for the Better?

One positive change is that the work reviewed here is the result of a serious research program. As evident from the chapters, educational neuroscientists are engaged in varied and sophisticated studies investigating hypotheses about brain maturation, brain plasticity, localization of function, and the possible relevance of these phenomena to subject matter learning, as well as to social and emotional development. Themes from the mid-1990s appear but are treated as scientific claims subject to revision and modification, rather than as dogmas of child development.

Developmental synaptogenesis is discussed in Chapters 6, 8, 10, and 12. As stated most clearly in Chapter 6, developmental synaptogenesis occurs, it cannot be reliably linked to behaviors, and there is considerable individual variability; however, any temporal correlations with behaviors should be noted. Chapter 10 notes that there is currently no direct way using functional magnetic resonance imaging (fMRI) to test the relationship between synaptic number, synaptic activity, and neural activity. The claim that the time of rapid synapse growth is a period of heightened brain plasticity, during which learning is easier or more efficient, does appear (Chapter 8). This remains pure speculation. Unless evidence can be cited in support of the claim, educational neuroscientists should stop making it.

The term "critical period" does not occur in the text of any of the subject matter chapters (Chapters 6–12). The authors of three chapters (Chapters 6, 10, and 11) use "sensitive period", and as one would expect it occurs most often in the chapter on language development (Chapter 6). In Chapter 10 "sensitive period" is given broad definitions: "a time of major opportunity for teaching and learning" or "periods of development in which the brain is particularly susceptible to certain environmental stimuli and particularly efficient at processing and assimilating new information – at learning." One can contrast this use of "sensitive period" with that of "critical period" in the mid-1990s as a biologically determined window of opportunity that slams shut. At the time I wrote "Bridge", second-language learning was the prime example of a critical period that educators were not exploiting. There is no doubt that with some aspects of second-language learning, such as phonology, earlier is better. The behavioral research favorably reviewed in Chapter 6 suggests that with appropriate instruction a second language can be acquired at any age, a substantial change from the view expressed in the 1990s.

More importantly, this broader understanding of "sensitive period" allows educational neuroscientists to connect their research more closely to one of the major findings of cognitive psychology: Ease and rate of learning is highly dependent on students' prior knowledge, a finding highlighted in the volume's introduction. One troubling lacuna in educational neuroscience, with its emphasis on when the brain might be sufficiently mature to learn XYZ or what brain area XYZ activates, is the lack of attention to the importance of background knowledge in learning. Background knowledge, prior knowledge, and rates of learning are not mentioned in the volume. If a sensitive period is period is a time when learning is optimal, then the sensitive period for learning Latin II is probably shortly after mastering Latin I, no matter the age of the student. Cognitive psychology has identified this phenomenon and made some progress toward explaining it, based primarily on associationist theories of memory. Here the work of computational modelers, as described in Chapter 3, might make a useful contribution to educational neuroscience by developing models, either symbolic or subsymbolic, that might lead to experimental tasks that could be used in the design of imaging experiments. One would hope that the insights provided by these models would go deeper than Hebbian hand-waving about neural firing and wiring.

Enriched environments and environmental deprivation make only a cameo appearance in Chapter 6. Environmental deprivation is contrasted with genetic factors that might cause language deficits. The author conceptualizes environmental deprivation as being either sensory (attributable to congenital problems) or social. Overall, the discussion of deprivation and enrichment portrays a generally positive picture of what might be done to address problems in language development. Gone from this discussion is the assumption that compensatory experiences only work before a certain age or during some optimal period in development. Environmental deprivation of the social variety is linked with socioeconomic status (SES). I am uncomfortable with this connection. One problem with using SES as an independent variable is discussed in Chapter 5 on methodology in educational research. SES is at best a proxy for numerous other causal factors that are more directly related to social development and school readiness. If so, relying on SES as an independent variable, while it may be a reliable predictor, is not contributing to an understanding of the causal mechanisms affecting language or social development. We use SES as a proxy because the data are relatively easy to acquire. Unless one is doing economic research, it may be time to scrap this proxy in favor of variables that have more causal, and remedial, value. A second problem with using SES as an independent variable is a normative one. It can conceal value judgments. It implies (or assumes) that economic disadvantage correlates with cultural disadvantage. This normative overtone can lead us to characterize the differences between low-SES children and middle-class children on entering formal education as *inequalities* (as stated in Chapter 6) in experience rather than as differences in experience. Different norms of language use prevail in different social and cultural communities, particularly immigrant and/or segregated communities. These differences are inequalities only when middle-class norms are given privileged status. There is no doubt that school is a paradigmatic middle-class environment. Some children are prepared for it; others need help to acculturate. Rather than providing enriched experience to the deprived, I would rather think of it as providing supplementary experience to those who arrive at school with different background experience and knowledge.

The treatment of synaptogenesis, sensitive periods and enriched environment presented in this volume is critical and informed. They present issues and problems within a larger research program, not talking points in a public relations campaign.

## The Methods of Educational Neuroscience

The breadth and depth of the methodology chapters (Chapters 2–5) illustrate the sophistication of the tools available to pursue research in educational neuroscience, as well as the pitfalls threatening the unwary. Judging from the methodology chapters on neuroimaging, computational modeling, genetics, and psychology of education, it will not be easy working in this field. The methodological challenges in each of these areas are daunting. Neuroimaging is a powerful tool but, despite the tsunami of imaging studies, it remains a difficult tool to master. There are many nuances involved in the statistical treatment of data, study design, and interpretation. Even the most sophisticated users and eminent practitioners in the field can be caught out by the subtleties of this technology. A recent example is the discovery of movement artifacts in resting-state fMRI that have called into question results on functional connectivity (Power, Barnes, Snyder, Schlaggar, & Petersen, 2012).

Computational modeling is another powerful tool; however, technical issues aside, models depend on one's understanding of the phenomena or behavior to be modeled. In the area of reading, there are computational models of both dual route (Coltheart, Rastle, Perry, Langdon, & Ziegler, 2001) and connectionist (Harm & Seidenberg, 2004) theories of word recognition. Both have been used in the design of imaging experiments and lead to interpretable results. Indeed, imaging results reported by Fiez, Balota, Raichle, and Petersen (1999) suggest that neither theory is consistent with their results. However, on a more fundamental level, there is continued debate on whether either model adequately accounts for the behavioral data (Coltheart, Curtix, Atkins, & Haller, 1993).

Genetics presents additional challenges. There have been countless failed claims of finding the gene for alcoholism, schizophrenia, depression, dyslexia, etc. As one neuroscientist recently commented, it is currently next to impossible to convince colleagues about particular effects of single genes. Where we do have adequate genetic explanations, for example Huntington's chorea and sickle cell anemia, we still lack adequate therapeutic interventions. Furthermore, genetics presents as many statistical challenges to practitioners as does neuroimaging.

Of the methodology chapters, the chapter on methods in the psychology of education was the most sobering. Designing studies of educational interventions and measuring their outcomes is exceedingly important for educational neuroscience, because it is these behavioral outcomes that the educational neuroscientist is attempting to explain and elucidate at the neural level. If the behaviors and causal factors generating these behaviors are not correctly and reliably measured, one would be attempting to explain spurious or nonexistent causal mechanisms. One does not have to look long in the psychology of education literature to find a study that violates one of the precepts set in Chapter 5. In reading studies cited in this volume, there are more than a few multiple regression models that do not have at least 15 cases per regressor or studies that conflate statistical significance with practical significance. The methodological sophistication required to work in and to interpret the work in educational neuroscience is no better exemplified than in the Hoeft et al. (2011) article on predicting long-term outcomes in dyslexia, cited in the literacy chapter.

Thus working in this methodologically diverse field and training young investigators for careers in it is a major undertaking. The research is difficult and the stakes are relatively high, particularly when scientists are asked for, or volunteer, research-based advice on educational policy and practice. Maybe one of the most important traits to encourage among young researchers in this field is to be critical not only of others' work, but also their own. Again the self-critique of functional connectivity results by Power et al. serves as a paradigm.

## Educational Neuroscience and Subject Matter

The subject matter chapters (Chapters 6–12) review some of the most important work in cognitive psychology and cognitive neuroscience published over the last two decades. A critical familiarity with this work is essential for anyone working in this field. I would characterize most of the work presented here as developmental cognitive neuroscience, albeit developmental cognitive neuroscience with potential applications to learning. On a spectrum from basic research to applied, I would place the work presented here as well toward the basic end, with some movement toward clinical applications in the diagnosis of learning disabilities. Based on my impressions of the work reported here, the most likely payoff of this research will be in the area of special education, addressing the needs of children suffering from special language impairment, dyslexia, dyscalculia, attentional deficit and related executive function disorders, and social and emotional disorders. Although there are allusions to eventual applications of these basic findings to instructional design, there are few, if any, examples of how this work has contributed to classroom instruction, which one would think is the goal and purpose of educational neuroscience. One should note that work referenced in the subject matter chapters is a mix of cognitive psychology and cognitive neuroscience. However, there is little indication that the inclusion of neural data is contributing much to the advancement of instruction and pedagogy. We know a great deal about the importance of phonological awareness in early reading. Indeed the imaging studies of the Shaywitz group, especially the study showing cortical changes in the brains of dyslexics after receiving phonological training, presupposes and exploits a long tradition of neuropsychological and cognitive psychological research on word recognition. We should also note that word recognition is necessary for reading, but it is not the only cognitive skill required to comprehend a text. Cognitive psychology also tells us a great deal about number processing, how the skill of number comparison is fundamental if children are to construct effective strategies for solving simple mental arithmetic problems, and the differences in solving such problems when objects are present as opposed to when they must be represented mentally (see the discussion of work by Siegler, Case, and Griffin in Bruer, 1993, and McGilly 1994) Recent work on teaching attentional skills (Posner & Rothbart, 2006), work not discussed in this volume, is also sometimes presented as a contribution of brain science to education. However, close scrutiny shows that the intervention itself is based on a cognitive theory of attention and the application of experimental measures of selective attention in a computer-based teaching tool. There may be changes in the event-related potential (ERP) responses in children after engaging with the teaching tool, but those changes are irrelevant to the effectiveness of the intervention in improving attentional skills and possibly raising IQs as the authors claim. One reasonable reply to these observations is to say that educational neuroscience remains at an early stage of development, where basic research predominates, and that these basic advances will one day lead to improved instructional strategies for all students, not just those suffering from learning disorders.

## One Bridge or Two: What Difference Does It Make?

As should be obvious by now, I remain an advocate of the two bridge solution to linking education to (cognitive) neuroscience, counter to one of the expressed goals of educational neuroscience. As stated in the Introduction, one of the goals of educational neuroscience is to construct a direct bridge from brain science and education. Advances in neuroimaging technology are seen as a new tool that will make this bridge a reality. I remain skeptical and will try, briefly, to explain why. In short, cognitive psychology and functional imaging (i.e., cognitive neuroscientific) research are highly interdependent. Overlooking the interdependence could be detrimental to the development of educational neuroscience.

The technological breakthrough that transformed cognitive neuroscience from a cottage industry to an international conglomerate was the development of positron emission tomography and subsequently fMRI. With the emergence of these technologies, one might even argue that cognitive neuroscience has become synonymous with functional imaging.

The first sentence of the abstract of Posner, Petersen, Fox and Raichle (1988) was "The human brain localizes mental operations of the kind posited by cognitive theories" (p. 1627). We might take this statement as the working hypothesis of cognitive neuroscience. Using examples from word recognition and attention, Posner and his co-authors illustrated how imaging studies could provide a source of direct evidence to allow cognitive neuroscientists to test hypotheses about the localization of cognitive processes. The insight was about the localization of cognitive processes, not the discovery of cognitive processes. The imaging work presupposed a theory of the cognitive processes involved and the existence of well-understood tasks that tapped these processes. The dependence or interdependence of functional imaging studies and cognitive psychology was further underscored by Posner and Raichle (1994). They argued that, if the challenge is to understand at deeper levels the actual mental operations implemented in brain areas, then the cognitive models used in imaging studies must be continually refined.

This interrelationship was a new development. Neural data became relevant to understanding cognition when neuroscientists began making connections between their measurements and prevailing theories of cognition. For example, Wurtz and Goldberg (1972) had observed enhanced neural responses to visual stimuli under certain experimental conditions in non-human primates. They interpreted these responses in terms of prevailing psychological theories of selective attention. They wrote: "We suggest that this enhancement of response in many neurons is the effect of the mechanism which on the psychological level is the phenomenon of attention" (p. 574). Likewise, the work of Hillyard, Hink, Schwent and Picton (1973) was one of the first ERP papers to interpret ERP components in terms of cognitive psychological theories. They interpreted the $N_1$ and $P_3$ components of the waveforms found in dichotic listening studies as "corresponding closely to the 'stimulus set' and 'response set' modes of attention, respectively" (p. 179), as described by the early selection theorists. Once this connection was made and further substantiated, neural data became relevant to testing cognitive theories about selective attention.

In one of the first imaging studies that tested theories of word recognition, Petersen, Fox, Posner, Mintun, and Raichle (1988) showed using tasks designed to activate different codes posited by cognitive models of lexical processing that the prevailing model in clinical neurology, the Wenicke–Geschwind model (Geschwind, 1979), could not account for the imaging results.

There is no better example of the dependence of imaging studies on underlying cognitive theories than the highly cited work of the Shaywitz group (e.g., Shaywitz et al., 2002, 2004, 1998). The results of these studies are well known. However, all these studies used a task hierarchy to isolate differences in phonological activations based on the work of Castles and Coltheart (1993) and Stanovich and Siegal (1994). This behavioral work to refine methods to identify subtypes of dyslexia was based on the assumption that "that the search for subtypes [of dyslexia] should proceed from psychological mechanisms that closely underpin the word recognition process."

The centrality of cognitive or functional models to educational neuroscience is evident in all of the subject matter chapters of this book. All the chapters refer to neural correlates, neural bases, or neural mechanisms of pre-defined psychological constructs. In addition to the word recognition models that are discussed in the literacy chapter, the following occur: Chapter 6, neural phenomena associated with selective attention and auditory processing; Chapter 8, neural phenomena associated with distance effects, the magnitude representation, and the spatial–numerical association of response codes effect; Chapter 9, neural mechanisms of analogical transfer; Chapter 10, neural phenomena associated with joint attention, gaze perception, face processing, and attribution of mental states; Chapter 12, neural correlates of executive functions and neural mechanisms of working memory. Chapter 11 refers to the neural correlates of substance abuse, where substance abuse seems to be presented as an unanalyzed behavior. So described, this research program would appear to be as ill defined and unpromising as looking for the neural correlates of playing chess. However, much of the work on substance abuse and impulsive behavior utilizes a task developed by psychologists, the stop signal reaction time task, a laboratory task for measuring inhibitory control (for an interesting example see Whelan et al., 2012).

Before leaving this topic, it would be helpful to the naïve reader if educational neuroscientists would define terms such as *neural correlate, neural basis, associated neural phenomena,* and *neural mechanism.* These terms appear to be used interchangeably. However, there would seem to be a substantial difference between a neural correlate that might serve as a predictive measure and a neural mechanism that would have some explanatory value. If there are differences in the kind or strength of evidence that support claims about a neural correlate versus a neural mechanism, it would be very useful to know what they are. If there are no such differences, educational neuroscientists might opt for the less loaded *neural correlate* over *neural mechanism.*

## Neuroprognosis

One of the more interesting developments discussed in this book is the "neuroprognosis" of learning problems. The idea is to use neural measures to supplement or supplant behavioral measures to predict future learning problems and learning trajectories. The neural measures are either ERPs or fMRI images. The Introduction and several subject matter chapters suggest that these prognostic studies are examples of a direct link between neuroscience and education.

First, let us look at the prognostic ERP studies cited in the volume. Again, the results of these studies are well known or can be read in the chapters above. Here, I only want to highlight the importance of giving the ERP components a psychological, functional interpretation, as Hillyard first did in the early 1970s. Pihko et al. (1999) interpreted the ERPs generated in their study as indicators of automatic stimulus change detection. Lyttinen et al. (2001) reports on the use of auditory ERPs to identify innate deficits in auditory cognition, speech perception, or categorical perception of speech in six-month-old infants. The pattern of ERP responses implied that children afflicted with dyslexia have an innate deficit in auditory perception. Molfese, Molfese, and Modgline (2001) used ERP components interpreted as measures of speech perception as independent variables in a regression model to identify which foundational skills, as well as demographic and social variables, predict later reading ability.

Maurer et al. (2009) present one of the more interesting discussions of the importance of understanding the functional significance of ERPs in predicting reading ability. This study reports that adding ERP measures to behavioral measures increases the variance accounted for in a regression model of reading ability by between 7 and 20% depending on the grade level assessed. The specific ERPs were late mismatch negativities (MMNs), which they call lMMNs, to tones and phonemes. However, as they state, the functional role of the lMMN for auditory processing is not fully understood. They suggest it may indicate interactions between preattentive and attentional mismatch processing following the MMN and may relate to preattentive processing of sound change or attentional reorienting. Here we are deep in the domain of cognitive constructs. Maurer et al. (2009) state the interesting research question quite elegantly: "Given the long-term predictive power for reading acquisition, clarifying the *functional* contribution of the lMMN to speech processing may also further characterize the nature of the processing deficits contributing to dyslexia and their neurobiological signature" (p. 346, my italics). Understanding the functional significance of the ERP might render it explanatory, rather than merely predictive.

Hoeft et al. (2011) present another compelling example of what cognitive neuroscience might contribute to neuroprognosis for dyslexia. They found that brain activation as generated by a rhyming task predicted with 90% accuracy which dyslexics would improve in reading accuracy 2.5 years later, although none of the behavioral measures employed in the study could identify this subgroup of dyslexic children. I want to focus only on the authors' discussion of the task they used in gathering the relevant imaging data. While in the scanner, children in the study were asked to respond with a button press to whether or not two printed words rhymed. Brain activations while doing the task were contrasted with activations while the children rested in the scanner. They acknowledge, in their discussion, that this is a relatively crude task. They also acknowledge that their result depends on this rhyming task. This rather simple task, the authors note, includes many reading processes, as can be gathered from the above discussions of the Shaywitz work. Rhyming occurred well up the hierarchy in the Shaywitz studies. Hoeft et al. state that it is unknown whether a more precise task derived from our current theory of work recognition would increase or decrease the predictive accuracy of their model. The interdependence of cognitive models and tasks derived from them with functional neuroimaging studies simply does not go away.

On a somewhat different note, Hoeft et al. further argue that their study illustrates that fMRI is not just a basic research tool, but that it can contribute to predicting future learning trajectories for dyslexics. This is likely to be true. The question is how will we use fMRI and fMRI data? One approach would be to develop a diagnostic protocol based on the Hoeft et al. study for imaging children at risk for dyslexia. Another, possibly more cost-effective, approach would be to use the results of imaging studies such as these to identify more specific and more sensitive behavioral measures. The former approach looks on imaging technology as the magic bullet. The latter approach recognizes the importance of continued refinement of our theories of mental processes as urged by Posner and Raichle (1994), if we are to fully exploit the imaging technology.

There is also a tendency in the reporting of these studies to diminish the importance of behavioral measures (even though the studies depend on them). For example, Chapter 7 describes these studies as having "successfully predicted reading performance based on patterns of cortical activation…." Hoeft et al. (2011) describe their study as well as that of Maurer et al. (2009) as suggesting "that brain measures may already better predict long-term outcomes in reading development than available behavioral measures" (p. 364). Hoeft et al. did not consider all behavioral measures, although their claim may hold for the measures they did examine. However, Maurer et al. (2009) and a similar study, Dumontheil and Klinberg (2011), do not show the predictive superiority of brain measures. Maurer et al. (2009) showed that when ERP data generated by a well-defined cognitive task were included as an independent variable in regression models already including behavioral measures, the neural data accounted for statistically significant increases in the variance accounted for by the model. Similarly, Dumontheil and Klinberg (2011) showed that adding a measure of activation level in left interparietal sulcus generated in response to a working memory task improved the predictive power of regression models and a discriminant function for children's arithmetical performance two years later. The regression models include both behavioral and neural measures as independent variables. Setting aside the question of whether the statistically significant increases associated with the brain measures have practical significance, these studies do not support a claim that brain measures alone already predict long-term outcomes better than available behavioral measures.

## Conclusion

For the reasons presented in these last two sections, I think it unlikely that neuroimaging technologies will enable us to build a direct bridge from neuro-science to education. Using brain imaging technology to understand the functional neurophysiology of memory, language, reading, math, science, executive function, and social–emotional development requires functional models of those phenomena, models of the kind provided by psychological research and task analysis characteristic of cognitive psychology. Cognitive neuroscience still seems the most likely link between brain and education, and if so cognitive psychology will remain central to the enterprise. We have to look forward to more imaging studies that, as Steve Petersen says, "close the loop," that is, where imaging data provide insights that allow us to improve the functional models.

More generally, this book provides a comprehensive survey of current work in educational neuroscience. It presents a serious and difficult research program, the results of which might eventually reach from basic science to clinical studies to classroom applications. Scientists and educators thinking about the brain and learning have overcome the simplicities of the mid-1990s. They are engaged on a wide research front that is attempting to investigate the relevance of (cognitive) neuroscience to education. Where it will lead, no one knows. This is part of the excitement of being involved in it.

Although progress has been made since the 1990s, educational neuroscience might still be suffering from the unfortunate hyperbole and unrealistic expecta-tions for brain science that were widely promulgated in the mid-1990s. I see two issues. One issue is the prominence given to brain imaging. Brain imaging is a powerful tool and brain images are compelling visual representations of highly processed experimental data. However, as I have tried to argue at least in the field of educational neuroscience brain imaging, cognitive models, and careful task analysis remain highly interdependent. We have to be careful that the prior fixation on developmental neurophysiology does not give way to a fixation on brain imaging technology per se.

The second issue is that since the Decade of the Brain (another highly success-ful public relations program) neuroscience has become increasingly prominent among the sciences and in the public imagination. One result is that everyone wants to be a neuroscientist: psychologists, educators, geneticists, psychiatrists, economists, ethicists, and even philosophers. In such a climate, it is much more satisfying to describe oneself as an educational neuroscientist than as a develop-mental psychologist interested in learning. As a result "neuroscience" is being used in the description of increasingly more research fields. Educational neuro-science is one such field. Although this book provides many examples of how neuroscience may be relevant to education, it is a little light on acknowledging the importance of cognitive psychology to this effort. As long as "educational neuroscience" is merely an example of a semantic creep and we are aware of the creep, I suppose relatively little damage is done. However, when we lose sight of the bigger picture, when we lose sight of the interdependence of the sciences of mind, brain, and behavior, the research program in educational neuroscience could suffer. Subsequent editions of this book will tell.

# References

Bruer, J. T. (1993). *Schools for thought: A science of learning in the classroom.* Cambridge, MA: MIT Press.

Bruer, J. T. (1997). Education and the brain: A bridge too far. *Educational Researcher, 26*(8), 1–13

Bruer, J. T. (1999). *The myth of the first three years: A new understanding of early brain development and lifelong learning.* New York: Free Press.

Bruer, J. T. (2011). *Revisiting "The myth of the first three years."* Retrieved October 31, 2012, from Centre for Parenting Culture Studies Website: http://blogs.kent.ac.uk/parentingculturestudies/files/2011/09/Special-briefing-on-The-Myth.pdf

Castles, A., & Coltheart, M. (1993). Varieties of developmental dyslexia. *Cognition, 47,* 149–180.

Coltheart, M., Curtix, B., Atkins, P., & Haller, M. (1993). Models of reading aloud: Dual-route and parallel-distributed-processing approaches. *Psychological Review, 100*(4), 589–608.

Coltheart, M., Rastle, K., Perry, C., Langdon, R., & Ziegler, J. (2001). DRC: A dual route cascaded model of visual word recognition and reading aloud. *Psychological Review, 108*(1), 204–256.

Dumontheil, I., & Klingberg, T. (2011). Brain activity during a visuospatial working memory task predicts arithmetical performance 2 years later. *Cerebral Cortex, 22,* 1078–1085.

Fiez, J. A., Balota, D. A., Raichle, M. E., & Petersen, S. E. (1999). Effects of lexicality, frequency, and spelling-to-sound consistency on the functional anatomy of reading. *Neuron, 24,* 205–218.

Geschwind, N. (1979). Specializations of the human brain. *Scientific American, 241,* 158–168.

Harm, M. W., & Seidenberg, M. S. (2004). Computing the meanings of words in reading: Cooperative division of labor between visual and phonological processes. *Psychological Review, 111*(3), 662–720.

Hillyard, S. A., Hink, R. F., Schwent, V. L., & Picton, T. W. (1973). Electrical signs of selective attention in the human brain. *Science, 182*(4108), 177–80.

Hoeft, F., McCandliss, B. D., Black, J. M., Gantman, A., Zakerani, N., Hulme, C., Lyytinen, H., Whitfield-Gabrieli, S., Glover, G. H., Reiss, A. L., & Gabrieli, J. D. E. (2011).

Neural systems predicting long-term outcome in dyslexia. *Proceedings of the National Academy of Sciences, 108*(1), 361–366.

Lyytinen, H., Ahonen, T., Eklund, K., Guttorm, T. K., Laakso, M.-L., Leinonen, S., Leppänen, P. H., Lyytinen, P., Poikkeus, A. M., Puolakanaho, A., Richardson, U., & Viholainen, H. (2001). Developmental pathways of children with and without familial risk for dyslexia during the first years of life. *Developmental Neuropsychology, 20*(2), 535–554.

Maurer, U., Bucher, K., Brem, S., Benz, R., Kranz, F., Schulz, E., van der Mark, S., Steinhausen, H. C., & Brandeis, D. (2009). Neurophysiology in preschool improves behavioral prediction of reading ability throughout primary school. *Biological Psychiatry, 66*(4), 341–348.

McGilly, K. (Ed.). (1994). *Classroom lessons: Integrating cognitive theory and classroom practice*. Cambridge, MA: MIT Press.

Molfese, V. J., Molfese, D. J., & Modgline, A. A. (2001). Newborn and preschool predictors of second grade reading scores: An investigation of categorical and continuous scores. *Journal of Learning Disabilities, 34*, 545–554.

Pihko, E., Leppänen, P. H. T., Eklund, K. M., Cheour, M., Guttorm T. K., & Lyytinen, H. (1999). Cortical responses of infants with and without a genetic risk for dyslexia: I. *Age effects. NeuroReport, 10*, 901–905.

Petersen, S. E., Fox, P. T., Posner, M. I., Mintun, M., & Raichle, M. E. (1988). Positron emission tomographic studies of the cortical anatomy of single word processing. *Nature, 311*, 585–589.

Posner, M. I., Petersen, S. E., Fox, P. T., & Raichle, M. E. (1988). Localization of cognitive operations in the human brain. *Science, 240*(4859), 1627–1631.

Posner, M. I., & Raichle, M. (1994). *Images of mind*. New York: Scientific American Library.

Posner, M. I., & Rothbart, M. K. (2006). Influencing brain networks: Implications for education. *Trends in Cognitive Sciences, 9*(3), 99–103.

Power, J. D., Barnes, K. A., Snyder, A. Z., Schlaggar, B. L., & Petersen, S. E. (2012). Spurious by systematic correlations in functional connectivity fMRI networks arise from subject motion. *NeuroImage, 59*(3), 2142–2154.

Shaywitz, B. A., Shaywitz, S. E., Pugh, K. R., Mencl, W. E., Fulbright, R. K., Skudlarski, P., Constable, R. T., Marchione, K. E., Fletcher, J. M., Lyon, G. R., & Gore, J. C. (2002). Disruption of posterior brain systems for reading in children with developmental dyslexia. *Biological Psychiatry, 52*, 101–110.

Shaywitz. B. A., Shaywitz, S. E., Blachman, B. A., Pugh, K. R., Fulbright, R. K., Skudlarski, P., Mencl, W. E., Constable, R. T., Holahan, J. M., Marchione, K. E., Fletcher, J. M., Lyon, G. R., & Gore, J. C. (2004). Development of left occipitotemporal systems for skilled reading in children after a phonologically-based intervention. *Biological Psychiatry, 55*, 926–933.

Shaywitz, S. E., Shaywitz, B. A., Pugh, K. R., Fulbright, R. K., Constable, T. R., Mencl, W. E., Shankweiler, D. P., Liberman, D. M., Skudlarski, P., Fletcher, J. M., Katz, L., Marchione, K. E., Lacadie, C., Gatenby, C., & Gore, J. C. (1998). Functional disruption in the organization of the brain for reading in dyslexia. *Proceedings of the National Academy of Sciences of the United States of America, 95*, 2636–2641.

Stanovich, K. E., & Siegal, L. S. (1994). Phenotypic performance profile of children with reading disabilities: A regression-based test of the phonological-core variable-difference model. *Journal of Educational Psychology, 86*(1), 24–53.

Whelan, R., Conrod, P. J., Poline, J. B., Lourdusamy, A., Banaschewski, T., Barker, G. J., Bellgrove, M. A., Büchel, C., Byrne, M., Cummins, T. D. R., Fauth-Bühler, M., Flor, H., Gallinat, J., Heinz, A., Ittermann, B., Mann, K., Martinot, J.-L., Lalor, E. C., Lathrop, M., Loth, E., Nees, F., Paus, T., Rietschel, M., Smolka, M. N., Spanagel, R., Stephens, D. N., Struve, M., Thyreau, B., Vollstaedt-Klein, S., Robbins, T. W., Schumann, G., Garavan, H., & the IMAGEN Consortium. (2012). Adolescent impulsivity phenotypes characterized by distinct brain networks. *Nature Neuroscience, 15,* 920–925.

Wurtz, R. H., & Goldberg, M. E. (1972). Activity of superior colliculus in behaving monkey. II Effect of attention on neuronal responses. *Journal of Neurophysiology, 35,* 560–574.

# Index

abused children 304–5
academic self-concept 118
academic self-efficacy 118
Academic Self-Regulatory Behavior
    Questionnaire 118
achievement goal theory 118
ACT-R (Adaptive Control of Thought -
    Rational) model 52–3
action observation 275–8
  motor experience effect 277–8
activity-based training 340–1
adaptive microworlds 45–7, 66–70
  example 69–70
  feedback 71
adolescence 278, 290, 309
  emotional development 309–13
    mental health concerns 311–13
    motivation 309–11
  language development 153–6
    educational neuroscience 155–6
    language behavior 154
    neural substrates 154–5
  social development 278–83
    theory of mind development 283–5
affective empathy 308

alcohol abuse 312
alexia 174, 175
  with agraphia 174
  without agraphia 174
algebra 228–9
amygdala 298, 305–8, 312
analogical reasoning 255–9
  analogical distance effect 258
  neural basis 257–9
  relational-complexity effects 257
analogies 255–6
  cross-domain analogies 258
  use of by scientists 256
  within-domain analogies 258
analysis of variance 124
angular gyrus 174, 203, 212
anomia 175
anterior cingulate cortex (ACC) 210,
    246–7, 248, 254, 303
antisaccade task 329, 331
aphasia
  conduction 174
  Wernicke's 174
arching of the back 301
arcuate fasciculus 174

*Educational Neuroscience*, First Edition. Edited by Denis Mareschal, Brian Butterworth
and Andy Tolmie.
© 2014 John Wiley & Sons, Ltd. Published 2014 by John Wiley & Sons, Ltd.

arithmetic
  development 210
  embodied understanding of 210–12
  individual differences 215
  *see also* mathematics
artificial neural networks 47, 50, 53–60
  capacity 58–9
  plasticity 58–9
atomic structure model 255–6
attention 337
  joint attention 273–5
  neuroimaging studies 20–3
  theories 256
  visual attention span disorder 184–5, 187
    remediation exercises 189
attention deficit-hyperactivity disorder
    (ADHD) 339
attitudinal research 128
autism 122
autistic spectrum disorders (ASD) 303–4

behavioral genetics 77, 79, 84
  cross-cultural research 102–4
  *see also* genetic studies
behavioral genomics 79
behavioral measures 111–17
  competence measures 111–12, 114–17
  performance measures 111–14
behavioral problems 304–9
belief-bias effect 252
bilingual children 195
  reading acquisition in the second
    language 195
  second language learning 157–8, 159–60
bivariate heritability 79, 92
blood oxygen level dependent (BOLD)
    imaging 35
brain
  emotional development studies 298
    adolescence 309–13
    lifelong learning 313–15
    middle years 303–9
    preschool years 299–303
  executive function studies 326–7, 337,
    338
    inhibition 330–1

switching 336
    working memory 333–4
  functional connectivity 190–1
    intervention effects 190
    maturation 138, 144, 154
    reading network 190–1
    sensory deprivation effect 159
  hemispheric lateralization 141, 144, 155,
    243
  mathematics neural basis 202–3
  maturation 138–9, 144, 154, 313
  reading impairment studies 186, 190–4
    brain activation 184–8, 192–4
  scientific reasoning studies
    analogical reasoning 257–9
    causal reasoning 243–7
    deductive reasoning 252–5
  social development
    action observation 275–8
    childhood and adolescence 278–83
    early development 268–78
    face processing 269–71, 279–83
    gaze processing 271–3
    joint attention 273–5
  specialization of neural systems for
    language 143–4
  structural development 36–8
  *see also* grey matter; neuroimaging;
    *specific brain regions*; white matter
brain damage studies 202
Broca, Paul 174
Broca's area 175
Bruer, John 5–6
bullying 289, 306

callostomy 242
callous–unemotional (CU) traits 305–9
Cambridge effect 176
CANTAB (Cambridge Neuropsychological
    Testing Automated Battery) 332
cardinal numbers 203–4
caudate 246
causal reasoning 240–9
  brain correlates 243–7
  causal inference 241–3
  causal perception 241, 242

causal reasoning (*cont'd*)
  data consistency effects 247
  theory plausibility effects 244–7
Cholesky decomposition 79, 92
classroom influence 89–90, 99
  *see also* environmental influence
classroom mapping measures 120
*CNTNAP2* gene 147
CogMed program 339
cognitive models 45–6, 48–63
  computational model elements 49–50
  evaluation 51–2, 60
  feedback 71–2
  future directions 62–3
  individual differences in language
    development 54–60
  subsymbolic approaches 47, 50–1, 53–4
  symbolic approaches 47, 50, 52–3
cognitive neuroscience 4–5, 6
competence measures 111–12, 114–17
comprehension assessment 23
computer modeling 46–7
  adaptive microworlds 45–7, 66–70
  cognitive models 45–6, 48–63
  feedback 70–2
  intelligent tutoring systems (ITSs) 45–6,
    65–8
conceptual change 261
conceptual knowledge 239–40
conduct disorders (CD) 304–9
  genetic influence 306
conduction aphasia 174
confidence measures 118
conflict monitoring 254
conflict processing 248–9
connectivity *see* functional connectivity
constructionism 67, 68, 69–70
constructivism 3, 220
  neuroconstructivism 60–1
contextualisation 61
conversational framework 64
corpus callosum 174, 242
cross-cultural research 102–4
cross-domain analogies 258
Cuisenaire rods 211, 222
Cyberball 286–7

Day–Night task 329, 330
deductive reasoning 249–55
  belief-bias effect 252
  content effects 251–2
  neuroimaging studies 252–5
deep dyslexia 179
Dejerine, Joseph Jules 174
demographic measures 119
depression 300–1
development
  neuroimaging studies 20–2, 27–8,
    36–8
  structural brain development 36–8
  *see also* language development;
    mathematics
DF extremes analysis 90, 93
diffusion tensor imaging (DTI) 35
Dimensional Change Card Sort 329–31
disbelief 248
dishabituation paradigm 207–8
distance effect 205, 208–9, 213–14
  nonsymbolic 205, 214, 216
  symbolic 205, 209, 214, 217
distributed connectionist reading
  model 178–9
dizygotic (DZ) twins 80, 84–5
  *see also* twin studies
DNA 79–80
  methylation 81, 99–100
domain-general reasoning 238–9
domain-specific reasoning 238–9
dorsal lateral prefrontal cortex
  (DLPFC) 247, 248, 254–5
dual-route reading model 176
Dunbar, Kevin 256
Dungan study, Kyrgyzstan 103–4
dynamic assessment 116
dynamic causal modeling
  (DCM) 281
dyscalculia 7, 69, 215–19
  5–12 years 216–19
  core deficit hypothesis 216, 217
  education approach 222–5
    training effect 223–5
  individual differences 217–18
  lifelong learning 219

mapping hypothesis 216–17
*see also* arithmetic; mathematics
dyslexia 6, 179–80
acquired 179
brain activation studies 184–8,
192–4
deep 179
developmental 179–80, 194
intervention studies 188–90, 223
neuroimaging studies 185–8
outcome prediction 192–4
phonological 179
phonological deficit hypothesis 180
psychology impact 3
surface 179
*see also* reading

education 8, 48
psychology collaboration 2–4
educational neuroscience 1–5
challenges 7–11
emergence of 5–7
policy 11
research 9–10
educational psychology research
methods 110–30
behavioral measures 111–17
demographic measures 119
environmental measures 119–20
experimental designs 123–6
nonexperimental designs 126–9
quasi-experimental designs 121–2
report measures 117–19
sampling issues 120–1
electroencephalography
(EEG) 13–16
electrode placement 15
filters 16
recording 15–16
emergent specialization 61
emotional development 297
adolescence 309–13
mental health concerns 311–13
motivation 309–11
cognition relationship 298
educational significance 298

lifelong learning 313–15
stress as an obstacle 314–15
undergraduates 313–14
memory enhancement for emotional
events 315
middle years 303–9
autistic spectrum disorders 303–4
behavioral problems 304–9
preschool years 299–303
emotion regulation 301–3
temperament 299–301
emotional intelligence measures 118
empathy 308
entity theorists 309–10
environmental influence 86–7,
96–100
family environment 96–7
genetic mediation 98
language development 134–5
multivariate genetic analysis
implications 93–5
MZ differences study design 98–100
relative contribution 86–7
teacher and classroom
contribution 89–90
environmental measures 119–20
epigenetics 80, 85, 99–100
error signal 72
event-related potentials (ERPs) 13–24
advantages and limitations 22–4
amplitudes 20
artefact removal 17–18
averaging 14, 17–18
components 14, 18–20
development studies 20–2
distribution 20
latencies 19
event-sampling technique 112
executive functions 325–42
academic achievement and 327–8,
337
evaluative processing 254
executive processing 254
inhibitory control 326, 329–31
neural bases 326–7, 338
structure 326

*Index*

executive functions (*cont'd*)
  switching 326, 335–6
  training effects 337–41
    complex activity-based training 340–1
    specific executive skills 339–40
  working memory 326, 332–5
exercise benefits 340–1
experimental study designs 123–6
eye contact 271
  callous–unemotional (CU) trait
    relationships 307–8

face processing
  childhood and adolescence 279–83
  emotional expression recognition
    279–80
  facial identity recognition 279
  infants 269–71
factorial designs 124
family environment 96–7
Fast ForWord program 149–50
feedback 68–9, 70–2
  extrinsic 71
  intrinsic 71
  negative performance feedback
    responses 310–11
finger gnosia 212–13
foreign language learning 157–8, 159–60
forward mapping 275
*FOXP2* gene 147
frontal gyrus 210
frontopolar cortex 258
frontostriatal tract 327
functional connectivity 190–1
  intervention effects 190
  maturation 138, 144, 154
  reading network 190–1
  sensory deprivation effect 159
  *see also* brain
functional magnetic resonance imaging
    (fMRI) 26–7, 35, 37–8
  *see also* magnetic resonance imaging (MRI)
functional near-infrared spectroscopy
    (fNIRS) 26–8
  *see also* near-infrared spectroscopy (NIRS)
fusiform face area (FFA) 280

gaze processing 271–3
genetic correlation 80, 92–3
  group genetic correlation 93
genetic studies 77–84
  cross-cultural research 102–4
  genetic influence estimation 86–7
  molecular genetics 100–2
  multivariate analysis 91–6
  quantitative genetics 81–2, 84–6
  sex differences 87–8
  specific language disorder 145–7
  terminology 79–82
  tools 84
  *see also* twin studies
gene–environment (GE) correlation 80,
    97, 98
gene–environment interaction 80
  relative contributions 86–7
genome-wide association studies
    (GWAS) 80, 101–2
germ theory 8–9
Gerstmann syndrome 212
glucocorticoids 315
Go–No–Go task 329, 330
Graphogame-Maths 222
grey matter
  conduct disorder relationship 305, 307
  developmental changes 138
  *see also* brain
group heritability 80, 91, 93

Hebbian learning 53
hemispheric lateralization 141, 243
  language 144, 155
hemodynamic response function (HRF) 26
heritability 81, 82–3, 86
  age relationship 94
  bivariate 79, 92
  environments 97
  group 80, 91, 93
  temperament 300
  univariate 92
hierarchical sampling 120–1
hippocampus 333–4
hypothalamus–pituitary–adrenal (HPA)
    axis 314

incompatibility effect 227–8
incremental theorists 309–10
individual differences
  cross-cultural studies 102–4
  dyscalculia 217–18
  dyslexia outcome prediction 192–4
  language development 54–60, 139–42
    addressing inequality 142
  mathematical achievement 213–15
    5–12 years 214
    12–18 years 214–15
    lifelong learning 215
  multivariate genetic analysis 91–6
  relative influence of genes and
    environments 86–7
  self-evaluation of mathematical
    abilities 95–6
  sex differences 87–8
  teacher and classroom influence 89–90
  working-memory training responses 340
inferior frontal gyrus (IFG) 174, 175, 182,
  209, 210, 217, 229
inhibitory control 326, 329–31
  academic skill relationship 331–2
  development in infancy 329–30
  development in school-aged
    children 330
  neural bases 330–1
  *see also* executive functions
instruction, mathematics 219–26
  dyscalculia and 222–5
  individual needs 221–2
  methods 220–1
insula 313, 337
intelligent tutoring systems (ITSs) 45–6, 65–8
  components 66
  feedback 71
Interactive Specialization theory 138–9,
  141, 280–1
interoception 313
intraparietal sulcus (IPS) 203, 209, 210,
  217–19, 337
ionizing radiation 28

joint attention 273–5
Joseph, Keith 201

KE family case study 146–7
Kyrgyz study, Kyrgyzstan 103–4

Landau–Kleffner syndrome 150, 153
language delay 139
  diagnosis 56–60
  *see also* specific language impairment
    (SLI)
language development 134–6
  adolescence 153–6
  continuity 144
  environmental influence 134–5
  genetic influence 135
  individual differences 54–60, 139–42
  infancy and early childhood (0–5
    years) 136–42
  intrinsic factors 136–9
  primary school (5–12 years) 142–53
  sensitive periods 156–60
    early deprivation impact 159–60
    foreign language learning 157–8
  socioeconomic status relationship 54–60,
    139–42
    addressing inequality 142
  specialization of neural systems 143–4
  *see also* language delay; reading; specific
    language impairment (SLI)
language processing 173–80
  cerebral function inference 173–5
Larmor frequency 31
lateralization *see* hemispheric lateralization
learning 7–8, 48
  Hebbian learning 53
  individual differences 3, 6–7
  memory and 4
  models 7, 48–63
  prediction error learning 68, 69, 72
  reinforcement learning 72
  self-organizing learning 71
  supervised learning 71–2
  *see also* cognitive models
learning disability
  multivariate genetic analysis 94
  twin studies 90–1, 94
learning goals 310
left angular gyrus 174, 203, 212

left dorsal lateral prefrontal cortex (DLPFC) 247, 248
left frontal gyrus 210
left supramarginal gyrus (SMG) 210
Lichtheim, Ludwig 174
lifelong learning
  emotional development 313–15
  mathematics 209–10, 215
    dyscalculia 219
  stress as an obstacle 314–15
Logo 67
longitudinal designs 127–8
  longitudinal cohort sequential designs 128

magic trick perception study 247–8
magnetic resonance imaging (MRI) 28–38
  blood oxygen level dependent (BOLD) imaging 35
  challenges of studying children 36
  components 29–31
  developmental studies 36–8
  diffusion tensor imaging (DTI) 35
  functional MRI (fMRI) 26–7, 35, 37–8
  image generation 32–3
  physics of 31–2
  safety 28–9
  structural images 34–5
magnetoencephalography (MEG) 38
magnitudes 203–4
matched-sample designs 122
mathematics 3, 201–2
  algebra 228–9
  development 207–10
    infancy and childhood (0–5 years) 207–8
    lifelong learning 209–10
    primary and middle school (5–12 years) 208–9
  distance effect 205, 208–9, 213–14
  embodied understanding of numbers and arithmetic 210–13
  importance of 201–2
  individual differences in achievement 213–15
    5–12 years 214

    12–18 years 214–15
    lifelong learning 215
  inhibitory control relationship 331–2
  instruction 219–26
    dyscalculia and 222–5
    individual needs 221–2
    methods 220–1
  negative numbers 226–7
  neural basis 202–3, 338, 357
  neural stimulation study 229
  place-value notation 227–8
  problem size effect 205–6
  self-evaluation study 95–6
  theoretical roadmap 203–5
  working memory relationship 334–5
    training effects 340
  *see also* dyscalculia
medial prefrontal cortex (mPFC) 273, 283
memory
  enhancement for emotional events 315
  working memory 326, 332–5
mental health concerns 311–13
mental lexicon 174
mentalizing 283
  *see also* theory of mind development
methodological interoperability 7
methylation 81, 99–100
Michotte paradigm 242–3
microarray studies 81, 102
microgenetic designs 124–5
middle frontal gyrus (MFG) 210, 217
mirror-neuron system 275–6
mismatch response (MMR) 137
  language development studies 137–8
mixed design 124
molecular genetics 81, 100–2
  genome-wide association studies (GWAS) 101–2
  quantitative trait locus (QTL) perspective 82, 100–1
monozygotic (MZ) twins 81, 84–5
  MZ differences design 98–100
  *see also* twin studies
motivational effects 118
motivational research 128, 309–11
mu wave activity 276–7

multilevel modeling (MLM) 129
multiple regression 129
multivariate genetic analysis 91–6
  learning disabilities 94
mutual gaze 271–2

N-methyl-D-aspartate (NMDA)
    receptors 312
natural pedagogy 288–9
nature of nurture 97
near-infrared spectroscopy (NIRS) 24–8
  development studies 27–8
  functional NIRS (fNIRS) 26–8
  principles 25–7
negative numbers 226–7
negative performance feedback
    responses 310–11
NetLogo 67
neural commitment 138
neurobiological maturation 138–9
neuroconstructivism 60–1, 220
neuroimaging 4–5, 13–38
  electroencephalography (EEG) 13–16
  event-related potentials (ERPs) 13–24
  hemispheric asymmetry 243
  magnetic resonance imaging
      (MRI) 28–38
  magnetoencephalography (MEG) 38
  near-infrared spectroscopy (NIRS) 24–8
  *see also* brain
neuroprognosis 194
neuroscience
  informing educational practice 5–7
  psychology collaboration 4–5
nonexperimental study designs 126–9
nonionizing radiation 28–9
nonshared environment 81, 86, 93–4,
    99–100
  *see also* environmental influence
nonsymbolic distance effect 205, 214, 216
Number Race game 222
numbers 203–5
  as labels 205
  cardinal 203–4
  embodied understanding of 210–13
  negative 226–7

ordinal 204
  *see also* mathematics
numerosities 203
  approximate 206

ordinal numbers 204
orthographic transparency 194–5

parahippocampal gyrus 246
partial representations of knowledge
    61–2
path analysis 129
peer evaluation 285–8
  rejection 287–8
peer relationships
  language development and 153–4
  peer learning 64–5
performance
  goals 309–10
  measures 111–14
  negative performance feedback
      responses 310–11
personality measures 118
phenotypes 77, 81
phonemic categories 136–7
phonological deficit hypothesis 180
phonological development 137–8
phonological dyslexia 179
Piaget's critical method 116, 119
place-value notation 227–8
planet discovery 249–50
pleiotropy 81, 92, 96
population-level modeling 55
posterior superior parietal lobule (SPL) 203
practice effects 220–1
precuneus 246
prediction error learning 68, 69, 72
prefrontal cortex (PFC) 203, 257, 259, 272
  development 326–7
  executive functions 326–7
  left 257, 274
    dorsal lateral (DLPFC) 247, 248
    medial (mPFC) 273, 283
    right lateral (RLPFC) 259
    ventrolateral (VLPFC) 287, 336
primary auditory cortex (PAC) 175

primary motor cortex (PMC) 175
problem size effect 205–6
prospective survey design 128
psychiatric disorders 312–13
psychology
    education collaboration 2–4
    neuroscience collaboration 4–5
psychometric measures 114–17
public health model 8–10

qualitative differences 87–8
quantitative differences 87–8
quantitative genetics 81–2, 84–6
quantitative trait locus (QTL)
       perspective 82, 100–1
quasi-experimental study designs 121–2
questionnaire measures 118

randomized cluster trials 126
randomized control trials (RCTs) 125–6
randomized designs 124
reading 172–3, 175–9
    distributed connectionist reading
       model 178–9
    dual-route reading model 176
    educational remediation 188–90
    functional connectivity 190–1
    inhibitory control relationship 331–2
    learning to read 3–4, 173
       language comparisons 194–5
    neural basis 180–4, 337, 338
    neuroimaging studies 5, 180–4, 338
    outcome prediction 192–4
    working memory relationship 335
    *see also* dyslexia
referential gaze perception 273
reinforcement learning 72
repeated-measures designs 124
report measures 117–19
    third person 118–19
research methods *see* educational
       psychology research methods
right fusiform gyrus (rFG) 203
right inferior frontal gyrus (rIFG) 203
right lateral prefrontal cortex (RLPFC)
    259

risk-taking behavior 311–12
Robo-Memo program 339

sampling issues 120–1
school action plus programs 304
School Life Questionnaire 97
scientific reasoning 237–8
    analogical reasoning 255–9
    brain correlates 243–7, 252–5, 257–9
    causal reasoning 240–9
    deductive reasoning 249–55
    domain-general reasoning 228–9
    domain-specific reasoning 228–9
    future directions 260–1
second language learning 157–8, 159–60
self-awareness 313
self-determination theory 118
self-organizing learning 71
self-report measures 117–18
sensitive periods 289
    in language development 156–60
       definition 156–7
       early deprivation impact 159–60
       foreign language learning 157–8
sex differences 87–8
sex-limitation models 88
shared environment 82, 86–7, 93–4
    *see also* environmental influence
shifting *see* switching
single-nucleotide polymorphisms
    (SNPs) 101
Smith, Adrian 201
SNARC (spatial–numerical association of
    response codes) effect 211–12
Snow, John 8–9
Social and Emotional Aspects of Learning
    (SEAL) program 289
social development 268–90
    action observation 275–8
    childhood and adolescence 278–83
    early development 268–78
    education implications 288–90
    face processing 269–71
    gaze processing 271–3
    joint attention 273–5
    peer evaluation 285–8

theory of mind development 283–4
social, emotional, and/or behavioral
    difficulties (SEBD) 303, 304
social rejection 285–8, 289
    sensitivity to 286–8
socioeconomic status (SES) 119
    language development
        relationship 54–60, 139–42
        addressing inequalities 142
special educational needs (SEN)
        teachers 222–3
specific language impairment (SLI) 135,
        139, 145–50
    causes 145–7
    changes in adolescence 156
    educational interventions 149–50
    screening procedures 147–9
    *see also* language development
statistical modeling 129
Stop Signal task 329
Strengths and Difficulties
        Questionnaire 118
stress hormones 315
stress responses 314–15
stressors 314
structural equation modeling 82, 87, 92,
        129
    sex-limitation models 88
substance abuse 311–12
superior temporal cortex (STS) 272, 280
superior temporal gyrus (STG) 174, 175
supervised learning 71–2
supramarginal gyrus (SMG) 210
surface dyslexia 179
switching 326, 335–6
    academic skill relationship 336
    development 335–6
    neural bases 336
    *see also* executive functions
symbolic distance effect 205, 209, 214, 217
synapse elimination 326
systematic observation 112–14

teacher influence 89–90
    teacher heterogeneity model 89
    *see also* environmental influence

teaching–learning environment 63–5
    computer modeling 67–9
temperament 299–301
    heritability 300
temporal ordering 127
test-based measures 114–15
theories of intelligence 309
    entity theorists 309–10
    incremental theorists 309–10
    learning goals 310
    performance goals 309–10
theory of mind development 283–4
    adolescence 283, 285
time-sampling technique 112
timing of developmental events 61
training
    activity-based 340–1
    dyscalculia management 223–5
    executive function skills 337–41
        complex activity-based training
            340–1
        specific executive skills 339–40
transcranial direct current stimulation
        (TDCS) 229
transcranial magnetic stimulation 202
triadic interactions 274–5
twin studies 84–6
    control twin method 99
    dizygotic (DZ) twins 80, 84–5
    genetic influence estimation 86–7
    learning disability 90–1
    monozygotic (MZ) twins 81, 84–5
    multivariate genetic analysis 92–6
    MZ differences design 98–100
    sex differences 87–8
    specific language impairment 146
    teacher and classroom
            contribution 89–90
    *see also* genetic studies
Twins Early Development Study 88, 89
TZ case study 150–3

undergraduates
    emotional experiences 313–14
    stress as an obstacle to learning 314–15
understanding, measures of 114–15

univariate heritability 92
universal grammar theory 51

ventrolateral prefrontal cortex
        (VLPFC) 287, 336
visual attention span disorder 184–5, 187
    remediation exercises 189
visual word form area 184, 186
vocabulary 138–9, 155

Wason four-card selection task 251
Wernicke, Carl 174
Wernicke's aphasia 174
Wernicke's area 175
white matter
    developmental changes 138, 327
        adolescence 154–5
        working memory and 333

reading network 191
    *see also* brain
Williams, Peter 201
Williams syndrome 145
Wisconsin Card Sorting Task 335
within-domain analogies 258
working memory 326, 332–5
    academic skill relationships 334–5
        math 334–5
        reading 335
    development 332
    neural bases 333–5
    training effects 339–40
        individual differences 340
    *see also* executive functions

zone of proximal development 68,
        116, 222